Down Alaska's Wild Rivers

Journals of an Alaskan Naturalist
Third Edition

FRANK KEIM

For my family who have enjoyed some of these wild rivers with me.

And special thanks to John Breiby for reading the manuscript and offering edits,
and to designer Dawn Serra for sticking with me in this wild river adventure.

Down Alaska's Wild Rivers. Journals of an Alaskan Naturalist. ©2024 by Frank J. Keim

Design: Dawn N. Serra

Aurora Books, an imprint of Eco-Justice Press, L.L.C.

Aurora Books
P.O. Box 5409 Eugene, OR 97405
www.ecojusticepress.com

Library of Congress Control Number: 2024937230
ISBN 978-1-945432-65-1

Third Edition

All photos by Frank J. Keim with the exception of:
"Bluethroat male" (page 164, by USFWS).

TABLE OF CONTENTS

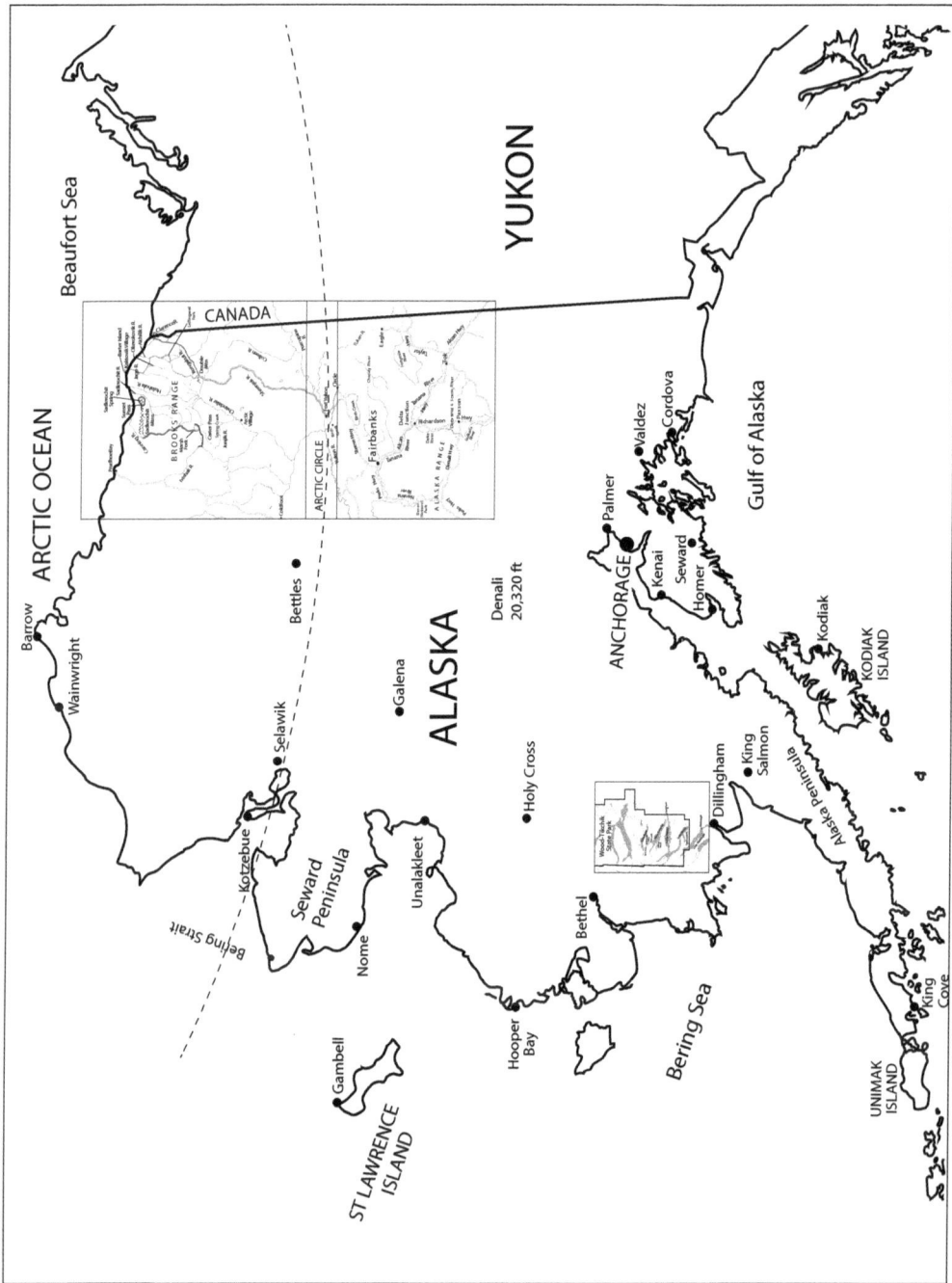

See insets for more details

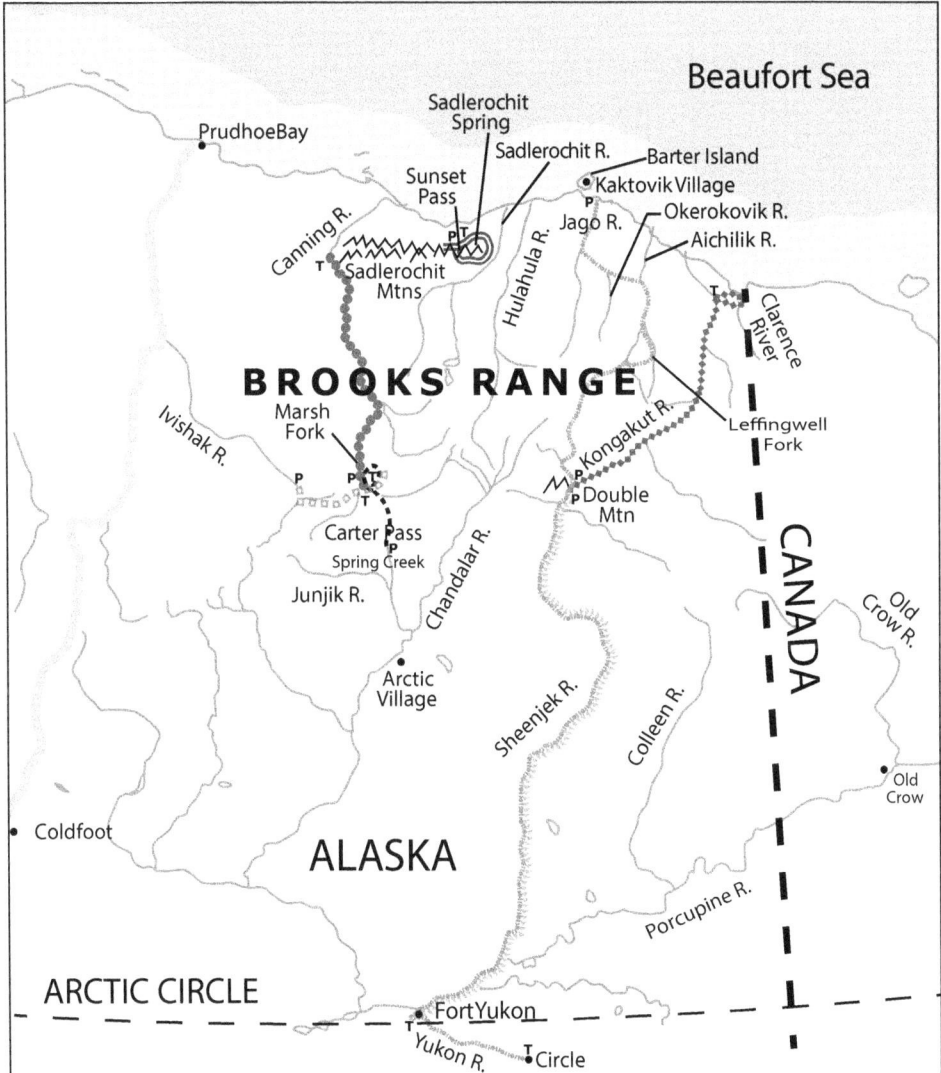

BROOKS RANGE RIVER TRIPS KEY

- High Water on the Sheenjek
- Three Men in a Tub
- Bluethroats & Brown Bears
- Caribou Rivers Journal
- Spring Creek to Marsh Fork
- Canning River Journal
- A Good Crew

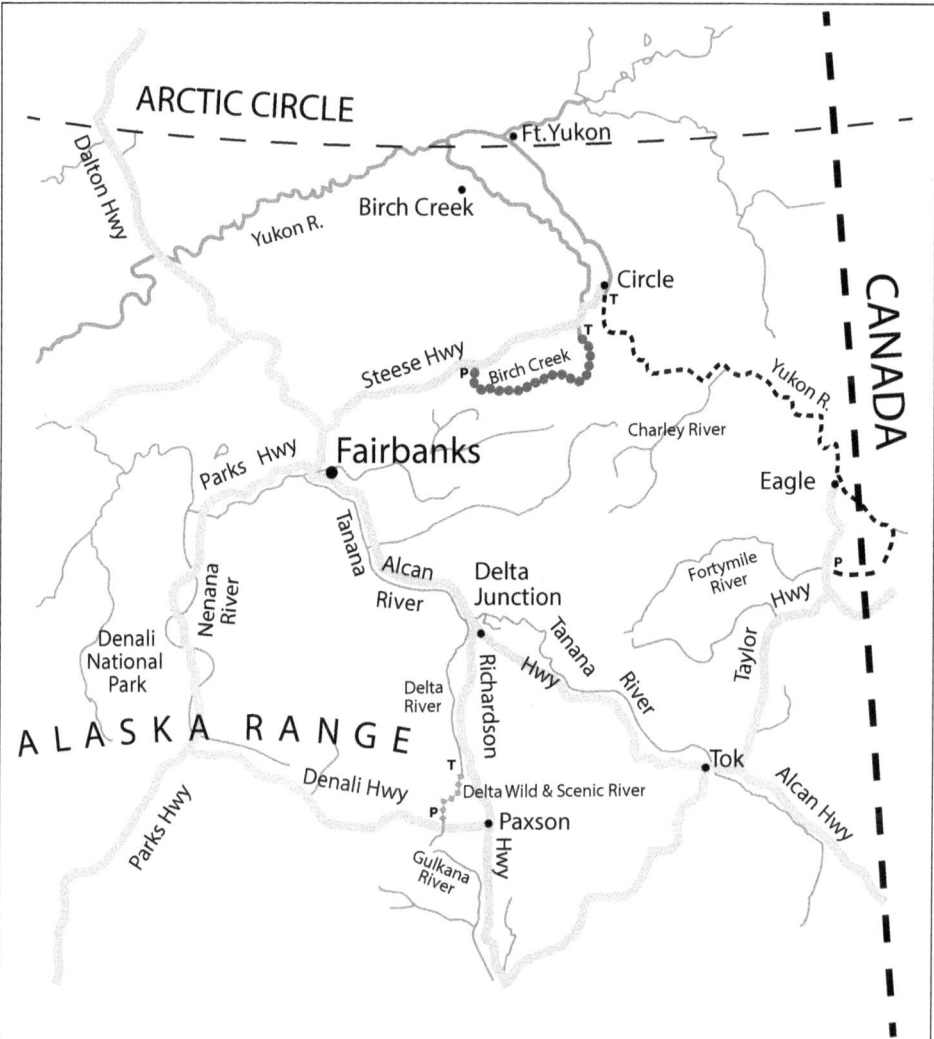

ARCTIC CIRCLE

Dalton Hwy

Yukon R.

Ft. Yukon

Birch Creek

Circle
T

T
P   Birch Creek

Steese Hwy

Yukon R.

CANADA

Charley River

Fairbanks

Parks Hwy

Eagle

Tanana

Nenana River

Alcan River

Delta Junction

Fortymile River

Hwy

Denali National Park

Delta River

Richardson

Tanana

River

Taylor

Hwy

ALASKA RANGE

T

P

Denali Hwy

Delta Wild & Scenic River

Paxson

Tok

Alcan Hwy

Parks Hwy

Gulkana River

Hwy

P

INTERIOR ALASKA RIVER TRIPS KEY

- On the Brink
- Rivers of Gold
- Music Men on Birch Creek

A Few Words

As I write, the earth's population is about 7.8 billion people and increasing exponentially every day. By 2050, demographers say there will be more than 9 billion of us on this planet. It is for this reason the wilderness and wild rivers we have left are not only important for the preservation of the well-being of other species but of our own as well. After all, since we came from wild nature not very long ago in terms of the scheme of evolution, it is still the place we find the greatest solace, both physically and spiritually. So, I agree with Thoreau when he said, "In wildness is the preservation of the world."

Certainly, Thoreau was referring to the larger world of species he came into contact with when he lived at Walden Pond, but being a human being he also included himself and others of his own species. For it is only we humans who can design nature to save it from ourselves.

My hope in writing this book is that the stories I've included about wild rivers and wild places will allow readers and others to love and respect (if only through the proxy of a book) wild places as much as I do and therefore defend and protect them into the distant future for the benefit of future generations. In his book, *Desert Solitaire*, Edward Abbey once said that a person could be a lover and defender of the wilderness without ever setting foot in it. In his words, "We need the possibility of escape as surely as we need hope; without it, life in the cities would drive all men into crime or drugs or psychoanalysis."

But there is nothing like the real thing, and that is my second hope, that some of you will get out there, as I did, with friends and family, and both challenge yourselves, and feel the physical and spiritual connection with nature that will further strengthen your desire to persuade others of the need to preserve, protect, (and restore, if necessary) wild nature.

As another of my culture heroes, Wallace Stegner, once wrote: "Something will have gone out of us as people if we ever let the remaining wilderness be destroyed; … if we drive the few remaining members of the wild species into zoos or to extinction; if we pollute the last clean air and dirty the last clean streams and push our paved roads through the last of the silence, so that never again will Americans be free in their own country from the noise, the exhausts, the stinks of human and automotive waste."

I could not have said this better, so I won't even try.

Read on.

Frank J. Keim
Fairbanks, Alaska
Fall, 2019

Author's Note

From the moment I first arrived in Fairbanks, Alaska, as a teen in 1961, I realized the State was dominated by rivers. Whether I drove or walked during summer, or cross-country skied in winter, there were always rivers to follow to get to where I was going—and so many of them with such intriguing names as Chena, Salcha, Chatanika, Tanana, Gulkana and Nenana. There were also others I found on maps that were much farther afield, like the Kobuk, Alatna, Fortymile, Birch, Delta and Sheenjek that fascinated me even more because there was no way I could get to know them unless I had a kayak or a canoe. It wasn't long till I asked my uncle Charles in Fairbanks if I could borrow his aluminum canoe and begin floating some of those rivers.

I used this shiny canoe for the first time in 1963 down what is now called the Delta Wild and Scenic River with my brothers, Dave and Mike. They had come over from Canada that summer to visit me in Fairbanks. From Round Tangle Lake on the Denali Highway, we floated through what my uncle had referred to in hushed tones as his "Hidden Valley." With its braided clearwater channel, snow-mantled mountains and rich wildlife, the country we paddled through was stunningly beautiful. This was an experience that changed my life and started me along a trail that continues to the present day.

Ever since that short four-day trip, I've floated and hiked scores of Alaska's rivers and creeks. Not all of them have been wilderness rivers, but none was a "civilized" river like those in the Lower 48 states. Even the tamest of Alaskan rivers still has more wilderness along its banks than any of the wildest rivers in the other states. There is no comparing our rivers, even to those in Canada or Siberia, both because of our unique geography and the protected status of many of the rivers.

After canoeing and walking so many of these riverscapes, I've gained a healthy respect and enduring reverence for them and the wildlife that depend upon them. About 40 years ago I started to keep journals of these experiences. Ten years later, I began rewriting the journals so they could be read by others to allow them to appreciate the rivers as I had, and also to learn more about them if they ever chose to float them in the future. With the fast disappearance of so much of the world's wild country, another important reason for writing about the rivers was to remember what they and the wilderness surrounding them were like in the past. It was also my hope that these personal stories would convey the message that wild rivers and wilderness have an essential value for the human spirit and therefore should be preserved and protected for future generations.

A friend of mine once said he was haunted by the sound of a river's flow. I couldn't agree more. Whether it's clear water running smooth and deep through verdant valleys, or a river frothing wild and white over stair steps of sunken rocks, or one like the Yukon, long and wide and pregnant with creamy silt, barreling cold and fast headlong for the sea, they all have the sound of flowing water, which is unlike any other sound on our planet. There is a poetic timelessness to it that kindles memories of adventures long past and fantasies of journeys yet to come. It's a sound that drives me mad in winter and sets me to planning my next river trek for the coming spring.

For ten years I lived in the village of Marshall on the lower Yukon River, and I often used to walk over to the high bank of the river to watch in awe as the huge expanse of water rolled ponderously towards the Bering Sea. It was laden with khaki-colored silt washed into its broad belly from thousands of tributaries cascading down steep slopes of hundreds of thousands of mountains in both Alaska and Canada. This is Alaska's longest river, I thought, almost 2000 miles long from its headwaters in British Columbia to where it ends in the Bering Sea. From my perch on the riverbank in Marshall, the Yukon was almost a mile across to the other side of its main channel, and at its mouth, just a hundred miles downriver, in spring it poured more than 600,000 cubic feet of fresh water per second into the Bering.

But the Yukon River isn't what this book is about. I've mentioned it because it was an intimate flowing part of my life for so many years and because it is the big river where most of the smaller ones I have written about finally end up.

I haven't included all of the Alaskan rivers I've ever traveled, but I have described some of the wildest of them. Hopefully, these stories allow others to feel some of the sense of wonder and excitement and unforgettable pleasure that I have had while floating or trekking these rivers with members of my family and good friends.

Frank J. Keim
Fall, 2019
Fairbanks, Alaska

CHAPTER 1

High Water on the Sheenjek
July 10-July 19, 1998

July 10 –

W e were flying up a wide valley crowded close by lofty mountains when Don Ross announced that we would be paddling the river at high water. Don was our charter pilot, and the river he was talking about was the Sheenjek, located in the far northeast corner of Alaska's Brooks Range. It was the only river in the Arctic National Wildlife Refuge designated as a Wild and Scenic River by Congress in 1980 when it passed the Alaska Lands Act.

There were advantages to the high water, Don said – not as many bad rapids to contend with because most of the boulders would be underwater. But, he added, it would run us faster out of the mountains and into the Yukon Flats,

Sheenjek River opposite Double Mountain

where there would be fewer opportunities to take side trips. Since one of the reasons we had chosen to float the Sheenjek was to do some hiking in the Brooks Range, Don advised us to slow down on the upper reaches of the river, then pick up speed on the lower river where the scenery was less interesting.

My canoeing partner, Andrew Benedetti, was in the front seat of the Cessna 185, and he was all eyes and ears as Don pointed out the land features that were so new to him. Nine years earlier, these mountains had been new to me also. Then, I flew over them for the first time with pilot Roger Dowding on our return south from a solo walk on the Kongakut River. When Double Mountain and the West Fork of the Sheenjek came into view, Don gestured toward Guilbeau Pass where Roger had run into some foul weather and crashed his airplane into the side of the mountain. Don had flown for Roger on various occasions, and after his death had bought his Yukon Air charter service.

Double Mountain was on our left as we began our descent toward a small box canyon and the tiny flat strip of gravel that Don planned to land us on. The Sheenjek River was almost completely covered with aufeis (seasonal overflow ice) from there on up, making it impossible to start any farther upriver. So this was the end of the line for us, where we would assemble our canoe and begin our float.

Don throttled his engine down and leaned the Cessna 185 east into the little canyon. He said the gravel there had been clear of ice for only a few days and was now firm enough to land on. To our right, a bull moose was feeding in the middle of one of the pothole lakes, and as he foraged on the bottom, ripples of water circled him and echoed endlessly outward on the black mirror surface of the lake. This peaceful scene contrasted sharply with the white water rapids we could see at the end of the aufeis only a hundred yards to the west.

Our attention riveted back to the box canyon when Don suddenly revved his engine to stabilize us for a bumpy uphill landing on the alluvial gravel that fanned out at the base of the canyon. Even with fat tundra tires it was a rough landing, but Don made the best of it and quickly brought his 185 to a noisy stop. This was it. From here on down the river, Andrew and I would be on our own.

Don opened his door and stepped down. Andrew was next, then I carefully pried myself out of the back of the little plane crammed to the ceiling with our Ally pack canoe, camping gear and two weeks of food for our first canoe trip down a river in the Arctic National Wildlife Refuge. As I stepped onto terra firma, my first thoughts were of the brightness of the sun and the diaphanous clarity of the air. The outline of the mountain peaks was knife sharp and the palette of wildflower colors on the ground defied words.

After unloading our gear, we chatted for a while with Don, then watched him ease back into the cab of his 185, start the engine, and roar off into the wild blue yonder toward Ft. Yukon, where we said we'd see him again in about two weeks. The little plane soon became only a moving mote of dust, and Andrew and I set about carrying our Ally pack and provisions to a suitable spot next to the river, where we could assemble the canoe and have some lunch.

In less than an hour we had the Ally together and floating. Three cheers for the Norwegian manufacturers of this humble little PVC-wrapped hull in which we planned to travel almost 300 miles down the Sheenjek to the Porcupine River, and from there to Fort Yukon, where we would disassemble it, pack it up again, then carry it over to the post office to send back to Fairbanks. It was a neat package, and if treated right, I knew it would take me down many more of Alaska's wild rivers. In some ways I liked it better than my solid-hull Mad River canoe. It was lighter, more buoyant and maneuverable, and I could take it wherever I wanted in Alaska, either by sending it through the mail or by carrying it with me on a charter.

But the Ally was only part of an enjoyable river trip. Even more important was the person who helped me knock it together. Andrew and I had been partners on several other wilderness treks, and we knew how to operate congenially and efficiently. We almost anticipated each other's next move. Although he was 20 years younger, he was a fellow teacher and a kindred spirit in environmental ethics, so we had a lot in common and a great deal to talk about during our many hours together on the river. The previous summer, when Sue Hall, Kristen Janssen and I had trekked south across the Brooks Range to the West Fork of the Sheenjek, Andrew had wanted to come along, but his dad had decided to visit him in Fairbanks at the last minute, and that put a crimp in his plans to go with us. This time, when I asked if he was interested in going back into the same country, he jumped at the chance.

I mentioned to Andrew that at the end of last summer's trek I'd left a unique limestone rock behind at the pick-up spot about seven miles upriver on the West Fork of the Sheenjek, and I wanted to try and find it again. It was the nicest coral fossil I'd ever found, and I could use it in my classroom. Unfortunately, it weighed fifteen pounds and would have overloaded the airplane during takeoff, so I set it down at the end of the airstrip, vowing to return the following summer to pick it up.

Andrew asked how long it would take to get to where I'd left the rock. I guessed maybe six or seven hours. So we ferried the canoe across to the other side of the river where we lined it up a small slough, then hauled it and our gear onto the high bank to make sure there were no surprises when we got back. At first, the walk seemed a piece of cake, but Murphy's Law quickly intervened, and we ran into the boggiest patch of country I had ever hiked in. More than once I thought of turning back, especially after my boots became soaking wet. So much for Gore-Tex! Every once in awhile we would hit a dry area and this encouraged us to go on, but by the time we got to the West Fork itself, we had already used up more than two hours of the day. We studied our map and decided that if we proceeded all the way to where my coral rock was stashed, we wouldn't be back to camp until well into the morning. So we cancelled our walk to get the rock and stopped at the top of some glacial moraine to have our snack and survey the surrounding country. On looking down towards the canoe, we could see why the land had been so damp. Rather than flowing directly east into the Sheenjek, the West Fork veered to the south almost parallel to the parent river. In the spring when it overflowed its banks the water created the large marsh responsible for our wet, prune-puckered feet. In spite of a fine rain beginning to fall, we marveled at the wonderful country on all sides of us. It didn't matter anymore whether we were able to retrieve the elusive coral rock. It was more important for us to simply enjoy this wild beauty of the Arctic National Wildlife Refuge. For who knew if we would ever be this way again.

I glanced upriver toward the headwaters of the Sheenjek. The aufeis we'd spotted earlier from the air outlined the river as it turned to the northwest, but I had to use my imagination to visualize how it dropped down from the high glaciers in the Romanzof Mountains. Its glacial origin mostly explained why it was now so silty, but other reasons were the heavy rains pelting the area just before our arrival, and warmer weather caused by climate change, leading to more glacial melting and higher water levels. But that was all right with us. Normally, in July the water is lower and the river slower and shallower, which would have meant more damage to the bottom of the Ally canoe.

On our way back we followed some old caribou trails, although they tended to peter out as we got farther into the marshy wetland. We saw no recent evidence of use of the trails, so the caribou must have headed for the higher mountain passes before the rains to get away from the bugs. Not that there were many mosquitoes. In fact, this was the most mosquito-free July I had ever experienced in the Brooks Range. There were a lot of warble flies, though, and it was those and the botflies that made the caribou seek higher ground to escape. Warble flies lay their eggs on the hair of the caribou's belly and legs, where the hatching larvae drill through the hide and migrate toward the underside of the skin on its back. There they grow during the winter until early summer when they cut through the surface and drop to the ground, where they pupate, emerge as adults, and begin the process all over again. Botflies are even worse, depositing their eggs near the nostrils of the caribou. After hatching, the larvae move up the nostrils into the animal's nose sinuses or onto the back of the throat, where they spend the winter. In heavy infections they may affect the animal's breathing to the point of suffocation.

Returning across the wetland, we were intercepted by the whistling of a species of curlew called a whimbrel. As he circled in the light rain, he called repeatedly in his high-pitched voice. I had run into these birds before in the Brooks Range and had learned how to fool them into coming down to within a few feet of me. So, as Andrew and I were plodding across the marshy tundra, I started playing with the whimbrel with whistles of my own. The second I whistled, he hesitated, then spiraled down for a landing and waited for us to approach a little closer so he could check us out. He probably suspected we were interlopers on his nesting ground. I wonder what thoughts were coursing through his little brain as we loomed larger and larger toward him with shapes that were anything but birdlike?

Finally, back at the canoe, we loaded up again and pushed off for the other shore of the river, where earlier in the day Andrew had found what he said was a good camping spot. Sure enough, in spite of a nearby grizzly rubbing tree, it proved to be just what the doctor ordered. Others had thought so too, and had pitched their tents and built campfires there in the past. There was no recent sign of human use, however, so our sense of being in wilderness was not unduly disturbed. Often, when I come to places in dedicated Wilderness where there are human tracks, I feel uneasy. If there is even more evidence of human intrusion, my unease becomes greater. It's not that I dislike people, but when on a wilderness trip I prefer to be in wild country without many signs of people around. That's why I take these trips down Alaska's rivers. They allow me and my friends to experience nature on her own terms, to be subject to her sometimes dangerous whimsy without any support system for hundreds of miles. Sounds foolish maybe because, really, in this day and age, support is never far away.

Before making dinner, Andrew suggested a walk up the gravel wash directly above our camp. I was game because I wanted to check out what was in our backyard, plus it would give us a chance to climb above the river valley to get a better view of the area. It also gave me an opportunity to familiarize myself with more of the wildflowers. Already I'd seen a lot of Siberian aster, Drummond's avens, Kamchatka rhododendron, dwarf fireweed, and grass of Parnassus. On this walk we came across shrubby cinquefoil, windflower, Indian paintbrush, and one I hadn't seen in a while, saussurea, which has a purple flower and belongs to the composite family. Another plant we found in bloom was the white-petaled wand lily, also known as death camas, *Zygadenus elegans*. Since Andrew asked me about its name, when we got back to camp I consulted my guidebook. The plant's bulbs contain the poisonous alkaloid zygadenine, it said, which is twice as potent as strychnine and has killed both livestock and humans. Most cases of human poisoning were because of confusion of the bulbs with those of edible species such as wild onion.

We were hungry when we arrived back at camp, so we built a fire and fried up some quesadillas, tortilla sandwiches with cheese in the middle that are always a gourmet delight when you're camping. And since the rain had stopped, we relaxed around the fire and munched and chatted about one of our favorite topics, the political status of the Arctic Refuge. So far, it looked good, with President Clinton vowing to veto any attempt by the Republicans to make it available for drilling by the oil companies. Now, with exploration for oil in the eastern sector of the National Petroleum Reserve highly probable, and the new lower estimates of the amount of oil under the Coastal Plain of the Refuge, it appeared even safer. The only wild card was the possibility of a Republican President in the year 2000. If that happened, it may mean the death knell for the area. I shook my head at the lack of vision of those who continued to advocate for drilling, since the burning of fossil fuels is one of the main engines behind climate change. But such is the short-sighted, capitalist nature of the United States at this stage in history. Although we are slowly evolving in the right direction, the change may not be fast enough to avert a worldwide catastrophe. We shall see.

Before we called it quits for the night we watched a squall on the other side of the valley amble slowly across the wetland we had trudged through in the afternoon. The billowing clouds and thick curtain of rain intermingling with the rays of the late evening sun made it appear as though the sky had thrown down a wide sparkling bridal veil that kept on spreading as the squall pushed itself in our direction. It was our last view of the sun. Soon it would begin its eastern roll across the northern horizon, and we wouldn't see it again till morning.

In the morning we discovered two little Arctic ground squirrels, known colloquially as parky squirrels, curiously checking out our empty tent bag, probably searching for a hidden tidbit of food. They must have recognized the shape of the bag from prior raids on the food supplies of other campers, because I had never used that stuff bag for food. We immediately checked our food containers to see if the squirrels had gotten into them. We were lucky, no holes, no missing food, not even any telltale gnaw marks. But, if we'd been in camp just one more day, I was sure the squirrels would have grown bolder and tried for the real stuff. As cute as those little guys were, the way they wrinkled their noses and dove in and out of the bag, their coy expressions belied their foxy personalities. They could do a lot of damage if left unsupervised.

As anxious as I was to get on the river, I proposed we walk farther up the draw in back of our camp to get a bird's-eye-view of the valley and take some pictures. Andrew told me to go ahead, and that he'd meet me on the mountain a little later. So I followed the creek for about a half-mile to where I could jump across to the other bank and then side-hill up the slope. First, though, I bent down and inhaled a few mouthfuls of the most delicious water I'd had in a long time. It was the sweet taste of tannin, the result of seepage through the tundra on the mountainside.

Then I was off up the mountain, following well-trodden sheep and caribou trails. Recent grizzly bear sign was everywhere, too, probably because there was so much to eat for them. The slope I was on was crowded with the white blossoms of bear flower all the way to the summit of the ridge. Also known as boykinia, it is Alaska's largest flowering saxifrage and one of the favorite foods of grizzly bears in the middle of the summer.

This reminder of griz hastened me along the narrow trail until I reached an overlook that gave me just the view of the valley I was hoping for. I could see right into the basin of the West Fork, where I had left the coral rock. I shook my head. How I had wanted to get that special stone! At that moment I felt like Gollum, the character who coveted the ring in Tolkien's book series, *The Lord of the Rings*.

While surveying the almost surreal mountain landscape on the other side of the valley, a gyrfalcon glided over, making a beeline upriver. I watched him briefly, then glanced up the valley, where the Sheenjek traced a meandering route from its headwaters in the north down through thick white aufeis, finally braiding for as far as I could see in the opposite direction. With the high water, though, the route looked easy enough, and when Andrew showed up I pointed it out to him, plus a number of landmarks I recognized from last summer's flyover of the area with Don Ross.

On our way back to the canoe, the mountain slopes and tundra were carpeted with alpine wildflowers still in bloom: the nodding Lessing's arnica, bearberry, spotted saxifrage, four-petaled gentian, and the lovely alpine, ground-hugging diapensia. If only paradise were this beautiful.

Once on the river, we were greeted by a skittish family of red-breasted mergansers. The tiny ducklings couldn't swim fast enough to elude what they probably thought was a killer river monster, so they headed for the protection of the overhanging bank. There they hid in a tangle of spruce roots and flotsam left behind by the high water of the previous few days. By the looks of it, we had hit the river just right. Any earlier, it would have been racing in flood; any later, we would have been doing a lot of lining in some very shallow water. Andrew pointed as a bald eagle swooped low over the river, his head craned toward us. Farther downriver, a female goldeneye, then a shoveller duck, flew off their nests on the riverbank. The juxtaposition of the two duck species was a good lesson for us. Where the shoveller darted straight up into the air the moment she saw us, the goldeneye flew only a little ways out on the river where she plopped down and did a sort of "poor-me" act until she felt she'd lured us away enough to be able to return to her nest. While on the river, we saw similar evasion strategies used by other bird species, ranging from green-winged teals, lesser yellowlegs, least sandpipers and semipalmated plovers. Since these species are still around today, it must work for them.

We'd been eyeing a round-topped mountain in the distance almost from the moment we set in. We wanted to do more climbing while still in the high country, but we found that most of the surrounding peaks and ridges inaccessible because of the sloughs, marshes and bogs separating them from the riverbank. The round-top looked different, though. On the topo map, the Sheenjek leaned inward on its shoulder, seemingly not presenting any boggy obstacles for us. If we could find a decent spot to camp, maybe we'd have a chance to stretch our legs after all.

The water was moving us downriver at a faster clip than we'd imagined, and it took us no time at all to reach the base of round-top. By 5:30 we had our tent pitched on a small jetty of sand in the middle of a large gravel bar within easy striking distance of the mountain. There was no firewood on the bar itself because of the recent floodwaters, so Andrew and I collected it from shore, built a small cook fire, and ate some of our usual fare of quesadillas and refried beans.

I was tired, probably because of the compressed nature of the trip so far. The first two or three days of any adventure are always exhausting, with so much to do in such a short period of time, and a lot of adjustment to new routines and different landscapes. Although I felt better after eating, I needed to rest and crawled into the tent early.

While writing in my journal, a DeHaviland Beaver on floats flew overhead, landing about ten miles upriver, probably on one of the many lakes to the east of the river. The best we could tell after consulting our map is that they'd landed on Ambrosevajun Lake (Last Lake). About two hours later we were awakened by the low roar of the same Beaver, apparently heading for the same destination. What they were up to was anybody's guess, but we imagined it must have had something to do with research. At that point I didn't care, and rolled over and went back to sleep.

Early to bed, early to rise, makes a man healthy, wealthy, and feeling pretty darn good. Good enough, in fact, to climb a mountain. Andrew felt the same way, so after a granola breakfast we started across the piedmont of wet muskeg and mosquitoes for round-top. Even though our steps were short and deep in the soft layers of mosses and lichens, we made it easily over to a creek, where we picked up a game trail used mostly by caribou and moose, then caught a rocky ridge, which would take us all the way to the summit. As we steadily climbed higher, we encountered a succession of wildflowers representative of each elevation. From coltsfoot and butterwort in the muskeg, and glacier avens, moss campion and lupine on the lower slopes, we found that boykinia followed us up the mountain almost to the top. Along the trail there was ample sign that Dall sheep had regularly climbed the ridge in the past and used it as a lookout. Although there was nothing recent, their trails and old beds were everywhere.

On top we could see all the way back up to the West Fork, and almost to the end of the mountains in the other direction. Only the eastward bend of the river prevented us from seeing the Yukon Flats. We also plainly saw Ambresvajun Lake, where the Beaver had landed the night before. There were now several tents huddled among the spruce a short distance from the lakeshore. Later we learned the occupants were U.S. Fish and Wildlife Service scientists studying permafrost levels in the area as part of the worldwide investigation of climate change. But we didn't know that at the time, and the tents and their occupants were a big mystery. About all we knew is that they chose what must have been the mosquito capital of the Sheenjek.

While Andrew studied our topo map, I wandered off along the ridge in pursuit of a pair of American pipits. Normally they're friendly birds, but now they were being elusive, and I figured it must be because they had young in a nest somewhere. As I glassed the pipits, my attention was taken back to the river. Directly below us the Sheenjek was now confined to one channel with only embryonic meanders, evidence the river was still close to its source and full of youthful energy. It was the kind of water I liked. So did Andrew and, as soon as he folded the map and placed it in my pack we started downslope again. Toward the bottom of the trail, a small falcon flew overhead, a male kestrel, probably hunting for unwary voles or shrews. He was one of only a few species of birds we saw during our jaunt up the mountain, but I was happy to see them all. A landscape would be impoverished without birds flitting or darting and diving through and above it. Birds give life to a forest and grace to the tundra, and they reward me with an ineffable sense of mystery.

Back in the Ally again, Andrew was humoring me about the canoe seat, saying it was the best seat in the house. I told him he hadn't tried the bear barrel yet. Not only was it ideal for protecting our food from hungry grizzlies, but it was also an excellent campstool. Made of hard, space-age plastic, and cylindrical in shape to prevent a bear's jaws from crushing it or hauling it away, its 18 inch length and nine inch diameter also served pretty well as a perch for my buttocks.

The water was moving fast at four or five mph without paddling, which meant six or seven if we paddled even halfheartedly. Things sometimes sailed by too rapidly, giving us barely enough time to savor them. Willows and cotton grass were ubiquitous and didn't stir our curiosity so much, but when we came across a family of green-winged teal, or nesting northern shrikes, or a bald eagle soaring, we glided away from them too quickly to take their full measure.

An animal we did get more than a fleeting glimpse of, though, was a variety of parky squirrel that had adapted itself to living along the banks of the river. I had never met parkies like this before. Normally they dug their holes in well-drained higher ground, on the sides of hills or mountains, but not down on the river bank itself. The first time Andrew and I noticed this was when we stopped to investigate a pair of wolf tracks. From what it looked like, we'd interrupted the efforts of two wolves trying to dig into a parky den. The story was told in the sand – the wolves sauntering upstream along the bank, the parky squirrel standing up to spot the danger, his sudden turnaround and escape down the hatch, the wolves running to the entrance, their furious excavation to try to get at the squirrel, finally their abrupt departure when they'd seen or smelled our approach.

I remember thinking how elusive wolves are. I hadn't seen one since the previous summer when I was walking up the Hulahula River with Sue Hall and Kristen Janssen. And then it was only at a distance. Sue and I howled to attract its attention, and for an instant the wolf stopped and glanced back at us, quickly resuming its stride and hurrying on to wherever it was bound. This time I was also tempted to howl to let the wolves know we didn't mean any harm, but then I thought, no, their distrust of our tribe was already too deeply imbedded, and it wouldn't do any good.

Shortly afterward we pulled ashore and climbed a small hillock of ancient terminal moraine to check out the country and get a little leg stretcher. Once on top, we had a 360-degree view of the Sheenjek, one unlike any yet because we were in the middle of the river valley. At this point we guessed the valley to be about six miles wide. In addition to the winding bends of the river, there were hundreds of pothole lakes of all shapes and sizes dotting the landscape. On the small lake directly below us, two green-winged teals peacefully dabbled among the sedges and juncus reeds, searching for edible tidbits in the mud. And from the surrounding tundra the high-pitched territorial calls of whimbrels echoed back and forth in a sort of musical dance.

Squinting toward the north, I thought I recognized the Lobo Lake of Olaus and Mardy Murie fame. Sure enough, somehow we had paddled by the lake without stopping to pay our respects to the man and woman who, more than any others, were responsible for the creation, in 1960, of the area that eventually became the Arctic National Wildlife Refuge. They had camped on the lake for two months in 1956 while they and other scientists like George Schaller and Brina Kessel gathered information about the wildlife in the Sheenjek River drainage. On looking more closely at our topo, I suddenly understood why we'd failed to stop. The name of the lake on the map was Kuirzinjik, not Lobo, and I hadn't put this seemingly unrelated information together in time. Never had I wanted to kick myself in the rear end more than at that moment. Now all I had was a distant image of a long, convoluted lake, plus passages from Mardy's book, *Two in the Far North*, to remind me that I had, in fact, retraced some of the Muries' footsteps along the Sheenjek River.

My attention was yanked back to the present when a short-eared owl fluttered across a meadow below us like a big butterfuly searching for nectar. On the other side of the river, a northern harrier hugged the green mosses and lichens of the tundra, probing for unwary prey. "No doubt about it," I thought out loud to Andrew, who stood beside me admiring the view, "the Sheenjek is rich in wildlife. Little wonder the Muries came to this spot to conduct their studies. And thank the gods they recommended it be set aside as a refuge!" Andrew nodded.

Paddling down the river again, we came upon a cow moose standing on the bank with a light brown new calf at her side. Then another mile farther and the sky above the river suddenly erupted in flight. Until now there hadn't been banks high enough or stable enough to harbor large colonies of bank swallows. But here was a bonanza, as more than a hundred of the nimble birds leapt into the air from their diminutive caves in the river wall, careening above us, curiously scrutinizing our intentions. I'd seen many other birds in the afternoon that had fascinated me, such as long-tailed ducks and red-throated loons fishing in the river, and a gang of bohemian waxwings flying randomly back and forth across the river, but none captivated me as much as these swallows, as they darted and pirouetted all over the sky around us. They were a part of the serendipitous natural rhythms that not only defined the Sheenjek River, but also gave clarity to my reason for being there; indeed, for my reason for being at all. Long live swallows!

For most of the afternoon we had been traveling on fairly calm water. In the early evening, though, we finally hit some real rapids. We ran some of them, but decided it would be more fun to run the remainder in the morning after we were rested. So, at the first comfortable gravel bar we pulled over and made camp for the night. By comfortable, I mean well drained with enough sand to guarantee us a cushioned sleep. The absence of mosquitoes was also part of our decision. It had been a long day, so right after dinner I went to our tent and fell asleep as I was writing in my journal. I didn't wake up till I heard bird song at seven in the morning.

"Sounded like a warbler," I mumbled. But Andrew was still asleep, so I didn't pursue that one with him. And it was time to start moving, so I opened the tent fly and crawled out into the sun-filled morning. Not only sunny, the sky was cloudless and the air transparent. The river shimmered, and its flickering light made my eyes blink so much I almost forgot what I was getting out of the tent for. Oh yes, the warbler. I was sure it was a warbler, but I didn't hear it again to verify. No matter, my attention swung to the river again when I noticed an Arctic tern hovering over one of its clear backwaters. It was my first tern of the trip, and as it dived toward the water. I remembered what a world traveler they were, migrating every year between Arctic rivers in summer and Antarctic seas in our winter. It likely had a nest not far away. I hailed it, then finished putting my pants on.

Two hours later we were back in the saddle, and it didn't take as long as we thought to paddle through the whitewater section of the river. Compared to some of the other northern rivers I'd paddled in the past, the Sheenjek so far was fairly mellow and caused us little anxiety. It had just enough flat water for us to enjoy the country and its wildlife as we slipped quietly by its low banks, and just enough rough stuff to make it a challenge.

Once we were beyond the last riffles, I noticed more Arctic terns on the river. In fact, the bird life in general became more abundant the farther downstream we got. Northern shrikes and bohemian waxwings were especially numerous. The hook-beaked shrikes usually perched on high willow branches above the banks, waiting for either unwary birds or voles to pounce on. If their victim is larger than bite-sized, they first impale it on a pointed twig before beginning to pick its bones clean. Later they disgorge pellets of fur, feathers and other indigestible parts of their prey, just as hawks and owls do. Waxwings are a different sort of predator, eating mostly insects and a few seasoned berries on their nesting grounds, increasing their consumption of berries as new ones begin to ripen in mid-summer. The many hundreds of waxwings we came across also showed more curiosity toward us than I'd ever seen before. They either lined up on the crowns of the tallest spruce and cottonwood trees along the banks and languidly watched us drift by, or they flew back and forth above us, drawn by our sudden strange appearance on the river.

The day continued sunny and clear, and it looked like we were in for a long-lasting high-pressure system. That didn't bode well for our exposed skin, especially for Andrew who had sensitive skin, although he had brought along a special sunblock formula called Bullfrog that he applied every morning before setting out on the river. Even I used it on my nose and hands to protect them from the strong sun. I usually wore gloves for extremely bright days, but since Andrew had forgotten his, I contributed mine to the cause. On long-distance canoe trips, paddlers' hands endure a lot of abuse. Constantly in sun and water, and paddling untold thousands of strokes, they become sun-darkened on top and calloused on the palms. But it's part of what a river trip is about, and one simply gets used to it.

When we started out in the morning, we noticed the lower part of the riverbanks were again alive with parky squirrels. And the more we watched them, the more we understood why they had made this special adaptation. It was a niche unused by other wildlife in the area and, in spite of the danger of periodic flooding, there was the advantage of protection from both winged and four-legged predators. All they had to do when one approached was dive under the overhangs of collapsed sections of the banks. I wondered how it might have been if there had been river otters living along the river. The otters would probably have amended their diets to accommodate a few fat parky squirrels.

As we rounded a bend, we came across two Canada geese on a sandy beach. I tried out the throaty goose call I'd learned on the Lower Yukon many years ago, but they didn't even seem to notice. They just stood there on the dry sand calmly watching us float by. Our attention quickly moved from the geese to a large white bird flapping low over a clearwater slough. It had a fish in its mouth and was being pursued by an Arctic tern. Osprey, I thought, or fish hawk, as it's commonly called, but I didn't think they lived this far north, and it was only after we saw two others farther downriver that I felt reassured in my identification of the first one. And, why was the tern chasing such a big bird? Maybe he had strayed too close to the tern's nest and was taking the consequences. There's nothing worse than the wrath of an Arctic tern, as I found out on the John River a few summers earlier when trying to photograph a tern nest. Both the male and female terns dive-bombed me, leaving a heavy splat of whitewash all over my backside. At that instant I was reminded of the limerick, "Birdy, birdy, flying so high, dropping whitewash in my eye. But I'm a big boy, I shan't cry. I'm just glad that cows don't fly."

Around noon we came across our first large sweepers. The taiga forest had by now become quite dense, with spruce and cottonwood trees growing right up to the edge of the bank. At flood stage the river undermined the root systems of many of those trees, causing them to topple over and just hang there "sweeping" the surface of the water. Sweepers are a constant danger for canoeists who must remain alert when they encounter them on the river. Birch trees make especially bad sweepers, but so far we hadn't seen any birch, probably because for as far as the eye could see the forest showed no evidence of having been burned and was still at its climax stage.

While we were stopped for lunch on a gravel bar, Andrew excused himself for a few minutes to pay his respects, as he put it. The next thing I knew, he was yelling for me to check out the caribou! I had been sitting on the bear barrel cutting my toenails when he called, and when I turned around there was a young bull caribou standing less than 50 paces away. We stared at each other for a few seconds, then he bolted and swam across one of the braids of the river to the other side. After climbing the bank, he shook the water vigorously from his glistening summer coat, glanced at us, then high-tailed it over an open patch of tundra. We knew he wouldn't stay out there for long, though, because of all the mosquitoes, flies, and whatever other dangers might be lurking in wait for him. He was a loner, and if he didn't find his band soon he would be a prime target for wolves or bear. Again, I wondered about the nature of solitary caribou. Were they like humans in that way, or was it only accident that left them behind to fend for themselves?

It seemed the day's excitement never ended, for soon after casting off we came across another "mouse that could." A few summers before, my brother Dave and I had met one of those mighty mice swimming across the wide lower end of the John River. We couldn't believe it and doubled back to take a look-see. As we came between him and the shore, he first attacked my camera when I lowered it to take his picture, then he dived under the canoe and surfaced next to the bank where he pulled himself out of the water and disappeared in the shadows. This Sheenjek mouse, also called a tundra red back vole, was cut from the same cloth. He was making a mighty effort to cross a wide cold river, even colder than the John River had been. We got in his way, though, and he started turning around in mid-river. Then he turned again and headed back in the same direction toward what was by now the nearer shore. We swung around too and paddled upriver to watch him drag himself out on the rocks and, step by halting step, search for some sort of shelter. He was shivering badly and looked like he might not make it. Then he closed his eyes and lay quaking like he had hypothermia. I could relate to that, since I had had a narrow scrape with hypothermia the previous summer after my son Steven and I overturned in the cold water of Birch Creek. Feeling instant empathy with the vole, I asked Andrew to stabilize the canoe while I jumped ashore to capture the little guy and warm him up before he died. I put him in my vest pocket with my hand over his body, and could feel him shake and vibrate, then slowly return to normal and begin to move around again. When I gently took him from my pocket to release him I could feel his heart palpitations but no more shivering. I said goodbye, wished him good luck, then let him go near a thick stand of willows that would protect him from any feathered predators that might be waiting to swoop down and grab him. Then we headed down the river, wondering if the vole would have done the same for us if the tables had been turned.

Next on the agenda were some fancy acrobatics by a hungry Arctic tern. I first noticed him diving repeatedly into the clear water of a small dead end slough off to our right. We soon discovered what he was after when he came up with a large minnow in his mouth. As he flew directly over the canoe, we could see the minnow was being held only by the thin edge of its tail and that it was still quite alive and kicking. Just then it wriggled completely free in midair, and we thought that was all there was to it. But quicker than a wink the tern pirouetted, swooped under the little fish and caught it in his bill. The minnow hadn't given up either and it wriggled loose again, splashing down almost beside us into the murkier water of the main channel. The tern was not about to lose his prize, though, and he dived steeply into the river two more times before finally beating a retreat back to the slough where he started. Not often, I thought, did the minnow get off that easily.

Not far down the trail we stopped again for a leg stretcher. We tried to do this every hour to iron out the kinks in our bodies or to check out some animal tracks we'd seen from the canoe. This time we came across fresh caribou sign, which is always easy to identify because of the opposing crescent moon configuration of the tracks and the rounder shape of their scat than that of moose. It looked like a small herd had crossed the river within an hour of our arrival. Nature is like that, subject to the whim of serendipity, and as unpredictable as the mew gull chasing a herring gull as we returned to the canoe. The much bigger herring gull was carrying a young bird in its beak. With the mew in hot pursuit, it seemed the herring gull had once again lived up to its reputation as a primary predator.

We understood why the herring gull was in such a predatory mode farther down the river when we spotted two of its bulbous gray-feathered young waddling quickly up the beach. What a job to feed them, I remarked. Suddenly, three adult gulls came screaming down at us, diving and swooping and, would you believe, crapping in the water on all sides of the canoe. The bombardment was so intense and so noisy I felt like I was in the middle of a war zone. We paddled hard to escape their wrath and were thankful when the gulls turned around and headed for home.

In late afternoon we came to the confluence of the Sheenjek and its East Fork. The burnished tannin clearwater of the smaller tributary scintillated in the sunlight as it flowed at a sharp angle into the main branch of the Sheenjek that we were on. I searched toward its headwaters and wondered if the river was ever floatable outside the season of spring torrents. We stopped paddling to chat about how it might be to canoe the East Fork, when a pair of loons popped to the surface on the verge line of the two rivers. Their slightly upturned bills and the red patch on their throats told me they were red-throated loons. They were taking advantage of the better vision in the clearer water where it purled off the cobbles of the East Fork into the main river. At first, they didn't seem to notice us, but all of a sudden there were a couple of loud burps, an explosion of wings on water, and the loons were flapping for all they were worth downriver till they finally became airborne. We thought they might keep on going, but they unexpectedly turned around, checked us out briefly, then winged their way back up the East Fork.

They weren't the first red-throated loons we'd seen that day. The many loons, along with numerous other species of birds, such as spotted sandpipers, tree and bank swallows, Harlan's hawks, and a Say's phoebe told me the Sheenjek was becoming more versatile in its ability to support wildlife. We only hoped the climate changes occurring worldwide wouldn't begin to fray the fabric of life up here, as they already had in other areas. We hoped, too, that President Clinton and his environmentally friendly Vice President, Al Gore, could convince the recalcitrant Republican Senate to approve the Kyoto Accord, signed by the President in December, 1997. Perhaps then we could stave off the extreme consequences of the human-caused climate change that was beginning to take its toll everywhere. (At the time of printing, this still has not been done, and the calamities caused by climate change continue to grow worse.)

By now, we'd been paddling for nearly eleven hours, and it was time to start searching for a place to pitch our tent. It wasn't long till we came to a gravel bar that had everything we needed: enough gravel for drainage, a patch of flat sand for the tent, a breeze to keep away the mosies and most of the moose flies, dry firewood, and the lovely fragrance of wild sweet peas in bloom everywhere. It couldn't get better than that, and in short order we had the tent up and supper on the fire.

We sat around the campfire only long enough to eat our polenta and beans and drink our decaf tea. By Arctic standards the evening was still young, and the bright sun reflecting off the river made it tempting to stay up, but we were bushed. So I closed the bear barrel, used it as a seat while I took a few cryptic notes, then headed down to the shore where I stood in the cool water and gently brushed my teeth. It had been a long day.

I awakened once in the twilight of the early morning. While outside the tent there were few mosquitoes buzzing about because of our location on the gravel bar, and I took my time to look around. A cameo full moon dangled in deep blue skies to the southeast while a tattered bank of clouds wrapped itself around the high mountains to the north, hiding the sun in its early morning roll across the Arctic sky. It looked like it was going to be another stellar day on the river.

The morning turned out as sunny and clear as I'd hoped, and I prepared pancakes for breakfast. These weren't just any old flapjacks, but a healthy whole-wheat mix I usually put together for extended river trips. It takes time to prepare a breakfast like this, so Andrew and I chatted a little longer than usual. He started off with chitchat about the weather, but eventually we got around to talking about our personal lives. We had known each other for eight years and had done a couple of long distance treks together. He and his wife, Monica, had been teachers in the Lower Yukon for a few years. They had recently left the Bush for Fairbanks, where Andrew hoped to be hired as a social studies teacher. I reflected on my own early experience as a teacher and was glad I didn't have to start all over again in another school district. I was enjoying my final years of teaching in the village of Marshall, even if it did mean separation from my family for a while.

We finished our last bites of pancake, and I changed the subject. Today would be our last day in the mountains, and we were really in no hurry to cast off. As always, though, we were curious about what lay ahead. Also, with the morning temperature increasing, the moose flies were beginning to show up, and we wanted to be on the river before they reached their peak. They, more than mosquitoes or black flies, were our nemesis this summer. Sometimes when we stopped in the heat of the afternoon we might have a hundred of them buzzing around us. One day I counted twenty dead in just a few swats on my bare legs, and they were still coming. I can understand why moose and caribou head for the hills when warble and botflies are numerous. The pesky critters reminded me of the horse flies that used to bother me when I was a kid in Canada. Their only redeeming feature is their eyes that when alive have the most brilliant green and gold miniature facets in them. After they're dead, though, the eyes no longer reflect light, and the bright colors fade away. But their bite cancelled out much of our fascination for their eyes, and rather than admire them we left the flies floating in the river as fish bait.

By afternoon we were quickly moving away from the high mountains, and also from the low moraine that dotted the valley everywhere. At one time, about 12-18,000 years ago, the Sheenjek Valley was a river of ice flowing out of the Brooks Range. Judging from the size of the moraine we'd run across, the glacier hadn't been very big, but it had enough of a presence to scour and weather the valley into what it is today. Now, all that is left of it and other remnant Brooks Range glaciers lies at the headwaters of the Sheenjek, Hulahula, Chandalar, Jago and Aichilik Rivers. Only the tallest of the mountain peaks in the range, such as Mt. Isto, Mt. Chamberlin, and Mt. Michelson, still harbor alpine glaciers. But even they grow smaller every summer as global warming takes its toll on the Arctic ecosystem, thawing more and more of the ice and letting gravity shoot the silty water down the river valleys and ultimately into the Arctic Ocean or Bering Sea, depending on which side of the Continental Divide the glaciers lie.

Evidence of the meltdown was under our canoe in the form of milky river water flowing so swiftly that at one point, just after we set out in the morning, we were almost overturned by its force. Right off the bat, the Sheenjek had braided, then suddenly joined again at right angles, catching us unawares. If it hadn't been for some quick countermoves, we'd have been swimming for dear life in a very cool river. As it was, we only shipped a few gallons of silty water, which we bailed out of the canoe with my cook pot as we floated downriver. We both breathed a sigh of relief and were glad I had roped down the load, "just in case!" Memories of a previous canoe trip down Birch Creek in Interior Alaska with my son Steven haunt me still. Then we hadn't secured our load completely before taking off in the morning and paid for it dearly when we overturned and lost many of our kitchen utensils.

The landscape continued to change as gravity shot us toward the sea. All the Drummond's avens were now in seed and sometimes blanketed the riverbanks with their fluffy mouse-colored twists. When the sun was just right, I told Andrew, we would pull over and take a series of pictures of those diminutive gems. We heard the telltale spishing of our first black-capped chickadees, who always make me feel at home, as does the high-pitched call of the Harlan's red-tailed hawk. The one we watched circling in the sky that morning was a light phase, lighter than any red-tail I'd ever seen before. No wonder ornithologists at one time considered them a separate species.

As we rounded a bend, I cocked my head and listened to the call of another familiar bird, an olive-sided flycatcher, and the first one of the trip. This is a species I've been concerned about, along with the Swainson's thrush, since their numbers had seriously started declining in the 1980's. Among the many flycatchers in Alaska, I never have a problem identifying the olive-sided because of its singular call, either "quick three cheers," or "quick three beers," however the listener happens to be inclined. When I finally spotted this elusive member of the Tyrannidae family, I was glad to see him as he raised his head toward the sun on his high cottonwood perch and ordered his three beers.

We were now floating through a heavily timbered forest, evidenced on the river by more sweepers and even a few log jams. With the fast water, these required us to be on our toes, if we didn't want to end up a casualty of the river. As we went into a steep turn, we spotted what looked like an old trapping cabin, but we couldn't stop to check it out because the river dog-legged too abruptly, then plowed into a confusion of sweepers that surely would have dumped us if we had tried going ashore. We knew a much larger building belonging to a Fairbanks friend, Richard Hayden, lay somewhere ahead of us, so we figured this had to be one of his outlier cabins used for emergency shelter or storage. We checked our map and found we were now outside the Wilderness portion of the refuge. That was why we were seeing signs of human habitation. I explained to Andrew that only tents were allowed in designated Wilderness areas.

Studying our map again, we were able to locate our position exactly because of a large massif named Shoulder Mountain that dominated the west bank of the river. The mountain's photogenic layers of plants made it one of the most inviting areas yet for climbing and walking. Its higher southeast-facing slopes were almost clear of vegetation, giving them the appearance of desert hills in the American Southwest. But in the narrow ravines trees reasserted themselves in the form of paper birch and white spruce. As these species grew closer to the Sheenjek River, they mingled with thickets of willows that crowded the lower banks and made Shoulder Mountain almost impossible to access. As much as we tried to get through them, the willows proved impenetrable, and we finally gave up our probing and simply settled for the wonderful view and a few photos to remember the mountain.

We stopped to have lunch just before the Koness River, one of the main tributaries of the Sheenjek. For a second time we raided our limited supply of hard-boiled eggs, which provided a welcome addition to our usual pilot crackers with peanut butter and jam or honey. Dessert was dried peaches, and we chased those with a cup of Red Rose tea. Then we ambled up and down the beach, studying the sand for animal tracks and examining the rocks for curiosities, as we did during most stops. This time we found a lot of fossils in the rocks, guessing them to be crinoids, corals, diatoms, sea worms and many others that a marine geologist would have a field day with. It was one more proof that the Brooks Range had been submerged under an ocean many millions of years ago, and it prompted me to reflect upon the recency of human life in the Arctic, and the tenuousness of our situation here. The only reason so many people can live in our northernmost city of Barrow is because of the availability of inexpensive fossil fuels. If these disappeared, they'd be back to the survival of the fittest all over again. The problem now is that everyone in Alaska has become so dependent upon them that when fossil fuels do finally disappear from the north in the next thirty or forty years, people will probably have to leave for points south in order to continue with their high standard of living. At the same time, very few of us will ever again be able to fly north to the Brooks Range to bushwhack in its breathtaking valleys or float on its remarkable wild rivers. Andrew and I were very lucky to live in the age of cheap fuels and thus be able to charter an airplane into the headwaters of this lovely northern ribbon of river.

Soon after getting back on the Sheenjek we were at the mouth of the Koness River. We came upon it suddenly because of the angle at which it cuts through Shoulder Mountain from the west. Glancing up the Koness, we could see no farther than a narrow canyon, which made us wonder about the mysteries that lay beyond. We didn't stop to explore them because we'd been told by Don Ross to look for his friend Richard Hayden's cabin, located just downriver from the Koness. So when we came to where we figured the cabin would be, we went ashore and explored the area. Across the river we could see the old clearing where Wright's Air Service had recently lost a Heliocourier while trying to land on the Haydens' makeshift runway. There was no cabin there, so we jumped back in the canoe and checked farther downriver. We were almost ready to cash it in when, "Eureka!" there it was off in a backwater. Not that we could see much of the cabin, since it was so neatly tucked away in the woods. What tipped us off was the rectangular clearing above the bank that only a Euro-American could have made. I reflected on how we are such slaves to our western geometry.

We paddled into the backwater, pulled our canoe up on the beach, then carefully approached the cabin, just in case there were other visitors of the furry four-pawed kind that may have had a similar visit in mind. Halfway along an old trail through the clearing, we stopped to listen. Hearing nothing but chickadees and gray jays to welcome us, we waded through ranks of old dog houses hidden by tall grass and fireweed until we stood in front of the log cabin and its cache. Since it was within the Arctic Refuge, Richard had had to obtain a permit from the Refuge office in Fairbanks to build the cabin and continue to use it for hunting and trapping. He and his Tlingit wife, Shannon, had raised their family there for over twenty years. Now that their kids were grown and gone, they no longer wished to remain in the cabin by themselves, so had moved to North Pole near Fairbanks where their children lived. Meanwhile, their cabin was already beginning to deteriorate, its blue roof tarps in tatters, hanging down the sides of the cabin. A spruce tree had fallen on top of the roof, contributing to the picture of entropy. We couldn't tell what condition the interior was in, since it was locked up tighter than a drum, but probably the red squirrels chattering nearby had found a way in and were using it as their headquarters. The raised cache was still in good condition, and nothing seemed to have climbed the legs and entered the locked door of the small storage cabin on top. We wondered why Richard had put so much focus on security. The type of people floating down the river wouldn't have done it any harm, and it could even have served as a warm dry shelter for those traveling in rainy weather. Maybe they were worried about boaters coming up the river.

As we were walking around the back of the cabin, we found an old Coleman canoe lying upright and filled to the brim with snowmelt and rainwater. There were also the remains of a vintage snow machine and three dogsleds. Out in front of the cabin we counted nineteen doghouses, which meant that Richard and his family had been kept busy hunting and fishing to keep all those dogs fed. Among the high grass and dog kennels, I picked up what was left of a plastic toy telephone. More than anything else, this little stained and broken toy brought the Hayden place alive for me. I imagined young children playing while older kids and adults busied themselves with chores necessary for their survival in such a harsh climate. It was one thing to be traveling down the river as we were, quite another to have lived and survived there as the Haydens had for so many years. But the toy telephone was still somewhat of a paradox and showed that even in the wildest country one couldn't get away from this icon of communication. Another thing the Haydens couldn't get away from was Blazo fuel cans. There must have been a hundred of them lying around, each now a piece of trash that tarnished the wild landscape. It wouldn't have taken much effort to break the cans down and fly them out to civilization, or to simply bury them, rather than let them wash down the river in the spring floods as they were. Andrew and I shook our heads, took a couple of pictures, then headed back to our canoe.

On the river again, we wondered if we could ever live in wilderness like the Haydens had. As attractive as the idea might be, we had to admit that we probably couldn't do it. Our wives wouldn't go with us, for one. And the isolation, in spite of toy telephones, would just be too great. I could do without modern conveniences, but I don't think I could manage without the social interaction.

Downriver from the Haydens' place we came to some high bluff country that reminded us a lot of the Birch Creek area to the northeast of Fairbanks, except for one difference: there were no birch trees. White spruce covered the summits of the hills and ran helter skelter up and down the numerous gullies and ravines. The entire area had climaxed out, and birch trees were absent because there had been no forest fires to start the succession process all over again.

With the spruce bluffs in the background, I again noticed a visual phenomenon that had always intrigued me. While floating down the river, although the backdrop of high country seemed to rush by even more quickly than we were paddling, the willows in the foreground showed no sign of simultaneous rapid movement. We supposed it was just another of those optical tricks that Mother Nature liked to play on us mere humans, but I wondered what could really explain it. But it was getting late, so when we came across a lovely gravel island opposite a high hill named White Snow Mountain we decided to call it a day.

During dinner I heard a loud burping sound. I glanced at Andrew, and he glanced at me. Nope, it wasn't us. Then there was wailing echoing from across the river, followed by another round of burping. Red-throated loons, of course. I glassed them with my binocs, and saw a mated pair performing what had to be their ritual water dance. As they swam toward each other, one would burp and lift itself up from the water with outspread wings. Then its mate would respond in the same way with a counterpoint. It looked like a sort of gentle sparring back and forth as they both burped and danced, then burped and danced again on the surface of the water, reminding me of the common loon's spring mating ritual. I finally decided it had to be the summer version of a more spirited dance performed in early spring. It wasn't long till both loons returned to fishing, one diving below the surface, the other following close behind. Sometimes they would come up with a prize, but mostly they didn't. And I never saw them catch anything as big as the fish one of their kind did the previous summer while I was camped on a small lake above the Hulahula River. I still wonder how that loon swallowed the fish without suffocating.

Just as both loons dived again I noticed a Harlan's hawk descending to the far shore with prey in its talons. It made an attempt to land on top of a spruce tree, but it was too heavy for the branches and took off again, finally landing on the other side of the willows where it feasted on what looked like a small rodent. As they soar and hover in the sky, these northern buteos hunt using telescopic vision, then suddenly swoop down and snatch voles, lemmings or young hares from the tundra or anywhere they can find them. They might even stoop falcon-like on a small bird. Most often, though, they watch for their prey from a perch in a tall tree from which they take off with powerful wing beats, then silently glide down and snag it with talons sharp enough to rip out the eyes of a grizzly bear.

After those violent thoughts I was ready to hit the sack. The sun was well into its roll across the Arctic sky and Andrew was just finishing a midnight swim, so I got my toothbrush and towel and went down to the shore to prepare for bed. I could still hear the burping and wailing of the loons who were now hunting beyond the bend of the river. Bank swallows wheeled in wild abandon above us, and Bohemian waxwings flew randomly back and forth overhead, curious about the human activity below. It was hard to believe there was so much action on the river so late in the day, and that at midnight I was watching the final reflections of the sun play off the rippling waters of the Sheenjek as it continued its endless push toward the Yukon River and Bering Sea. At that magic hour the forest, sun, river, birds and sky all seemed to merge into one great cosmic harmony. Then I turned and headed toward the tent.

Morning greeted us with feathery clouds in the southern sky and a pregnant moon floating high over White Snow Mountain. A crowd of bank swallows swooped over our camp, then suddenly veered away, separating into two smaller flocks. When they came back around again to check us out, many of them looked like young ones that had probably never seen humans before.

Since it was windless and warm, and the sun was shining radiant on the river, I decided it was high time I took a bath. Andrew had already taken his the night before, and I didn't want to sully the fresh air in our canoe, so off with the duds, on with the suds, and into the cold water I leapt, at least for the few seconds it took to rinse the soap from my body and hair. Then lickety split I was out again and drying myself in the smiling sun. It felt refreshing to be clean, with the oil and sweat off my body and the sand and grit out of my hair. Not that the sand and grit were so bad, but there's something about the oil and sweat that builds up on my body over time that I have a hard time getting used to. I wouldn't have waited as long as I did to take the plunge except for the frigid water on the upper river. It was still cold, but not so bitter as it was up there. Now I was ready for a hearty breakfast.

It wasn't long after we started paddling again that we came across the setting I was searching for to take some good pictures of Drummond's avens in seed. I saw a procession of them on the right bank, flickering in the lambent light of the river, and I knew those were the ones I had to photograph. After landing I marveled at their unusual beauty. All of the flowers had lost their petals, and the seed heads had transformed into fluffy whorls radiating from a luminous central crown. They reminded me of little feathers waiting to be taken by the wind. When Andrew came up the bank to see what I was doing, even he was taken by their magic.

Down the Sheenjek from White Snow Mountain the country reminded me of the bluffs along the Porcupine River. With bold shoulder

patches of low scrub and spruce-accented sideburns, the bluffs were a striking contrast to the east side of the river, which was now flat and wooded
for as far as the eye could see. On one of the tall spruce I spotted my first
Townsend's solitaire of the trip. A member of the thrush family, this bird is
infrequently seen in Alaska. I usually spot them during my river trips, when
they sit like waxwings on the tiptop of white spruce trees. Just as we left the
solitaire behind, I caught sight of two bulbous gray-feathered birds trying
to scurry for cover toward a cluster of logs stacked like pick-up-sticks on a
wide gravel bar. They were young herring gulls and so round and fuzzy they
reminded me of guinea hens. We both laughed at their awkward attempts to
escape through the narrow cracks and crevices in the pile of logs, but such are
the trials of youth even among us humans.

It was soon time to stop again for another leg-stretcher, and the river cooperated by offering us a wide loop that interfaced perfectly on the
right with a tall bluff, which we itched to climb. While beaching the canoe,
though, we were immediately set upon by our constant hungry companions,
the moose flies. They were so big and noisy they sounded like motorboats,
and we had to step lively up the slope to avoid them.

As we climbed, I was amazed at the variety and succession of plant
life from the river to the top of the bluff. In the ribbon of woods next to
the bank I found our first paper birch, quaking aspen and spreading juniper.
Where the trees ended there was a narrow swath of Labrador tea, then on
the dry part of the slope were two members of the parsley family, yellow
thoroughwax and northern goldenrod, along with several others, including
Alaska sage and kinnikinnick, which is also known as bearberry. Although
kinnikinnick's perfectly round red berry is pithy to my taste, bears will eat it,
perhaps mistaking it for its sweeter cousin, the lingonberry.

Once on top, we took out our map and surveyed our surroundings.
Burnt Mountain lay behind us to the northeast, and about 25 miles west lay
the Christian River and the old gold mining camp of Christian. We wondered if any miners still had active claims there. North of us was White Snow
Mountain and a maze of braids we had just canoed through. To the south
was the last high spot on the lower river, Outlook Point, which we hoped to
climb later in the day. In that direction also was the first sign of forest fire
along the Sheenjek. Not far away, a lone cow moose was taking advantage of
some of the new browse growing after the fire. She was looking in our direction, probably wondering what we were. We remarked on the absence of a
calf. Did a bear or wolves get it, as happened so often, or was she simply one
of those rare barren cows that never found a mate? By the way she suddenly
turned and moved away from us, we suspected it was the former.

With my binocs I could just make out the sinuous outline of the Porcupine River, which according to the map came fairly close to the Sheenjek

at that point. We had mixed feelings about getting there. It was much bigger and siltier than its tributary, and completely unexciting for fast water, but the peregrine falcon survey I had done on the river with Fran Mauer a few years back left me with pleasant memories. It was also an inevitable part of the last leg of our journey down to the historic Kwich'in Athabaskan village of Fort Yukon. Andrew wondered about the early role that the village had played in the history of the territory.

Remembering some of the information from James Wickersham's book, *Old Yukon*, I explained that the village had been founded in 1847 by the Hudson's Bay Company as a fur trading post. When the U.S. purchased Alaska from Russia in 1867, the British owners of the post had to move their trading operation up to what became known as New Rampart, located downriver from the present day Canadian Kwich'in village of Old Crow on the middle Porcupine River. There was never much gold found in the immediate area, although for many years after the Klondike Gold Rush of 1898, Ft. Yukon was a regular stop for the mail sleds and sternwheelers that plied the Yukon River.

While eating our snack on the bluff, we heard the thin "tseetsee" buzz of what we were convinced were grasshoppers. I got up and poked around the grass a bit, then came back with an affirmative. They were grasshoppers, although half the size of any I was familiar with. We wondered if global warming was responsible for them being that far north, or was it simply that the heat of the sun on those south-facing slopes had made a cozy home for this species of small grasshopper for countless eons? Even during cooler times, we guessed the sun's rays must have been warm enough to create microclimates capable of sustaining many of the insects we knew from more southern climes. "Not only insects," Andrew commented, "people too! It's no wonder Athabaskan Indians have such swarthy skin!" He appreciated their protective dark skin, since he had the same "cheap white skin" that my wife Jennifer claimed she had.

It was hard to leave that bluff above the Sheenjek, because we knew it was our last opportunity to climb a hill. We were now officially out of the Arctic Refuge and in the Yukon Flats National Wildlife Refuge. From here on it would be as flat as one of my flapjacks. So we took our time stepping down the dry slope through the sage and goldenrod and buzzing grasshoppers. Suddenly I put up my hand for Andrew to stop. "Whoa, what have we here?" He probably thought I'd seen a bear below us. I reassured him it was only a harmless bunch of pink wild carnations. I was about to go on when I realized I'd never seen wild carnations anywhere before, much less in the Arctic. (They weren't in my flower guide either, so when I got back to Fairbanks, I looked them up in my encyclopedic book on Alaska plants by Eric Hulten and identified them as *Dianthus repens*, a species of wild carnation found only in a few isolated northern locations in Alaska.)

Another mystery was the species of mosquito buzzing around us as we returned to the canoe. I'd first noticed them while exploring the Haydens' cabin, but then there were just a few among a horde of others attacking us. Now, though, all the mosquitoes I was killing were the same, with transparent wings, making them almost invisible, and an anesthetic that made their "bite" painless. They were also nearly silent, allowing them to sneak up and nail us from behind.

We were roasting hot when we got back to the Ally, so we waded into the shallows and doused our heads in the refreshing coolness of the river. We thanked the glaciers upriver for the cold water, but we were not thankful for the moose flies that showed up again and zeroed in on our wet heads and arms and legs. Rather than fight them, we jumped into the canoe and paddled down the river like a couple of rustlers escaping a posse. As we left the flies and mosquitoes behind, we noticed that almost all the herring gulls we encountered on the river were wading knee-deep in the water, and we speculated they were either cooling off or protecting their already pink legs from getting any pinker. If I were a gull, I'd be doing the same thing. There wasn't even a wisp of cloud in the sky, and the sun was blisteringly hot, with the temperature probably about 110 degrees. Slathering on more Bullfrog and pulling my visor lower on my forehead, I wished I had brought an extra pair of gloves for my own hands, because already they were browner than coffee beans. Later in the afternoon, when we spotted a giant thunderhead to the southeast, we hoped some of the clouds would spin in our direction and cool us off.

Just in case we got more than we bargained for, though, we thought it might be prudent to eat our dinner a little early, so we pulled into a backwater, hauled our kitchen gear and food out on the cobbles, and made a small fire. Andrew said he would cook this time, and he fixed us another tasty meal of polenta and beans. As we ate, I heard the telltale territorial call of our first blackpoll warbler of the trip. There's no mistaking his song, a thin mechanical zi-zi-zi zi-zi-zi-zi-zi-zi, on one pitch, becoming stronger, then diminishing toward the end, much like the sound of a sewing machine.

Back on the river again, Andrew yawned, saying that after such a big meal he felt like taking a Mexican siesta. I told him to go ahead and indulge himself, and that I'd be okay now that we didn't have any more fast water to worry about. So he leaned back, closed his eyes, and prepared to rest. All of sudden, without warning, a female herring gull swooped down from out of nowhere, shrieking like a banshee. As Andrew jerked up, he narrowly missed being stabbed by the gull's sharp yellow bill. What a wakeup call, I joked. And that was the end of his siesta. We understood the mother gull's ire a few seconds later when two young gray-jacketed gulls jumped off their perch above a log jam and flew directly overhead. Digging our paddles deeper and faster in the water, we soon left the three big gulls milling in the air behind us.

As we rounded a bend and entered some slow water, we heard the loud "kerplash!" of a beaver. There were actually three of them working right on schedule at 5:00 p.m. Most river beavers I've encountered have been in the late afternoon, and they are active all night. Here they were working in a maze of logs, which explained why the current had slowed to the pace of molasses. There were so many logs that it seemed the river might clog up completely, and we would either have to line or portage around them. It reminded me of Birch Creek when several years ago my son and I had to climb over a big pile of them that was choking the river. We were more fortunate this time, and by following the main current we managed to find a slow trail through the shambles of floating logs and debris that surrounded us.

"The best laid plans of mice and men gang oft aglay," I announced to Andrew, quoting Robert Burns, when we realized we were not going to be able to climb Outlook Point. Its summit was farther from the main channel than we'd thought, but even if we could have made it across the wetland, its topknot was completely canopied with tall trees, which made us wonder why it was called Outlook Point in the first place. Probably prior to when it was named there had been a forest fire and the top had afforded a better view of the flatlands we were paddling through. And I mean paddle, since the river had now slowed to a crawl and had become a wide, meandering, back-looping channel hemmed in on both sides by tall spruce. We were lucky, though, because if conditions had been normal with lower water we would have been paddling much harder from the start.

The sky continued cloudless, the sun searing hot, and the water sparkling like quartz crystals. I was thankful for the dark glasses that Don Ross had loaned me in Ft. Yukon, but by evening the relentless glare of the sun proved too much for us and we pulled off the river. Andrew complained he had been "sun-fazed" and had started to lose focus, so he disrobed and dove in the river for some instant reenergizing. I stopped short of jumping in and only doused my head with cold water. Then, gluttons for punishment, we stepped back in the canoe and went on our way again.

Thankfully, the swirling vestiges of the thunderhead we'd seen in the afternoon finally caught up to us. By the time it was directly overhead, though, it had lost much of its energy, and all we got was one anticlimactic clap of distant thunder and a wimpy whisper of rain on the river. But, at last, there were clouds! I lifted my arms in thanks to the darkening sky, then took off my sunglasses so I could see things in their natural light. And see things, I did. As soon as the sun went under cover, the beaver came out in force, and by the end of the day we saw eleven of them assiduously carrying sticks in the direction of their lodges. The herring gulls were also flying around again, and even an eagle cruised across the river, his bald pate craned downward closely checking us out.

By 9:00 p.m. we still felt lively, so we decided to stay on the river. For a change of pace, I gave Andrew the stern, and I took the bow. But, try as I might, I could not get used to being a bowman. My strokes were either backwards, or I overcompensated, since it takes more effort to steer from upfront than it does in the stern. Then we found ourselves in tough water again. First, another labyrinth of floating logs where the water slowed to a snail's pace, and we never knew from one moment to the next if we would hit a dead end and have to back-paddle to find another channel, or what? But then the river would narrow and run more swiftly, at one point grabbing us and almost sucking us into a big whirlpool. Several times we were swung broadside to the river by an unseen current and had to dig deep to correct our heading. We wondered what it was under the surface that caused the river to produce such whirlpools – large logs, tree roots, giant fish, plesiosaurs? My guess was waterlogged tree roots, but by then I would have settled for plesiosaurs. I was completely frazzled from being in the bow, even for an hour, and I finally asked Andrew if he was ready to call it a day. He was, and just where we saw our eleventh beaver we found a spot that suited our needs perfectly. Since it was late, we weren't met by our usual welcoming committee of moose flies, and there wasn't a single mosquito either. Strange, but okay with us, and before we hit the sack we had a leisurely midnight cup of mint tea around a small fire. It had been a long day.

We awoke to a hazy morning sky, and wondered about forest fires. It reminded me of those smoke-filled days the summer before, when the visibility was so poor on the West Fork of the Sheenjek that my walking partners and I doubted the pilot could make it in to pick us up. But, as on the West Fork, the smoke began to dissipate in a favorable breeze, and by the time we were on the river again the sky was almost clear. Since we were now on the lower stretch of the Sheenjek, Andrew ventured that we might make it to the "big river" by late evening. The problem was that even with a map we didn't know exactly where we were. There were just too many loops and bends in the river, and our topos were ten years old. I mentioned my reservations about topos to Andrew, telling him that in the past I had sometimes run rivers "cold," without the benefit of maps, just to see how it felt. Rivers, of course, are governed by gravity and always flow seaward, so I knew I would eventually reach my destination. But my Western mind could not get used to it. I felt more comfortable using a map and "knowing" where I was at all times – the element of faith in what's written on paper. And there is the real benefit of being able to take advantage of the knowledge of those who have gone before. I truly enjoy stopping to explore points marked with interesting place names that still might be important to the Native people living in the area. The name Sheenjek is a good example, I said. It means "salmon river" and refers to the salmon that swim up the river to spawn. By the time they got to their destination they were probably pretty lean, but the Kwich'in people who once lived there used to eat them or feed them to their dogs.

On the river we began to smell the fragrance of balsam poplar, also known as cottonwood. It is so fragrant that it reminds me of the tropical forests of South America. There is a difference, though, between jungle smells and those on northern rivers. Where the jungle is so redolent with aromas that they almost overwhelm your olfactories, the sweetness of cottonwood comes suddenly as you float down the river and just as suddenly disappears.

By mid morning we seemed to be out of herring gull territory, because from then on we saw only mew gulls. "Mewies" are much smaller than herring gulls, and they also seem to be more friendly. Both the immaculately white adults and gray-flannelled young curiously sailed overhead and alongside the canoe as we quietly drifted downstream. While watching them I spotted a bald eagle soaring high above us in the uplifting thermals, and I remembered my dad and how he'd wanted to be reincarnated as an eagle. Maybe I could come back as an eagle too, I told Andrew, but then wondered why we naturalists always wished to return as avian predators? We'd be at the top of the food chain, to be sure, and free to drift and soar in the vaulting heights of the endless sky, or to dive toward the earth in quest of either a meal or a mate. But what about reincarnation in the form of a more humble bird, such as the affable boreal chickadee or Says phoebe? Maybe I'd reconsider.

In no way did I wish to come back as a lowly moose fly, though. Right on schedule, at about ten a.m., they were out in force again, zooming at us from all angles, even in the canoe. Where mosquitoes generally head for cover when the day begins to seriously warm up, the much larger moose flies seem to prefer the heat of the day. They must regulate their body temperature differently, or perhaps they have less glycol in their system and perform better once their body fluids are heated by the sun. They certainly disappear during cloudy days and when it starts cooling off in the evening. There was nothing about this in my insect guide, but it did say that, as with mosquitoes, only the females of this tabanid sucked blood. The female also might live all summer, while the male only hung around for a few days to mate with her, then died.

Our attention was taken from the flies by a movement on shore. A sleek cross fox was striding along the bank like he was on a mission, but when we came into view, he stopped and sat down on his haunches to watch us pass. We watched him, too, and remarked on how handsome he was. Most of his fur was a rich dark brown, and there was a marbling of blacks and russet reds that made him look like he had rolled around on a painter's palette. But, like "red" foxes everywhere, his white-tipped tail was the flag that differentiated him from all other wild canines. Since we hadn't seen much mammal life on the river for the past two days, this little guy was a visual treat.

Good mosquito-proof gravel bars were becoming more scarce the farther down we got on the river, so when we finally came to one that met our standards we went ashore for a leg-stretcher. Right away we noticed the tips of two thin spruce logs sticking diagonally out of the sand, and we thought we'd try out the ancient Greek concept of the catapult. Try as we did, though, we couldn't get their notion of motion to work. The problem was the shape of both the logs and the stone missiles we were trying to hurl. Roundness, we learned, doesn't make for good outward propulsion of a heavy object.

Shortly after putting in again we bumped into a large gaggle of Canada geese. We counted 25 young and six adults waddling like barnyard geese on the shore and gravel bars, then finally wading into the water and swimming for all they were worth downstream. The adults frantically flapped their wings and headed in opposite directions from the goslings, to try to lure us away from them. We noticed they only had stubs for wings, indicating they were in the middle of their molt. Finally everything became quiet when they found hiding places under willows at the edge of the cutbank. Their frenzied evasive action told us that hunters from Ft. Yukon probably used this area for subsistence. Otherwise, their attempts at escape from two men in a little boat might not have been so frantic. Like other waterfowl, Canada geese have an excellent memory, and this usually helps them avoid hunters in motorboats. It's their size that causes them problems, along with their molt all at once in the middle of summer.

In spite of the slower water we were on now, there was never a dull moment. From their high perch in the spruce or cottonwoods Hammond's flycatchers called to us with their abrupt tse-beek!...tse-beek! Or red-throated loons burped loudly, then silently submerged. Once as we rounded a long bend we ran into five of the loons fishing in one of their "hot spots." They all burped in unison, then took off running on top of the water until they were airborne, gaining elevation for a few seconds, then beginning a lazy circle back in our direction. Within minutes all five loons had splashed down where they had originated. It wasn't only the birds that captured our attention. There were other humbler things, like the root systems of the cottonwoods that fell through the bottom of the overhanging cutbanks into the water, reminding me of mangroves I'd seen on the coast of the Yucatan Peninsula in Mexico. Roots act the same everywhere.

By late afternoon we came to a large clearing on the right bank. We were curious, so we tied the canoe to some willows and went up to take a look around. We were greeted by a loud crashing through the brush of what we guessed was a moose hurriedly vacating the area. Doubt knit my brow a few moments later when we discovered a grizzly bear rubbing tree with copious amounts of amber-brown hair clinging to it, along with the "ecstasy bite" marks located at the bear's mouth level. As we explored what was probably an old Kwich'in hunting camp, we found more grizzly sign, which probably explained the large man-made clearing. The Kwich'in have a healthy respect for grizzlies and don't like surprises.

After picking up some garbage left by hunters, we cast off, wondering aloud why we still hadn't seen any bears. And what about the clearing we'd just come from? We had to admit that it was only a tiny wedge of land in a gigantic wilderness, a seemingly insignificant attempt by humans to keep Nature at bay. But so had things begun in the same way only a few hundred years ago in the Lower 48. Now, four million miles of roads later, there are few wide-open spaces left down there. And the situation is not getting any better.

We have Olaus and Mardie Murie and other dedicated naturalists to thank for advocating the setting aside of large tracts of land such as the Arctic National Wildlife Refuge to preserve wildlife populations in Alaska. I only hope future generations realize the purpose those wilderness areas serve in relation to their own survival. Unfortunately, we don't have much time left to change where we seem to be headed. Soon there may be so many threads of Nature's fabric torn and broken that earth's biosystems will begin to irretrievably shut down. Andrew and I are lucky to live in this mostly wild State, but even Alaska is not completely safe, and if present trends continue, it will experience destructive changes similar to those happening elsewhere. The jury is still out, but the writing seems to be on the wall. I have hopes for such international meetings as the Kyoto Conference, but as someone once said, "biology is on the side of gluttony and compulsive growth!"

We stopped for the night on another "comfortable" east-facing gravel bar, although we had to use our paddles to shovel sand to build a level platform for our tent. After that, we prepared a quesadilla dinner that Andrew said was fit for the river gods, and watched slate gray skies threaten us for the first time with some serious lightning and thunder. At the last minute, though, Thor only sent a whispering pitter-patter of raindrops across the expanse of river in front of our camp. The rain was so light that we were able to sit around the fire and watch the storm swirl past us to the south, then quickly dissipate into wispy feathers of clouds. It's not often a person has a chance to watch the evolution of a storm cell like that. The only other times I can remember were in the Minto Flats near Fairbanks and in the Yukon Delta. Now the Yukon Flats. All of those places have one thing in common. They are pancake flat.

When the rain passed, we studied our topo and found that in spite of the slow current and all the long loops and bends, we had gone about forty-five miles since setting out in the morning. By assiduously checking the map as we paddled down the river, we had finally figured out where we were. The Porcupine still eluded us, but there was no hurry; we'd be there the next day. The closer we got to the "big river," though, the more the mosquitoes found us, even on the gravel bars. These were the same species that had introduced themselves just below the Koness River, smaller, almost translucent, with a higher whine and a "new improved anesthetic," as Andrew put it.

In the tent we chatted awhile about the philosopher Joseph Campbell's notions of myth, and the endless conversations about them I used to have with a Jesuit priest named Ed Flint in Marshall, where I still taught school. Ed was a great source of intellectual stimulation. Together we viewed Bill Moyer's video series, *The Power of Myth*, about Campbell's life and thoughts, and afterward had some great discussions that ran the gamut from evolution to atheism.

Before closing my eyes, I read a few pages of naturalist Sigurd Olsen's lovely book, *The Lonely Land*, about a canoe trip he took with some friends in central Canada in the early 1950's. His writing style is more matter of fact than that of modern nature writers who tend towards the sentimental and lyrical, but he still has a way with words and some very good descriptions. His writing reminds me a little of Aldo Leopold's in *A Sand County Almanac*. He and Leopold were close enough in age to be contemporaries, and it's possible they even knew each other. But, as good as Olsen's book was, my eyelids became droopier and droopier, finally closing as I listened to the sound of the river purling by. The night before, the current had been full of the noise of riffles and eddies, but now there was only the whisper of the water folding into itself, and a final roll of thunder in the distance.

We knew this would be our last day on the Sheenjek River, and it was so clear and sunny again that we just took it easy eating breakfast around an almost smokeless spruce campfire. I remembered a story my Fairbanks friend Evert Wenrick once told me about his solo trip from the headwaters of the Porcupine River to the Yukon bridge, and I wondered how it had been for him during the month it took to canoe that far. It was probably a satisfying opportunity for introspection, but it must also have been just a little lonely for him. Andrew admitted he still wasn't at the point where he could enjoy a solo trip as long as Evert's, and I thought I probably wasn't either.

Back on the river, we paddled in the lethargic current past a Harlan's hawk nest in a tall spruce tree, with two curious fledglings perched gawking at us, while one of their parents stood sentinel, complaining in slow squeals of our uninvited presence. A little farther down a great gray owl surprised us, lifting off a dead tree that jutted into the river. As its heavy bulbous form melted into the shadows of the forest, a loud trail of vocal complaints from other birds followed its flight through the trees.

I'd just finished remarking on all the kingfishers we'd been seeing when the river suddenly picked up speed and cut abruptly through the narrow neck of a big loop. This was a new channel, probably carved the past spring, and the water rushed us by piles of logs jammed up on either bank. "Heads up, Andrew," I yelled nervously. "This may be a tricky one!" But we made it to the other side unscathed, and breathed a little easier when we checked our map and saw how much river the short cut had saved us. We weren't so concerned about the distance, but by the stiff east wind we'd have to face as we rounded the big bend. We still had to work hard for the rest of the morning, since the river was now flowing as slow as spruce sap and gave us little headway against the wind.

By mid-afternoon the current had almost stopped moving, and we sensed we were close to the mouth of the river. There was now barely any riverbank, and willows and balsam poplar filled the horizon on all sides. Sweet fragrances in the air told us the poplar were still in bloom and would soon throw their cotton. Waterfowl abounded everywhere, and a young horned owl perched on an outstretched willow branch, watching what soon could become a tasty meal caught by one of its parents. At the moment we passed him, the owl was being noisily harassed by a varied thrush, one of many we had seen on this lower stretch of the river.

On our final leg on the Sheenjek we became a little confused by the immense tapestry of channels and islands the river had formed over the millennia. At that point, though, our topo map offered us reassurance, indicating we were headed in the right direction on a long westward arching tongue of the Sheenjek that finally entered the bigger river to the right of a narrow gravel spit shared for almost half a mile by both rivers. Then, almost anticlimactically, we were on the Porcupine.

Before entering the Porcupine, we came to a sandbar projecting into the river like a sharpened stick. At its tip was a derelict spruce tree, completely denuded of branches, bark and most of its gorgon-like root system. Eleven adult Arctic terns, all facing upriver, perched on the stubs of its tentacles and along its trunk. They reminded me of commuters waiting for the morning train, and all I could think was, what a place to be waiting for the train.

Our stomachs started to grumble, so we headed across the muddy waters of the big river to the far shore, where there was a gravel bar larger than any I'd seen since I was on the Porcupine with Fran Mauer doing the falcon survey in 1994. As we unloaded our little gas stove and lunch-makings, we noticed a steady stream of Arctic terns orbiting us like oversized black-capped chickadees. Glancing up and down the beach, I could see an almost endless string of them sharing the cobbled edge of the river with mew gulls. Most of the standing terns had the lighter markings of young birds. I hadn't seen so many terns since I was camped on a big lake near Arctic Village almost ten years earlier. So many juveniles meant the gravel bar was a nursery where fledglings were raised. As we watched, the adults caught large dragonflies and fed them to their young. It only took three voracious gulps and the insects were down the hatch, head, wings, and all. During a walk along the beach, one of the adults repeatedly dove at my head, narrowly missing my hat as it swooped upward at the last instant. Within a minute, five other adults joined the onslaught, hovering overhead, attacking frontally, veering abruptly skyward, and screaming at me loudly. I pitied any stray fox or errant eagle.

It was another hot afternoon, so we decided to take a quick dip in the river before hitting the trail. But it turned out to be more than a quick dip because when we got in the water we found it to be so warm we ended up going for a real swim. I waded slowly up to my waist, then swam downstream with the gentle current. The water was turbid, but the temperature was so perfect that I stayed in for the longest Arctic swim ever. We got out only when a red canoe came into view. Just in case they might care to make a spontaneous visit, we thought it best to at least have our skivvies on. When the canoe paddled up the mouth of the Sheenjek, though, and the occupants started fishing, we dove into the warm water again for another swim.

Back in the Ally, the current was stronger than we'd imagined, and we moved rapidly down the wide avenue of the river. It was so much wider than the Sheenjek, and the wildflowers and bird song were so far away from the main channel that we felt strangely disconnected from the river – very different from the personal relationship we had developed with the smaller river. I especially missed the bird song we were always so in tune with on the Sheenjek. But the Porcupine gave us some of the best panoramas yet of the sky above the Yukon Flats, especially of the many storm cells growing like mushrooms all around us. It was fascinating to watch them start in the east as white shafts of hot air pushing thousands of feet into the sky, finally building into gigantic thunderheads that unleashed their fury with streaking bolts of lightning and crashing thunder. We watched spellbound as a dark mushroom quickly built in front of us, then whirled across the Flats and dissipated in only an hour. A little later we glanced astern and saw another storm sneaking up on us. It was a really big one this time with a lot of black clouds, and it was moving very swiftly. Jagged lightning bolted helter skelter all over the sky, and Thor's thunder roared, warning us we'd better get off the river and start searching for shelter, NOW!

And after taking one more picture of a flotilla of baby canvasback ducks with their mother, that's what we did. We headed for the right bank and found a well-drained spot on a wide gravel bar where we erected our tent just in time to escape a full-fledged deluge. Only short minutes after we'd battened down the hatches, the storm poured buckets of driving rain on the tent, proving beyond the shadow of a doubt that my rain fly had seen its better days and would have to be replaced when I got back to Fairbanks. The leaks weren't disastrous, but they needed to be tended to before I took my son, Steven, down the Forty Mile River in two weeks.

While the raindrops beat like sledgehammers on the tent, I tried to read my book about Sigurd Olsen's canoe adventures in Canada. Our own trip was in wilder country than his, but the river system he paddled through was filled with much more white water. As I read, I glanced at my wrist to see how late it was. To my surprise, my watch was gone. Somewhere between getting out of the canoe and pitching the tent, I had lost it. During a lull in the storm, I was just about to jump out of the tent to look for it when I saw a tall, black, four-legged silhouette ambling along the shore of the river right in front of us. I stopped and whispered to Andrew to take a gander at the young bull moose, now standing still on the beach. He must have heard us because he turned around and started moving back toward the willows upriver. As we watched him fade into the woodwork, the sky suddenly let loose again. This time it meant business and pounded us like never before, continuing in waves of intensity for almost two hours. A steady drip near my right shoulder plagued me until the storm subsided, and I was thankful for my air mattress, which kept me dry even as I catnapped during the rain.

Andrew awakened me to say the tempest had spent its fury, and would I like to join him in a bowl of polenta and beans? "Con mucho gusto, señor," I replied. First, though, I went down to the shore to wash my hands and spill some cool water on my face. As I bent down, a familiar shape caught the corner of my eye. My watch! It looked like it had been through a water war, but it was still ticking, and right on the mark. This led to a discussion of time and its importance to most of us Westerners as a way to measure efficiency in everything from work and play to eating and space travel. Sometimes I wondered why I even wore a timepiece on trips like this. There was certainly no need for one. But, who knows, there might be some psychological baggage from my Kobuk River trip in 1971, when neither my friend Steve Grubis nor I had worn a watch and we had lost two full days while floating on our log raft down the river. Then we chatted about all the expressions of time we had in the English language, finally "killing" so much time we felt it was "high time" we officially got some shuteye.

When I crawled out of the tent the next morning, the air was like crystal. What haze and dust there had been the day before was completely washed away by the deluge. I gave the river my usual salutation, then slowly let my eyes rove 360 degrees around the camp. No bears, no moose, no animals of any kind, in fact, except a few birds flying in the willows. But even they were silent because of their young hiding somewhere in expectation of being fed. This would be our last day on the river, and I wondered what surprises it held in store for us. Mystery and surprise are a quintessential part of a trip like ours, since there is always something new around every bend. The Porcupine was such a big river, though, it didn't seem like it could have quite the same personalized brand of mystery as smaller rivers like the Sheenjek. We'd just have to wait and see.

Not far downriver we came across another osprey lazily flapping overhead. It was the third of the big raptors we had seen, and the sightings were spaced far enough apart so that I was reasonably sure they were all different birds. For a predator that had been so scarce in Alaska only thirty years before, I'd say that was a fairly good comeback so far north.

On the river I noticed a predator of another kind – a large dragonfly hovering above the surface, suddenly pouncing on the water, then helicoptering back up again. He repeated this many times, and we thought he might be hunting some sort of submerged insect larva invisible to our own eyes. It was behavior I'd never witnessed before and gave us one more glimpse into how dragonflies survived in the north. It also explained why the Arctic terns the day before were able to catch so many dragonflies to feed their young at the river's edge. They must have been easy targets for the highly versatile terns.

Where the main channel bumped into a high cutbank, I could make out the song of not one, but two, olive-sided flycatchers, which brought a smile, since they are such a rarity anymore. Their winter habitat in western South America is being fragmented so rapidly that I wondered if this bird would escape extinction. Close to the end of the cutbank I smiled again when we ran into a mama black bear grubbing for food along the shore with her two small cubs. As she methodically climbed the bank into the woods, only one of the cubs was successful in hauling itself up and over the tangle of roots and branches of trees that had fallen to the river's edge during spring floods. When the sow saw us approaching the shore to get a photo she climbed back down and stood guard until the little cub navigated its way to the top of the bank. We came so close to shore we could hear her grunting as she urged the cub on, close enough even to see her gray snout twitching in an effort to determine just how dangerous we were. Slowly, and with mighty effort to pull its furry little body through the clutter of debris, the cub climbed to the lip of the bank and into the thicket of prickly rose next to the forest. There he and his sibling waited for their momma who, after a few hops and jumps, was soon over the top and beside her cubs again. Then a quick glance back at us, and the bears all turned as one and disappeared into the trees.

Andrew thought this brief encounter was pretty cool. He had never seen anything like it before, and actually neither had I. Every meeting with wild animals is different from the last and teaches me more about their behavior. This one led to a chat on the river about the Native American idea of "tribes" of four-leggéd animals. Species of wild animals were often likened to tribes of humans and, in many cases, legend claimed that humans had originated from animals. In more traditional times, Native Americans were much closer to "four-leggéds" than they are today. So were our own ancestors, for that matter. And what a tragedy it is that we have all grown so far apart.

While we were philosophizing we noticed three mew gulls hovering around some low willows on the edge of the cutbank. Time after time they would swoop down on the trees and pluck moth larvae from the leaves. Neither of us had ever seen this before either, and we marveled again at the survival strategies of northern birds.

As the fluttering gulls faded in the distance, we spotted a dragonfly skipping awkwardly over the surface of the river, hardly able to stay in the air. Suddenly it dropped into the water, only making feeble attempts to extricate itself from what looked like a final watery grave. I wondered if we should lend a hand, and decided it was worth a try. I lifted the little downed whirlybird out of the river with my fingers and placed him on top of the canoe thwart where I hoped he would dry out in the sun. After a few minutes I picked him up and gazed directly into his green multi-faceted eyes, bulging like miniature watermelons, and I wondered what he was feeling as he peered back into my own blue eyes.

I felt his four lacy diaphanous wings, which appeared so fragile, but were really made of some very tough stuff. They were also independently powered, which enabled him to hover, fly backward, and attain speeds of up to 30 mph. No wonder dragonflies were the source of inspiration for the concept of the helicopter. But one thing their amazing wing design allows them to do that helicopters will never be able to match is fly together in tandem, with the male grasping the head of the female with his tail. Of course, dragonflies have different imperatives. They do this to discourage competing males that would otherwise try to extract his sperm from a storage pouch inside the female and replace it with their own. Helicopters are also dependent upon fossil fuels for their propulsion, whereas dragonflies depend only upon themselves. The fuel, however, allows the machine to be thousands of times bigger than the insect. The largest dragonflies only had a wingspan of two-and-a-half feet, and those lived 180 million years ago during the Jurassic Period. I wondered what it would be like canoeing on a river with such large insects coursing above us, landing momentarily on the canoe to check us out and ponder the prospects of a tasty meal!

After five minutes our little dragonfly friend lifted off from the thwart and headed downriver. At first, we thought he was going to be okay, but then he abruptly took another dive and ended up in the drink again. Since he was directly in our path, I scooped him up a second time and put him on the floor of the canoe so he wouldn't be able to take wing so easily before he was fully dry. He waited about ten minutes, then made a beeline for the near bank on our starboard side. We really thought he was going to make it this time, and rooted for him as he started helicoptering at full speed towards the bank. But suddenly he veered around and headed back out into the river where he began bouncing and skipping on and off the surface, as we'd seen him do at the outset. Then, kerplunk!, he was down and under again, and we resigned ourselves to his fate – probably a good square meal for some young gull or tern.

Our attention was taken from the dragonfly by the sound of a motorboat growling up the river. We were about twelve miles out of Ft. Yukon and just rounding a big bend when we spotted a flat-bottomed aluminum skiff heading in slow motion towards us. There were two men aboard, and as they came alongside we stopped paddling and hailed them, asking their names, giving them ours, and small-talking about the river. Their names were Harold and Tommy Ward, brothers, and they were going upriver to their homestead. They were friendly fellows, but their toothless faces told us they had probably been through at least one or two drunken brawls. After giving us directions to Sucker Creek, our backdoor into Ft. Yukon, they told us they had to get going because they were low on fuel.

We wanted to enjoy our last hour on the Porcupine, so just before Sucker Creek we pulled over on a big gravel island where we'd spotted a flock of more than fifty ducks, mostly mallards and teals. We watched the ducks until they suddenly spilled up into the sky, crossing the river in a whistle of wing beats, and finally vanishing over the spires of tall spruce on the far bank. Then we relaxed and indolently ate our lunch and absorbed the sounds and smells and colors of the Porcupine. Listening, we heard the spishing of chickadees in the black-green spruce of the forest, mingled with the faint gurgle of the cream-colored river as it butted against sweepers hanging from the bank on the other side. Breathing deeply, I could smell the guano left behind by the scattered wanderings of the ducks that had just vacated the island.

Then, too soon, we were off again in search of the entrance to Sucker Creek, which, according to the Ward brothers, we were to paddle up for two or three miles until we reached a campground visible from the creek. There was no problem finding Sucker Creek, since I remembered the sand bar at its mouth from our flight over it with Don nine days earlier. With barely any current, canoeing up the narrow creek was a piece of cake, and there were no mosies, which really surprised us. We just knew there had to be millions of them hiding in wait for us somewhere, but as we paddled farther, not a single one graced us with an appearance. So we relaxed and enjoyed the calm water, its mirror of reflections of blue sky and cumulous clouds, and the return of bird song. As we rounded a bend, Andrew spotted a horned owl perched on an old snag projecting from shore. The owl was eyeing a flotilla of young teal, and didn't see us until we'd floated to within just a few yards of him. When he finally spotted us he stretched his long wide wings, leapt into the air and fluttered away like a giant moth.

When we saw an opening in the forest to our right, we figured it must be our take-out spot. It didn't look like a campground, but we knew there had to be a trail nearby that led to Ft. Yukon. So we pulled out for the last time, broke down the canoe and stowed it in its bag, then prepared for what we thought would be a long hike into town. Don Ross had offered to help us transfer the canoe and our equipment from the landing to his place, but first we had to walk the four miles into Ft. Yukon to let him know we were back.

Serendipity has a funny way of intervening on my canoe trips, and it happened again. We heard the telltale *put put* of a four-wheeler on the trail heading in the direction of town, so I quickly ran out and hailed the driver, asking him if he could take me to Don's house. No problem, he said, and I jumped on behind, telling Andrew I'd be back in an hour.

The driver was Dick Miller, the local physician's assistant, and when we arrived at Don's screen door he and his wife Kyoko were just starting to eat dinner. They invited me to join them for moose teriyaki, and as we ate I recounted some of the highlights of our adventure down the Sheenjek. Then Don and I jumped into his rattletrap pickup and hurried back to the landing to pick up Andrew and the canoe. We were thankful there were no mosquitoes, since he had to wait more than an hour for us. It was worth the wait for him, though, because when we got back to Don's, Kyoko had the moose teriyaki all warmed up and ready to eat. Andrew dove in, relishing every last bite. I joined him for a tasty Japanese fruit dessert. We went to bed well fed that night.

July 19 –

After a hearty breakfast the next morning, Kyoko told us that Wright's Air had a special flight coming into Ft. Yukon at about 10 a.m. with some of Don's clients aboard. It was then going on to Arctic Village and from there back to Fairbanks. Would we be interested in getting on it? Since Andrew had never been to Arctic Village before, we jumped at the chance and quickly loaded our gear into the little trailer hitched to Don's three-wheeler. We thanked Kyoko for her gourmet cooking, and away we went.

It didn't take long until we were in the air bound for Arctic Village. On the plane were a group of ecotourists heading for the Okpilak River, where they were going to do a cross-country trek over to the Jago River. Two of them were originally from India and worked with the Centers for Disease Control in Atlanta, Georgia. Since their projects were the Ebola virus and the Hong Kong chicken virus, I thought they might be interested in our new "Sheenjek mosquito." They found it fascinating, but I could see that mention of the word "mosquito" brought a look of worry to their faces, which led to a question and answer session about mosquitoes in the area of the rivers where they were headed. They had heard all sorts of horror stories, and we confirmed them, but I told them this was probably their lucky year because of the conspicuous absence of mosquitoes everywhere along the Sheenjek and Porcupine Rivers. By the time they stepped off the plane in Arctic Village they were all smiles.

I had my fingers crossed for them as they went out the door. But, I thought, bugs or no bugs, the couple would have an unforgettable experience, just as we had had on the Sheenjek River. The memory of insects and other minor inconveniences would soon fade, and only the radiant images of the land and its rivers would remain.

PHOTOS

1. Andrew above Sheenjek River
2. Andrew on Shoulder Mtn. above Sheenjek Flats
3. Thunderhead over Porcupine River

CHAPTER 2

Rivers of Gold The Fortymile and Yukon Rivers
July-August, 1998

All of the rivers I've traveled in Alaska are natural wonders, carved out of country so wild and beautiful they've often left me speechless. The Fortymile is somewhat of an exception. Although it was wild more than a century ago, before the discovery of gold in the region, today it is only a scenic river, lacking the quintessential beauty that true wilderness rivers have in Alaska. Still, it has a quality that makes it fascinating in its own right – its history as the first Interior Alaskan river to generate a gold rush. For it was in September, 1886, that Howard Franklin and others struck gold on the river. Until gold was discovered in much larger quantities ten years later on the Klondike River in the Yukon Territory, the Fortymile was the only real action for miners in the Interior.

Sunset on Yukon River

I had canoed the river twice before, and each time had learned something new about its character and history. Over the years I had also watched it change. When I floated it the first time with my oldest son Eric in 1980, there were many more cabins on the river – some of them used by miners working active placer claims on shore. That was the summer before the passage of the Alaska National Interest Lands Conservation Act (ANILCA), when the Fortymile was declared a National Wild and Scenic River and officially placed off-limits to shore-based placer mining. Thirteen years later, in 1993, when my brother David and I did the trip again, only the miners' cabins that had been grandfathered in under the ANILCA were still occupied. During this trip with my fourteen-year-old younger son Steven, we spotted just two cabins that still seemed to be a going concern. There was still evidence of past mining activity, but small floating suction dredges were doing the only mining we could see this time on the American side of the border. Our hope was that one day these operations, too, would disappear and the river would again return to its original state.

But enough talk of history and dreams. Let's get on with the story.

July 29 –

My teacher friend Andrew Benedetti was our driver as we rattled across the gravel washboard on the road through the gold diggings of the old mining community of Chicken. We were headed for the bridge where Steven and I were to start our canoe adventure down the Fortymile to the Yukon River, stopping at the ghost town of Fortymile to meet a couple of friends, canoeing with them along the Yukon, then finally ending up 250 miles later at the Kwich'in Athabaskan village of Circle.

When we arrived at the bridge in early evening, the sky was dark gray with rain clouds threatening a sudden deluge, so we quickly made preparations to depart down the river in our Mad River canoe. A young miner at the landing glanced at the sky, then at us, and warned of the fickle nature of the river – how, after a heavy rain, it could rise as much as ten feet above its normal level. I actually saw this happen in 1993 when I floated the river with my brother David and his daughter Oceanelle. In the space of only a few days, heavy rains raised the water level almost eight feet! I downplayed the sinister implications of the miner's warning to Steven because I didn't want to spook him.

We glanced at the moody sky, finished cinching down the load in the canoe, thanked Andrew for the ride, then cast off into the clear tannin-colored water of the Fortymile River. The water level was the lowest I'd ever seen it, and when I stuck my hand in its dark brown luminosity I commented to Steven that it was also warmer than I'd ever felt it. It was warm enough to swim in, I told him. He looked at me like I was a little nuts, but I assured him that if the sun was out the next day I would go for a swim.

This stretch of the river moved quickly, but there were no rapids and I was able to take in the nature of the wild country we floated through. It reminded me of the uplands around Fairbanks, although the hills were higher and more rugged, sometimes approaching the size of small mountains. The tree cover was also the same, mostly mixed forest composed of white spruce, paper birch and quaking aspen. Willows and alders crowded the banks of the river, providing perfect nesting and feeding habitat for many species of warblers and flycatchers. Although it was mid-summer, wildflowers such as the mustard-yellow tundra rose and white-petalled grass of Parnassus studded the shorelines.

Only a half-hour into the float, as we rounded a wide bend in the river, we came across a young bull moose standing knee-deep in the water, watching us as we drifted silently toward him. He wore a small rack of antlers still sheathed in soft velvet, and his eyes bulged with curiosity. But his fear of the unknown got the best of him, and he wheeled and moved off into the willows with the sprangly stride of the teenager he was. When he disappeared, Steven wondered how the moose might have interpreted what he had seen while peering at us. What did we really look like to him? Were our proportions bigger than life and murky around the edges? Was he truly afraid of us?

Not long afterward, we came to a spot on the inside of a bend that looked ideal for a campsite. We stopped on the gravel beach, and I walked up the high bank to check it out. "It's just about perfect," I yelled down to Steven. It had a soft bed of moss for the tent and protection from any possible rainstorm by three wide overarching white spruce. After helping me pitch the North Face tent, he gathered wood for our cooking fire while I hauled up some large rocks to contain the flames and serve as a platform for our grill. We built it on the edge of the bank so it would catch the breeze and not blow back in our faces, as so many fires seem to do. Soon we were ready to cook up some quesadillas and feed our growling stomachs.

The deluge we were worried about never did materialize, and there were no mosquitoes around to swat, so we chatted by the fire for a spell after finishing our tea. While looking around I wondered aloud what kind of terrain lay behind our campsite. Soon my curiosity got the best of me, and I ambled back into the woods to do some exploring. I immediately came across an ancient birch studded with polypore fungi, sometimes known as Horses Hoof, running helter skelter up and down the gnarled trunk of the old tree. There was one quite fat one toward the base of the tree, and I kicked it off to take back to the village of Marshall, where I taught school in the Lower Yukon Delta. These "punks," as they're called there, are used by Yup'ik Eskimo elders with their chewing tobacco. They first dry and burn them, then pulverize the ash in a coffee bean grinder, finally blending it with ground-up Black Bull tobacco leaves. The Yup'ik name for it is "araq" (pronounced with a French "r"), and it acts as a catalyst to speed up the action of the nicotine in the tobacco. Since the punk ash is expensive, because of its unavailability in most villages on the Delta, I thought I'd make a gift of it to an elder, as I had done over the years there.

When I returned to camp I showed the plump piece of punk to Steven, then picked up my toothbrush and headed down to the river to do my teeth. Since I'm a peripatetic tooth brusher, while I brushed and rambled around the gravel beach, I discovered some interesting rock specimens I thought I might take back to my classroom. The question was, which ones? When Steven saw me hefting each one, he reminded me that we already had a big enough load in the canoe. So I settled on just two round cobbles of marble and a heavier angular rock of streaked granite that I placed in the stern as ballast to counter Steven's weight up front.

Before we returned to the tent, I asked Steven to help me secure the canoe right side up to a stout willow close to the bank. Just in case it did rain and the water level rose dramatically during the night, at least the Mad River wouldn't float away. Many years before, on Birch Creek, the river had risen two and a half feet overnight, and if it hadn't been for a little foresight, my buddy and I would have been up the creek without a canoe.

This was bear country, so we had brought our bear-proof food barrel with us in which to store our "fragrant foods." In all of my canoe trips, I had never had a problem with bears stealing food, but there was no use tempting fate so far from home. Since bears fear fire even more than humans, we also built a smoky fire to discourage them from checking out our camp. As an added precaution, we loaded the short-barreled shotgun Andrew had loaned us and pushed it into the tent ahead of us.

For breakfast the next morning we had one of our "fragrant foods," steak and potatoes, that Jennifer had thrown in for our first day on the river. I seldom have such lavish meals in bear country, but the storage barrel made me a little less careful than usual. It would probably be our only red meat of the trip, so we ate it slowly, relishing each bite, knowing we would need the protein to keep our paddling muscles strong. The river had risen about three inches, so I knew we'd get a little assist from that, but the current would still be slower than usual because of the low water level, and we'd need to use more elbow grease to get down to the Yukon.

With the heavy granite rock as ballast, the Mad River rode better in the water. I've found that having my stern lower in the water than the bow makes for better steering. Our first real test of the idea came within a half-hour after we set out. We heard the roar of rapids ahead of us, and soon we could see the frothing dance of white water as the river took an immediate jog to the right. About fifty yards before the turn the channel split in two, then crashed together again in a confusion of rushing water directly in front of a high rock wall on the other side of the river. It was too much for us to handle this early in the game, so I yelled for Steven to head for shore. Together we stepped out of the canoe, then towed it over to the top of the little gravel island and across the right fork of the river. From there, using both bow and stern ropes, we lined the canoe past the toughest rapids, then jumped in and rode over the rest of the white water and around the bend. It was an adrenaline rush for both of us, and an introduction to the unpredictable wiles of the river.

We began to relax. It was a lovely sunny day, with pellucid blue skies punctuated by vagrant wisps of cloud. We were alone on the river, and it was now perfectly calm and peaceful. As we paddled, we noticed that many of the south-facing shores had sparkling sandy beaches on them, maybe, I thought, because of past gold mining activity on the river. But the negative association didn't lessen their beauty. River beaches are like magnets for me, and I want to stop at every one of them and go for a swim, or do some fishing, or build a fire and make a cup of tea. So stop is what we did on a wonderful stretch of sandy beach just down from another rapid. We stayed only long enough for Steven to catch and release a pan-sized grayling, and for me to heat up some tea water under a luminous sun.

It was good we took out where we did because around the next bend we were in the middle of an ugly placer mining operation. We wondered how mining was still allowed on this river dubbed "Wild and Scenic" by the ANILCA. The only explanation might be that it had been "grandfathered in" as a preexistent active claim before the Act was passed in 1980. But, why, we asked, had it not been taken by eminent domain, or simply purchased outright by the Bureau of Land Management (BLM), the agency that managed the river? The only conclusion was that the BLM, even under the Clinton Administration, was still in cahoots with the mining industry, as they were in most other parts of the American West. It was a lesson in "laissez faire" for Steven, confirmed again downriver a number of times, not only by shore-based mines, but also by oversized "recreational" dredging operations. I had seen small suction-dredging machines on other rivers, but these larger ones were masterpieces of deception. On the surface they appeared to be recreational, but when I looked more closely I could see by the size of their hoses that they were in the murky realm of the commercial. Any way you cut it, dredges destroyed both the wild character of the river and any credibility BLM had left for me. Fie on laissez-faire!

Just downriver from the dredging we came to a small stream called Canyon Creek. Knowing that our first really dangerous white water, Deadman Rapid, was just ahead of us, we stopped at Canyon Creek to eat lunch and study our map. With such low water, there was a possibility we could run the rapid, but we'd just have to see when we got there. As it turned out, the big rapid was a little tricky, and Steven decided he didn't want to try it. He was still a little gun shy from a spill we'd taken the previous year on Birch Creek, when we had to swim for our lives after going over a small waterfall. So we lined the canoe for about 300 yards along the rocky shore until we were where Steven felt confident with the river. As we lined, I showed him where we could have shot it on the right side, but that would have to wait till the next time. Meanwhile, we both enjoyed the kinetic energy of the racing current, then jumped back into the canoe and bounced down the remaining rapids to calm water again.

From my previous trip I remembered a spot just down from Deadman Rapid, where there were three cabins built illegally on an old gold claim. It was such a flagrant violation that the BLM served the miner with an eviction notice. I was curious to know whether the cabins were still there and, if they were, what condition they were in. When we came to the site, the cabins were no longer visible from the river, and I wondered if the miner had indeed taken them down. Steven waited for me on the gravel bar while I checked. As I suspected, the three cabins were still there, but their windows were broken and their roofs trashed. They were such eyesores that I had the urge to set a match to them, but I resisted and went back to the boat.

Before pulling into shore, we'd noticed a tent pitched just upriver from the cabins. I was curious and climbed the bank to check it out. What I found was an unholy mess! The occupant had been doing some mining, then suddenly abandoned ship. His tent had two holes ripped in it, probably by a bear, and his dirty clothes, tools, rifle and fishing gear were strewn about everywhere, along with many cans of food. There was no recent evidence of bear, but the small aluminum boat still on the beach made me wonder if the miner had been eaten by the same bear that had torn open his tent.

When I returned to the canoe Steven had a worried frown on his face. He was afraid the owner might come back while we were there and be angry for our intrusion. When I described to him what I'd found he seemed reassured, but I admitted there was a time when I wouldn't have walked up to a tent like that. The first trip I took on the river with his brother Eric, in 1980, just before it was included in the Wild and Scenic River system, was during a dangerous period. The miners knew what was about to happen and were suspicious of anyone who even looked at them sideways. We only found one family on the entire river who welcomed us in for a cup of coffee. Now, eighteen years later, emotions had cooled, and people were at least civil to one another again. I mentioned a book, *Coming into the Country*, by John McPhee, that graphically described some of the bitter confrontations between miners in the Eagle-Fortymile area and the National Park Service who, along with BLM, managed the land in the region.

Steven listened to those stories as we continued down the river. I stopped talking only when I heard the telltale cries of peregrine falcons, the third family we'd identified so far that day. Their warning calls reminded me of the falcon survey that Fran Mauer and I had done on the Porcupine River in 1994. I'd learned much about their behavior from Fran. Talk of peregrines with Steven led to observations about other wildlife, especially certain species that were conspicuously absent on the river. For example, there were no dragonflies, but this was the end of July and there were few mosquitoes for them to eat, so little wonder we didn't see them. There were also no bank beavers, and no sweepers, even so close to the Yukon, probably because of the sudden high water levels that occurred on the river, which would make short work of both of them. But we were seeing a lot of ducks, including green-winged teal, common and red-breasted mergansers, and even a few female canvasbacks, with their long sloping head profile. Most of the birds led little flotillas of ducklings, so they were nervous about our presence, skittering away from us over the surface of the water as fast as their fluttering wings and paddling feet could push.

While I ogled birds on the calm stretches of the river, Steven lay back and watched the clouds that had begun to materialize in late morning. He pointed at one combination of white fluff that reminded him of "Santa Claus with a Russian hat on," morphing quickly to Popeye's head, then into a bear's face, all of which showed how fertile the imagination is of a teenager. Later in the afternoon he pointed to a towering thunderhead that looked "evil" to him because it might rain on us, but as we moved down the river dissipated and finally disappeared into the boundless vault of sky above us.

A cloud with horns on it led to a discussion of our family trip to Spain the past June, and the brutality of the bull fight there. And while we were on the topic, I told Steven how, when I attended college in Mexico City in 1962-63, I used to go to the bull fights almost every Sunday for the first couple of months. The Ernest Hemingway mystique was popular at the time among young Americans living in Mexico, but the mystique soon wore off and I stopped going. It was just too bloody and unfair for the bulls.

Suddenly, a flock of green-winged teal flew up directly in front of us, and just as suddenly splashed back down into the water. We wondered what had gotten into them, thinking they might just be inexperienced young practicing their landing skills. Then Steven pointed at a peregrine falcon on top of a nearby spruce, intently eyeing the flotilla of ducks. As we approached, the teal exploded into the air for the second time, but when the peregrine pushed off from his perch and swooped down toward the ducks, they all dove for the water again, causing a huge collective sploosh! That seemed to be enough to dissuade the peregrine, and when we heard the plaintive hunger call of a young falcon high up on the bluff, the parent bird veered away to try another strategy elsewhere.

By late afternoon we were encountering more big rapids, and since we felt more confident of our paddling abilities together, we ran all of them we came to. Even though we had to do a lot of bailing after each run, Steven enjoyed every one of these new adrenaline rushes. The Mad River performed like a charm. I'd made the right decision about putting the ballast rock in the stern for better balance and quicker response time.

When we knew we'd crossed the Canadian border, we decided to seriously start searching for a good campsite. It didn't take long till we came across a freshwater creek and some good flat ground that suited us just fine. While Steven carried our tent and supplies up the bank, I cleaned a grayling he'd caught upriver where we'd last filled our water bottle. It was a perfect pan-sized fish, but since I never fry grayling in a pan, I laid it on a length of aluminum foil, doused it liberally with olive oil, lemon pepper and onion flakes, then carefully wrapped it in the foil and waited for our fire to develop some hot embers to cook it on. Fish always taste best broiled that way, although you have to be careful not to burn them on the red hot coals. About ten minutes on each side is enough for my taste. Along with the grayling, we also prepared our usual quesadillas, plus a dried lasagna dinner.

After dinner, as we were drinking our tea, Steven wondered what to do if a bear surprised him while he was in the woods paying his respects. I said to simply yell, "bear!" and I'd come-a-runnin' with the shotgun ready for action. He was quick to suggest that I ought to tape a pair of earplugs on the gun barrel, so I could protect my ears. I smiled at that one. Then he jogged onto the topic of highways, wishing there were more of them in Alaska, so he could travel to more places by road. Almost instantly, he backtracked, admitting he must have sounded like our three stooge Congressmen, in saying what he did. We chatted a while longer about highways and how quickly they destroy wilderness and the rivers that flow through it. Soon we realized time had sneaked up on us again, and we went down to the creek to brush our teeth. It had been a good day on the river, and a varied thrush singing in a spruce tree above us made it even better.

"Daylight in the swamps!" I yelled up at the tent. I had just finished washing my face in some cold water down at the creek, and I figured I should roust Steven from his slumber. It was time for breakfast. As smoke from the fire drifted in the direction of the tent, I heard the fly unzip, and Steven popped his head out to ask if we were going to have pancakes. He must have been hungry because the next thing I knew he was dressed and standing next to the fire waiting to eat.

Over our pancakes, I mentioned that I'd been thinking about the grayling he'd caught the day before. Even though he'd told me in no uncertain terms he didn't want to clean it, I decided to back off my usual policy of, "if you catch it, you clean it, or you don't catch again," because I had failed to trim the barbs off the Mepps treble hook he'd been using. When the fish swallowed the lure we weren't able to extract it without a severe bloodletting, and I thought it would be better to eat it than let it go. After talking out what had been our first disagreement on the river, we got the collapsible fishing rod, snipped the barbs off the Mepps, then struck camp.

We were on the river by 10:30, but it wasn't long until we stopped again on one of those sparkling Fortymile beaches. I'd spotted a stand of weeping birch trees and wanted to try to find a sapling to take home to Fairbanks to transplant in our yard. While I searched, Steven fished along the edge of the beach, this time with a barbless hook. As much as I probed and poked in every nook and cranny for a young tree, though, I couldn't find any and headed back to the canoe. Above me I heard the telltale *tse-beek* of a family of Hammond's flycatchers in the tops of the weeping birch. I knew some of them were young birds because their call was not as distinct as that of the adults, who were probably trying to keep track of their hungry brood. When I haled Steven he pointed at yet another peregrine falcon circling above the river. "Right on the money," I told him, "You're getting to be a good falcon spotter."

The river slowed to a crawl after that, and I let us drift so I could jot down a few lines of poetry I'd been playing around with in my mind. At first, they were only random thoughts relating to my hopes for the rest of our trip on the river, but as I wrote, it became a challenge to put the words into some sort of rhyme and rhythm. I rearranged the lines a bit as time went by, until I came up with this:

> May the wind be ever at our back,
> and the water levels high,
> and there only be sporadic rain on our neck,
> and the sun cool in a cloudy sky.
>
> May the sandy beaches be many,
> and the water warm to swim,
> and our cooking fires never smoky
> and hot enough to fry our fish in.
>
> May the moose flies be few
> and the black flies far between,
> and nary a mosquito in view
> to zap us in the mainstream.

I read it aloud to Steven, joking that it sounded like sympathetic magic, which I explained was something written or drawn in an effort to have it actually come to pass. Well, we'd just have to see if it worked.

By early afternoon it was time to take another break. While Steven fished, I climbed a steep bluff overlooking the river and a big placer gold mining operation on the other shore. We had spotted some of the tailings piles from upriver, but we couldn't get a good view of the mine because of the barrier of trees they had left along the riverbank. From my 300-foot perspective above the canoe, though, I could see right down into the maw of the ugly mine. It was evident the Yukon Territorial government didn't care much about the sanctity of the Wild and Scenic River status of the Fortymile in Alaska. I could see where a big dozer had torn up the ground for almost a half-mile parallel to the river. The machine, parked next to a little trailer, flew a skull and crossbones flag above its cab. There was no activity in the neighborhood, and no one appeared to be home. Then again, maybe there was someone there. We'd just have to stop by and find out. It would give me a chance to take a closer look at the operation and, if anyone was home, to ask a few innocent questions.

I took my time climbing down the bluff, stopping to check out the wildflowers still in bloom on the slope. Golden arnica, purple lupine, a little yellow umbel called thoroughwax, and Alaska sage and yarrow with their aromatic herbal smells were all there. Near the river were other blooms, such as blue Siberian aster and magenta-colored fireweed, both of which we'd already seen along stretches of the river that had been burned by forest fires. Right next to the water itself, dapples of grass of Parnassus were just sending up their white-studded spikes from the damp ground. On close inspection, the veined petals of this saxifrage reminded me of small gemstones.

By the time I returned to the canoe, Steven had only caught one medium-sized grayling. He said the barbless hooks were working fine, and he was able to release the fish immediately after catching it. And, yes, he said, he had wet his hands before touching the fish, just as my grandfather Morse had instructed me to do when I was young. It's a rule I've never forgotten.

Back on the water again, I informed Steven I was going to stop and check out the gold mine I'd seen from the bluff. He looked concerned, but I reassured him, and we put in next to the trail that angled up the bank toward the trailer and dozer. There didn't appear to be any recent tracks, and when I reached the trailer no one responded to my "halloo's." I peered through the window next to the door and saw only filth and disorder, with newspapers strewn in every direction. I wondered whether there had been a drunken free-for-all, and if someone had to be evacuated. I looked for evidence of bloodstains, or even recent signs of foot traffic, but there was nothing that gave me any clues. I went over to the dozer and checked for activity there, but again there was only the skull and crossbones flapping pathetically above the cab. The flag was so symbolic of the desolation surrounding me that I wanted to tear it down and bury it in the mud, but I thought of the possible consequences for future canoeists by these spoilers, so I walked back to the river. I stopped to examine some fuel tanks along the way. More desolation. In front of the tanks were extensive diesel oil stains that led down the bank to the river. I threw up my hands. Miners! I glanced at the skull and crossbones one final time, and fervently wished the price of gold would plummet to oblivion so this once wild country could someday be wild again.

Steven could tell I was upset when I reached the canoe, but he only asked if anyone was home. As we pushed off, I described a little of what I'd seen, then my attention was taken by the screaming and careening around and around of alarmed adult peregrines from what was now our sixth aerie. We could hear the young announcing their hunger to the world. The cacophony of strident cries told me this nest had been quite successful, with perhaps as many as four downy-feathered fledglings peering out from behind some lofty crag on the cliff face.

We knew we were getting closer to our biggest challenge of the trip, Canyon Rapids, and we wanted to be totally ready for it before we started through the canyon, so when we found another sandy beach we pulled in for a long lunch break. While Steven fished for "catch n' release 'ems," I took a bath in the warm water. By "warm," I mean maybe sixty degrees, but as I told Steven, that's ten degrees warmer than I'd ever experienced it at this time of year. The water stimulated my appetite, so to my usual peanut butter and honey on crackers, I added a power bar to give me enough extra calories to get through the canyon. I encouraged Steven to eat a bar, too, but he could only stomach part of one, since they don't really have a taste that turns on a teenager.

Sooner than expected, we found ourselves on the approach to Canyon Rapids. We could hear the deep-throated roar of the rumbling water around the next bend, and I felt us grow more nervous as we got closer to the mouth of the narrow canyon. Just as we were on the brink of the white water, we pulled ashore on the left bank. We both jumped out, and while Steven anchored the canoe to the shore, I walked downriver to see what we had gotten ourselves into. I found no place on the left bank to line through the canyon, but it looked like we could make it most of the way on the right side, so we lined the canoe back upriver about a hundred yards, faced it into the current, and ferried across 150 feet or so to the opposite side. We lined downriver the same distance, then unloaded the heaviest gear on the rocky shore.

Grabbing bow and stern ropes, we towed the canoe along the boulder-strewn edge of the river. With our new sandals, we were able to rock hop in and out of the water on some very slippery surfaces, where one mistake would have meant serious injury. Slowly but surely we proceeded through the maw of the canyon, stopping often to stand in awe of the force of the rapids. They appeared much more powerful than I remembered them, maybe because the river was lower than the last time I went through. I estimated the worst section to be class 3 1/2, and I would never have attempted it with a full load. By now, the roar was almost deafening and we had to yell to communicate. I couldn't help but wonder how it must be in the canyon at flood stage. There wouldn't be a chance in hell of getting through there alive. Finally, after much slipping and sliding and toe stubbing on sharp stones in deep water, we found a place in the middle of the canyon where we could reload the canoe and prepare to shoot the rapids the rest of the way out. To make sure it was possible, I climbed above the canyon to get a bird's eye view of the situation. With luck and skill, I knew we could do it, so I gave Steven the thumbs-up.

We left the canoe on the rocky shore, then packed back the gear we'd left upriver. At some point Steven stumbled and bloodied his foot, but he said he barely felt it at the time, probably because of his high stress level and the cold water. We loaded up, roped the gear in, then I climbed the bank again to chart the route we would take. I briefed Steven on what he would have to do to help get us around the giant boulder promontory directly to our right and to avoid the class three rapids in the middle of the narrow channel. If we could get around the bend without taking much water, we'd be home free. Before jumping in the canoe, I studied the motion of the rapids as they rebounded from the boulder. I could see there was a three to four second hiatus between each crash-and-rebound, and if we were to escape unscathed we would have to push off at the precise second the wave energy left the rapids.

Steven was the bowman, so he got in first, went into a kneeling position, and held the canoe poised and ready to go with his paddle. Watching the water, I yelled, "On my mark, get set, go!" After a mighty push, I quickly knelt on the floor of the canoe, then paddled hell-bent-for-leather to escape the echo of the waves off the boulder. In just seconds we cleared the promontory and were in less chaotic water on the other side. We had escaped the maw of the dragon. But, in an instant, I steered us back onto the dragon's tongue to have some fun riding its flame, until finally it petered out and the water became more peaceful again. Then we began to relax and enjoy what was left of the walls of the canyon and the return of silence to the river. I reflected for a bit, remembering the naturalist Sigurd Olsen's book I was reading and his own experiences with rapids in the Canadian North. I announced, half to Steven, half to the canyon walls, "Sigurd, you would have loved that one!" Steven glanced back at me and wondered for a moment, then he knew what I was talking about.

In his next breath, Steven complained he was "wiped out!" I understood and told him to go on cruise control while I took the helm. Before he could lean back on the load and relax, though, I pointed over to the left bank at the twisted and broken remnants of an old barge that early miners had probably lost many years ago. It had either been taken by flood conditions from upriver and finished off by the violent water in the canyon, or lost while being towed through the narrow gorge during high water in spring. Whatever the reason, mother nature was in the process of burying it with sand and gravel, and in a few more years it would be gone forever, a symbol of the ultimate impermanence of man's artifacts.

After this brief lesson, we both went on cruise control. Steven closed his eyes while I watched the wildlife below the canyon. Just beyond the derelict barge, we encountered our first small flock of tree swallows, most of them young birds, diving and swooping on insects over the river. Farther down, a family of Bohemian waxwings checked us out, fluttering overhead like big butterflies. When Steven asked about the name, I told him it was from the red, waxy tips of the secondary wing feathers and the way it travels like a Bohemian gypsy during the winter, seemingly carefree and without a permanent home. Even today no one understands the reason for the waxy feathers, another mystery of nature.

Soon we began to see signs of beavers working on the river – at first, a lot of gnawed and felled trees in the water, and then the beavers themselves, making their presence known with loud slaps of their long, flat tails on the surface of the water. The first slap was so loud it startled Steven and he sat straight up in his seat, wondering what in heck made that obnoxious noise. By then we had come to the next set of rapids. Even though they were minor compared to those in the canyon, the sound alone was enough to put him on full alert, ready to take instructions.

Not long afterwards we found an island that promised us a good camping spot for the night. We put in on a sandy shore, and, although we had to excavate a site for the tent higher up on the island, it was just what the doctor ordered, and we unloaded our gear, started a fire, and started preparing dinner. As we ate our quesadillas we began one of those typical fireside chats that braids back and forth like a river, about every topic under the sun, including such things as evolution. While we were on that one, he made the most original analogy I'd ever heard about the role man's acquisition of language played in speeding up his evolutionary process – "kind of like a propeller," he said, "that allowed man to think so much better." He also wondered how it would be if, instead of raining, it began "phlegming," in the foulest sense of the word. Then we had a spelling quiz where I nailed him with the word "gonorrhea," and he confused me with "gobstopper." He also got me on the modern meaning of "cybernetics," which he said was the study of mechanical-electrical communication systems that included computers and robots. Then we were silent and just listened to the crackle of the fire and the rhythm and flow of the river and our own thoughts.

On the other bank, we could hear the nervous chatter of red squirrels, and wondered what the source of their worry was. I hoped it wasn't a bear, although I knew that our campsite on the island made us safer than if we were on the riverbank itself. I also hoped for the return of the Canada geese that had been feeding on goose grass where we'd beached the canoe. During an after dinner walk around the island I spotted their telltale tracks in the wet sand and mud. Following them, I found where the grass had been bent and clipped by their hungry bills. On the gravel bar I gathered cobbles of marble, gold-bearing quartz, and greenstone, which geologists say is the most ancient rock on earth. The magenta blooms of dwarf fireweed were everywhere, and in the angular light of the setting sun the island glowed like it was on fire.

On the way back to camp, I came across a thicket of wild raspberries, and filled my hat with the little red gems to share with Steven. I found him in the tent reading his book and gave him the berries, then got ready to call it a day. While brushing our teeth next to the river, Steven pointed at the sky. An ivory half-moon was emerging from behind a bank of clouds to the south. It rose higher and brighter in the pallid sky as we zipped our sleeping bags shut, and its increasing whiteness told me the days were beginning to get shorter. We were now at the end of July, and almost halfway through the summer solstice. Tempus fugit!

Our alarm clock the next morning was the loud chatter of a little red squirrel ensconced in the branches of one of the spruce trees just behind camp. As I listened to him, I could also hear alder flycatchers on all sides of us. I seldom saw these birds, but recognized them by their characteristic *rree-Be*, a call I remember because it sounds like, "three beers!" As with all flycatchers, the bird's call never varies because it is genetically inherited from its father, unlike those of songbirds that are learned from their fathers.

Breakfast was an orange and pancakes, chased by some hot chocolate, but Steven was engrossed in his novel, *Gunslinger*, by Steven King, and took his time extricating himself from his sleeping bag. No hurry, I told him, since we were a day ahead of schedule in our arrival date at the old town of Fortymile, where we had promised to meet my old friend, John Breiby, and his canoeing partner, Will Miles. I did a little reading myself, about some of the recent young recruits to the Northern Environmental Center, a Fairbanks organization I'd been a member of for more than 25 years. I was glad to see there were young people who were passionately helping in the battle to preserve and protect what we still have left of the world's wild lands.

Finally, Steven stirred into action, and we were soon on the river again. Right away, we heard the raucous cries of our seventh family of peregrines. Both adults were languidly circling in the air when quicker than an eye blink the smaller male dove on two ducks that had taken off from the river. He was fast in his stoop, but just in time the ducks took evasive action, and the falcon missed them by only inches next to the surface of the water. He gave chase, but didn't catch them, and when he swooped back up toward his mate, she started scolding him, as if to say, "You missed! Can't you do better than that? My babies are hungry, and you missed!" Then two falcons of a different species hurried out of the forest to see what was going on. "Kestrels," I whispered to Steven, and young ones, judging from their curiosity and clumsy flight directly over our heads, so close we could see the sun glittering from their black eyeballs.

"What's that, dad?" Steven pointed at a metal cable stretching across the river. I remembered learning from a previous trip on the river that it was the remains of an old tram used many years ago to service a gold mine on the west bank of the river. It was no longer needed when the new bridge was built to access the Clinton Creek asbestos mine nearby, so, there it hangs and rusts to the present day. I told Steven some of the history of the infamous asbestos mine, and how, when it was forced to close down by the Canadian government, the company had to reclaim the land and dismantle the buildings in the town. As with all big mines in the north, the Canadian Government had subsidized this one, too, and it left a huge ugly crater in the ground that will be around forever.

I wanted to stop at the new bridge to check if my brother Dave's old Datsun pickup truck was still where he had abandoned it three years before. He'd put his canoe in the river there, then floated down to Eagle, where I picked him up and took him to Fairbanks. He said it was only a junker on its last legs, anyway, and he didn't mind parting with it. Needless to say, the truck wasn't there, so someone must have found a use for it. While I was on the bridge, I noticed how much its timbers had deteriorated in the 15 years or so since the asbestos mine had shut down. Only gold miners used it anymore, probably including those from the "skull and crossbones" mine we'd run into upriver. We hoped the bridge would soon fall and be hauled off to the dump in Dawson City, thus depriving miners of access to their gold mines. The offensive smell of creosoted timbers assaulted my nose hairs, and I couldn't help contrasting that ugly odor with the fresh fragrance of the river. For me, it was yet another example of how man's works pale in comparison to Nature's, and I hurried back to the canoe.

About a half-mile downstream from the bridge we parked our canoe behind a rock shelf and walked up the steep bank to a log cabin that I remembered had been unlocked on my last trip, with a welcome note to travelers. I wanted to show it to Steven as a model of a well-constructed cabin. But this time it wasn't open, and we could only peek through the windows to get an idea of how the owner had crafted the interior. After a few minutes, though, Steven mentioned he felt uneasy about peering into someone else's house, so we walked once around the cabin to get a feel for how the logs were put together, then wandered back down to the river.

Before casting off, we went over to the rock shelf, where I couldn't resist diving into the river. The sun was just too hot, and the glistening surface of the tannin-black water too inviting, so I doffed my clothes and took the plunge. The water was surprisingly warm, and I dove back in two more times. I tried enticing Steven to join me, but he never took the bait and remained on the rocks watching me have fun. I knew it was the last chance I had to swim, because we were so close to the muddy Yukon River, and, as I've often thought about other special places I've visited, I might never be that way again.

We had our paddles up while we watched a Harlan's hawk flutter awkwardly toward us, as only young ones do after they've first fledged, when I noticed a log cabin I didn't remember from my last trip. We went ashore to see how it was constructed and found it to be quite different from the one upriver. All log cabins have a similar ground plan, but each is as unique as its builder. This one hadn't been occupied for at least a couple of seasons because the squirrels had had a free-for-all with the couch during the winter, and the stuffing was scattered all over the house. As always, I checked out the books on the shelves, and found some very good ones, including many by Shake-speare, and one by the British explorer John Lloyd Stephens, in which he tells of his travels in the Yucatan Peninsula during the 1830s. The cabin owners appeared to have been latter day hippies with kids, who had tried to make a go of it in the wilds of the Fortymile. They had left a big teddy bear behind, and I wondered if the kids missed it.

Finally, we came to the last big bend on the Fortymile, and we found ourselves gazing at the wide, cream-colored expanse of the Yukon. I saw Steven's head move ever so slightly and his eyes fix on a pair of big birds hobbling after each other on the left shore. Bald eagles, I whispered. He took a peak at them through the binoculars, and remarked that they didn't appear as regal squatting on the ground as they did when perched high in the branch of a tree. I agreed, saying that the bald eagle's wimpy call alone would have dis-qualified it as my choice for the national bird.

I glassed the mouth of the Fortymile again and spied a green canoe beached on the shore in front of the old gold mining town of Fortymile. It was a dead ringer for John Breiby's homemade cedar strip canvas canoe, and I wondered if he and Will had arrived a day ahead of schedule, too. As we came closer, I saw a figure ambling down the bank, and I hallooed, asking if it was John Breiby. He replied that it was, and after our initial greetings explained that he and Will had made it to Fortymile the previous night. While unload-ing the canoe, Will greeted us and helped us with our gear to the campsite, then excused himself to continue reading a book he'd borrowed from the custodian's cabin in the old town. John had kidded him about taking the book from the cabin while the caretaker was away, so Will decided he'd finish it before we all took off the next morning. Meanwhile, John heated up some tea water, and we visited some more about our travels. John hadn't seen Steven in more than a year and was surprised that he was already taller than I was. After finishing our tea, I took Steven for a tour of what was left of the old town. Until a few years ago, the Yukon Territorial government had taken great pains to restore and maintain some of the original structures, but because of budget cuts had allowed many of them to fall into disrepair.

Most of the buildings were still intact, however, and we especially en-joyed poking through the remains of the Northwest Mounted Police post, the Anglican mission building, a few of the warehouses, and the caretaker's cabin, which had a sign on it that read, "General Store." The building had been broken into by a black bear that had wreaked havoc with the inside of the cabin. Bears are pretty smart, but when this one had come to the wel-come sign outside the front door it hadn't bothered to read the instructions, which asked anyone who stayed in the cabin to please keep the place neat for the next guy. Instead, the bear had broken and entered through the window, scattering glass everywhere, then dumped the table over on its way to the kitchen, where it tore down a tall set of shelves and all of the food items on them. Shards from shattered gallon-sized jars lay everywhere, along with their contents of beans, rice, flour and macaroni. Books from the shelves had been added to the pile, and insult was added to injury when the bear pulled the mattress off the bed and tossed it on top of everything else. Steven and I cleaned up some of the mess before we went out, but left most of it for the caretakers to deal with.

Not far from the cabin we came to a large sign the Yukon Government had erected that told the story of the old settlement, which, it said, had been established in 1886, after the big gold strike along the Fortymile River. It was then that Arthur Harper and Alfred McQuesten came down the Yukon from Stewart City and built a trading post at the mouth of the Fortymile to service the many miners operating there. In its heyday, the town of Fortymile had a population of almost a thousand people, and was served by six saloons, several brothels and restaurants, doctors, blacksmiths, a library, theater, and the territory's first post office. The trading post prospered there until the rich Klondike River strike in 1896, near Dawson City. Then the Fortymilers all struck out for the Klondike, where they unfortunately found little room left for new claim staking, so returned to their old claims on the Fortymile. There they continued to use the A.C. Company trading post for both their gold sales and grubstaking. The community that had grown up around the post lasted until the 1930s when the gold petered out in the area, and the miners drifted off to other parts, where the pickings were more promising.

As Steven and I wandered through what was left of the settlement, we were constantly amazed at the fine quality of the wood that had been used to build the interior of structures like the Mounted Police headquarters and the Anglican mission. Even the warehouses that were still standing had originally been so well constructed that they had not needed much renovation. But we couldn't find any of the original cabins, probably because they had been hastily and poorly constructed so the miners could get on with their main business of mining. The caretaker's cabin looked like a recent addition. In that regard, John was right when he said, "the place was a good example of the ephemeral nature of man's work."

When we got back to camp, John and Will were waiting for us with a plan to canoe across the Fortymile to search for the remnants of the original Han Indian village that was there even before the miners discovered gold. It was the location where the Indians intercepted the Fortymile caribou herd during the fall as they crossed the Yukon to the south shore, as well as a major grayling and salmon fishery in spring and summer. But the place was now so thickly overgrown with tall trees and willows and prickly roses that we couldn't find any evidence of the old village. Besides, as John pointed out, almost everything the Han had used at the time was organic, made of animal skin, bark or wood, and, therefore, subject to rot and decay. The only objects that would have survived a century of this sort of entropy would have been stone and bone tools and maybe a few trade items, such as metal pots, cups, bowls and spoons. Recent bear tracks on the sand and a sudden crashing noise through the brush further discouraged us from venturing beyond the prickly roses.

While returning to the canoes, we came across a wandering tattler strutting next to the river and poking its long bill in the wet mud in search of tiny tidbits of food. At first, I thought it was a spotted sandpiper because the two shorebirds sound so much alike, but when I glassed it I could see it was much larger and grayer, with a longer bill, and green rather than yellow legs. The reason it's called a "tattler," I told Steven, is that when it's a little nervous it starts a non-stop "wheeting" as it forages along the pebbly shore. Its call brought back pleasant memories of other canoe trips I'd taken on creeks and rivers in Alaska.

Back in camp again, John used his Dutch oven to bake a nut-loaf bread from a mix he'd put together before he left home. It was a tasty dessert and a welcome change. Then Steven and I went for another walk through the old town and along a trail I hadn't noticed the last time I was here with my brother David. When we heard voices I wondered if there were other canoeists camped on the upstream side of Fortymile, but it turned out they belonged to a young couple who had parked their car at the end of a spike road from the Clinton Creek road to a trailhead on the Yukon River, only a mile from the old town site. He was from Dawson, his girlfriend from Prince Edward Island, and he confirmed the road and trail were new, built to allow tourists easier access to Fortymile.

They weren't our only visitors. Later in the evening, two canoes pulled up to the bank just down from our camp. They were an older couple and their two grown sons, who said they'd made it down from the Fortymile Bridge in just two days. Their mother was looking for a secure place to sleep, so after John told them of the General Store cabin, they cleaned up the bear's mess inside, and she and her husband stayed there for the night. I seldom sleep in cabins on the river because they're either too full of mosquitoes, or they have the musty smell of mold and decay. Besides, a tent puts me closer to the sounds and sights I came to find in the first place. That evening, Mother Nature didn't disappoint me, presenting one of the most beautiful sunset displays I'd ever seen on the Yukon. The midnight-sun sky cast a reflection on the confluence of the two rivers as a peach-pink mirror image of the forested hills on the opposite shore. A gauzy haze over the mountains in the distance accented the scene and made it hard for me to finally zip up the tent fly and prepare for bed.

I awakened to the song of a white-crowned sparrow just outside the tent. They had been quiet upriver. With fledglings flitting around in the brush, they didn't want to reveal their whereabouts. But here was one singing. I lay in my sleeping bag listening to the sweet song that Eskimo kids in some western Alaskan villages say sounds like, "Don't want to go to school no more!" because they show up in spring just before school lets out. In most of Alaska they are a harbinger of spring and I look forward to their arrival. I always hear the birds before I see them, although when I finally locate them I can never mistake the adults for any other species. Their badger-striped head pattern gives them away every time.

It was another sunny day, and when I crawled into the sunlight I stoked up the gas stove and put on some tea water. By then, John and Will were up, wondering if we needed a can opener to pry Steven out of the tent. We didn't, and he was present and accounted for even before the tea water finished boiling. We were eager to strike camp and get on the river, so breakfast was only granola and a cup of tea. We'd stop later for something more substantial.

We were on the river by 7:30, angling steeply across the clearwater current of the Fortymile and entering the Yukon River almost parallel to the direction of its flow. We knew the moment we crossed the visible line dividing the clear water of the Forty Mile from the Yukon, because the river was now the color of creamy coffee and the silt-laden water sounded like raspy sandpaper on the bottom of the canoe. At first, we had a slight head wind with scattered clouds in a light blue sky. A Harlan's hawk soared above us, and across the river we could hear the hungry cries of young peregrines echoing from a high bluff. It was near there that my brother Dave, his daughter Oceanelle, and I came close to disaster after visiting an Indian fish camp on the north bank of the river. While paddling out into the mainstream from the back-flowing eddy next to shore we were tipped on our side by the force of the oncoming current, and shipped half a canoe of silty water. Dave hadn't realized the danger and kept paddling, so I yelled for Oceanelle to bail for all she was worth. The current was pulling us straight toward some really turbulent water just out from the face of the bluff, made worse by the Yukon Queen, a powerful jet boat filled with tourists that had roared upriver only moments before. I thought for sure we were headed for Davy Jones' locker, but at the last minute the high waves miraculously subsided and the river allowed us to pass unscathed, except in our minds. It was the closest shave I'd ever had on the Yukon.

As in a revisited nightmare, while we rounded a big bend, the Yukon Queen came barreling by us, heading downriver for Eagle. This time we simply turned into its wake and sat out the oncoming swells. I cursed the boat as it passed. We knew we would have to deal with the jet boat only one more time, in the afternoon during their return trip to Dawson City. The wake would be much more dangerous then, because it would be plowing upstream against the current, and we would have to be alert as to how we handled it.

At noon we pulled over for some lunch on a large sandy island. I figured it was time for a leg stretcher, but when I suggested we hike around the island, only John took me up on the offer. As we walked, we found more river-rounded cobbles of marble, which I thought might have rolled down from the Fortymile River. We also came across some of the largest horse's tail (*Equisetum*) I had ever seen that far north, and I wondered if it was yet another manifestation of climate change. We also wondered how islands like this were formed, and decided it had to be from the bow, or downriver end, especially at high water in spring. As the stern was worn away by the erosive force of the water, the bow continuously replenished itself by deposition. In this way, the islands actually moved downriver from year to year, just like a ship.

In the middle of our walk, we stumbled across a wonderful example of how spiders adapt to their surroundings. On a puffy spike of northern goldenrod, a small yellow crab spider blended perfectly with its host, except for traces of rust on the top of its abdomen that resembled a smiling face. Of course, a smile to us might seem like a frown or threat gesture to a predator. I thought it was worth a photo, so I carried the little guy and its goldenrod home back to the canoe, where I'd left my camera. I later learned that this species of crab spider can change color according to its host plant.

On the river again, we now had a strong tail wind, but there were times, as we rounded the long looping bends of the river, that the wind began hitting us from the side, and we were forced to paddle closer to the leeward bank. There I asked Steven to stop paddling for a moment and listen to how it whipped through the treetops, making them sound like a thunderous waterfall. At one point, John asked me if we shouldn't pull over and wait the storm out somewhere. I replied that I didn't think it was enough of a problem yet, as long as we took precautions, like always making a dash for the leeward bank of the river so we wouldn't be blindsided by strong gusts, and, of course, keeping our life jackets tightly cinched.

We came across our first fish wheel at the base of the third tall bluff down from the Fortymile on the north side of the river. I wanted to check it out, but Steven was anxious to catch up to John and Will, so he could talk more to Will about computers. I asked, why the hurry, and told him I was curious to see how fishermen were doing on this part of the river. He wasn't interested and didn't want to stop, so we continued on down the river. I slowed my paddling, though, to explain that I'd hoped the trip could be mostly a father and son outing. Besides, I didn't think John and Will appreciated it when our canoes were hitched together as we rolled down the Yukon, and all we talked about was IBMs and Macs! In retrospect, he probably felt I was an old fuddy duddy, and I promised myself the next time we went on a trip together I would bring along someone his own age.

About five miles down from the fish wheel, Steven pointed to a second one on the same side of the Yukon. Just across from it I spotted a new log cabin, and motioned to John and Will that we were going to make a stop there. They waited for us to catch up, then we angled our canoes toward a sleek aluminum riverboat parked out front. When I knocked at the door, the owner gestured through the window that he was on the phone and would be out shortly. As John and I waited, we reflected on how the concept of "roughing it" had changed in the nearly forty years we'd been in Alaska. It was a nicely constructed cabin, and far from "civilization." But a telephone!

The owner turned out to be a French-Canuck named Gaeten, on contract with the Canadian Fish and Wildlife Service, doing research on the salmon run. He informed us that the government fish wheel across the river had only caught four king salmon, making this season the worst on record so far. No wonder, he said, with the water temperature at the warmest ever. In June and July, he had measured the temperatures at a consistent 19 degrees C (66 degrees F). The Yukon River was also extremely low, he said, at six feet below normal. I jokingly blamed the poor fishing season on "El Niño," but seriously suggested it was probably due to climate change and the warming of the earth's oceans and rivers. To which John added that, "The cold water-loving krill the salmon feed on in the open sea were probably driven too deep for them to reach, so it may be they were starving to death." John was a fisherman over on Bristol Bay, and had just come from a poor season there.

We thanked Gaeten, then went back down to the shore where Steven and Will were waiting, anxious to get going again. Heading out, we noticed the current was running faster than usual, probably a good six or seven mph, and with our paddling we estimated our speed to be about 10 mph. We kept on at this pace past the Alaska-Canada border, which was marked by a 20-foot swath of clear-cut that started at each bank of the river and snaked for as far as the eye could see in both directions. I had heard a funny story about the logging outfit from Washington state that had contracted to cut the trees in the early 1990s, but had underestimated the difficulty of the terrain and finally had to resort to helicopters to finish the job, thus losing all of their expected big profits from the operation. Since the first time the job had been done in 1911, I reflected on how expectations can change over the years.

Once we were on the other side of the border, we knew it wouldn't be long till we'd be on our approach, first, to the small Athabaskan Indian village of Eagle, then to the non-Native town of Eagle itself. Everything was going well, the country seemed more familiar, and I began to feel almost home-free, when the east wind picked up again. I glanced over my right shoulder and saw the skies darkening and the tops of the cottonwood trees blowing so hard their leaves made them look like giant sails. I knew then we would have to get to the other bank of the river before things got any worse. At that point we were hugging the north bank, and the river was bending at an angle where, if we didn't cross to the south side right away, it would be dangerous to do so later and land at my friend Julie Waugh's place in Eagle. I motioned to John and Will to come over for a parley and told them what we had to do before the wind got any worse. Then Steven and I dug in for all we were worth and raced for the opposite shore. When I looked back and saw the waves were already white-capped and moving quickly in our direction, I yelled for Steven to paddle harder. The river was almost a half-mile across there, but we were traveling so fast I knew we'd make it before the really big waves caught us. Even so, the wind-tossed breakers were hard on our heels, and we were pitched and shaken like rag dolls by the buffeting wind until the river began to slowly bend to the west and take us into calmer water.

There had been only one other time when I had been in rougher water, and that was five years earlier during a canoe trip with a teacher friend, Dennis Lenssen, on the lower Yukon River. While on a long straight stretch between the old village of Ohagmiut and Marshall, where we taught, a head wind came up so suddenly and with such force that we couldn't put ashore, and we had to keep paddling into its teeth. Fortunately, it was blowing toward us at a diagonal to the current, and we were eventually able to find our way into a slough and hug its leeward bank the rest of the way home.

Now that we were under the leeward bank of the Yukon, we could relax again and enjoy the remaining few miles of our last leg into Eagle. I soon recognized the high cutbank where some friends, Wayne and Scarlet Hall, had once built a log cabin. The long ladder hanging from the lip of the bank was still there, although they no longer were, having recently sold their place and moved down to the Nation River, where they were planning to buy someone's homestead and build another cabin.

On our approach to Eagle Village, we continued along the south bank of the river. The roar of the wind as it bounced fiercely off the bluffs on the opposite shore told us we were fortunate to have crossed the river when we did. None of this seemed to worry a young bald eagle, though, as he stood on the cobbled beach tearing strands of meat from a rotting king salmon carcass. Although we floated to within just a few feet of him, he made no attempt to move away from his prize. Three ravens hunkering nearby like vultures waiting for road kill undoubtedly had something to do with his possessiveness. Every few seconds he glared at the ravens, as if to say, "Stay away from my fish!"

Soon we were on the outskirts of Eagle Village, where we began to see some very attractive log homes. I didn't remember them from my last trip, so they were probably the ones the Halls told me about when I visited them there in 1996. They said the Han Athabaskans from the village had been sell-ing off their Native land allotments piecemeal to non-Natives. Wayne Hall had acquired his own land this way and, although it was a shame the Indians were selling their heritage, he admitted it was good luck for him and his family, who wanted to be as far away as possible from civilization. Most of the Indians had sold out and gone to Fairbanks to live, he said, leaving fewer than fifty residents in the village. It sounded like something out of the history books about the westward movement and the way the Indians had lost their lands to the advancing flood of pioneers. As in those times, the Indians of Eagle Village were also ill-equipped to adapt to the changes, suffering the scourges of unemployment, alcohol abuse, violence, disease and dependency. The same pattern was being repeated in many parts of Alaska, with notable exceptions where the subsistence way of life was still strong.

While drifting past what was left of the Indian village, it didn't seem to have changed much in appearance from the last time I floated by, except for a few more derelict cars and pickups that one finds in every road-accessible Native community in Alaska. But there were no new houses, as one normally sees in other villages. Only a handful of children played in the streets, and there were even fewer adults doing things outside. In Alaskan villages, boats and motors are a measure of affluence, and a good indicator of the robust character of a river community, but judging from both the number and con-dition of the boats parked on the beach, Eagle was no longer a healthy place to live.

Steven asked me about the school, the largest building in the village, but it had all of its windows broken. I told him that a few years ago the state had merged the village and town schools because there weren't enough vil-lage children anymore to justify maintaining two separate schools so close to each other. It had caused hard feelings between the two communities, but that was nothing new. There had been bad blood between them ever since May 28, 1898, when a group of disgruntled miners, disgusted with Canadian mining laws, crossed from the Yukon to the Alaska Territory and established the town of Eagle. They named it after a pair of eagles that nested on a nearby promontory, which they called Eagle Bluff. We could plainly see the bluff in the distance, and it brought back memories of the many times I had climbed to the summit of the peak behind it that most people now referred to as Eagle Mountain.

When we arrived in the town of Eagle, I motioned to John and Will to land just upriver from the metal bulkhead, constructed by the Army Corps of Engineers a couple of years before to arrest the erosive action of the river. Spring floods had already taken a hundred feet of the waterfront, and it was hoped the seawall would keep the rest of the town safe from future floodwa-ters. (Which it did not do. Eleven years later, in 2009, the town was almost totally wiped out by a record-breaking flood.) Just above the bank was Julie Waugh's log house, and I headed in that direction to let her know we had arrived. I found her sitting on her upstairs deck, convalescing from a bad fall she had taken in early spring. She got up to greet me with the aid of a cane, and instructed me to put the tents toward the edge of the bank, since she was having her lawn cut by one of the local boys.

After all the gear had been carried up the steep bank from the canoes, and the tents pitched, I brought everybody into the house and introduced them to Julie. Then, while John and Will took Steven over to the local greasy spoon for a hamburger, I caught up on the news with Julie. She told me she had recently sold her house to Skip Jorgenson from Tok and was planning to spend her remaining years in Ketchikan in an apartment owned by her son, Dan. He had just arrived in Eagle from Utah with his wife, she said, to help her move. Just then, he and his wife Monica came in from the guest cabin, and he and I had a chance to talk over old times. When I'd last seen him he was a callow teenager, and full of mischief. I remembered how, when I was working as a packer for his big game guide father, Hal, in the early 1960s, he had gotten me in trouble at their hunting camp in the Alaska Range by eating too many of the candy bars that Hal had set aside for his clients, and I had been blamed for the overindulgence. Even though I'd had nothing to do with the purloined bars, I never mentioned anything to his dad about it.

When Steven returned from the restaurant, he helped me move Julie's fiberglass canoe from the gully behind the house, where it had been moldering for twenty years, up to a location beside the original log cabin that she and Hal had built in the late 1950s. There we placed it on top of four metal drums, and cleaned the moss and lichens off it so the next owner of the property could use it. Then we searched for John and Will, who still hadn't returned from their walk through town. We found them at the local store making telephone calls to their wives. John talked for a long time with lines of deep concern written on his face. Later, he told us his wife Anecia had had a dizzy spell the doctor thought might have been a minor stroke, and it worried John so much he had trouble sleeping that night. Not so, with Steven and me. We were dead tired, and slept even through the rain that started to fall in the early morning.

Although the rain stopped by morning, it had soaked everything, including John's sleeping bag in Will's leaky tent. But Julie came to the rescue, offering her dryer to John to rehabilitate his soggy bag. Later, we walked through old Fort Egbert, built in 1899 after martial law was declared in that part of the territory to keep order among the miners and traders who had moved to Eagle. Martial law ended in 1900, but the fort remained until 1911. By then, Eagle had lost much of its population to the booming Fairbanks area, so the Army pulled out its troops to cut its losses. Only five of the original forty-six buildings still stood, and we found just one of those open to the public in the morning. The quartermaster storehouse was the oldest structure left at Ft. Egbert. First constructed in 1899, to store a six-month food supply for those living at the fort, it now served as a small museum.

On our way back to Julie's we walked by the old courthouse, built under the direction of Eagle's first judge, James Wickersham, in 1901, the same year the charter was approved that made Eagle the first incorporated city in Interior Alaska. Judge Wickersham was quite a colorful character, as I discovered when I read his book, Old Yukon. Having to cover the Third Judicial District, which stretched from the Arctic Ocean to the Aleutian Chain, and included about 300,000 square miles, would have been enough to make a character out of any judge.

As we passed in front of the restaurant, we met my friends, Wayne and Scarlett Hall, with their client Charlie Moore, whom Wayne had just guided down the Porcupine River in a canoe. They were getting some supplies together to head back to their fish camp near the Nation River, where their friend, Tim McLaughlin, was taking care of their dogs and fish wheel. They told us they didn't think they'd be able to make it down till the next day, but we were welcome to stay there with Tim. Then we returned to Julie's, where we thanked her for her hospitality, loaded up our canoes, and hit the trail.

By the time we were on the water it was close to noon and had started to drizzle again. But at least there was no wind, and the mist that hugged the surrounding hills lent a mood of mystery to the river that was intensified by the constant hiss of raindrops on the mirrored surface of the water. About ten miles down, a huge outcropping named Calico Bluff was a graphic reminder of how violent the Earth had once been. Its convoluted stratigraphy and variegated colors, ranging from rusty reds and ocher yellows, to slate grays and heather browns, came straight from the canvass of a mad artist. Steven thought the tectonic upheaval that had taken place there must have been devastating for the ancient animal life.

Just then, an example of some recent animal life caught our attention on the right bank. Trotting along the water's edge with a snowshoe hare hanging from its jaws was a handsome black and red cross fox. Although we paddled almost right next to it, the fox paid us little heed and marched resolutely forward like it was on a mission, probably to deliver its catch to hungry kits. If we'd been patient enough, we might have spotted its den, but we decided to let the current take us and floated on down the river. I wondered whether any species of fox had lived during the period more than 250 million years ago, when Calico Bluff had gone through its throes of earthquake and upheaval. Steven didn't think so. The peregrine falcons we saw just past the Tatonduk River on Montauk Bluff conjured up similar questions about ancient birds.

But I didn't think the first bird species evolved before 150-160 million years ago. And what about the physical shape of the country then? There's something about floating on a big river like the Yukon that makes my mind drift back into geologic time and contemplate the earth's beginnings. As I do, I become acutely aware of how brief and insignificant our human presence has been on this planet.

The rain stopped in late afternoon and the water became a mirror again. Even without paddling we were making good time. For a river that dropped an average of only two feet every mile in these parts, it moved us along at a rapid pace. Including our desultory paddling, we calculated our speed at about seven mph, although we probably could have made better time if it hadn't been for some of Steven's mischief making with Will's paddle. He'd traded the cambered racing paddle he'd been using for Will's long-handled paddle, and liked it so much he kiddingly told Will he'd keep it for the rest of the day. But Will said it would discombobulate his paddling rate of 250 strokes every five minutes, and he wanted it back.

While this game between Steven and Will was going on, John and I had some good close-up chats about everything from fishing to the environment. We both felt strongly that the Alaska Lands Act of 1980 had done the right thing when it set aside the area we were now passing through as the Yukon-Charley National Preserve. It would have been more protective of the wildlife if it had been designated a Wilderness area, or even a national park, but with its peculiar history of human use there was little wonder it was designated as a preserve. In this way, there could be minimal human occupation and use of the hunting resources, while still protecting the land and wildlife for future generations to enjoy. Amazingly, although the area was the size of New Jersey, it only had a population of about thirty human residents, all located on in-holdings that had been registered before the Lands Act was passed. Hunting was allowed by permit, as was the gathering of firewood and subsistence fishing with fish wheels and nets. But neither logging nor mining was allowed in the preserve except on a few grandfathered in-holdings such as Woodchopper Creek, located farther down the river, and those leases would expire after the deaths of their owners. The owner of the lease on Woodchopper Creek, Joe Vogler, had been the victim of a grisly murder committed by one of his fellow miners in Fairbanks just a couple of years before, so that claim would soon be void. Slowly but surely, those ravaged areas would be on the way back to their original natural state.

Steven and Will continued to haggle over the paddle for a few more minutes until finally Steven relented and gave it back. But he still held on to the side of their canoe and bantered back and forth with Will about the latest information on computers. As each minute went by, I could see John growing more impatient, so I simply told Steven to set the talk aside for a while and push off. As soon as he did, John and Will quickly paddled away from us, and we went on our separate roads again. Steven and I immediately fell behind, but that was okay. He was pulling his weight better than ever, and I was proud of how well he was doing.

In the distance we began to hear the sound of an engine that seemed oddly familiar. The noise grew louder as we paddled. When we rounded a bend I suddenly recognized what it was – a Go-Devil outboard motor. The last one of these I'd seen was in South America two summers before on a Bolivian tributary of the Amazon called the Alto Beni. Most of the Indians owned them there because of their shallow draft capacity, which meant they could be used on rivers or sloughs that were only inches deep. The sound made by their single piston earned them the name "pecky pecky" in Bolivia. Only within the past few years had they become popular on Alaskan rivers. It wasn't long till the boat passed us, headed for a homestead across from the Nation River. The long angular shaft of the Go-Devil was as strange as the choppy syncopation of its engine noise, and if I hadn't already seen them in operation in Bolivia I might have been scratching my head, wondering how the devil the contraption worked. The six- or seven-foot length of its shaft permitted its low angle to the water and allowed the large prop to push the boat forward.

It wasn't long after the "pecky pecky" passed us that we spied Wayne's fish camp on the right bank. As we came closer his sled dogs began their mournful howling ritual, something Steven and I were familiar with, having lived for so many years in Yup'ik Eskimo villages on the Lower Yukon Delta. Just upriver from the camp, we spotted a pair of goshawks sitting on a branch partly overhanging the water. The big stripe-tailed hawks both remained there for a long time, but when a smaller bird suddenly darted across their path, one of them quickly spread its wings and pushed off after it. We watched the pursuit, and it was evident the smaller bird had escaped when the goshawk pulled up and headed back to its perch. By then we had reached Wayne's fish camp and were nosing our canoes toward shore, where the dogs were at full throttle into their wolf-like ululations. It was 7:00 p.m., and we were hungry.

We noticed Wayne's fish racks were full of king salmon and, since he had invited us to make ourselves at home, and we didn't see Wayne's friend Tim around, we cut up a portion of one of the big red-fleshed fish on the splitting table and prepared to cook it for dinner. It was then we heard another boat, this time heading upriver, with its bow angled toward our beached canoes. Soon we could see its single occupant, whom I recognized from my visit with Wayne and Scarlett in 1996 at their log cabin near Eagle. It was Tim McLaughlin, and he was driving a Grumman aluminum canoe powered by a small outboard motor. He was on his way back from the Hall's fish wheel, which he had helped them place downriver opposite the mouth of the Nation River. Wayne had told us in Eagle that they'd had a good season so far, averaging about fifty kings per day over the past several days. Tim confirmed the average, pointing to about thirty kings in his canoe just from the afternoon. He had picked an equal number from the fish wheel in the morning. He told us they were having better luck than anyone else on the upper Yukon, and hoped it would hold because they'd calculated they needed about 2500 kings and chum salmon for the dogs alone to get them through the year. Then there were also the fish he and the Halls would need for their personal use.

When Tim saw we were preparing a salmon on the work table, he replaced it with a Jack king, freshly picked from the fish wheel, saying it was not only fresher but cleaner, since he hadn't taken as much care filleting and hanging the fish destined for the dogs as he did with those used for human consumption. We assured him that we were so hungry for salmon we would have been satisfied with anything with red flesh that looked like a fish. Steven was especially eager to eat some of this "food of the gods," and we immediately filleted and wrapped it in aluminum, then set it on a bed of glowing embers on the beach to cook. Most of the praise for our finest dinner of the trip goes to John, whom Will nominated for sainthood after eating.

Tim told us to go on up to the main camp and make ourselves at home while he finished splitting and hanging his afternoon catch. We offered to help him, but he declined, saying he had a system and could manage by himself. So we grabbed our gear and took it up to where the Halls had erected their new 10 x 12 wall tent. Steven and I arranged our sleeping bags on top of their bed, then went outside where John and Will were busy building a fire in a metal container used to avoid the possibility of a forest fire. The kitchen area had been organized in front of the wall tent, and we settled into some comfortable lawn chairs the Halls had recently added to their outfit. Radiating out in every direction from the living area, sled dogs were tethered to tall spruce trees. These were the same dogs that had given us their spirited musical welcome as we pulled ashore. On the downriver side of the wall tent was a small dome tent normally used by the Halls' young son Garf. That night, however, John and Will would use it. Tim slept in a tipi he had built in the middle of the dog yard, for maximum bear alarm, he said, especially against grizzlies, which were plentiful around here at the height of the fishing season.

When Tim finished hanging his fish he joined us over a cup of tea, then sat for a long chat about his life on the Yukon. He'd come to Eagle from Ohio in 1995, vowing never to return to the rat race he had finally escaped. As soon as he arrived he acquired a dog team and learned how to fish for salmon. He admitted it was hard work, but he wouldn't trade it for a million bucks. He enjoyed the challenge and the wilderness he lived in, along with the friendship of the Halls and the company of his dogs. Since John was a fisherman himself, he was interested in the nature of their permit. Tim replied that it was a subsistence permit, allowing the Halls to camp and fish in the Yukon-Charley National Preserve for the duration of the fishing season, which would probably be for another two or three weeks, until both the kings and chums had passed by. We all envied Tim a little for being his own boss and being able to live according to the rhythm of the land and the river. It was with those thoughts that Steven and I finally zipped up our sleeping bags and called it the end of a long day.

"Top o' the mornin', Tim," I yelled from inside the tent. I'd heard him rustling around outside, and figured I'd join him for a cup of coffee. As I got dressed, the smell of the new wall tent's treated canvas took me back 37 years to my first summer in Alaska. My Uncle Chuck had hired me as a packer to work in Hal Waugh's South Fork hunting camp in the Alaska Range, and whenever I was at the main camp on Post Lake, I slept in a wall tent exactly like the one the Halls called home on the Yukon.

My reverie ended when I stepped out into the fresh aroma of newly brewed coffee. I accepted the cup offered by Tim, then invited him to share some of my special Yukon pancakes. He hesitated, but eventually ate two of them when he realized we had more than enough batter for all of us, including a tidbit or two for Wayne's lead dog Ginger, the only one of the team allowed full run of the camp. Being the progenitor of the majority of the 22 dogs in camp evidently gave her a few privileges. Ginger's appearance prompted Tim to ask if the dogs' howling had awakened me during the night. I told him it had, but that I was used to the sound, having lived in the Lower Yukon for so long. Besides, their wailing had only lasted a few minutes, and it reminded me of wolves, which I always enjoyed listening to.

Before we took off, Tim showed me more of the camp. Wayne had strung copper wire in every direction behind the wall tent, so they would have better radio reception. Scattered the way it was, the wire looked haphazardly placed, but it did the trick because their radio signal came in loud and clear. Even so, Tim said the best aerial they'd ever had was an old bicycle Scarlett had strung up in a tree in a camp they'd made at Doc LeFevre's old cabin the previous winter, farther down the river. He also pointed out their shower, which featured a steel beer keg hung in the trees, and a green plastic tarp for privacy. Finally, the outhouse included a toilet accessory with handles used by the elderly in rest homes. I didn't ask where they got that one.

After the tour, I grabbed my gear and joined the others down at the canoes. Since John was still worried about his wife Anecia, he was eager to set out. Just prior to casting off, Tim offered us another king salmon, telling us to pick it up from their fish wheel downriver. Then we waved goodbye and paddled out into the main current of the Yukon. Our destination was Slaven's Cabin, located on Coal Creek, about 50 miles from the Nation River. We weren't paddling for more than ten minutes, though, when Tim motored up to us waving a book in his hand. Will recognized it right away as one he'd been reading the night before and forgotten on the kitchen table. We thanked Tim, and were off again, commenting on how friendly he was, undoubtedly the result of living in wilderness for long periods of time.

When we reached the Hall's fish wheel, we marveled at Scarlett's abilities, for it was she who had built it. For some reason the wheel was not revolving and, although it was probably only jammed by a submerged log, we decided not to fool with it. It must have happened overnight because there were just 10 kings in the storage box. Since Tim had indicated he would soon be down to collect the fish, we figured he knew more about his own rig and could take care of the problem without our bumbling help. So, after choosing one of the smaller fish, John gutted and cleaned it on the spot, and away we went again.

It wasn't long till we came to the cabin Tim had told me about that morning. Located on a high bank on the left side of the Yukon, it had been built in the 1960s by Fairbanks Doctor LeFevre. At his death, it was donated to the Park Service and is now used as a shelter for canoeists on their way down the river. The Halls had camped at the cabin for a few weeks the previous winter, and it was during their stay there that Scarlett had discovered the inimitable powers of radio reception of an old bicycle they'd found in the neighborhood. Just before our arrival at the cabin, Steven and I watched another avian drama unfold on the other bank. A peregrine falcon had bulleted into the woods close to a perching goshawk. Quicker than an eye blink the goshawk dropped from his forest parapet and took after the peregrine. The falcon easily escaped, then in turn gave chase to a family of mallard ducks flying over the river. But the mallards instantly dove into the water with a big sploosh! and, at least for the moment, cheated the falcon of a dinner. Since peregrines must catch ducks in the air, this one would have to wait for another chance, which I knew wouldn't be long in coming, especially after his mate showed up a few minutes later. Shrill screams of their young from a nearby nest spurred them into action again, and they both circled above the river, waiting for the right opportunity to pounce.

Shortly after pushing off from the cabin, Steven pointed at a large brown animal hurrying toward us on the left shore, and we paddled closer for a better look. At first, I thought it was a young grizzly bear, but the nearer we got, the more it resembled a blackie. He kept on, marching resolutely, and didn't see us until we were about a hundred feet in front of him. He suddenly stopped in his tracks, stared straight into our eyes, then wheeled around and raced in the other direction. "By golly," I said to Steven, "we've just seen our first brown blackie ever in Alaska." He was a young bear, with naîveté written all over his fuzzy face, and his instant, terror-filled reaction told me he'd probably been shot at before. Only a few moments later we came across a porcupine waddling along the same bank, and Steven commented that this was the second animal he'd never seen before in the wild. He was excited and his excitement made me happy I'd brought him along.

It's curious how things can go so well one minute, and in the next fall to pieces. I wanted to add a few notes to my journal in reference to the bear and porky encounters, but Steven wanted to keep up with John's canoe so he could continue visiting with Will about computers. I took the notes anyway, and we fell hopelessly behind, which didn't make Steven a happy camper. When I saw a channel I thought might be a short-cut, I steered us into it, but it turned out to have a much slower current and to be laced with gravel bars.

There was no way we were going to catch them, I told him, so we may as well pull over and take a break for a while. Besides, I reminded him, this was supposed to be a father and son outing. On shore, the situation didn't improve, and getting stuck on the gravel bars at the lower end of our "short-cut" made matters worse. When Steven became petulant, I lost my temper and said things I still regret. Finally, when we got back into the main channel, and ate some trail mix to restore our depleted blood sugar levels, we felt much better. If only we'd eaten the trail mix earlier! Since I was the adult and had lost my cool, I apologized to Steven. We talked about the problem more sensibly then, and he finally agreed that it wasn't important to be so close to John and Will all of the time. We would see them again when we got to Slaven's Cabin at Coal Creek, and there he could chat with Will about computers to his heart's content.

When we came to the Kandik River, which emptied into the Yukon on our right, we spotted John's green canoe on the bank, just downriver from the confluence. Since we were clear on the other side of the main channel, it would have been too much of an effort to paddle over to them, so we pulled out on the south bank to inspect a couple of cabins we'd spotted from the river. One was brand new and locked up tighter than a drum, but the second cabin was an old-timer and open for visitors. It also had a large library, and I took some time checking out the many titles on the shelves. I soon found the owner was more into light adventure and mystery, though, and headed back to the canoe.

We ended up not seeing John and Will until evening at Slaven's Cabin. Meanwhile, I recounted to Steven a little of the history of the Kandik River that I remembered. Few Natives had actually lived in the area since 1914, when a bad flood had wiped out the Han Indian community located near the mouth of the Kandik. The people from the settlement, which the miners called Charley Village, moved down to Circle, where their descendants still live today. From then until the Second World War, Whites dominated the area, first, placer mining for gold, then trapping fur for a living.

With the beginning of World War II, the region was virtually emptied of its population because gold mines were deemed to be "non-essential" to the war effort, and the conscription of men and rationing of gasoline assured that most mines would close. Only with the rise in gold and fur prices in the 1970s, and the lure of the last frontier, did a few people return to the area. Many of them settled along the Kandik and Nation Rivers, using the old cabins built many years earlier by gold miners and trappers. It was too late for the majority of these new settlers, however, because the 1980 Alaska Lands Act required that they move off the land set aside for the Yukon-Charley Preserve. This didn't sit well with them, and there were numerous confrontations between Park officials and local "residents." Things have simmered down since, but there are many in the Eagle area who still hold hard feelings about how the Park Service treated them.

The Charley River was the next major drainage we came to. In 1994, I had floated the Charley from its headwaters with Steven's brother, Eric, and my own brother, David. Its upper reaches had proven a real challenge because of their infamous rock gardens, but after getting beyond them the river proved to be one of the most scenic I'd ever been on. It was also a swift river almost all the way to its mouth, where it slowed and finally merged with the silty expanse of the Yukon. It was at the mouth of the Charley that Steven and I stopped our canoe and switched ends. He wanted to take a crack at paddling in the stern so he could practice the different strokes he would have to master to be a good stern man. Two hours later we pulled into the landing at Slaven's Cabin, about a half-hour behind John and Will. Like I told Steven, "No use hurrying, since the river would get us there anyway. Meanwhile, enjoy the glitter of the late sun off the edges of the moving water, listen to the bird song, breathe deeply of the sweet and lucid air, sit quietly and contemplate these precious moments on the river, because, soon enough, our time here would be up, and all we'll have left is memories."

John and Will helped us carry our gear up to Slaven's Cabin, and while they were settling in I took a short walk up the trail to Coal Creek, where I found the water at flood stage. It was running the color of tannin, and racing in haystacks and rooster tails. Chaos reigned supreme. It was very different from when I was there four years earlier and the water only bubbled and flowed in a timid stream. It must have been raining much harder in the Coal Creek area than it had farther up the Yukon. On my way back to the cabin the rain started in earnest again, and I changed my mind about sleeping in the tent. The cabin didn't offer such poor accommodations after all. During my previous trip it had been loudly buzzing with mobs of bloodthirsty mosquitoes, but this time there was virtual silence.

As I soon learned, Slaven's Cabin was more than just a "cabin." It was really the old two-story log roadhouse that a miner named Frank Slaven had built in 1930 to cater to other miners, mail carriers and travelers, who had business on the river between Circle and Eagle. The Park Service had rightly decided to restore the old structure for use by canoeists and other recreationists plying the river in summer, and for dog mushers racing in the Yukon Quest in winter. They had done a good job with the reconstruction, especially the log work, but they fell down when they got to the kitchen, which for some crazy reason they placed upstairs. They had provided campers with the luxury of a working propane stove, and a counter to prepare meals and eat on, but they had failed to add a sink with running water or even a simple drain for disposing of dirty dishwater. So we had to throw our wastewater out the upstairs window, which we'd left wide open to cool us off, since a young couple staying in the roadhouse when we arrived had overloaded the drum stove on the first floor with wood. Even with the window propped open, the roadhouse felt like the inside of an oven, and made us old timers head downstairs to get some fresh air. It was pouring rain outside, so we took refuge in the still relatively cool entry room of the roadhouse. Since that's where we'd stashed our gear, we decided it would also be where we slept the night.

By then Steven and Will were into a pretty intense conversation about computers, which even included a few philosophical references every once in a while. It later transitioned into a game of chess. Meanwhile, John and I chatted with the young couple who liked hot fires. Jason was from Buffalo, New York, and Millie was an Israeli he'd met while hitchhiking in Alaska. They'd rented a canoe in Eagle and were on their way to Circle. Jason was an adventurous young fellow in his mid-twenties, and reminded me of myself when I was his age. I could see Steven was taking in a lot of the conversation, even though he was pretending to think deeply about the next move in his game of chess.

After our visit with Jason, I read some of the interpretive materials provided by the Park Service, learning that Frank Slaven had sold out, lock, stock and barrel, in 1934 to A.D. McRae and Ernest Patty, who then constructed two big dredges on Coal Creek and nearby Woodchopper Creek, which they put into operation in 1935. These continued to operate on the two tributaries of the Yukon for almost thirty years, although the Coal Creek dredge shut down a few years before the one on Woodchopper Creek. When we were here in 1994, Dave, Eric and I had walked up to where the Coal Creek dredge now sits, slowly rusting into oblivion. When we nosed through its innards, it was like time-traveling to an age when all that mattered was the quest for gold. Health and safety precautions for the workers never even entered the equation. We wouldn't see the dredge this time, though, due to the rain and John's worries about Anecia. Circle was our goal, and we would be there the next day, come hell or high water.

W e were up at the crack of dawn, and I heard John singing halle-lujah that the rain had stopped. He was anxious to hit the trail. But a person can't race through breakfast granola, so as I crunched I scanned the small library upstairs. The many travelers who had stayed in the roadhouse had left books on everything from light romance and mystery to a miner's manual and travel guides to the Yukon and Alaska. There were novels such as, *Hawaii*, by James Michener, and narrative journals like John McPhee's, *Coming into the Country*. I also found a couple of Japanese "pocket novels" that I took with me to show my students in Marshall. I thought the peculiar reverse reading structure, from right to left, would be interesting for them to see.

Steven and I were on the river ahead of John and Will, so we had a chance to ruminate on things just between the two of us. As with his dad, Steven didn't like the enormity of the Yukon. And it simply wasn't as exciting as the smaller rivers he'd been on, like Birch Creek, the Fortymile and the Delta Wild and Scenic River. I added that these rivers were also more personal because you could hear the birds sing and actually see the owners of the songs. I never heard them sing on the Yukon, unless it was while we were stopped for the night near a grove of trees. Just as I spoke, a pair of ravens flew directly over us, doing some of their usual aerobatics. When one of them suddenly "bell croaked," I laughed, since technically the ravens just proved me wrong. Ravens are, after all, big song birds, and while gyrating overhead they had performed only one of their many songs, which varied from the bell croak we'd just heard, to *quorks* and *toks* and *coos*, along with *prruks* and *cr-r-rucks* and a few prosaic crow's *caws*. I think it was Bernd Heinrich who said in his book, *Ravens in Winter*, that only human speech exceeds the spectrum of sounds ravens can make.

I dug my bird guide out and read aloud that northern ravens, *Corvus corax*, weigh three to four pounds, have a wing span of four feet, and wield a powerful three inch-long "Roman nose" beak that they use for everything from poking holes in tin cans to amorously stroking their mate's own beak during spring courtship rituals. In North America, they nest from the high Arctic, south to Nicaragua. They have a higher metabolism than most other birds, and it is this trait that allows them to survive Alaska's long cold winters. They also live for decades, and are probably the world's most intelligent bird. "Fascinating, eh Steven?" "Yeh," is all he replied. So much for birds....

Downstream about ten miles from Slaven's place we came across an area of high bluffs and ridges, mantled in low clouds and tendrils of mist that stretched almost to the edge of the river. It reminded me of a river trip I'd taken two years earlier through the jungles of Bolivia. The tree species were different, but the verticality, in combination with the tags and tatters of fog, took my mind for a roller coaster ride through time and space. Then, suddenly, I was back on the Yukon again. John and Will had caught up to us, and we were nearing a cabin I had stopped at during my last trip. We were now 15 miles from Slaven's Roadhouse, and I reckoned that since we were making such good time we could stop there again for a short break. The two-story log cabin was owned by a Fairbanksan named Richard Smith, who had left a note on his still unlocked door, welcoming all who felt the need to use the building. We went in so Steven could see yet another of the wide range of log cabins on the river. John and Will were just as curious to see how people lived along the Yukon, and we were all interested in what sorts of books the owner read. Richard's library, as it turned out, was filled with adventure novels, most of which we'd already read, so we only cracked a few of them and returned them to their shelves. Then we ate a snack and headed out the door, thanking Richard as I dropped the nail through the hasp.

On our way down to the canoes, I pointed at what was probably the original miner's cabin. But it was only built of thin logs, prompting John to comment that it must have been a real bear to heat during the winter. He had lived in such a cabin for two years in the early 1960s and knew first-hand what a cold experience that could be. The fact that the cabin was located on the same lot as the new one made me wonder about the history of what had to be an in-holding patented in the early 1900s. I read later that at the turn of the century there had been an old cabin located on the property called Webber's Roadhouse. Judge James Wickersham, who often traveled from Eagle to Circle and Rampart for court sessions, had a lot to say about roadhouses in his book, *Old Yukon*. Webber's Roadhouse was not one of his favorite places to rest because old man Webber was cantankerous and a slovenly housekeeper. In Wickersham's words:

> "The one-room log tavern stood at the edge of a dense forest of tall straight evergreens. The sidewalls of the cabin, built of small round logs, were head high, and the central roof-log was just above the outstretched finger tips. The roof was constructed of small round poles laid from the ridge pole to the top logs on the side walls, then covered a foot deep with moss and weighed down with sod and gravel. The tavern was about ten by sixteen feet square inside. It was finished with one clapboard door hung on wooden pins, and one window sash. The dining table consisted of rough boards nailed to poles, about three feet long, driven into auger-holes about four feet apart just below the window. Two pole bunks of similar design adorned the back wall. The dirt floor was spattered with grease from the stove. There was one chair of riven slab set on three pole legs. The two other chairs were boxes, one marked in large letters, 'Hunter's Old Rye,' and the other, 'Eagle Brand Milk.' A dog stable, much smaller than the tavern, stood alongside."

On our left just downstream from the Smith cabin, we passed Takoma Bluff. John had read this was the traditional boundary between the Han and Kwitch'in Athabaskan Indians. The boundary changed, though, after the big flood of 1914 wiped out the Han village site near the mouth of the Kandik River. Then the Han moved to Circle, where they joined the Kwitch'in and began to mix bloodlines. Although Takoma Bluff is on the left bank of the river, it was connected at some point in geological time to the formation on the opposite bank. Both sides are composed of thin layers of reddish brown limestone and dolomite, and have needle-like spires that were formed by dissolution over millions of years. Limestone is a soluble material and, when water penetrates through vertical fractures, slowly dissolves the surrounding bedrock. The river narrowed at this point, spawning swirling eddies close to the face of the bluff and a series of rolling waves in midstream. We speculated about these disturbances, figuring they could be anything from benthic river demons to an irregularly eroded extension of the limestone of Takoma Bluff below the water surface. I bet Steven five bucks on the former.

A few miles downstream from Takoma Bluff we spotted another familiar cabin. I couldn't forget this one because a huge land slump had narrowly missed the cabin in 1983. When I first saw it, my guess was that it occurred as a result of abusive mining activity prior to the Lands Act in 1980. However it had begun, on its way down the tumbling earth took everything with it. Spruce and birch trees had been uprooted and thrown like pickup sticks all over the side of the mountain. Amazingly, some were still alive, although crooked from new growth searching for the sun – which made us wonder why trees always sought a 90-degree angle to the earth? Was it some average angle of sunlight they were after? Or a weight to balance ratio? Or gravity? None of us knew the answer, so it would have to remain a mystery till we got home.

At this point, we were roughly halfway to Circle from Slaven's Roadhouse. The intermittent slow drizzle we'd been having since we started in the morning was a welcome change from the blazing sun and river surf pushed by gusty winds. After traveling in it for a while, I actually began to enjoy it, even seeing poetry in the fine drops as they sifted down from the gray sky, dimpling the flat sheet of the river. The poetry began to dissipate, though, as the clouds lifted, leaving a high overcast sky and a warm breeze blowing from the west.

Shortly after the rain stopped, a lot of noisy flapping off to our right grabbed our attention. I glassed toward the bank and counted almost 150 terror-stricken Canada geese running at top speed along the shoreline. I told Steven they were in the middle of their molt, and vulnerable to predation because they couldn't fly. Most of the birds were probably pre-adults that had been lollygagging around there for the entire summer. But I hadn't seen a flock react so furiously before. They were waddling, splashing, swimming, and even sporadically trying to fly as fast as their bulbous half-feathered bodies could carry them. Needless to say, we didn't stick around to feed their frenzy.

Just down from the molting geese we came to another familiar location where I remembered my brother Dave and I, on our earlier trip, had been racing a big electrical storm and, after seeing bolts of lightning strike next to the river, quickly headed for shore to make camp. None too soon, for within minutes after getting our tent up the sky unleashed its full fury on us, including fierce winds and bucket loads of driving rain. After sharing that memory, Steven and I were glad the rain clouds had lifted, and we hoped they would stay that way until we got to Circle.

Speaking of which, it was time to be on the lookout for the village, and we caught up to John and Will to tell them to start watching for signs. John said he'd noticed the country had already become markedly lower, especially on the left bank. Pointing at his open map, he told me the maze of islands and channels before Circle looked complicated, and he wanted to be sure we didn't miss the turn and continue down the river toward Fort Yukon. I didn't want this to happen either, and reassured him that the best way to the village was via the main channel. In any case, I said, if they wanted, we could go ashore at the last bluff and climb to an overlook to get a bird's eye view of the area.

As we floated closer to Circle the land became even flatter on our left side. In my mind's eye I imagined the large expanses of wetlands out there, including pothole lakes, interspersed with muskeg and paisley pattern stands of black spruce. Up until now, I told Steven, most of the trees we'd been seeing were white spruce, *Picea glauca*, the tall conifers found in Interior Alaska mostly on the banks of rivers and sloughs, as well as on the south sides of mountains and hills. Out in the marsh and muskeg country, such as the Yukon Flats ahead of us, another spruce tree predominated. Known as *Picea mariano* to scientists, and black spruce to us commoners, it is shorter than its cousin and grows where few other trees do, in extremely acidic, low oxygen conditions, often over wide areas of muskeg-capped permafrost. To conserve nutrients, black spruce retain their needles from year to year, and also make them unpalatable to herbivores. A characteristic they have in common with white spruce is that their lower branches can take root and sprout new trees if they come in contact with the soil.

Steven wasn't as interested in my litany of "fartless facts" as he was in trying to get home by sometime that night, which meant we would have to call Jen as soon as we got to Circle to ask her to come and get us. He pointed out that, if she did, he would be able to begin work on his Spanish project a full day earlier. I smiled, and simply said, yeah!

The last time I was on this stretch of river with Dave, I was worried about finding our way through the labyrinth of channels just before Circle. On the map there were two possible routes, but to avoid any doubt we climbed the last tall bluff on the right bank to plot the remaining ten miles or so through the Yukon Flats. From the top, we could see the metal roofs of the village reflecting in the distance, and as we let our eyes twist and turn along the many braids between the bluff and the shining roofs, we decided the main channel would be our best route. Since Circle lay on the inside left bank of a wide west-swinging loop of that channel, the trick would be to make sure we didn't get carried by the current down any of the other branches of the river before arriving there.

This time, the four of us stopped below the bluff to ponder whether we, too, should go to the top to scope out our route. My past experience would be enough, everyone agreed, and we chose not to. Meanwhile, we had an interesting encounter with a young Bonaparte's gull. We first saw him swimming upstream on the river, and as he paddled close to the shore we could see the color-coding that made him uniquely a Bonaparte's. His narrow black bill and gray mantle, the dark spot behind each of his eyes, and his black tail and wing tips were all telltale markings. It would be another year until he acquired his ebony black hood and orange-red legs. Then he would be much more wary of humans and, when he began nesting, the most aggressive gull species in Alaska. What will make him most distinctive of all, though, is where he and his mate build their nest: high in a branch of a spruce tree near the water's edge. No other gulls nest in trees.

John and Will followed our lead down the river, but somehow became separated from us. They took a braid that was so shallow they had to jump out and drag their loaded canoe through three inches of water for almost 300 yards until they reached us at the other end of the braid where we'd stopped to wait for them. I was pleased when Steven voluntarily walked up the beach and helped pull their canoe through the worst stretches of the shallows.

On the final leg to Circle we caught some fast water next to a cutbank on the left side of the river and rushed by a tangle of cottonwoods torn from their roots and thrown into the river. We wondered why it was so much faster here, speculating that maybe there was a slight elevation drop associated with the high bluff country we were quickly leaving behind. As we rounded a wide bend I glanced up to see an adult bald eagle peering down at us from a tall cottonwood. Leaving the eagle in our wake, we drifted toward the middle of the river, where Steven pointed at the reflection of rooftops in the distance. Now all we had to do was favor the left shore and follow our noses straight to the village. I stopped paddling to savor the last mile of the river. So did Steven.

Just as we pulled into Circle a huge black storm cloud swirling in our direction from the northwest started to pick up speed. I knew there would be some serious rain to contend with shortly, so Steven and I unloaded the tent first. John and Will did the same as soon as they hit the boat ramp.

Lickety-split, we put the tents up, hurried over to the local store to call Jen to let her know she could come pick us up, then started dinner before the first tentative drops began to fall on our sizzling frying pan. Beans and rice were our fare, along with the last of our flour tortillas and cheese. Although everything was a little soggy when it came out of the pan, it tasted really good at the end of our long river trip. John and Steven and I ate in the downpour, while Will took cover to read inside his tent. By this stage, we were happy for the rain because it kept the midges, aka "no-see-ums," and mosquitoes at bay. The midges, especially, had been increasing in numbers the closer to Circle we got, and in the village we found them in multitudes and swarms. I don't mind mosquitoes, but no-see-ums crawl up your sleeves and pant legs and into your nether parts, and their bites cause welts.

Rainstorms don't last forever, and we used the drops that were still falling to clean the silt and sand and gravel out of our canoes. John found a pay phone to call his wife Anecia, and when he found out that her dizziness had been caused only by a temporary inner-ear imbalance, he joined us on a walk through the old village. As many times as I had visited Circle, I'd never actually explored the Indian village. Although the sign at the landing said there were 73 residents in Circle, you'd hardly know it by the number of cabins at the old site. In fact, the majority of the Han-Kwich'in Indians now lived in the new HUD housing area situated along the highway just out of town. But, even with the new houses, the community wasn't what it used to be. In 1896, during its heyday, Circle had a population of 700, most of them miners, with two trading posts, saloons, brothels and dance halls, an Episcopal church and school, a newspaper called the *Yukon Press*, and even a library with books brought from Fortymile by Jack McQuesten when he set up his store in town. It even had an entertainment center, located in a two-story log building called the Tivoli Music Hall that hosted entertainers from as far away as San Francisco. During our walk we saw none of the celebrity of the old town, but such is the way of all gold discoveries in Alaska. The boomtowns have all gone bust and become ghost towns, and the buildings and accoutrements of those who once lived and worked in them have slowly moldered into the ground, along with the miners themselves. Only the Indians, who were there before them, and the earth, trees, and the Yukon River that sustained them, now remain.

After strolling back to the landing, John and I packed up the rest of the gear, then settled into our tents to get away from the no-see-ums and wait for Jennifer's imminent arrival. Somewhere along the line, Steven and I nodded off, but we were awakened when a vehicle drove up at about midnight. Will looked out the tent and reported it was a white Jeep Wagoneer. I yelled back that ours was a Toyota, and lay down to listen to the sporadic pecking of raindrops on the tent shell. Just as I began to close my eyes again, a familiar woman's voice boomed from the car, "Are you guys going to lie there all night?"

PHOTOS

1. John Breiby (stern) opposite Calico Bluff
2. Steven Keim (right) feasting at Halls' fish camp
3. John Breiby at Halls' fishwheel

CHAPTER 3

Three Men in a Tub Kongakut River Trek
July-August, 1998

June 22 –

It felt like déjà vu when Andrew Benedetti and I were dropped off at Wright's Air Service on the east ramp of the Fairbanks airport. We were headed out on another summer adventure together, although this time Andrew had invited a California buddy of his along. Dan Hatfield was from the Sacramento area and had backpacked a lot on trails in the high Sierras, but he had never done any serious hiking in Alaska. This imbalance in his life would change dramatically as we embarked on a trek that took us from the Sheenjek River headwaters, across an alpine saddle, then almost all the way down the Kongakut River to the edge of the coastal plain in the far northeast corner of the Arctic National Wildlife Refuge. On the lower half of the Kongakut a small raft would be waiting for us to travel in, but on the upper portion of the river we would hoof it like the caribou we hoped to see along the way. We would be on our own, with no roads, no trails, no picnic tables or latrines. Best of all, there would be no other people – only the three of us, and a lot of wilderness for hundreds of miles in every direction.

Andrew and Frank on aufeis

At 9:00 a.m., our pilot Ken announced the mail flight to Arctic Village was ready to leave, and we could now board the Cessna Caravan parked on the tarmac.

We arrived at the Arctic Village airstrip just in time to miss a big thunderstorm moving off to the south. A small traffic jam of rafters at the airport had not missed it, though, and they were still a little damp from its onslaught. Our charter pilot Don Ross, for the next leg of the trip, and his helper Dirk Nickisch were both there cramming their Cessna 185's with passengers and gear. The weather had set them back a bit, and they were scrambling to catch up on their busy schedules. We would have to cool our heels on the tarmac until Don returned from delivering the rafters to their destination on the middle Kongakut River.

While we waited we walked along the shoreline of a nearby lake. Many years before, in early July, I had camped overnight by the same lake while waiting for my flight back to Fairbanks. I remember the surface of the lake was alive with almost a hundred Arctic terns, probably snagging small minnows to take back for their young.

Finally, at 6:30 in the evening, Don flew in, packed us in his airplane like duffel in a bag, and whisked us away in a roar for the upper Sheenjek River. Forty-five minutes later we were flying over Double Mountain, then landing on the uphill slope of a wide alluvial fan that gently dropped from the east side of the mountain to the valley below. After un-cinching the load, Don handed us our packs and, seeming very tired at the end of a long day, asked, "Now you're going to come back alive, right, so you can pay me?" I assured him we would, and he eased back into the cockpit of his Cessna 185, taxied toward the river, turned, then poured on the power and took off the same way he had landed – uphill. I was worried about his tired eyes and remembered what had happened to Roger Dowding, the pilot who had taken me into the Kongakut in 1989. Roger finally pushed himself beyond his limits and paid the ultimate price.

"What a fantastic place," Dan remarked quietly, as we stood and gazed in awe at the snowy peaks that dominated the Sheenjek River Valley. Those few words only scratched the surface of my own feelings about those mountains. I had walked in the area before, and felt a strong reverence for its wild qualities. My feelings hadn't changed. There was still the deep respect coupled with the thrill of being in true wilderness where the word "survival" had real meaning. Don had meant what he said. This country was not kind to the unprepared.

Once down at the river's edge, we searched for a stout piece of wood to use as a staff to help us cross the still high, murky waters of the Sheenjek. But being right at the tree line, we couldn't locate anything on our side of the river sturdy enough to do the trick, and had to use a makeshift walking stick I had brought along, an old ski pole I had used for many years for similar river crossings. But it worked just fine as we linked arms and carefully waded in our sandals across the maze of cobble-bottomed braids of the river ahead of us. We chose a ford that had looked a little tricky from the alluvial fan where Don had landed us, but that's where I figured the river would be at its shallowest point, so that's where we crossed. The water was cold, but not nearly like it had been a couple of weeks earlier down on the lower Kongakut River, where I had spent seven days with two other Fairbanks friends, Andy Keller and Sue Hall.

After putting our boots back on, we walked in sparsely forested tundra to the edge of the spruce trees, where we found a dry flat spot that beckoned us to set up our tents and rest the night. There was a creek nearby, so we did just that. As soon as we had our water, I made a fire with some dry spruce branches, helped Dan set up my old North Face tent (now with a new blue fly to keep us dry if it rained), then began dinner. We had hardy appetites and were looking forward to a batch of my mountain quesadillas. As we ate, conversation around the campfire turned to bear encounters that Andrew and I had had during our past treks and canoe trips on Alaska's wild rivers. When I saw Dan getting a little nervous, though, I changed the topic to other things, like the pair of Upland sandpipers hanging close to camp. Dan had never seen these sandpipers before, and I showed him how they reacted to my rendition of their shrill whistle. He agreed that the whistle sounded like a "cat-call," one that men sometimes used in the presence of pretty women. When I imitated the whistle, both birds drew closer, curious about these strange looking interlopers. Since the sandpipers were the only entertainment in town, we watched and listened to them until we stuffed ourselves into our sleeping bags at about midnight.

By then it had turned cool, and my sleeping bag felt really good. I was happy I had brought my cold weather bag with me. I started to zip up the tent fly, but stopped mid-way, since there still were no mosquitoes. We were lucky, and before calling it quits, we watched with unimpeded view as the dull yellow orb of the sun rolled behind the opposite mountains. Dark puffs of gray cloud lined with fringes of white light stood as a backdrop to the highest peaks, funneling the sun's rays down on our side of the river. Dan had seen some very pretty alpen glows in the California Sierras, but this one on the Sheenjek was special to him, both because of the angle of light and the clarity of the skies.

The upland sandpipers were shrilly "cat-calling" at us again during the next day's breakfast. We were probably camped only yards from their nest, and they wanted us out of there pronto. We capitulated and broke camp early, heading up over the tundra to the continental divide that separates the Yukon River watershed from that of the Kongakut River. Now above the tree line, we would not see spruce trees for the remainder of our trip. The tundra was dry and the walking easy, and we were soon standing on the saddle, looking back and forth in both directions, north toward the Kongakut and south toward the Sheenjek River. We were fascinated by the idea that if we took a few steps one way we would be in a drainage that finally ended up in the Bering Sea, and if we took the same number of steps the other way we would be on the Kongakut River, which drained into the Beaufort Sea.

As we surveyed our surroundings, I spotted a merlin cruising overhead. If I hadn't brought along my fancy Zeiss binoculars, I might not have been able to identify the falcon so quickly. I thanked my dad again for making a gift of them to me before he died. With them I also identified a pair of American golden plovers, worried about our intrusion through their backyard. "*Too-lee, too-lee,*" they piped. I could plainly see their black aprons and gold-flecked hoods and backs. I mentioned their marathon winter migration to Andrew and Dan, how they first travel southeast from Alaska across the Canadian north to Labrador and Nova Scotia, then south over the Atlantic Ocean and Brazil, and finally to the pampas of Argentina and Bolivia, where they spend the winter months. They return to Alaska by flying over western South America, Central America, the Mississippi Valley, and the Canadian Prairie Provinces. Altogether, they travel nearly 20,000 miles round trip, averaging a constant 60 mph all the way down and back. "No wonder they're referred to as champion long distance migrants," I remarked.

A little farther along I found the remains of a dead upland sandpiper. It was missing its breast meat, and we wondered if the merlin we'd seen earlier had anything to do with it, or perhaps the immature golden eagle just then soaring high above us. I discounted the eagle, since it wouldn't have been worth spending the energy to hunt such small prey. "Probably the merlin, then. An upland sandpiper is just the right size for them," I said.

"Yeah, speaking of eating," Dan added, "let's have a bite ourselves. I'm hungry." So we found some dry tundra tussocks and settled down for a light lunch.

The sky was cloudless in every direction and the sun dazzlingly bright, making for torrid walking up to the top of the saddle, so we were happy to be able to take our packs off and relax for a while. It also gave me a chance to check out the wildflowers. There was conspicuous bloom everywhere, including a white rose called mountain avens that studded the slope, bunches of bell-shaped cassiope, and the wonderfully fragrant Lapland rosebay, pink parrya, and moss campion, which grows in a compact mat on the dry tundra. Even a few forget-me-nots and rock jasmine poked their diminutive blue and white noses above the lichens and mosses.

There were no large trees to be seen anywhere, but when I got down on my hands and knees I found tiny willows known as *Salix phlebophylla* and *Salix reticulata*. The first is commonly called skeletonleaf willow because of the way its old leaves persist brown and partially skeletonized at the base of the plant for one or more years. The latter's common name is netleaf willow because the veins of its leaves have a net-like pattern. The catkins of the skeletonleaf willow grow taller than its stem and leaves, qualifying it as one of the tiniest trees on earth. Both of these willows are among 37 species found in Alaska, making it the largest genus of trees in the state. Although their size may vary from one inch to more than twenty feet tall, willows all have two things in common: catkins, and a bitter quinine-like taste of their bark, which was traditionally used by Alaska Native peoples as a patent medicine to relieve pain. Salicylic acid, used in aspirin, was originally a derivative of the willow bark.

These were the sorts of things we talked about, as Andrew and Dan and I munched on our bagels and cheese or peanut butter. Quickly, though, the topic changed to Dall sheep when I started glassing the verdant southern flanks of the surrounding mountains. Only two weeks earlier on the lower Kongakut River, everything had been brown and gray after a long cold winter. Now the slopes were green with all sorts of forage for wild sheep to feed on, and I counted 23 ewes and lambs doing just that. About a quarter of the flock was made up of first year lambs, so it seemed they had survived the winter and spring fairly well.

We were soon on our way again, this time downslope toward the Kongakut River, seen glittering like a shiny snake in the distance. Although we were moving downhill, tussocks and surface water turned our walk into a slog, and with heavy packs and our first mosquitoes it was a challenge for us. But, such is the nature of tundra, and after a couple of miles we decided to side-hill above the morass. It was a good decision, for as soon as we gained some elevation the terrain turned drier and easier to walk on, and with more wind the mosquitoes abated and we felt much better – good enough, in fact, to take another break. I saw what looked like a large glacial erratic rock about 300 yards away, so we aimed for it.

When I pack long distances across country I like to take as many breaks as possible. Even so, one look at Dan told me I would probably have to double my usual number. Although Dan had a positive outlook, he was definitely not in good physical condition, so Andrew and I decided to travel more slowly until he had lost a few pounds and was a little leaner and meaner. There was no need to hurry anyway, and maybe if we took a little more time we would see more wildlife.

No sooner had we stopped than a short-eared owl flew overhead, fluttering like a giant moth. Since these owls don't have much choice during the Arctic summer, they hunt mostly by day. They are also very curious birds and investigate anything that remotely looks edible. I wondered aloud what it would be like to be the size of a lemming when a short-eared owl flew over. Something tells me we wouldn't be sitting on the rock jabbering the way we were.

After yet another break near a fresh pile of grizzly bear dung, we headed for the north side of the quickly widening Kongakut River Valley. There were just too many tundra tussocks, or "Watt heads," as some of my friends pejoratively refer to them, (after James Watt, President Reagan's infamous Secretary of Interior, who committed so many environmental atrocities while in office). These tussocks were particularly difficult to walk in, and I figured it would be easier to traverse along the side of the mountain again. It turned out to be even easier when we encountered a well-traveled caribou trail that flanked the edge of a ridge, finally leading to such a lovely flat spot overlooking the Kongakut Valley that we decided to park our tents there for the night. We also found some convenient pockets of water nearby that we could use for drinking and cooking. They were full of tiny wriggling mosquito larvae, but after scooting the critters to the bottom with a swirl of the finger, the water tasted sweet, and that's what counted most for the moment.

Since there was no wood on the ridge, we used our gas stoves to fry up some whole-wheat quesadillas. Over dinner, Andrew commented that President Thomas Jefferson would have loved this trip. I had been telling him and Dan of Steven Ambrose's book, *Undaunted Courage*, about the Lewis and Clark Expedition of 1803-1804. Jefferson had commissioned that journey of exploration partly because of his thirst for knowledge about new country. Ours wasn't an expedition of that magnitude, but it was through country as thoroughly wild as that which Lewis and Clark had explored. Yes, I agreed, Jefferson would have reveled in this wildness.

We chatted over cups of tea as upland sandpipers whistled at us from the tundra below our camp. The slanting rays of the late evening sun reflected brightly off the 6500-foot-high mountain massif paralleling the valley on its south side. It was a long mountain with rugged canyons and ravines carved out of its north slope, and was now almost as white as chalk. I guessed it to be of limestone, and probably once part of an ancient ocean that covered the area about 200 million years ago.

Just as the sun slipped behind our side of the valley and began to cloak the limestone massif in twilight shadow, I caught movement out of the corner of my eye. I turned to see two caribou, a cow and maybe its yearling calf, quickly hoofing it up a shallow ravine next to our camp. It was evident the animals knew of our presence and kept on going, heading north toward the Coastal Plain, following an imperative as old as the land itself. We wondered how they had managed to make it this far alone, especially through bear country. All around our camp were grizzly diggings, where they had feverishly clawed down to bedrock after parky squirrels, trying to add some spice to their usually bland diet of roots at this time of year.

Dan was tired, so toward midnight we hit the sack, Dan and I in my North Face, and Andrew in his own tent. We chatted for a while about Dan's climbing experiences in the California Sierras, but soon he drifted off to sleep while I wrote in my journal. I crawled out of the tent briefly to take a picture of the limestone mountain, which by now had turned the color of yellow chalk, as the sun shone through a pass behind us, completely illuminating the opposite slope of the valley. I stood in awe, pondering what Thomas Jefferson would have thought of this land.

When I awoke, I lay in my bag listening to the upland sandpipers whistling. More than anything else, except for the land itself, these long-necked, short-billed sandpipers, called by scientists, *Bartramia longicauda*, (literally, "long-tailed Bartram," after the naturalist for whom it was named) provide continuity for me from day to day, week to week, even from summer to summer. I never grow tired of them, as I never grow tired of the white-crowned sparrows who are also my constant companions during these northern treks.

At breakfast we noticed all the water was gone from our mosquito ponds. Overnight the underground dam of seasonal ice must have thawed and released its hold on the water above. In a way, it was a symbolic event, representing the end of the long winter and the beginning of what at this latitude is a very short summer. We wondered if any of the mosquito larvae had been able to hatch in time to escape. No matter if they hadn't, I thought. The fewer mosquitoes, the better.

After breaking camp, we headed up to a high ridge that gave us a broad view of the Kongakut River Valley. To the east, the river doubled in size after joining a southern tributary that drained the backside of what I came to call "Chalk Mountain." The Kongakut then took a dogleg to the north, which we hoped to shortcut by continuing down the other side of the ridge we were on, thus saving us several miles of trudging through damp tundra.

Somehow during the hike up to the ridge I had tweaked a muscle in my back and had to stop on top and do some serious stretches. Andrew and Dan apparently felt the need to do the same and shucked their own packs to join me in my regimen of hip rotations, dog tilts and butt lifts. The exercises helped, but the pain lingered, and as we walked I tried to take my mind off the constant throb by thinking up descriptions of the surrounding landscape. One that Andrew joined me in was conjuring up colorful words to describe the forget-me-not wildflowers, which we ran across every so often in the alpine tundra. I started with "stabbing" beauty. He continued with "piercing," and I finished with "penetrating," as in, "little blue and yellow eyes suddenly gazing up at us from the tundra, penetrating our collective consciousness." It worked.

We climbed a bald-faced outcropping that reminded me of a rockscape out of the Arizona desert, especially with the noonday sun blazing down at us. On the north side we found a place in the shade of some large scree and stopped for a bite to eat and a long swallow of water from our canteens. The temperature felt like it had already passed the 100-degree mark, and we were parched. While I was drinking I noticed two golden eagles swimming in the thermals above us. I thought of vultures, which would have completed the analogy with the southwest, but mew gulls coursing along the river below us, and two giant ravens sitting on a nearby bluff shattered the comparison.

The shade felt good, as did the snack and rest, but soon it was time to hit the trail again. Just before donning our packs I spotted an animal trail leading along the edge of the talus slope. It looked well used and led in the direction we were headed, so we followed it.

It was a good trail, and by the double crescent shape of the tracks had been recently used by hundreds of migrating caribou. We followed it for several miles as it snaked along the base of the mountain to our left, up through a stretch of tundra tussocks, then down again to the valley bottom where it meandered and braided like the river itself across flat meadows of mountain avens and cobbled islands interspersed with thick stands of tall fragrant willows. I was enjoying the pleasure of a good trail so much I hadn't noticed how Dan had started to lag behind. Finally, Andrew asked me to slow down so Dan could catch up. When Dan came alongside he told me in no uncertain terms that he couldn't keep up the fast pace I was setting. I apologized and promised to walk more slowly.

Since we were near the river, I proposed a short break and a swim, if the water were warm enough. It wasn't, so I only soaked my lily-white feet in the cold clear water long enough to refresh them for the next leg of the journey. I also checked the condition of my left heel, which had bothered me since the previous Christmas. *Plantar fasciitis* is what the doc had called it, and I had purchased a special insole to help me fight the tenderness when I stepped on it. I had changed my gait, too, putting more pressure on the ball of my feet rather than on the heel – "walking like an Indian," as my dad used to say. The strategy seemed to be working because the foot felt fine. It felt even better after soaking it in cold water, and we were soon back on the trail again.

By now our trail showed much recent use by both caribou and wolves, and we hurried along, hoping to catch sight of the animals up ahead somewhere, but as much as we tried, we never did get a glimpse of them. No matter, though, because the wildflowers in bloom everywhere were enough to satisfy me, especially the alpine lupine that carpeted the slopes of the mountains in deep indigo blue. There were other species, too, such as the white-petaled mountain avens, found mostly on flat expanses of the riverbank, and Sudeten lousewort, with its handsome reddish-purple head of flowers. According to my field guide, Siberian Natives picked the lousewort in early spring and boiled the young shoots in soup.

As I stooped to admire the peculiar spur shape of the lousewort's blossom, I noticed the huge tracks of a grizzly bear that had recently passed our way. When I announced my find to Andrew and Dan, they were instantly on the alert, their heads searching like swinging compass needles for the source of the fresh pads in the mud and sand. The discovery of the bear tracks led to a discussion of our own gait, and Andrew contributed the words "supinate" and "pronate" to my vocabulary. The first meant "walking flat-footed," and the second, "tending to walk on the inside of one's heel," as I apparently did.

Our blood sugar levels were getting low, so we stopped for a snack in the neck of a windy notch where the river narrowed through a rocky canyon. We also took our bearings. To the south, we had a good view of our first large expanse of glistening white aufeis – dense ice left behind from last winter's overflow. Beside the river, braided caribou trails converged and formed one wide diagonal path up the incline to our vantage point. To the north, the river zigzagged, first left, then right, where it disappeared from view. Around that final bend we decided there had to be a place where we could camp for the night. It was still early, but we had been sweating profusely all day long and wanted to take a bath in the worst way.

Sure enough, a few tussocks and river bends later, we found an ideal gravel bar with just enough sand to put our tents on, and there we dropped our packs and called it a day. There was also plenty of dry willow, so while the guys put up the tents, I gathered wood and built a little Indian fire to boil some tea water over, then to fry up the remainder of our tortillas and cheese for dinner. We felt so good, and the river water looked so inviting, we decided to take a full bare-naked bath, our first since the beginning of the trek.

After an exquisitely cold bath, we sat around the fire and checked out our neighborhood. Although we were surrounded by a completely new vista, the mountains here, too, were mostly composed of limestone and shale. But these mountains had steep, roughly hewn faces with few green slopes or sheep trails on them. And, as expected, there was no evidence around of any four-legged animal life – only the cry of mew and herring gulls coursing above the river and the lonesome sound of whimbrels in the tundra. Later, we heard a few redpolls twittering in the willows and a rock ptarmigan growling on the face of the mountain opposite our camp. Two spotted sandpipers came teetering along the edge of the river in search of freshwater crustaceans, then a raven cruised by, head craned down, curious about the strange creatures sitting around a plume of smoke below. Far above, two golden eagles soared, probably scrutinizing us with their telescopic vision and wondering whether we were anything good to eat. High above, feathery wisps of clouds drifted northwest, finally dissipating into clear blue sky, victims of the much drier Arctic air pattern. We wouldn't have any rain this night, I predicted. By now there was also virtually no snow left in the mountains, quite a change from the thick mantle of snow that lay everywhere only three weeks earlier.

Just as it had done the evening before at about 8:00 o'clock, the direction of the wind changed from upriver to downriver, probably because of the warming influence of the sun by day on the mountain air, causing low pressure, then the reverse pattern setting in by night – a practical lesson in meteorology for all of us. Both winds were greatly appreciated because they kept the mosies at bay and allowed us to walk barefoot around camp, and to take our time without putting any dope on. We took advantage of this opportunity, and sat around the fire listening to the sweet warbling of robins and the riffling of the river, chatting quietly about sundry topics, like recent puma sightings in Alaska. I told them there had even been a puma spotted on the Lower Yukon River the previous summer by some Eskimo friends of mine.

As I listened to Andrew and Dan compare their puma experiences in California, I studied the river. It was no longer in spate and had narrowed to a cobbled channel only forty feet across, as clear as spring water. I glanced around, half expecting to see my canoe resting on the beach. Most of the time, when I'm camped at the river's edge, I have the security of my canoe with me. But, at least for now, it was pure leg power, although we hoped Don had dropped my little Sea Eagle 8 raft farther downriver at Drain Creek.

Soon it was time to sleep, and Andrew and Dan decided to bunk together in my North Face while I used Andrew's tent. My last image before closing my eyes was of the midnight sun sinking ineluctably behind the mountains to the northwest and the half-moon rising in the southeast. I wondered what surprises the river held in store for us the next day.

Happy Birthday, Jen! It was June 25, my wife's birthday, and I wished she were with me to share the wild beauty of this river and these mountains so far away from the humdrum of civilization. After building a fire and heating some tea water, I saluted Jen with my white plastic cup of Red Rose tea. The guys still weren't up and I enjoyed this time alone, watching mew gulls as they cruised and called above the purling sound of the river. Some of their calls were muted, others higher pitched, while they searched for food to fill their empty stomachs. If they were looking for fish, I couldn't imagine there were many in this part of the river. But suddenly one of them dropped to the river's edge and stared at the riffle in front of him for the longest time. I wondered if he knew something I didn't about this river.

The sun was already hot, and I could hear Dan and Andrew beginning to rustle around inside the tent, earnestly complaining about the heat. It didn't take them long to get out into the cool air, where I suggested they jump in the river to refresh themselves. They glanced at the river, then at each other, but finally decided to forgo the swim and came over to my little fire where they poured some hot water for their breakfast coffee. We chatted about many things, finally landing on the topic of Bill Bryson's often hilarious book, *A Walk in the Woods*, which I had been reading while they were still sawing logs. Bryson, in his tale about his journey along the Appalachian Trail, spoke of the many hardships he had while walking parts of the trail. As I read excerpts from the book, none of us was very sympathetic. The difficult conditions he described paled in comparison to those we were experiencing on our own trek.

Talk about books drew us into a discussion of Ambrose's book about Lewis and Clark and their benefactor, Thomas Jefferson. As much as Jefferson may have been a free thinker for his time, he was still very much a product of the customs of his era, many of which we frown on today. His dependence upon slaves for his income, and his slave mistress, whom he never accepted as an equal for fear of social condemnation, were two examples. Another was his destruction of ever increasing acreages of the native forest to dedicate to the production of cotton and tobacco, so he could maintain his upper class style of life. Even his attitude toward Native Americans was not correct for our times – to subdue them so the fur trade could reign supreme all the way to the Pacific Coast. As we are today, Jefferson was a victim of his times, and did not actively challenge most of the accepted norms of early 19th century American society.

A pair of twittering upland sandpipers interrupted our morning gossip, and continued to fly nervously in the tundra as we broke camp. Moving downriver, we came across more of those fascinating sandpipers, once regarded by ornithologists as plovers, both because they nest like them in alpine tundra and because they move like them on the ground. We also saw another species of sandpiper, the lesser yellowlegs, which is about the noisiest bird in the North Country when you inadvertently approach their nest.

Just around the bend from the yellowlegs, the river bounced off a high rock abutment and took an abrupt jog to the right. As we stood above the water, I noticed a shadow and some movement in a deep pool just upriver from the jog. On glassing the shadow, I couldn't believe my eyes. It was a huge grayling slowly patrolling what must have been his favorite summer hangout. I never in my wildest dreams thought there were grayling in the Kongakut River. Arctic char, yes, but not grayling. There he was, though, with his long dorsal fin, cruising back and forth, every now and then hitting the surface for small floating insects. It was yet another of our many surprises on the river.

After crossing a long meadow of tussocks, we came to our first stand of stunted balsam poplar that followed the banks of a deep tributary creek of the Kongakut. It was strange, finding tall trees so far above the Arctic Circle. And wouldn't you know it, the windbreak they offered us also provided an opportunity for the mosquitoes to try their luck on our bare legs as we carefully forded the creek in our sandals. Not for long, though. We quickly dried our feet, put our boots on, and stepped out of the shadow of trees and back onto the breezy floodplain.

This time there were no tussocks to contend with, only a maze of willows, which we easily wended our way through by following the braided patterns of trails left by migrating caribou. Then suddenly, the willows ended and we entered a gently sloping alluvial fan studded with avens and other wildflowers. The flat ground offered such a superb walking platform that we were able to avoid the brushier more uneven terrain of the riverbed. When we came across tufts of beige fur, shed on the ground by a passing grizzly bear, we were glad we were out in the open where we could see for miles in every direction. We often stopped to survey the area for these elusive creatures. Here the valley was at its widest point yet, one alluvial outflow turning into the next. We wondered how long our good luck could last.

When the valley finally did begin to narrow, we were forced back down to the riverbank, where we found another copse of balsam poplar. Our faces were burning up from the sun's relentless rays, so we took a short break under their welcome shade to smear sun block on our noses and ears. Andrew and I had experienced this Arctic heat before and were prepared for it, but Dan was incredulous. The hot sand next to the river, bright reflections from the running water, and the way he sweat "like a pig," he said, were totally beyond what he had expected during the trek. He was ready for the raft. The problem was that, although the river had widened considerably, it was still not deep enough for us to even think about a raft. Besides, our rendezvous point, Drain Creek, was still days away.

A well-traveled game trail took us along the edge of the river for a few miles, and Andrew and I unintentionally picked up our pace. We soon noticed Dan lagging behind again, and slowed down for him to catch up. Not wanting to alienate him, we decided to take more breaks. Besides, with more breaks we could search the country for any animal life in the neighborhood and admire the surrounding mountains for their spectacular beauty and unusual geology. Formed of limestone and slate, their upper extremities were angular and rugged, and their lower ridges as jagged as bear teeth. We glassed them for signs of Dall sheep, but saw nothing more than a few thin trails crossing the talus slopes.

Soon the river narrowed even more, and the caribou trails led us back up on the mountainside just below the talus. Once, as we were threading our way through a rocky area, a short-eared owl flew over us, so close we could hear the luffing of its wings. It was searching for voles and lemmings in the soapberries and kinnikinick that matted the slopes we were walking along. There were other wild flowers, too, such as wintergreens (*pyrolas*) and louseworts, among them capitate lousewort, which we hadn't yet encountered. Their three vertically pendulous, creamy yellow flowers were typical of those

I had seen on other trips in the Brooks Range. They seemed to like these calcareous piedmonts, as did the other plants and bushes we found there.

When the river took an abrupt dogleg to the left we decided to follow our caribou trails to the top of another ridge to save a few miles of walking. When we reached the summit we could see the big bend of the river on both sides of us. On the south flank lay the stretch we had walked since morning. To the north lay our next day's challenge. Meanwhile, we were ready to call it a day and began an earnest search for a good spot to put our tents. Following the still well worn game trails, we dropped down from the ridge top, skirted some small alpine lakes, finally stopping at a rocky overlook, where we rested and glassed the country for a campsite. To our left, a large tributary creek flowed out from between two craggy ridges and ended in a huge field of glowing white aufeis. This field joined another much larger one on the Kongakut River, forming the most massive platform of winter overflow ice I'd ever seen. There the valley widened again and the aufeis filled the river for as far as we could see. I told Andrew and Dan that maybe the next day we could use it as a highway to save some bushwhacking through soggy tundra and brush.

We continued down the slope, aiming for a small knoll overlooking the aufeis, where it seemed like we might be able to set up camp. The creek crossing was easier than I had anticipated, and when we reached our destination, the knoll was just what we needed. There was no wood handy, not even willows, but that's what our gas stove was for, so after pitching the tents we cooked dinner and heated some water for a cup of Red Rose tea.

When Andrew and Dan retired to their tents, I took my cup of tea and ambled down to the edge of the aufeis to watch a pair of semipalmated plovers scurrying around near the ice. They appeared tiny next to the vertical blue and white ice abutments. Just then, the sun shone from behind threatening rain clouds and intensified the glacial blue colors in the ice. Along with alternating lines of white ice, the combination became almost ethereal, and I hurried back to camp to fetch my camera. The plovers were gone by the time I returned, but the colors were still intense, and I hoped for the best.

My boots were beginning to show some wear above the soles, so on returning to the tent I grabbed my Shoe Goop and smothered the ragged edges with the awful smelling stuff. I was glad I had brought the glue along, and somehow I knew this wouldn't be the last time I'd have to use it. As I waited for them to dry I was visited by a midget grasshopper, our first this far north. He was as all grasshoppers are in southern climes, just five times smaller. He even spat "tobacco" on my fingers.

When the breeze stopped, another insect began to visit me – many of them, all having a sharp proboscis and a terrible appetite for mammalian blood. They finally got a little too pesky, so I retired to the tent, where Dan was already ensconced. It was late, and with the sound of mosquitoes (which I call, "mosies") thumping the tent fly, and the thin whistling call of whimbrels in the distance, I lay back and closed my eyes. I informed Dan that we were now more than halfway to the raft. He grunted his approval.

After a short rest, I read my book, then crawled inside my sleeping bag, and again lay listening to the magical sounds of the country. Two snipes were diving and winnowing overhead, and a red-throated loon wailed on a small lake behind our knoll – for me, a fitting end to another great day on the Kongakut.

I awoke to the noisy barking of a parky squirrel behind the tent. When I heard a hissing sound, I popped my head out the door to find Andrew hovering over the gas stove with a small kettle of hot water. He was getting ready to brew his morning cup of strong Columbian coffee. It smelled so delicious that I crawled out of my bag, greeting the day with a wide arm stretch to the sky. The sun was shining again and there were only a few clouds downriver. The signs looked auspicious for another fine day of hiking.

When Andrew offered me a cup of his coffee I was quick to accept and sat down by the stove to get my bearings. I could see the silhouette of the parky squirrel standing on top of a small bump of ground behind camp. He continued to bark as a snipe winnowed high above him, invisible against the rays of the morning sun. The aufeis was still blue and white on the river, and when I went down to the shore to wash up, the rhythmic dripping of melt water from the edge of the ice was punctuated by thundering booms of giant chunks of ice crashing into the river in the distance. The glare of the sun was intense, and I had spots in my eyes when I stared a little too long at the shadings of glacier blues reflecting from the surface of the water. There were a few mosies hanging around, but nothing a little breeze couldn't take care of.

The wind came up as ordered on my way back from a walk over to the little lake behind camp, where I had heard the loon the evening before. The loon wasn't on the lake now, but there were three pintails, a male and two females. When they saw me they flew straight up in the air, the male pintail showing off his long neck and handsome plumage. They headed downriver, the direction we were preparing to go ourselves very shortly.

When we were finally on our way again, we trekked through meadows of mountain- and yellow avens that were so level I referred to them as "the avens trail." After we ran out of these flat areas, we tried our luck on the aufeis, but were able to walk on its uneven and sloppy wet surface for only a half-mile or so until forced to drop down to the river, where we found an easy caribou trail to follow. While on the ice we came across numerous small light brown piles of what appeared to be limestone dust. I took a pinch of the material and touched it gently with my tongue. It had the bitter soda-water taste and crunch of calcium carbonate, and when Andrew and Dan tasted it we agreed the dust must have been blown down in winter from the eroding mountains around us.

The breeze was just what we needed to keep the bugs off our backs so we could take our time and savor what we found along the trail – the tantalizing designs on the river cobbles, bearberry leaves already turned a vivid autumn red, the mustard yellows of arctic arnica, lines of cottonwood trees punctuating the horizon, the pendulous pink flowers of arctic pyrola hugging the ground, and the green mats of kinnickinik and juniper blanketing the southern edges of the knolls on the mountain outwashes we were crossing.

On the other side of these outwashes, we were back on the river again, this time among some tall bushy willows. Suddenly, a cow moose with her newborn calf almost stumbled into us, scaring us half to death. The calf was so close I could clearly see the rich deep brown and russet tones in its fur. Turning abruptly in the willows, they ran off up the bank where the cow, hackles raised, stopped momentarily to try to make some sense of who we were. Since the wind was blowing into our faces, she and her calf hadn't smelled us, thus causing the mutual sudden surprise. We were lucky. A cow moose with calf can be deadlier than a grizzly bear.

We stopped for a lunch break on a high breezy bluff where we could keep the bugs at bay and watch the country for any sign of moving animals down below. Then, to stay in the breeze and away from the willows and possible dangerous encounters with other moose or grizzly bears, we followed a caribou trail high on the flank of the mountain. I wondered aloud if caribou originally made their trails for a similar reason, to escape would-be predators and the hordes of mosquitoes waiting for them on the bottomlands.

We took another break to "wet our whistle" at a sparkling rivulet of fresh water where we found small clusters of wild rosemary. The leaf of this small plant resembles that of its relative, Labrador tea, and is sometimes mistaken for it by Native children sent out to gather tea for their parents. Like many other wild members of the heath family, rosemary contains the toxic chemical andromedatoxin, which lowers blood pressure and causes breathing difficulties. The pink globe-like hanging flowers and top vertical leaves distinguish it from Labrador tea, which has white flowers and horizontal leaves. At this rivulet we also listened to the voices of our constant companions, the whimbrels and upland sandpipers. Without larger animals around to pique our interest, these little guys gave us the gift and flow of wild uninterrupted bird song.

Then it was back down to the river again, following the path of least resistance along game trails that, like the river, would ultimately lead to the Coastal Plain and the Beaufort Sea. A few miles later we found a gravel bar with enough flat patches of sand on it to make a comfortable location for our tents, and it was there we called it a day. By now we were into a routine, so while Andrew and Dan put up the tents I built a fire and started supper. I soon turned the operation over to Andrew when he suggested cooking his specialty, polenta and beans. We still had a lot of Frank's Hot Sauce left, and we used much of it to make an already zesty meal even zestier.

After dinner we put a few more sticks of dry willow on the fire, and I told some stories from my Peace Corps experience in Bolivia during the mid 1960s, including one about my arrest by the Bolivian military for being a "comunista." Those were the days when Che Guevara was roaming the jungles of Bolivia and anyone working with the Indian people was suspect. As I finished the story and we went on to other subjects, I took a look around. On all sides, the mountains were heavily skirted in gray and yellow talus. High white lenticular clouds flowing fluidly across the summit of the mountain provided a backdrop and started me speculating about what they might mean for the next day's weather. Would there be rain?

Early in the morning I awoke from a dream where I'd been trying to cross a bridge overflowing with floodwaters caused by heavy rains upstream. Raindrops were pecking staccato-like at the ripstop nylon fabric of the tent fly. Our first rain. My suspicions proved correct about the high white clouds of the night before.

When the rain let up, Andrew and I painstakingly built a small fire by cutting and shaving miniature tidbits of willow kindling, then slowly coaxing the flame by blowing at its base while adding ever larger pieces of damp wood. It wasn't easy, but within ten minutes we had enough fire to heat water for our tea and a lentil chili brunch. Not a very thrilling meal, but with cheddar cheese melted on top it tasted pretty good – one of those "stick to your ribs" type of meals. As Andrew and Dan chatted about winter driving strategies, I watched a parasitic jaeger flit gracefully overhead, reminding me of a big arctic tern. He disappeared down the valley, hidden by miasmic strands of fog that slithered above the surface of the river.

We struck camp at midday, deciding to try to hike across the crunchy surface of the largest field of aufeis we had encountered yet. It wasn't long, though, until we came to where the ice was so irregular we were forced to climb back down to the riverbed, then up a high steep bluff, at the top of which we hoped to be able to do some serious hiking again. But scaling the bluff proved a real challenge, and we had to use willow branches as an aid to pull ourselves up an almost seventy degree incline. It was dangerous, especially with heavy packs strapped on our backs, and I checked the strength of every willow I grabbed, making sure every toehold in the rocky earth was completely solid. After I was up, Andrew took his turn, then Dan. What

I remember most about the climb was the smell of Alaska sage, growing everywhere on the south-facing slope. When Andrew joined me he brought a piece of it with him to let me smell. It reminded me of the Arizona desert and sparked a storm of memories of my many walks there.

It was good I had those memories to keep my mind occupied because soon after we began walking on the high bank the sky let loose with a downpour like I hadn't experienced since my hike five years earlier through the Gates of the Arctic with Andrew Benedetti and Sue Hall. Even with a double raincoat on, the water seeped through the fabric to my vest and shirt. Fortunately, my rain pants held up as we waded through the thick wet underbrush. We couldn't have picked a worse spot to run into heavy rain. Not only was the terrain rough, with many ravines and small canyons to cross, but also the willows and alpine birch were chest high in places. After a couple of hours the rain finally stopped, leaving rags and tatters of dense fog in the valley similar to those we'd seen near camp in the morning. Stretching across the aufeis still smothering the river, they eventually dissolved into a thin miasma, gradually dissipating as the sky cleared and the sun shone again. Although my shirt was damp and skin clammy, my spirits improved when I glimpsed a wandering tattler pecking for food along one of the streams we had to ford. Bobbing and teetering at the edge of the water, it sang out its clear *whee-we-we-we*, reminding me of the call of the spotted sandpiper.

When I checked my inside vest pocket for my notebook and map, I found they had absorbed some of the moisture that had seeped through my rain jackets. This would not happen again, I mumbled, and I determined to invest in a quality raincoat as soon as I got back to Fairbanks. Walking conditions soon improved, though, and I quickly forgot about my wet notebook and clammy skin. At least I was warm and the trail was getting better every minute.

Good trails promote a good walking stride, and again I found myself moving too quickly for Dan. Andrew was just ahead of Dan, keeping him company, and when he yelled that it was time for another break I shucked my pack and bent down to smell the wild Labrador tea flowers in bloom along the trail. I smiled as Andrew strode up with a small bouquet of the fragrant tea hanging from the top of his raincoat zipper. He knew a good source of natural perfume when he saw it. I didn't have to remind him of the psychic uplift that a "nose hit" of the stuff gave a person, especially when the going got rough. But it was a new idea to Dan, and we introduced him to the concept right there and then. He was a quick learner and immediately picked a white flower head and began sniffing.

Dan continued sniffing as we followed the trail up to the crest of a ridge, where we stopped to take in the lay of the country. "I've never seen anything like it," I commented to the fellas. "I never thought we'd find aufeis that just goes on and on like this. It's gotta have at least a minor effect on the climate here, maybe even causing some of the fog and rain because it's so cold." They thought that was a pretty good Keim theory, as my musings have come to be known. At that moment a merlin cruised smoothly above us, wings stretched back sharp and unmoving, diving into the valley. What did it see that we didn't, I wondered.

A little farther along we came to a huge gaping hole, recently torn out of the side of the ridge by a grizzly bear with an appetite for parky squirrel. Rocks and earth were strewn in every direction, and the hole was almost big enough to fit all three of us inside its gaping maw. I ventured that the griz may even have used it as a winter lair. Andrew was so impressed he took a picture of me inside the hole, pretending to be a bear waiting for unsuspecting human prey to stumble into his dagger-like claws.

"Speaking of grizzlies, Dan," I said, as we continued our ridge walking, "here's what they eat when they can't find humans or parkies." I pointed out a plant called bear root. With the scientific name, *Hedysarum alpinum*, bear root is in the legume family. Its roots are edible and when cooked taste a little like young carrots. Especially in spring and fall, they are a favorite food of grizzly bears, which are experts at distinguishing them from their poisonous close cousins, the wild sweet pea, *Hedysarum mackenzii*. Dan was curious and dug up the root of one of the plants to try a morsel. We all took a nibble, and decided it had a tangy taste. It would probably taste better cooked, especially in spring or fall when most of the sugars were still in the roots. I told Dan how Yupik Eskimos in Hooper Bay used to gather these roots from vole nests in the tundra and make delicious soups of them.

We came to the edge of a deep, east-trending canyon, where we stood for a while checking our bearings. The sky was still overcast and, with the walls of the Kongakut River Valley growing steeper and darker in the distance, we had the urge to find a campsite and start dinner. We were tired and hungry. Since the only way to go was down, down we went, following another well-worn caribou trail along the knife-edge of the canyon rim all the way to the bottom of the river valley. From there I walked quickly ahead to scout for a good camping spot, finally locating one around a wide willowy bend in the river below a small knoll that I judged would be just high enough to keep the cold coastal breeze off us and still discourage the mosquitoes. By then Andrew and Dan were ready to call it quits, saying they had followed so many trails they were beginning to feel like caribou.

I was amazed to find that even after the heavy rain the dead sticks lying at the base of the willows were still dry enough to kindle a fire for Andrew to cook dinner on. His special fare that night was almond chicken and polenta, and we were looking forward to it. Meanwhile, I took my map out of its plastic ziplock container and checked it for our progress. Dan and I went over it millimeter by millimeter, concluding that we were just a hair away from our destination. We reckoned the raft should be stashed somewhere within a mile of camp. When I got up on top of the knoll and spied what looked like a bright yellow tent only a few hundred yards downriver, I knew we were close.

After a quick dinner, I hoofed it down to what was indeed a tent pitched in the middle of a gravel bar surrounded by running braids of the Kongakut. I hallooed across the water, then watched a corner of the door flap open and a young man's head peer out. I carefully forded two braids of the river and walked up to the tent, reassuring the two people inside that I was only a fellow traveler and telling them what I was up to. They must have been terrified because they didn't make any attempt to come out and kept the flap open only enough to watch me with their wide frightened eyes. In a few minutes, the man finally introduced himself as Rob and began to talk nonstop through the open flap, telling me they had come from Washington, D.C. to float the river in their Klepper kayak all the way to the Arctic Ocean. They were worried about bears, he confessed, and about the level of the water, which seemed to be on the rise due to the heavy afternoon rains. I finally had to interrupt him to ask if he had seen a raft, life vests, and two bear barrels hanging from a tree, as Don Ross had indicated he would do for us on one of his backhauls. He had, he said. They were on the large gravel bar about a hundred yards upriver.

After visiting through the tent flap for another five minutes, I re-crossed one of the braids and checked for our equipment. Everything was intact, but Don had placed the items in a location we probably never would have found if the yellow tent hadn't been there to flag them. I yelled back that I had found the stash and that I would return the following morning with my buddies to inflate the raft and start our own float through the canyon. They were welcome to join us in their Klepper, I offered. Then I crossed the river again, retracing my steps to camp, where I made my report to Andrew and Dan. Dan was elated.

To bed, to bed, where it seemed like I'd slept for only an hour before raindrops started pelting the rip-stop with a fury worse than we'd experienced in the afternoon. For almost half the night I was able to sleep in only fits and starts, until finally, at about 4:00 a.m., the rain suddenly stopped. I zipped down the tent flap and peered outside to see the mountains on all sides of us heavily blanketed in immaculately white snow. Beautiful wasn't the word for it, I thought, but then reality clicked in as I realized that we'd have to get going early in the morning to beat the high water over to our raft.

We didn't get packed up and out of camp until mid morning, and just as I'd thought when I'd seen all that snow earlier, the river was already two feet higher than the day before. With the water racing, turbid and daunting at our feet, we stood staring, wondering how we could cross to the island where our raft was stashed. We walked up and down the bank, trying different possibilities until finally we found a wide riffle we felt we could ford safely. The water was only up to our thighs and we made it across without incident, then quickly hiked down to where I had found the raft the previous day. Andrew and Dan agreed that we never would have spotted it if the pair from D.C. hadn't camped on the gravel bar close by.

As we spread out the flat gray hulk of the Eagle raft on the edge of the gravel bank and began to blow it up with a foot pump, the couple inside the banana yellow tent began to rustle around inside, finally zipping their flap all the way down and stepping out into what had become an intermittently rainy day. Rob put his hip boots on, forded one of the minor braids, and came over to watch us prepare for our trip downriver. In the course of the conversation, we learned he had been recently married, that he had used his Klepper only once before on a much mellower Alaskan river, and that his new wife had never floated with him in the kayak on a serious river like the Kongakut. Andrew and Dan glanced at me quizzically, and I knew what they were thinking – a disaster waiting to happen, especially with the water as high and fast as it was. I remembered the fresh set of wolf tracks we had just run across upriver, thought it better not to mention them, and again offered to let the couple tag along behind us. Rob thanked us, but said they'd probably wait another day or so until they started down. Meanwhile, would I mind checking out the zippers on his tent before leaving?

I examined the zippers closely and found two of the three were hopelessly faulty and would not work at all, meaning Rob and his wife had to depend on only one zipper for the duration of their trip. I advised them to treat that zipper with kid gloves, and gave them a tip on how to lubricate it with soap. I wished them luck, then crossed back to where Andrew and Dan were waiting for me to do a final safety check on the raft. That done, we carefully placed our packs and bear barrels in the middle of the raft and organized ourselves so that Andrew and Dan were sitting on the left and right sides of the big tube to paddle, and myself on the stern to do the steering. With only eight feet for three big men and all of our gear, I marveled that we were actually able to fit. My first thought was of the old nursery rhyme, "Rubadubdub, three men in a tub...!" When I recited it aloud, the three of us laughed. Then we bid Rob and his wife adieu, and cast off down the raging river. As we raced by the banana tent, I glanced up to see a golden eagle soaring above us. We had watched one fly over earlier in the morning. It was probably the same eagle, but I wondered what odd scene he was imaging at that instant. Three men in a tub, indeed!

For the first couple of miles, all went well. The river ran swiftly and there were no difficult rapids. After getting down our paddling technique, we were able to deftly move away from large boulders that often crowded the river with their roiling gray domes. Rounding bends was tricky because of our heavy load, but we soon mastered them. With the right combination of strokes, we scooted from one side of the river to the other like a big bubble. Even a little rain didn't dampen our spirits, although the sky didn't remain overcast for long. Soon it began clearing again, the wind calmed a bit, and things seemed almost perfect. It didn't matter how crowded we were in the boat, or what dangers lay ahead down the canyon. We were on our way to our final destination, Caribou Pass.

It was getting late in the afternoon when we realized we hadn't eaten lunch yet. We also felt the need to stretch our legs, so when we came to a spot that seemed to have the right qualifications, we headed for shore. After securing the raft and building a small fire in the lee of a wall of tall willows, we boiled some tea water and ate a snack, but as we chatted about the fortuitous events of the last two days the wind began picking up and dark clouds started rolling over the mountains. We didn't want to press our luck too much, so we pitched our tents on a flat span of fine gravel and gathered more wood for the fire. Our supper was part of the cache of tortillas and cheese that had arrived with Don, and the fresh food lifted our spirits. Now that we had our paddling and steering system under control in the raft, we were looking forward to what the next day would bring.

Just as we finished our last quesadillas the rain started again. We sat around the fire for a while, listening to the slow pitter-patter of the drops on the willow leaves and their frenetic sizzle as they hit the burning wood and hot stones in the fireplace. But when the drops got heavier, we packed the food back in the bear barrel and headed for our tents. Dan and I both reeked of the strong burnt-carbon smell of smoke, which I thought might have been due to the influence of the rain. All smells seem to be accentuated by rain.

Once inside my sleeping bag I scribbled a few journal notes, then fell asleep. But the hard whack of rain on the tent woke me up after an hour or so. As it was still light, and since I couldn't go back to sleep, I read more of Bill Bryson's book, *A Walk in the Woods*. I couldn't help smiling at his complaints about the difficulties of walking on the Appalachian Trail, and I wondered if he would enjoy a trip such as ours. Twice, as I read, I heard the drone of a small plane overhead. Poking my head out in the rain, I recognized Don's Cessna 185 cruising low under the rain clouds, probably heading for Caribou Pass to backhaul some passengers. The second time I looked out I noticed the mountains were again mantled in snow. The next day there would be a lot of new water added to the river, and I hoped the D.C. couple would be smart enough to transfer their little yellow tent and all their gear to higher ground.

A thin veil of mist hung over the valley as I built a small breakfast fire and put some water on to boil for our early morning tea and granola. In spite of my gentle admonishment, Dan drank his tea black without first eating something or spiking it with powdered milk. Immediately, he dashed for the willows and vomited it all back up. When he tried again, he did it the proper way, first eating his granola, then drinking the tea with milk in it.

The river was running three or four feet higher than normal, and we knew we were in for a wild ride that morning. We were off by 10:00, and down we went through the turbid, boulder-strewn millrace at a faster clip than I'd ever floated in a raft before. The walls of the canyon were quickly closing in on us, and we recalled Don's warning about the Kink, infamous for its tricky hairpin turn and the current that tended to ram even large rafts up against its vertical walls. The problem was we didn't know exactly where the Kink was, so at each steep bend in the river we prepared for the worst. But the worst never came. Only at one point did the river twist at a precarious angle and bounce off a steep rock face, though even there we were able to take the inside of the bend and avoid the precipice. Not that the river wasn't tricky, even dangerous at times, but with our precision system of paddling and steering, we managed to get through the morning still dry and in one piece.

For bend after tortuous bend we slid and bounced down the racing river, once skirting too close for comfort to the vertical walls of a field of aufeis spreading from one side of the canyon to the other, allowing us just enough room to slip through a narrow opening in the blue ice. Then, as the river turned in a wide arch to the northwest, it divided into a confusing maze of shallow braids. Once, when the raft got stuck on the bottom and Andrew jumped out to try to free it from the gravel, he lost his balance and fell part way into the icy cold river. His rain gear prevented any serious penetration of water, but it was a warning for us to be more careful. When we were grounded on yet another shallow braid we all had to jump out, but this time we only got wet feet. At about noon the wind picked up, making maneuvering even more difficult, in spite of our combined strength and three paddles.

Things began to improve a little as the channel narrowed, funneling us through a small canyon filled with a whimsy of turtleback boulders and foaming rapids. Next to a sheer rock face a small flock of cliff swallows surprised us, milling around the mud nests they had recently built on the vertical shale of the rock wall. Dan wondered why they built like this, but before I could answer him an immature golden eagle flapped over our heads pursued by an angry mob of mew gulls, one of which abruptly changed course and veered toward us, just missing Dan's hat. Then lickety-split, my eyes darted over to the shoreline where an American dipper dashed out from its nest on the steep bank, flew low over the water and landed at the edge of the river. I remarked that I'd often seen these little birds that feed underwater on the south side of the Brooks Range, but never north of the Continental Divide.

We stopped for lunch to watch the dipper and dry our socks and boots. To hurry the drying, I kindled a little willow stick fire near a clear-running creek. Tall willows protected us from the onslaught of the cold wind, and soon we felt warm enough to take a short jaunt to the crown of a nearby knoll. We wanted to see the summit of Mt. Greenough, one of the highest peaks in this section of the British Mountains. After bushwhacking through the willows, we followed the deep ruts of a caribou trail up the shoulder of the knoll. Once on top, we ducked behind a rock outcrop to escape the fierce wind, then peered into an eastward trending valley that according to our map stopped just short of the Canadian border. We could also see down the Kongakut River, where another maze of braids and a lot of whitewater awaited us. We weren't looking forward to that.

On our way back to the raft, we again wrestled with the choice of either continuing on the river or camping where we were for the night. We chose the river, and when we reached the raft, quickly jumped aboard and pushed off for what we hoped would be a fast ride down to a good campsite. As soon as we were back in the saddle, though, we knew we were going to have to work hard for any rest at the end of this leg. The wind raced up the middle of the valley, causing choppy water, often throwing spray in our faces, and the wild rapids made it difficult to steer the raft. Twice we hit colossal waves generated by huge boulders that sloughed us off to the side, filling the raft with silty water. We bailed, trying to keep ahead of the water, but finally it got the best of us, soaking both our packs and ourselves.

Luck was with us when we spotted a clear-water creek rushing in from the west side of the Kongakut. The bank looked promising as a campsite, so we angled the raft into the jade-colored shallows in front of the creek, hopped out, and pulled the raft ashore. We hastily unloaded our packs, hefted our big inner tube onto the gravel bank and searched for a place to pitch the tents.

We found it in the lee of a line of willows paralleling the creek. There was even enough sand to serve as a good platform for both our tents, and we had a lovely view of the valley and of 7200-foot Mt. Greenough, glimpsed across the river through shifting veils of mist and cloud. Its summit and slopes were white with new snow, fallen over the past three days of summer storms.

Almost everything in our packs was damp except for our sleeping bags, which we had wrapped in plastic trash containers, so we spread it all on the ground to dry in what turned out to be a wonderful sunshine-filled evening. But it was still windy and we were shivering cold, so we gathered sticks for a bonfire and crouched close to the licking flames to warm up. I don't usually build bonfires, but this time the occasion called for one. The radiant heat from the fire was just what we needed, and soon we were comfortable enough to be curious about other things around us. As we stood by the fire, we watched a mixed flock of mew gulls and mergansers fishing at the mouth of the creek. We knew arctic char swam this far up the Kongakut to spawn, and wondered if the birds were eating their eggs. Or was it grayling? It was a mystery that would remain a mystery. And that was okay. To delight in the natural wonders of the Kongakut Valley didn't mean we had to understand everything about them. For the three of us, it was enough just to be here.

The sky continued to clear, and the stiff breeze kept the mosies away. After such a rough afternoon, this was a great change. Dan was particularly amazed at the green water of the creek rushing pell-mell into the turbid Kongakut – which somehow reminded us of Rob and his wife upriver. We had an ominous feeling about their luck with the river, half-expecting pieces of their Klepper and accompanying gear to come floating past us at any moment. We hoped Don Ross was keeping a close eye on them each time he flew up or down the valley. Speak of the devil, as Dan was recounting some adventures he had in India and Nepal a few years earlier, Don buzzed over again, staying high enough to keep the noise of his 185 at a minimum. Little did we know, he had just performed a rescue operation that had probably saved the D.C. couple's lives.

As every fire must burn down to its embers, so every day must finally come to a close. My day always ended with a good meditative tooth brushing at whatever water source we happened to be camped by. This one was particularly lovely. The sparkling cold green-water creek rushing and splashing on my hand when I bent down to wet my toothbrush made me feel like I was on top of the world. The clearing skies added a luminescent quality to the raw wilderness surrounding me that made the mundane brushing of my teeth a special event. I lifted my gaze from the creek, turning it toward the summit of the mountain behind our tents. I wondered if Dan and Andrew would want to climb it the next day. When I asked them, they glanced in the same direction I had and replied, "Good idea. Let's do it."

High cirrus clouds filled the blue arch of early morning sky. It was an auspicious day, and the pinnacle of mountain behind our camp teased us like the proverbial carrot on a string. Since the wind was still blowing hard up the valley and the water level on the river was dangerously high, we had already made up our minds to stick around for a day. So why not go for a long stroll up the mountain? A pair of golden eagles diving steeply on something above the summit further enticed us. I wondered aloud if there were Dall sheep up there. No sooner had I said it than three ewes rounded the bend of the talus slope above us. Then several more put in their appearance. There didn't seem to be any rams among them, but you never knew what might lie around the corner.

After stowing our smelly food in the bear barrels, we started up the green-water creek, gaining elevation gradually, then doubled back, aiming for an overlook I'd spotted with my binoculars, where we could look directly down at the sheep and hopefully get a few good pictures of them. Dan and I immediately fell behind Andrew who set off at a rapid pace. I wanted to photograph some of the wildflowers that were in full bloom, so I hung back to do that. Dan was content just to climb at his own speed, since there was no hurry to get anywhere except on the mountain someplace above the sheep. Because I was moving more slowly, I began to see varieties of flowers I'd missed before, like bladder campion, sandwort, and a number of different species of saxifrage, which is one of Alaska's largest families of wildflowers. Only when we could no longer see Andrew, did we pick up speed and try to catch him. A well-traveled caribou trail helped us make better time up what had turned out to be a rather brushy mountainside. Soon we were crossing a rugged zone of talus, but still no Andrew.

We whistled, yelled his name and glassed every inch of the flank of the mountain, but no Andrew anywhere. Finally, I spied him about 300 yards below us, standing in some thick brush, and we whistled again as loudly as we could. He saw us and waved, then started up the rocky slope to join us. As he angled up the mountain, we angled down, but not too far because we still wanted to be above the sheep when we reached the ridge where we'd seen them in the morning.

Andrew met us on a small overlook, where we decided to have our lunch and watch the sheep, by now in full view on a grassy slope below us. Several ewes and lambs had joined the original band, and all were feeding and resting, with no idea we were spying on their private lives from above.

While we glassed the sheep, I saw we had a little winged visitor spying on us from a nearby rock. A black and white thrush known as a wheatear was nervously watching us as he flitted from rock to rock, fanning its tail and bobbing up and down. Wheatears are unmistakable in this behavior and also in the color pattern on their tail that forms a black inverted "T" on a white field. Their common name refers to their distinctive white rump, and is a euphemism of the Anglo Saxon word meaning "white arse." They are a unique Alaskan bird in that they migrate in fall in a southwesterly direction all the way to sub-Saharan Africa. This one was a male and scolded us a few times with a *chack-chack*, *chack-weet*, before flying away up the mountain. Soon after, we headed down the slope to see how close we could get to the sheep before they spotted us.

When they finally did see us, the ewes and lambs didn't seem very concerned. They slowly ambled off to rockier ground on our left. As they followed a trail through a copse of alders, two of the ewes rubbed themselves against the branches of the alders to get rid of some of the winter hair hanging in rags and tatters from their summer coat. It was fascinating to watch them do this, and it explained why we had found so much sheep hair hanging on the brush along the trail.

After watching them for a little longer from behind a large limestone outcropping, we headed back to camp. It was already getting late and our stomachs were starting to grumble. We had to stop one last time, though, to admire a meadow of blue lupine just behind our tents. It reminded me of another trip many years earlier while walking alone down one of the tributary creeks of the Kongakut. Then I had also been awed by the lupine that carpeted the north side of the valley with a velvet blue.

Back at camp, while drinking my tea and chatting with Andrew and Dan next to the fire, a lone bull caribou came into view, ambling slowly along a bluff on the other side of the creek. Something was wrong with him, though. He was limping on his right side. Judging by his antlers, already in dark velvet, he appeared to be about four years old and, except for his limp, in pretty good shape. I remembered my uncle Chuck telling me once that sometimes caribou ruptured their Achilles tendon while running over sharp talus. If that were the case, he probably wouldn't make it any farther than the nearest wolf den. But such is the tenuous life of a caribou. That's why they are so gregarious. Their large numbers usually save them from a myriad of dangers lurking behind every willow bush and tundra rock. Loners and wounded animals like this one don't stand much of a chance. But he didn't know that, and after stopping for a moment to check us out he continued up the valley we had just come down.

Before dinner we all wandered over to the river to study the level of the water. It was starting to go down, and we thought that by morning maybe it would be low enough to think about putting in again. Not far away, on one of the opposite mountains, were five more ewes feeding casually on the herbs and forbs studding the slopes. Later, as we ate our chili dinner, we continued to watch them through a thin rainbow arching from one edge of a local rain shower to the other. Above the rainbow, snow-clad Mt. Greenough hugged the darkening sky. "I've got a hunch we're in for some more liquid sunshine tomorrow, fellas," I announced. At almost that precise instant, a female red fox trotted up to the edge of camp, stopped, and stared at me as if she were wondering what I had just said. Then, completely unconcerned about who we were, she trotted over to Andrew's tent, urinated, and faded into the willows and alders. She was losing her winter fur, and her ribs showed beneath her summer coat. We guessed she probably had a den of kits somewhere and was out hunting for them.

Towards midnight, after zipping myself tightly into my sleeping bag, I still had the scrawny image of that little vixen in my mind. As I finally closed my eyes and began to drift off to sleep, I heard myself say to Dan, who was probably already in dreamland, "Slim pickin's for fox this far north, Dan. Slim pickin's."

I awoke feeling a little bleary-eyed from lack of sleep. Dan's snoring was part of the reason, but the other was my incessant worry about the high water crashing through the canyon as a result of all the rain and snow. While descending the mountain the afternoon before, I'd glassed what I could of the canyon below and I didn't like what I saw of the big rapids I'd heard about. As much as I tried, I couldn't see what some called the Staircase, so I could get a feeling for its power. Maybe it was better that way because if I'd known what was ahead I may not have slept at all.

So it was with some trepidation that we broke camp earlier than usual and prepared to take our chances with the whim and fancy of the Kongakut. Although the day was overcast and threatening rain, at least the wind was in our favor, heading downriver for a change. While getting the raft ready, I theorized that a polar low-pressure front out on the Beaufort Sea might explain the wind direction.

After cinching in the packs, down the river we went, swept away like a feather in the wind by the racing current, hardly even able to cast a glance back at the green-water creek where we'd camped for the past two nights. Following the sinuous route of the river, we paddled hard to avoid the dangerous rocks and rapids I had peered at the day before. But around another bend we were abruptly in new country, which I hadn't been able to see from the mountain, and heading into some really big water. The current was taking us so quickly that we barely had a chance to react as boulder after boulder raised its huge foaming back, pitched and tossed us to one side, then sped us down the narrowing chute of the river. Each time we dodged and bounced off the boulders, we took in a large dollop of water, but with my trusty old cooking pot I bailed for all I was worth, somehow managing to get through more than a mile of standing waves and rapids. Suddenly, though, we didn't react swiftly enough. We were shot right up onto the butt-side of a huge boulder, the raft pushed forcefully down into the eddy of its backflow, angled broadside and almost overturned. Andrew missed being thrown completely into the river by the skin of his teeth, and so much water poured over the side of the raft that our only choice was to head for the left bank immediately.

I ordered us to shore, and with powerful draw strokes by Andrew on the left, quick paddling by Dan on the right, and hard ruddering by me in the stern, we found an opening in the fast water and skidded onto the rocky beach just in time. Andrew and Dan hopped out and hauled the raft up on the bank as far as they could, then I jumped out myself. "That was too close for comfort," I yelled.

While doing a reconnaissance of the river, I found it was even worse for a full half-mile beyond where we'd taken out, with a dangerous combination of narrow canyon walls, drop in elevation, huge boulders and a lot of foaming whitewater. This was probably the Staircase, I guessed. When I got back to the raft, I told Dan and Andrew the best thing for us to do was portage the entire half-mile around the bad water. Dan said he thought we could line around it, but I repeated what I'd seen downriver and looked at Andrew for support. Andrew backed me, and we started unloading the raft.

It took two loads, but at the end of the portage we all felt we'd made the right decision. Lining would have been much more arduous and may also have damaged the raft. At first, Andrew and I tried carrying the raft between us, but it finally proved easier for him to simply hoist it up on his head and back and portage it that way. It was actually quite light, not weighing more than 25 pounds. Every once in awhile the wind tried to knock him off balance, but with rope in hand I was able to keep him and the raft steered in the right direction, and soon we were ready to launch again.

Just down from where we stood planning our next move, the river crashed into a high abutment, preventing any further portage on our side, and we could see the water was too rough to float down the stretch in front of us, at least as far as the next bend. So we figured the best thing to do was to ferry directly across to the other shore, check out the rapids around the bend, then portage again as far as caution required. After settling ourselves in the raft, I yelled, "Go!" and we paddled for all we were worth toward the opposite bank. We were surprised at how deftly we managed to thread our way through the obstacle course of boulders and standing waves on all sides of us. When we finally bumped to a stop at the edge of the rocky shore, we leapt out again and hogtied the raft to some alders. While Andrew and Dan unloaded the gear, I took off to inspect the lay of the river. I soon returned with the good news that our portage would be a short one this time.

Andrew again carried the raft along with his pack while Dan and I hauled the rest of the gear, allowing us to do it all in one trip. When we'd crossed the narrow neck of a loop in the river, I pointed out a tricky, potentially dangerous double eddy ramming headlong into a cliff, not once but twice, then shooting out into the mainstream like a stone from a slingshot. After studying the eddies closely, we decided it was worth a try, and much better than having to pack everything another quarter of a mile up and around the brush-entangled bluff between us and the next tame part of the river.

For us to have enough time to make our turn and escape the eddies, we had to put in above a long, turbulent stretch of rapids. From there we would have to do some fast paddling to get through the whitewater and avoid being pushed into the vertical walls of the bluff. By now, though, we felt confident and skillful enough to do this, and poised the raft and ourselves for the big test.

With Andrew drawing to the left, Dan paddling on the right, and me holding at the stern, we zigzagged back and forth through the maze of rooster tails and turtlebacks, pulled and pushed hard one way, then the other, until we were through the rapids and on a collision course with the cliff face. In the nick of time, with exactly the right combination of stern and paddle work, we narrowly missed being forced into the first, then the second slate rock wall, finally being taken by the current and spit back into the mainstream. The whole maneuver occurred so quickly we hardly knew what had happened.

It wasn't over yet. The river kept rolling along through rock garden after rock garden of churning whitewater, then divided around a small island and wrapped around it in a tight hairpin turn. We pulled out on the island to try to spot any potential dangers lurking in wait for us around the corner. Dan stayed with the raft while Andrew and I bushwhacked through the willows to the other side of the island where the two braids joined, then back up along the edge of the channel to the raft. As we fought the underbrush, we studied the whimsies of the racing river. The rapids would be a real challenge, but our adrenalin levels were up and we made the decision to go for it.

Only 100 feet or so from the raft, I flushed a red-breasted merganser from her nest under the willows. It had six buff-colored eggs in it, and I stopped briefly to photograph them. This was the first merganser nest I had ever found and I was impressed with its construction. It was circular in shape and made mostly of downy feathers, probably plucked from the female duck's own body, mixed with bits of grass, twigs and leaves, a combination designed to keep eggs and ducklings warm even on the coldest days.

Just as I put my camera back in its case, I heard the hard sound of raindrops on the surrounding willows. To avoid the wet leaves, I quickly waded along the edge of the river to rejoin Andrew and Dan and help them drag the raft back upriver a ways so we could get a better shot toward the middle of the channel where there were fewer dangerous boulders that might upset us. As we pushed the raft beyond the near-shore rocks and jumped in, it began raining with a vengeance, but the long narrow chute of rooster-tails that followed focused our attention so completely on the river that we barely noticed the gusty rainsquall. Around the hairpin turn we went, narrowly missing the sharp slate canyon wall, rocking back and forth in the spume and froth of the raging whitewater, finally being tossed out of the canyon into a widening river where there were more calm sections between splashing boulder fields and furious chutes of churning rapids. We still managed to hit a few big standing waves and take in a bucketful of water, but the river seemed to be mellowing out, and we now had time to think about how fiercely it was raining on us.

My feet were soaked and getting colder in the four inches of frigid water in the bottom of the raft, so I asked the fellas to paddle for shore where we could dump the heavy load of water and stretch our stiffening leg muscles for a few minutes.

Then we were on our way again, going round and round the incessant bends, wondering how the big ecotourism rafts floated this length of river with its huge boulder fields and narrow channels. Three ewe sheep watched us intently from a rock precipice as we came out of one of the final big bends. At this point the mountains seemed more familiar to me. Sure enough, on looking downriver, I saw what my friend Roger Kaye once referred to as Velvet Creek, issuing from a wide valley that I had hiked through in 1989. There I had discovered the velvet blue color of the blooming alpine lupine, and it was also where I had been attacked for the first time in my life by a big chocolate colored male grizzly. He and I both escaped with our lives, but it was a hair-raising experience for the two of us. And there at the mouth of Velvet Creek was the big molar tooth outcropping I had used as a landmark that same year.

Speeding quickly past these places, we soon reached Fire Creek on our right and the massive hulk of Whale Mountain, where I had started my solo walk in 1989. Then I spotted the Whale Mountain gravel airstrip, where Andy Keller, Sue Hall and I had camped for a week just three weeks earlier. I almost felt like I was coming home as the valley opened up and we could see all the way to our final destination, Caribou Pass. It was 1:30 p.m. We could have made it to the Pass, but we still had a few days left of our stay on the Kongakut, so we decided to pull out at the Whale Mountain strip and camp the night there. By then we were all pretty cold anyway, and needed a fire to warm up. Dan was especially cold, "not winterized like us," in his words.

Nature is truly remarkable. Only moments after we pulled the raft up on the cobbled beach at the Whale Mountain landing, the rain stopped, allowing us to pitch our tents and light our fire in comparative comfort. My first fire died a slow smoky death because of the damp willow sticks I'd used. On my second try, though, after scouring the neighborhood for "skeleton willows" (dead age-dried willow limbs), I had a hot fire going in no time at all. We ate our lunch as near to the licking flames as we could get, remarking on our close calls in the morning. Since we'd set up camp in the lee of a clump of willows, which kept the cool breeze to a minimum, we soon felt like we were among the living again.

When we were all warm enough, I showed Andrew and Dan where I had camped three weeks earlier. By now, any evidence in the sand that I had once been there was obliterated by the double crescent tracks of hundreds of caribou that had recently passed through the valley, heading for the coastal plain. Fresh wolf sign was also abundant, and hairy remains of their prey in the scat indicated they had had a successful caribou hunt. This prompted me to suggest a walk back upriver a mile or so to search for traces of the pair of wolves I had seen there the last time I was in the area. Andrew was enthusiastic about going and, although Dan was tired of walking, mention of the wolves tweaked his interest enough for him to change back into his hiking boots and come along.

We followed the route I had taken so many times with Andy and Sue during the first week of June. We crossed the wide stretch of gravel bar along the river where ground-hugging Pallas' wallflower (*Erysimum pallasii*) still studded the cobbles, but by now were all in seed, trailing long curved spear-like pods from their green rosette of leaves. I remember kneeling down on the cobbles in those days to sniff the fragrance of their pink blooms, knowing it was the only way we could truly appreciate this lovely Arctic mustard.

The wonderful smell of Pallas' wallflower was history, but there was another fragrance that now permeated the air, one that Andrew recognized from previous trips he'd been on with me at this time of year: wild sweet pea. Known also as northern sweet vetch, and to botanists as *Hedysarum mackensii*, this flower's delightful smell belies the poisonous quality of its roots. It is not an edible plant and is avoided by humans and bears alike who distinguish it from its edible cousin, *Hedysarum alpinum*, known commonly as bear root or licorice root. The sweet pea also has a very lovely dark pink blossom that decked the gravel bar with lively color everywhere we looked.

Our destination was a high knoll in the middle of a tundra meadow, not far from where I had first seen the two wolves back in early June. We searched for them for some time from this vantage point, but our hopes of finding them didn't pan out, so we headed back to camp. The walkabout wasn't wasted, though. They never are. I always see something new whenever I'm on one. This time was no different. In addition to finding countless wildflowers and many bird species, while we were on top of the knoll we had a lovely view of the Kongakut River and the rugged mountains paralleling both sides of the valley. Most wonderful of all was the field of blooming cotton grass blanketing the tundra meadow below. No wonder the caribou used these river valleys as travel corridors. This sedge, with the scientific name *Eriophorum vaginatum*, is one of their favorite foods, necessary for pregnant females, since it provides their milk with added nutrition for their calves. Unfortunately, it wasn't so important for the cows this summer because deep snow in the Brooks Range prevented transit for most of them and they bore their calves in Canada and then lost them to predation and flooding river waters.

Back at camp we ate another Mexican dinner of rice and beans, then moved a bunch of old rusty aviation gas cans from under the willows near our tents over to the airstrip where we hoped they would be backhauled to

Ft. Yukon by Don Ross or some other pilot with an empty cargo hold. They had been there at least since my trip to the Kongakut in 1989, and probably for many years before that. It was time for them to return to civilization where they belonged. Afterwards, we sat by the fire, watching nearly fifty ewes and lambs feeding on the east bank of the Kongakut. The late evening sun was shining on them as they grazed along the southwest-facing flank of the mountain, and they gleamed snow-white on the dark green backdrop. It was a fitting end to another exciting day on the river.

This was to be our last day on the Kongakut, and over breakfast it looked like Mother Nature would cooperate. Above all, there was no cold wind whipping up the river, and we didn't have to worry about the canyon or high water anymore. There were a few mosquitoes buzzing around us, but we knew that as soon as we started down the river, they would quickly disappear.

As we pushed off from shore, a parasitic jaeger cruised over, first heading upriver, then following us for a ways toward the coast, searching for a choice morsel that may have washed ashore during the high water. It made me wonder about Rob and his wife back at Drain Creek, and I hoped they hadn't met with some tragic fate. The way the channels were beginning to braid, the bird also made me wish I had wings so I could check out our route down the river. Soon, though, we were opposite the Pagilak River, flowing into the Kongakut from the east, and our attention turned to a large flock of ewes and lambs grazing and cavorting on a high meadow above the west bank of the river. There the bank became a ruggedly steep outcrop of tilted limestone. A few young rams, that I thought might be feeding at mineral licks, perched precariously along the face of the rock, and I wanted to approach them more closely to verify my hunch. It was time to get out and stretch our legs anyway, so we beached the raft and slowly walked toward the cliffs.

Indeed, the sheep were licking moist spots at the edges of steeply angled strata of limestone – probably mineral salts oozing out from between the layers, and it was just what the sheep needed to satisfy their desire for salt. We were amazed at how nimble the animals were while climbing on the irregular rock face. Andrew and I had seen these gymnastics before, but they were completely new to Dan and kept him in a state of awe. At one point, a bevy of six newborn lambs started playing on the cusp of the cliff, capering, jumping and hopping around, having a good old time, coming so close to the brink that I thought they might suddenly fall to their death. The little dickens reminded me of rebellious little boys challenging the fates with their daredevil antics.

We could have watched the sheep all day long, but at about noon sudden gusts of cold wind began pushing up from the coast. It was time to jump back in our raft and head for Caribou Pass. By then the wind was blowing with such a vengeance it was difficult for us to paddle and steer, even with a swift current helping us along. Every few minutes we had to hop into the turbid icy water and line the raft to prevent it from beaching on the sand and gravel bars. Sometimes we were blown completely off course down the wrong braid and got hung up on shallow gravel shoals. When this happened, and the water was too muddy and unpredictable to take our chances jumping off the raft, Dan and Andrew had to belly forward along the top of the raft and spread their weight as evenly as possible to get us through the tricky spots. As big as they were, that was not an easy task, but they took it in stride, and slowly but surely we made our way down the river.

Cold wind wasn't our only challenge. Soon misty rain and fog set in, and I had a hard time recognizing the landmarks I'd planned to use to guide us to the landing at Caribou Pass. For long periods the mountains would disappear altogether, and I had no idea where we were. I could reckon only by gut level feeling, and things got worse when the rain on my glasses prevented clear vision even for near distance. I was worried, but my mood lightened a little when six large bull caribou suddenly loomed out of the mist beside us on the right shore. At first, their antlers looked like giant wings, and I wasn't sure of what I was seeing. Then as quickly as they appeared they melted back into the fog again and were gone.

I took out my compass and checked to make sure we were still heading in the right direction. I had already decided that the minute we started bearing toward the northwest we would go ashore and camp until the fog dissipated. The Caribou Pass airstrip lay on a major northwesterly bend in the river, and we did not want to miss it. Just as I was taking another compass reading, the mist lifted enough for me to see an expanse of aufeis that I recognized from my over flights three weeks earlier. A familiar tall snaggle-toothed rock made a fleeting appearance on the slope to our right, and I knew we were near the end of our trip. The fog gradually thinned even more, and I could make out the dim outline of the valley as it began its slow tack to the west. I told the fellas we were very close and to watch for a narrow cobbled runway that terminated right at the river's edge. I felt better, and much more so when an Arctic tern flew directly over us, his forked tail tilting back and forth in the stiff wind to keep him headed downriver. In quick succession, three red-breasted mergansers popped up in front of us on the river, fleeing with rapid wing beats as soon as they saw us. These fish ducks indicated the presence of clear water somewhere nearby, and I guessed it was coming in from the creek that flowed down from Caribou Pass.

My stress level went up again briefly when the main channel began to narrow as we floated between the vertical banks of the overflow ice. Surely it wouldn't abruptly close on us and swallow us alive this near our destination. It didn't, and our attention was diverted from the ice by three golden eagles that appeared above the river, cavorting in the thermals generated by wind bumping off the high slope to our right. Somehow those eagles told me we were home free. And we were. Dead ahead, perched next to the gravel runway was a yellow tent. We had arrived.

By then I was shivering cold, and to avoid onset hypothermia I marched down the airstrip to get the blood rolling through my anemic limbs. On my way back up, I found the occupants of the yellow tent, two women, Nancy Munro and Debbie Hicks, both from Anchorage, who told me they had just completed their trip down from Drain Creek by Pak Canoe. It had taken them seven hours to line the Staircase, the same spot we had portaged around. It was a real adventure, doing it during high water, they said, in fact, the most hair-raising adventure they had ever had on a river, which put things squarely in perspective for us.

When I returned to the raft, Andrew and Dan had already pitched the tents, so I immediately blew up my Thermarest, threw my sleeping bag on top, then dove under cover from the still falling cold misty rain. Dan and Andrew did the same.

At about 6:00, I opened the tent fly and peeked out. The rain had stopped and the mist was rising. Still feeling cold to the bones, I put on my wet boots and marched down the airstrip, again at high speed. The mist was quickly fading, its diaphanous tattered edges against the mountains reminding me of a torn and ragged wedding veil. It brought back memories of the mists and fogs and low clouds of Cordova, on the south coast of Alaska. I couldn't shake the clammy feeling I'd picked up earlier, though, and knew the only thing that would do this would be a nice bonfire. But, as much as I searched and searched for dry wood, there was none to be found anywhere. Previous groups of river farers with the same idea had completely cleaned the area out. So, while Dan and Andrew were chatting with the two women, I started the gas stove and put on some tea water. It was my last hope to warm up.

While drinking my tea, Nancy came over and began disassembling her Pak Canoe. Andrew and Dan volunteered to make dinner, so I went over to give Nancy a hand. She recounted that they had been part of a two Pak Canoe party and that the other group had had an especially gruesome time of it because of their huge load. When Debbie came over to help out she told me about their trip down the Alatna a few years back. They had been rained and snowed on, she said, and it was an unholy nightmare. The floodwaters of the Kongakut weren't nearly so bad, yet bad enough to turn back many caribou cows and calves they had seen wanting to cross to the west bank. After packing the canoe tightly in its big sack, the two women examined my Sea

Eagle 8 raft, and marveled several times at how we were able to float the river in such a small craft. We marveled at the idea ourselves.

By now, the mist had retreated, and we admired the spectacular view across the river. The long sloping valley was completely blanketed in cotton grass and looked like it had been dusted with new snow. It was similar on the gentle slope rising up from the airstrip on our side, but patchier.

After our dinner of piping hot potato soup, I took a photograph of Andrew and Dan next to the deflated hulk of our humble raft. "What a miserable looking little mess," I cracked, as I framed the rather unflattering picture of what now resembled an insect crushed on the windshield of a speeding car. I felt slightly awkward when I said it, though. As miserable and small as it was, it did get us down the river in one piece.

It was still overcast and wet when I finally zipped up my sleeping bag and closed the tent flap for the night. We all wished for sun in the morning, both to dry things out and provide us with drier tundra to walk on during our trek over to the Clarence River. We had noticed a couple of men heading that direction shortly after we arrived at the landing, and fervently hoped not to have to travel under those sopping conditions.

As I closed my eyes, Dan and I chatted about the best way to be a minimalist during walkabouts like ours. He referred to me as the most quintessential example of a minimalist he had ever met, adding that someone could write a good magazine article on how I did it. I knew he said it tongue in cheek, but I agreed anyway. "People just don't need all the crap they take with them on trips like this," I told him. And I cited Rob and his wife as an example.

We changed the subject to how grubby he felt and how he was going to really appreciate a shower when he got back. I felt the same way, I said, re-calling a passage I had recently read from Bryson's book, *A Walk in the Woods*. In it, he wrote,

> *"Each time you leave the cosseted and hygienic world of towns and take yourself into the hills, you go through a series of staged transformations – a kind of gentle descent into squalor – and each time it is as if you have never done it before. At the end of the first day, you feel mildly, self-consciously, grubby; by the second day, disgustingly so; by the third, you are beyond caring; by the fourth, you have forgotten what it is like not to be like this."*

All night I slept fitfully because I simply wasn't getting enough fat in my diet to keep me warm. So when Nancy came over after breakfast and offered us their leftover food, I asked if she had anything with fat in it. She responded that she had plenty of salami and nuts and that I was welcome to them. I eagerly accepted. Dan requested only a little toilet tissue, since he didn't feel right about "asking for favors," as opposed to "being asked for one." I then advised that accepting an offer wasn't quite like asking for a favor, but that, in any case, there was nothing wrong with either one, since they both made the other person feel good. He had never looked at it that way, he said.

As we were philosophizing, my attention focused on a small bird flitting around the willows behind Andrew. I glassed it with my binocs and found it to be a Smith's longspur. It was the first one I'd seen since my visit to the Kongakut in 1989. Then I had unwittingly camped almost on top of the longspur's nest, and listened to the male's sweet warbling song all night in the bush next to my tent. Seeing this bird now brought back that memory and lifted my spirits. At the same moment the sun broke through the overcast, shedding its wonderful warmth on us. We were ready to begin our trek over to the Clarence River.

Just as we shouldered our packs, we heard the drone of a familiar airplane. I recognized Don's dark blue and white Cessna 185 and, before we knew it, it was circling to land. It was only 11:00 o'clock. Don was an hour early, so Nancy and Debbie were feverishly scrambling to get ready for their departure. We removed our packs and helped the two women finish breaking camp and hauling their gear over to the airplane. As I passed Don their packs, he recounted the story of Rob and his wife, whom he said he had rescued from a serious upset in their Klepper kayak. He had flown over them right after they had capsized only a hundred yards downriver from where their tent had been set up at the gravel strip near Drain Creek. He immediately landed, helped pick up the pieces, then flew the couple back to Arctic Village, where they waited for the next flight to Fairbanks. "So they escaped with their lives, and I won't have to worry about them anymore. Rob was a hardhead and should have taken my advice about floating the Sheenjek River instead. Their Klepper was much better suited for that slower-moving river," he said.

After we had crammed the final bit of gear into the 185, and Nancy and Debbie squeezed in, Don and I furtively shook our heads at the huge load they had brought to the Refuge with them. We waved goodbye to everyone as Don revved his engines, then roared down the gravel runway and up into the rapidly clearing blue skies. As the airplane turned steeply to the left, we shouldered our packs again and headed up the cotton-studded slopes for the Clarence River. By the time we were on top of the ridge, the skies were a transparent blue, and we had to shed our outer layers to keep from overheating. "From frigid cold to boiling hot, that's what you've got to be prepared for during the Arctic summer," I remarked to Dan. We stood on the ridge, retracing the route we had taken down the river the day before. We could see the limestone bluffs, now on our right, where we had watched the sheep, then the braided part of the river where we had been buffeted by the polar wind, and finally the section of aufeis where we had momentarily feared for our lives. The meadow of cotton grass across the river was resplendent in the glorious sunshine, and nearby four caribou ambled slowly along, eating the cotton on our side. A golden eagle soared above us – a good omen, I said, of lucky days ahead.

I set a steady pace for Andrew and Dan, but they must not have cared for my route, for after a couple of hours they took their own trail along the base of the mountain to our left. I continued to follow the creek bank I had originally started along, finding it soft and damp in some places, but free of the tundra tussocks I suspected they were walking in. They eventually rejoined me at the edge of the creek as I ate my lunch and photographed the lovely broad meadows of shining cotton grass that blanketed the tundra in every direction. The cotton was so thick and so white that from a distance it reminded me of a field of snow. Through the field marched a mixed band of caribou, first, two large bulls, then six cows hurrying to keep up with the bulls. Possibly, like humans, the females felt safer being near the much bigger males.

Continuing on up the creek toward the Clarence River, we had to climb over a wide saddle studded with cotton tussocks interspersed with standing water. We searched for other routes, but decided this was our best bet. Our feet were already wet, so it didn't matter if they got even wetter. Down the other side the walking improved and we were soon on a solid caribou trail that led along the edge of a steep valley spangled with more wildflowers than we had seen since beginning our trek at the headwaters of the Kongakut. Purple lupine and lemon yellow arctic poppies were especially evident, but rosebay, cassiope and weasel snout were also sprinkled everywhere, as were mountain avens and pink moss campion. I proposed a rest break so I could photograph some of these colorful wildflowers.

While taking a picture of a photogenic group of poppies, I heard the loud raspy squall of a rough-legged hawk. Glancing up into the limpid sky, I could see two of them circling around a tall lichen-matted chimney rock. "There has to be a nest on top," I speculated to Andrew, "and I'll bet there are one or two young in the nest." When I trained my field glasses on the pinnacle of the rock, there were indeed two little heads peeking over the lip of a large nest made of small sticks. I had seen many of these nests while living in Scammon Bay on the Bering Sea, and knew they were well built, usually of willow sprigs mixed with mosses, lichens, feathers and various other materials. After laying her two or three eggs in the nest, it would take a full month of brooding by the female until they hatched. It would be another forty days or so before the young would be ready to fledge for the first time. As they learned to hunt and put on fat for their long migration south, they would never really stray very far afield from the nest. The circle would be completed the following year when surviving adults returned to the same nesting area, sometimes to the very same nest, to begin the next generation of rough-legs.

Before shouldering our packs again, I heard a pair of wheatears *chak chaking* behind us. Glassing them with my binocs, I thought about the origins of this little thrush and how, like humans, they had migrated to North America from Asia during Pleistocene times when there was a solid land platform joining the Eurasian continent to Alaska. Not that they walked, mind you. It was just a lot easier to hop from hill to hill as they searched for new nesting grounds and an abundant food supply.

Andrew and Dan had their packs on and were ready to go, so I loaded up and joined them as they prepared to glissade down a steep flush of snow that still hadn't melted from the long winter. Leaning slightly forward on our boots, we slid down the still firm snow, then toward the bottom we lowered our heels, skidded to a halt, and jumped onto the tundra again. Even Dan, as tired as he was, thought it was fun. Then away we went, following a caribou trail down the canyon. Just before heading out, I heard Andrew comment to Dan, "No rest for the wicked, huh, Dan?" To which, Dan sardonically replied, "I must be pretty wicked then!"

Not long after he spoke, though, I pointed in the direction of the Clarence River. I could just make out the river at the end of the canyon we were in. When I glassed it I saw overflow ice on the riverbed. The reflection of the ice coming through the narrow canyon stirred me to remark, "There's light at the end of the tunnel, after all, eh Dan?" The dour expression on his face changed almost instantly, and he grinned. So did we.

Our pace picked up, and soon we were near the bottom of the canyon. We stopped briefly at its entrance to examine the tattered remains of an immature golden eagle that had somehow missed his turn during a steep dive into the canyon. As with the six capering lambs we had watched on the Kongakut, it seems that the young of all species tempt their fates, and sometimes lose.

Once out on the Clarence, we had to find a place to cross the river to the opposite bank, where it looked like there might be a good camping spot. We carefully climbed onto the aufeis, now composed of a lot of candle ice in an advanced state of melting. We jumped from section to rotting section, finally fording a channel of swiftly flowing water to the other side. Our boots were already so wet we didn't even bother to take them off before we waded through the clear cold water. Then we were up the bank and onto the green tundra, where we shucked our packs and boots and let the bottoms of our feet feel the soft grainy texture of mosses and tundra flowers. We couldn't have picked a better place to call it a day.

A fistful of mosquitoes joined us, but the gentle wind kept most of them at bay, and we took a few moments to check out our surroundings. To the north, we could clearly make out the Beaufort Sea, still mostly mantled in ice, but with some wide reaches of open water inside a partial span of barrier islands called Icy Reef. High "tombstone" rocks on the other bank of the river were now in deep shadow because of the westering sun. Just downriver from the tombstones a lone caribou grazed, probably still unaware of our presence. Somehow this solitary animal and its wilderness backdrop symbolized all of the intangible values of the Arctic Refuge. As the three of us rested under the warm sun, we chatted about these values. Freedom was one of them, surely. The desire to return to our evolutionary beginnings was another. Spiritualism was yet another, and, for me, the most important of all, for it is in wilderness where I am able to feel closest to what is truly sacred in life.

After some tea, we prepared one of the dehydrated dinners that Steve and Kay Grubis had given us the previous summer when Andrew and I floated down the Alatna River with my son Steven. It wasn't the best of fare, but we were so tuckered out we didn't much care about the quality of our food. As long as it filled the holes in our stomachs, that's all that mattered. I was especially weary because of the little sleep I'd gotten the previous night, and idly watched a cloud of flies swarming above our tents. I pointed, referring to them as "smoke flies" because they resembled smoke. Their frenetic movements reminded me of crowds of people in big cities, and I remarked, "Just like the rat race, eh fellas?" They simply nodded.

I took out my map and binoculars and glassed to the north again. Icy Reef was plainly visible. To the west, it formed a spindly arch with an old Inupiat Eskimo site on it named Kulurak. To the east, the reef seemed to be joined to the shoreline and was called Demarcation Point. The open body of water inside the barrier reef was named Demarcation Bay and, according to the map, was only about eight and a half miles from where we were camped. Toward the southeast shore of the bay, a long flat boat was grounded in the shallow water. I later learned it was a Canadian supply barge that had broken loose during a fierce storm back in the 1980s, and was now hopelessly irretrievable. What an ugly reminder of civilization it was in this otherwise unsurpassable wilderness.

Beyond Demarcation Bay was a solid blanket of sea ice, with a thick fog rising above it. I retired early, but when I awoke at midnight and peeked out of the tent, the fog had obscured the open water in the bay and, aided by long strips of gray scudding clouds, blotted out the midnight sun. There was still clear sky above us, but the clouds seemed headed our way, and I wondered what lay in store for us.

July 4 –

At 3:00 a.m. I heard the sound of rain spitting on the tent. Then suddenly the wind picked up, gusting to nearly 25 mph, and Dan and I thought we might have to move our camp to a more protected spot somewhere across the river. The tent was doing some pretty serious pitching and yawing, and I was snagging every bit of ballast I could find to weigh it down. Packs, boots, everything came in to keep the tent from blowing away. Then, just as we were thinking about abandoning ship, the wind stopped dead, though a light rain continued. It was 3:30, and we waited with bated breath to see what would happen next. Nothing did. Complete calm returned to the early morning, so we tried going back to sleep. It took me a while, though, because I had visions of waking up again to overcast and drizzle and a drenching cold trudge back over the pass to the Kongakut. But the rain soon tapered off after the wind stopped, calm weather prevailed, and I returned to the wonderful world of sleep. When I awakened at 8:30 and crawled out of the tent, the tundra was dry again. I was a happy man.

I was even happier when I spotted fourteen caribou crossing the river right in front of our camp. I quickly grabbed my binocs and counted an equal number of bulls and cows in the small band. Above them an adult golden eagle floated lazily in the still air, heading for the tombstones, where he spiraled upward in the thermals generated by the tall rocks. I wondered if the eagle was related to the dead one we'd found the day before almost directly below him. A little later, as we ate breakfast, a semipalmated plover frenetically flew around and around like a panicked moth above the gravel bar below our camp, landing, then flying up again, over and over, all the while shrilly piping as though something big and dangerous was about to swoop down on him. We soon learned why when another plover bounced into view, briefly landed on the gravel, and was chased zigzag back and forth out of what was probably the original plover's nesting ground.

It got even better as we were breaking camp. While glassing the other side of the river, I spotted a large animal ambling slowly upriver. At first, I thought it was a caribou, but on closer inspection it looked furrier and squatter to the ground. And much bigger! I handed my binocs to Dan. "Take a gander at your first wild grizzly, Dan," I said. Then Andrew took a turn glassing as the grizzly bear stopped to dig in the gravel and eat roots, probably from the *Hedysarum alpinum*, appropriately given the common name, bear root. The wind was in our favor, and we watched as the bear wandered up on the high bank, then down again to the river bottom, where he alternately sat on his haunches and stood up near a large snow flush. Since the bear seemed preoccupied with this behavior, we took advantage of the lull in his movement upriver to shoulder our packs and start for the other side. We didn't want to wait until he was directly opposite us, since he would probably block our return to the Kongakut, at least the way we had come. We finally lost sight of him after he ambled up the bank into some willows and disappeared from view.

We were just starting to ford the river in our bare feet when we noticed a bull and cow caribou browsing on the riverbed. When she saw us the cow walked right on by, headed downriver, but the bull wandered onto the overflow ice and lay down, curiously watching us cross. As we were putting our boots back on he stood up, still studying us carefully. Only when we got up on the ice and began wending our way through the maze of small channels lacing the aufeis did his nerves get the best of him. He turned swiftly, ran back and forth as though confused about which way to go, then finally jumped off the ice, climbed the east bank of the river and ran at top speed in the tundra toward the Beaufort Sea.

We quickly marched back along the same trail we'd hiked over on, hoping the bear wasn't right behind us. Dan was especially anxious about Bruno, and it spurred him on at twice his normal pace up the canyon trail. In no time flat we were at the rough-legged hawk aerie, where the female was perched on the edge of the nest feeding her young. From there we took a detour to the right up a small ravine to bypass the cotton grass tussocks and boggy tundra in the saddle we'd slogged through the previous day. When we reached a rocky bench that leaned to the west, we followed it, keeping as high a contour as we could to avoid the softer ground below. Lupine and yellow arctic poppies grew in profusion everywhere on the south slope, and it was hard to resist photographing them. When I came across a spray of Siberian phlox, though, I stopped, got down on my knees, and out came the camera. These phlox have a delicate pink color that brings a certain zest to the drab gravel they grow on. They're among my favorite arctic wildflowers.

A lone bull caribou grazed in the ravine below us as we continued walking along the high bench. A while later, after stopping at an overlook for a snack, we watched a small cow amble by, taking a course that led her over a long patch of snow. As she tried crossing it, she fell in several times up to her haunches and had difficulty lifting herself out. When she finally got to the other side, we clapped and whistled at her determination. She stopped and gazed at us for a moment, then trotted off, flushing a pair of golden plovers, the first we'd seen since starting over from the Sheenjek River two weeks earlier.

At shortly after noon, we arrived at the top of a small pass that we knew would eventually take us back down to the Kongakut. It was a longer route than the one we'd followed the day before, but easier walking and more interesting, since it took us through the mountains that fronted on the coastal plain. Looking east from the saddle of the pass, we could trace our trail almost all of the way back to the Clarence River. Demarcation Bay was visible, as were the barrier islands and a strip of blue water in between the mainland and the islands. I could also just make out the headwaters of the Turner River, somewhat to the west of the Clarence. With my binocs, I watched a golden eagle soar into view, and I followed him inland toward tall bumps of mountains that must have been on the Canadian border and beyond, into the Yukon Territory. There the Canadian government had set up two national parks to protect the Porcupine caribou herd from the incursions of oil and gas development. To the north was Ivvavik National Park and, joining it to the south, was Vuntut National Park. The hundreds of inverted conical bumps I was seeing were in the northern park.

After taking some pictures, we headed down the other side of the pass, where we encountered the same cow caribou we had clapped and whistled at earlier in the day. At first, she ran from us, but then returned, "as if she were lonesome and wanted to join our band," I joked to Andrew. But she ran off again across a boggy tundra meadow, which we, too, had to cross to get over to a mountain we called Big Roundy, because of its shape. While circumnavigating this mountain, we came across three more "boos," as Andrew called them, grazing in the cotton grass. As they munched, we realized how important this sedge was for them. Anything contributing to its deterioration would ultimately lead to the decline of the Porcupine caribou herd. I wondered if the retreat of the permafrost deeper into the ground, as was now happening with climate change, would contribute to these changes.

We wanted to have one last willow fire before heading back to civilization, so we slogged down to the creek that entered the Kongakut near the Caribou Pass landing strip. Along the way I almost stepped on a baby parky squirrel right in the middle of the caribou trail we'd been following. I stopped dead in my tracks and pointed down, so Andrew and Dan would know what I was doing. The squirrel hugged the ground as though frozen there, barely seeming to breathe. The only way I could tell it was alive was by the reflection from its glistening wide-open eyes. Carefully, I took out my camera and snapped a couple of quick shots of the little brown fur-ball, which didn't seem to faze him at all. He remained on the trail as still as stone. But I was a little worried about aerial predators, so just before leaving, I nudged him gently into the brush. It was a first for me. I had never seen a baby parky before.

After searching for a flat spot on the gravel bottom of the creek where we could set up camp, we gathered enough willow sticks for a small fire and got down to the business of cooking our dried bean dinner. It wasn't half bad either, and we sat around chatting and scanning the hillsides for more signs of caribou. Only a few moments later a cow came running along the face of the hill just to the west of us. She raced at top speed toward a bull caribou, passing him in a whirlwind. She had been spooked by something we couldn't see, and it was contagious. The bull started running too, following right behind the cow like his heels were on fire. We thought a bear might be in hot pursuit, but nothing ever showed up. Whatever it was, it didn't bother a small band of fourteen caribou entering the scene only a few minutes later.

Among the mixed band of cows and bulls was a solitary newborn calf, one of the few that had escaped all of the adversities brought on by the terrible spring snowstorms. We all felt sympathy for the little guy. He would not have many playmates.

We hit the sack at about 8:00, so we could rise early to finish our trek back to Caribou Pass. We didn't know when Don would be in, but we didn't want to push our luck, especially since storm clouds were gathering again, threatening us with yet another bout of foul weather. I had to admit to Dan that there was always the possibility we wouldn't make it out the next day.

"Que sera, sera," I said, and closed my eyes.

I was suddenly awakened about 1:00 a.m. by what I thought was Dan's loud snoring. But as I started to nudge him, I heard it again... and again. It was a sound I recognized. Not a bear, but caribou, and a lot of them, heading fast down the creek. By the time I opened the tent fly, though, they were already out of sight. Gazing downstream, then up at the sky, I didn't like the looks of the low cloud cover. It had the ominous appearance of rain, or even snow.

I awoke again at 6:00 when I heard the repeated thwack of heavy raindrops on the ripstop nylon fly. So much for rising early. There was nothing I could do but try to go back to sleep. Then, when that didn't work, I read Bryson's book about his travails on the Appalachian Trail. Three hours later the rain started to let up a bit, and I yelled over to Andrew in the other tent, "Daylight in the swamps, Andrew. We may as well take advantage of this lull and hightail it for Caribou Pass."

"Roger, roger," he replied.

The heavy rain held off as we broke camp and hoofed it to the top of the ridge overlooking the airstrip. Halfway up, we suddenly flushed a spotted sandpiper from its nest. I stopped briefly to peek at the eggs. There were four of them, all buff-colored with brown spots, and neatly tapered at one end so they fit perfectly in the middle of the nest. When I later researched the "spotty," as my dad used to call these birds, I found it was the male I had scared off the nest, since he's the one who is exclusively in charge of incubating the eggs. It is the same sort of role reversal found among phalaropes, and, as with that species, the female is usually polyandrous, having more than one mate.

The morning rain had left the tundra soggier than a wet sponge, and by the time we reached the ridge top my boots felt like sponges. They were so wet and so heavy I was glad to see the little airstrip that was our final destination. Before heading down, though, I took a few moments to watch and listen to a black-bellied plover as he vigorously called, *tloo-ee, tloo-ee.* Then the rain picked up again, and I started for the landing. My raincoat was beginning to leak, ever so little, but enough to make my skin feel clammy.

That was enough for me to realize I had to put up the tent fast and climb into my bag to warm up. In my haste to do this, Andrew later told me I had completely missed a band of 20 caribou standing together in the brush at the end of the runway. But I knew what I had to do, and lickety split the tent and fly went up, in flew my Thermarest and sleeping bag, and I followed immediately afterward. Once inside, off came my soaking boots and rain gear, then I dove into my bag and zipped it tightly around me. I was cold.

Since Andrew and Dan were younger and had better central heating systems than I did, they stayed outside in the drizzle to stoke up the gas stove and put on some tea water. When the drizzle turned to slushy snow and then to legitimately big flakes, even they finally felt compelled to drink their tea under cover. So, in they piled, and all three of us sat inside the North Face like hunched buzzards in a cave, and drank our hot tea and ate a snack of crackers and peanut butter, which is about all we had left.

We fervently wished Don would make it in that afternoon, but hope for that dwindled when the rain and snow got even worse. For two solid hours it kept falling, landing on the tent fly with the sloppy sound of something between wet and dry. While waiting for it to let up, I dug out Bryson's book again. In times like these, it's such a pleasure to have a good book to read. Since neither Dan nor Andrew had brought one along, I read passages of the book to them aloud, and couldn't help remarking that, "If Bryson wanted a real walk, he should have come with us!" They nodded. I was feeling a lot better with both of them in the tent generating so much extra body heat. It's amazing how warm a little dome tent can get with three big guys inside.

At 6:00 p.m., the slushy snow stopped, and we piled outside to take a look. There was no actual snow on the ground where we were, but on the ridge above us a heavy layer had fallen to within 200 feet of the river level. In spite of the inconvenience it had caused us, it was an awesome sight to behold. While Andrew and I ran back and forth on the airstrip to keep warm, we noticed that upriver the low ceiling of snow clouds was beginning to lift. Gradually the sky brightened and the snow-wrapped flanks of the mountains glowed with an almost magical light. As the valley opened up, we could see the snow had completely blanketed every mountain within view. Directly opposite us, on the other side of the Kongakut, it had come so far down the mountain that it merged with the wide meadows of cotton grass, and we couldn't tell where one started and the other left off. It was a wonderland none of us had ever seen before, and we were speechless as we beheld it.

But while the clouds lifted higher and higher upriver, a heavy fog began sluggishly creeping toward us from downriver. By now I was becoming a little impatient and muttered, "Oh, Mother, you do like to play tricks on us, over and over again!" When tentacles of fog started enclosing us in a slow misty rain, we resigned ourselves to staying put for another night. I headed for the tent again as Andrew stoked up his gas stove and prepared dinner. He had just brought over a steaming pot of polenta and beans to be served inside the tent when we heard the steady drone of an airplane coming down the valley.

We couldn't believe it, but suspected it was Don. Still, how could he see through the vault of mist that had encased us? Andrew, who was still outside the tent, confirmed it was Don, though, reporting that, as we spoke, he was touching down at the end of the gravel airstrip. After we heard the wheels hit, we wolfed down our food and hastily started packing up. Bowl in hand, I ambled over to greet Don. He looked tired, but said he was in no hurry, since we were his last charter of the day and would be heading directly back to Ft. Yukon. We slowed down a bit, and Don and I chatted about the weather and various caribou sightings of his on the way over from Ft. Yukon. When our gear was stowed and cinched down inside the plane, we motioned to Dan and Andrew to load up. After buckling in and putting on our earphones, the little Cessna fired to life, then with a roar raced along the gravel through the thick fog. In less than a minute we were airborne, banking off to the left toward the river.

Don had landed and taken off from this strip so many times, he probably could have done it blindfolded, but I was still a little anxious as we leveled off over the mist-enshrouded river and made a run between the mountains for the south. It didn't take long until the fog began to clear off, and the valley soon exposed its braided belly of muddy water, gravel islands and willow groves, all still in heavy gray shade. By the time we were over the tiny Whale Mountain strip, the fog was totally gone. The sun popped through the clouds like a bright spotlight and the world below was transformed completely into one of sharp contrasts where the intense green color of summer foliage showed through the immaculate white of the recent snowfall. Along a familiar slope we flew so close we were able to count a mixed herd of forty caribou dashing up the mountain. I was mesmerized, the more so because we were flying over the same route we had walked and rafted down for so many days on end. We had come through the country so slowly that we recognized every one of the major landmarks and many of the minor ones now below us. It was still hard to believe that we had covered so many miles in so little time, and most of it on foot.

The rest of the trip to Ft. Yukon was anticlimactic. The snow eventually disappeared, rugged gray mountains gave way to gentler greener slopes, and willows and alders were replaced by sparse forests of paper birch and white and black spruce. We flew just to the west of the Colleen River, then over the lower Sheenjek and Porcupine Rivers and, ever so suddenly, we were back on the ground again in Ft. Yukon. Civilization!

PHOTOS

1. Andrew and Dan after pulling out at the Staircase
2. Caribou along Kongakut River
3. Dall sheep along Kongakut River

Chapter 4

Bluethroats and Brown Bears in the Sadlerochits
June 13-30, 2001

One of the reasons I love to be in wilderness is that the surprise of the unexpected is always present. Whether it's on a wild river or a mountain trail, you just never know what's around the next bend or rocky slope. And so it was during this trip to the Sadlerochit Mountains in the northeast part of the Brooks Range with my wife, Jennifer and her friend, Cindy Wentworth. Not only did we encounter more brown bears (aka grizzlies) than on any previous trek of ours in the Arctic, but we also discovered the nest of a special bird, the bluethroat, a small Old World thrush that spends only three months nesting on Alaska's northwest and Arctic coasts, then heads south to southern India and north Africa for the rest of the year. Since our camp in the Sadlerochits was a base camp, we were able to observe this nest and its little family over the course of our 2 1/2 weeks there. It was an experience the three of us will never forget, along with so many other things.

Jen and Cindy at Sunset Pass

The journey began on June 13 in Fairbanks. After collecting Cindy in our little Toyota pickup, we filled up with gas and coffee, then headed north for 254 miles on the Dalton Highway to Coldfoot, where we had chartered Dirk Nickisch to fly us into the Sadlerochits. It was 5:30 p.m. when we left Fairbanks.

We found the gravel highway in only fair shape, although the final 25 miles had been paved the previous year with "chip and seal" and was in much better condition. On the north side of the Yukon River Bridge, a lynx crossed the road in front of us. He stopped on the shoulder for a moment, appearing long and lean in his thin summer coat, and he peered at us like he had never seen human beings before.

Jen and Cindy had never been to Coldfoot before, and when we arrived there at midnight they were unimpressed with the scattering of ugly buildings and parked trailer trucks en route to Prudhoe Bay. Although the sun was still circling to the north, the cafe was closed, so we drove over to the airstrip where we found our pilot, Dirk Nickisch, and his dad Willard, transferring aviation gas from their fuel truck to blue plastic drums for trans-shipment the next day to a refueling point in the Arctic Refuge.

Dirk assured us of good weather in the morning and said that he'd be good to go at about eight, so we put the truck in four-wheel drive and drove over to the Koyukuk River to find a place to pitch our tents on a gravel bar. We finally hit the sack at 1:30 a.m., anxious to begin our flight into the wilds of the Arctic National Wildlife Refuge.

June 14 –

Dirk was late getting started, but after helping him load his new orange and white Beaver, we were finally rumbling down the runway by mid-morning, headed for the Sadlerochit Mountains and our destination, Sunset Pass.

As we lumbered over Chandalar Lake, Dirk told us that when the Tobin gold mine at the head of the lake was abandoned a few years earlier, 20,000 gallons of liquid cyanide were left behind in drums in a storage bunker. The State DEC said they didn't know about it when Dirk reported it, although when he checked with the Federal EPA, they had already listed it as a Superfund toxic waste site! Seeing the gross disregard of the environment by miners was one of the things that turned him into an activist, he said.

Over the constant drone of the Beaver's single engine we chatted through our headsets about the hard spring the Porcupine caribou herd had had this year. It was the second bad year in a row for the herd and would probably result in the death of thousands of calves as it did the previous spring. Dirk also told us of his many flights during the winter months, ferrying media people of every nationality, from as far away as Australia, over the Refuge Coastal Plain to give them a better idea of what the country looked like. Recently, he and another pilot, Kirk Sweetsir, had flown more than 40 photographers and reporters into Caribou Pass to try to intercept the caribou herd as it migrated through there. It was the most crowded that area had ever been, and he could only imagine the problem with human waste that went along with the crowds. He added that the middle Aichilik River was also concentrated with people, including our mutual friend Don Ross, who had been enlisted to guide several photographers through the area, also in search of the elusive Porcupine Herd.

The Beaver had no heater, so Cindy and Jen were a little cold in the back seat. Dirk said he had taken the external heater off because of the drag and lower fuel efficiency that resulted. He apologized for their feeling like a couple of popsicles. Shortly afterward he apologized again as the airplane suddenly lost power and lurched downward. "Sorry," he said, "the left tank's empty," and calmly switched to his right wing tank. Jen and Cindy later told me that when it happened they just about swallowed their tonsils.

After two hours of flying over some of the most awesome mountains in the Brooks Range, including a couple of the highest peaks, Mt. Chamberlin (2749 meters) and Mt. Michelson (2699 meters), and two of the range's largest lakes, Peters and Schrader, both still locked in ice, we floated through the portal of Sunset Pass in the Sadlerochit Mountains (*Sadlerochit* means "area outside the mountains" in Inupiat Eskimo, an apt name for this northernmost island of mountains in the Brooks Range). As we landed on a makeshift airstrip opposite Weller Creek, it brought back memories of the last time I had been in the area in June, 1997, and I was excited to be there again. It was a clear sunny day, and in the distance we could make out the flat white line of the pack ice of the Beaufort Sea, only 19 miles away. Jen and Cindy were happy to be on the ground and thrilled to be in such wild country.

It wasn't until Dirk had disappeared behind the mountains to the south that Cindy realized he had forgotten to offload her blue food bag, but we figured he would probably discover it when he got back to Coldfoot that night and then deliver it to us as soon as he could. No use fretting about it, we decided. We would just have to do without the snack foods and some of the breakfasts she had been assigned to bring.

We set up our two teal-colored tents about a hundred yards from where we had unloaded the Beaver and settled down to prepare lunch. A small stream of clear water, part of the larger north-flowing Itkilyariak Creek, flowed in front of our campsite, and there were plenty of dry willows for cook fires. We were amazed there was so much willow growing in the creek bed, and it made us feel better about burning the dead wood.

After lunch we hiked up a ravine to the top of a saddle, located about a mile to the east of camp. On the south-facing slopes were bright patches of blooming wildflowers, including glacier avens, moss campion, mountain avens, and purple mountain saxifrage. All of these grew in colonies and illuminated the mountainside with sprays of vivid color. The mustard yellows of the glacier avens were especially beautiful to Jen and Cindy. My favorite was the diminutive purple mountain saxifrage, which seemed to be one of the first flowers to blossom in Sunset Pass. En route, we also saw five long-tailed jaegers, and many Smith's longspurs, with their telltale song, so sweet at this time of year. Hidden in the grass we found a nest of this little bird, containing seven brown-splotched eggs, and soon after, a White-crowned sparrow's nest, with six well-camouflaged dark, mottled eggs inside.

From the rocky top of the saddle we could clearly see the outline of Camden Bay as it rounded on both sides into the Arctic Ocean. Just to the northeast the meanders of both the Sadlerochit and Hulahula Rivers snaked their way toward the ice pack. A sliver of blue water along the edge of the coast showed where they pushed into the ocean. Spring was late here.

We returned down the mountain much faster than we went up and reached camp an hour later, hungry for dinner. We weren't able to prepare anything substantial, though, as heavy clouds had moved in from the west, threatening to dump rain on us by the time we got back. We only had time to fry up some tortillas and cheese before diving into our tents to escape the rain. The drops came down hard until about midnight, when the rain stopped and turned to heavy overcast. But by then we were comfortably ensconced in our sleeping bags, chatting about what we might do in the morning. We hoped for a sunny day.

We awoke to a thick fog blown in from the pack ice by a cold breeze. Not to worry, I told Jen and Cindy, the fog would be gone by noon. Then I built a small fire of dry willow sticks and put on a pot of water for tea, hot chocolate and a bowl of granola.

After breakfast, while Jen and Cindy visited around the fire I walked out toward the Coastal Plain. About a half-mile from camp two long-tailed jaegers began swooping down over my head. When they came closer and closer I figured I must be near their nest. I crouched and waited and watched until I saw the female land and gently position herself on what I presumed were eggs. The moment I stood up, though, she flew into the air again, and I immediately hurried over to see how many eggs she had. On only a shallow scrape in the tundra I found two large eggs (about 2½ x1½ inches) with tapered ends, each with a different color, one light green and the other camouflage-brown. As I photographed the eggs, the female attacked me so aggressively that I thought she might peck the top of my hat. She swooped back and forth like a giant tern, and I had to hold my arms above my head to keep her from hitting me. Even as I ran from the nest she chased me, diving over and over from both front and back. I was astounded at how quickly she could turn in midair, but when I was about 50 yards away she suddenly broke off her charge and went back to sedately brood her eggs. Only once before had I been attacked that fiercely, by an Arctic tern on the John River, near Bettles, many years ago.

As I ambled north along the edge of Itkilyariak Creek, I wondered about its name. I suspected it might stem from *Itkilik*, meaning, "louse nit," a pejorative term used by the Inupiat to describe Athapaskan Indians living on the south side of the Brooks Range. Perhaps the two peoples hunted caribou there in the past.

Not long afterward I stumbled on the remains of two broken metal skis from an Elan snow machine. One was black and the other yellow, both neatly broken across the front third of the skis. I surmised that probably many years earlier an Inupiat from the village of Kaktovik, located less than 30 miles to the northwest, had been hunting in the area during a spring snow storm. He couldn't see where he was going and ran head-on into a large rock, which the skis were lying right next to. There was a dent in one of the skis, matching perfectly the edge of the rock it was propped against. Perhaps a friend on another snow machine put the rest of the Elan on the back of his sled, and they returned to Kaktovik when the storm was over.

At about noon I took Jen and Cindy over to see the jaeger nest. We just barely escaped with our lives from its renewed attack, but they were able to see the eggs and were as amazed as I was at their different colors. We were going to proceed down the creek so I could show them the broken skis of the Elan, but soon after we left the jaeger nest I spotted a large blonde male grizzly nonchalantly heading in our direction. We watched him digging for bear root, a staple part of the bear's diet at this time of year. The plant is a member of the legume family, and still has a lot of starch in the root in the early spring just before it begins to sprout stems and leaves. It is also eaten at this stage by many Alaska Natives. We later tried it ourselves and found it to be quite sweet tasting.

The bear kept on lumbering toward us, so we decided to walk slowly back to camp, just in case he took an interest in our tents and food cache. It was still quite cool due to a low overcast sky, so when we reached the tents we built a fire and waited for our grizzly (whom we called Blondie) to appear. It wasn't long until he did just that, walking in the direction of our camp so nonchalantly that we became a little worried and began banging our pots and pans to give him a message. He was a curious bear, though, and watched us casually for a while, sometimes standing, sometimes seated on the tundra, until finally he changed his course and resumed feeding. By then he was less than 100 yards from us, and we could plainly see him digging for bear root and at least one parky squirrel. He also searched and pounced for voles and lemmings, which it looked like he caught every once in awhile. I don't think I've ever studied a grizzly for so long, mostly because he wasn't the least bit afraid of us. I thought maybe this was because he'd never been trained by his momma to be fearful of humans, or that he'd never had a bad run-in with the hunters in Kaktovik.

We waited until Blondie had traveled a fair distance away from our camp before preparing an early supper of quesadillas and potato soup, but kept a close eye on him as he slowly ambled in a random zigzag pattern up Itkilyariak Creek, beyond Weller Creek and then out of view.

By the time we finished our supper we decided Blondie wouldn't return to camp, so headed for the hoodoo rocks above Weller Creek. But we stopped a short ways up the creek when the bear came into view again. At one point, he started running in our direction, totally unnerving Jen and Cindy. He must have caught our scent, though, because he suddenly stopped in his tracks and resumed his zigzagging in the opposite direction up the creek. By now Jen and Cindy had lost their desire to hike up to the hoodoos, so we turned back toward camp, then followed my morning trail down to where I'd found the broken skis.

It was mid afternoon, the sky was crystal blue, and the sun warm again like the day before, so we took our time, pausing often at the creek's edge to bask in the arctic sunshine. At one point, we stopped to smell a patch of moss campion atop a large lichen-studded rock, and I took a picture of Jen and Cindy next to the flowers. On the way back we watched a pair of pipits take a bath in the creek then mate on a nearby rock. We also surprised a pair of Baird's sandpipers. The female was alternately crouching in the tundra and doing a "broken wing act," trying to distract us from her nest. A little later it was our turn to be surprised when a rock ptarmigan "growled" at us as it flew up and away.

Back at camp, we built another small "Indian fire" and put on some water for tea. While waiting for the water to boil, Jen spotted a small bird flitting around just below camp, no more than twenty-five feet from our fire pit. She guessed it had a nest somewhere close by, so she and Cindy sneaked down and carefully searched for it. They soon found the nest tucked neatly under a stunted willow and inside a small hollow of dead grass. They called me down to take a look, and we counted seven creamy-green eggs in it. Then we quickly returned to our fire and tea and waited for the bird to go back to her nest. It didn't take long until we spotted her furtively sneaking back through the willows, cautiously entering the entrance to her nest, turning around and finally settling down atop her eggs. I peered closely with my binoculars and excitedly identified her as a bluethroat. I had only seen this species once before, over near the Hulahula River, during my 1997 trek to the headwaters of the Sheenjek River. This was the first nest I had ever come across. The bluethroat is a fairly rare bird in Alaska. It is a member of the thrush family, nesting only in northwest and Arctic Alaska as far east as the Canada border. We wondered where the male was, and kept watch as we drank our tea, chatting about the trek we were going to begin the next day.

By late afternoon the limpid blue sky was empty of clouds in every direction. We only hoped it would remain that way for the next several days as we hiked around the east end of the Sadlerochit Mountains in search of the Sadlerochit warm springs and the muskoxen that lived in the neighborhood. We only had a light snack for dinner, since we were now concerned about our limited food supply, then did some preparations for the next morning's trek.

That night, as I wrote in my journal, I began to hear a sporadic melodious warble mixed with other sounds like cricket chirps, twitters and whistles coming from up the creek. I had never heard this combination of song issuing from one bird, and I wondered if it could be the male bluethroat. My Peterson's guide only described the "cricket-like note," so I really couldn't be sure what I was hearing unless I could see the bird itself. The problem was that even with the midnight sun I couldn't find the bird. Much as I tried, his voice shifted like a phantom in the willows, seemingly another example of avian ventriloquism.

I wrote until 1:00 a.m., popping my head out of the tent every now and then to search for my phantom bluethroat, and to watch the sun as it slowly wheeled across the Arctic sky. In every direction the combination of acutely angled light and long shadows on the mountains revealed golden hues of color seen only in this part of Alaska at this time of year. We were indeed lucky to be here.

Today was a long hard day, especially for Jen and Cindy. Over breakfast we watched the female bluethroat on her nest and earnestly searched for her mate, but we neither saw nor heard him. Not even a chirp. I hoped we would have better luck finding him when we got back from our trek around the end of the mountains.

Meanwhile, we broke down our tents, stuffed our sleeping bags and air mattresses in our packs, made room for six or seven days of food, then set out on a southerly course toward the top of Sunset Pass. The first three miles or so didn't take long to walk because of the hard dryas terrace underfoot. We also found the old Inupiat tent and cache site, including the stone seal oil lamp, that I had located back in 1997. As then, I shook my head in wonder and admiration at the nomadic way of life of those traditional Inupiat. How things had changed for them since the advent of oil development on the North Slope!

About three miles up the pass we came to some wet tundra that made for hard slogging the rest of the way to the top. Our consolation, though, was the wonderful weather, with blue skies and long vistas up and down the Sadlerochit River Valley, including snow-peaked Mt. Chamberlin to the south, where the sun reflected brightly off its glacier fields. During breaks we watched long-tailed jaegers gracefully sweeping the skies above the tundra, their heads craned downward in search of edible tidbits hiding in the grass. Once, I noticed a jaeger land on the tundra and hunt and peck for caterpillars and other insects. I hadn't realized they ate insects, but considering the difficult environment they nested in, and how successful they were adapting to it, it seemed they would be as opportunistic as any other Arctic bird species.

Toward the top of the pass we came across a nesting pair of black-bellied plovers, upset with us for our rude intrusion, and whistling their loud alarm call, *toolee, toolee*. They look a lot like American golden plovers, and with their black belly and silver-flecked wing feathers are quite a handsome bird. Almost hidden at the base of some stunted willows I found the recently dead body of a willow ptarmigan, probably the victim of a gyrfalcon attack. Carrion beetles had just begun to eat into the wound on its breast, reminding us of the harshness of life in the Arctic.

We took a detour over a low saddle to the east to avoid the wet tundra country along the Sadlerochit River below. I had trudged across it back in 1997 on my way south to the Sheenjek River with two friends, so I knew what it was like. On top of the saddle we took a long rest break to savor the glacier-mantled massif of Mt. Michelson dominating the Hulahula drainage to the southeast. It was a glorious view on a sparkling day. I could clearly see the trail I had taken back in 1997, first across the Sadlerochit River, then following the Kekiktuk River and Karen Creek, and finally over a tundra plain to the Hulahula River. The remainder of the route was behind the mountains, but in my mind's eye it was still as big as life. Hiking the trail the way my companions and I had done made it unforgettable.

A slow trudge down the steep mountain slope took us across more wet brushy tundra, thickly populated with dwarf birch and willows, to a point next to the Sadlerochit River, where we thought we'd camp for the night. I found a flat spot for the tent, but it was only after I started hammering the tent pegs into the ground that I realized we were perched squarely on top of a tundra polygon, a flat, angular circle of mosses and lichens separated from other polygons as a result of freezing and thawing of the underlying permafrost. The ice was just two inches below the surface and the pegs would only enter the ground with a few good wallops from a hammer stone.

We were bushed, so we all took a short nap. I woke up before the women, so got my book out and read a few pages from Gordon MacCreagh's story about a misbegotten scientific expedition he accompanied through the Bolivian selva in the 1920's. Although the expedition was doomed from its onset, the book is written with a great sense of Scottish-American humor.

I prepared dinner, the last of the tortillas, with cheese, fresh tomatoes, onions, and a side dish of chicken noodle soup. It's amazing how such simple food tastes so good after a long day of strenuous hiking. While we ate we watched a porcupine waddle along down on a gravel bar, probably searching for something to eat himself. It was the first porky I had ever seen this far north. Normally, they stay in the taiga where they have a little more to eat. Like every other form of life in the Arctic, though, the porky is an adaptable creature. Another animal in the same category, the spotted sandpiper, was peeping down on the river's edge as we chatted about the possibility of seeing muskoxen the next day. I remembered, back in 1997, when my two friends and I had camped near four of the strange bent-horned animals at the confluence of the Kekiktuk and Sadlerochit Rivers. We had watched them browsing on willows and grasses next to the river all evening. Even after we had turned in for the night they were still shuffling around just below the riverbank.

Cindy was a little worried that her tent was located on a bear trail, so Jen and I helped her move it next to ours. I told them a story about how, many years earlier, while working as a packer for hunting guide Hal Waugh, he had placed his big tent in the middle of an animal trail. What a surprise when, later in the dark of night, a big bull caribou had stumbled into it and scared the living daylights out of us. We at first didn't know the identity of the animal that had crashed into us, but even when we discovered it was only a caribou it left us chastened.

As I brushed my teeth and prepared to call it quits for the day, I wondered about the high cirrus clouds moving in from the east. They looked like they might be harbingers of rainy weather. But only time would tell.

We awoke to slightly overcast skies, meaning cooler walking for us as we hiked east toward Sadlerochit Spring. After breakfast and striking camp, we climbed the high bluff above us to avoid a long cutbank, created by the river as it bounced off the south flank of the mountain. It was tough going for about 3/4 of a mile while we slogged through some brushy tundra. To make matters worse, as Cindy jumped across a deep tundra creek rushing down the slope she slipped and fell in up to her waist. It gave her quite a fright because there didn't seem to be any bottom to it. She quickly pulled herself together, though, and changed clothes, then we headed back to the river where we were able to find a much easier route on its willow-studded gravel bars. The muskoxen must have felt the same as we did because they, too, had climbed down to the river in search of a better trail. In doing so, they had left their tracks and quiviut, the fine layer of wool they grow next to their skin to keep them warm in winter.

Along with muskox sign, there were also wolf and caribou tracks, as well as recent piles of dung and droppings left by grizzly bears and moose. Through the willows we spotted a small antlered moose in velvet, browsing on the side of the mountain. He didn't notice us until we were fairly close to him, but when he did see us he bolted and ran. Since the wind was in our favor, the only explanation for his fear that I could come up with was that hunters had either shot at him during the winter or spring, or he thought we were bears.

We had to weave our way in and out of the tall willows on the gravel bars, but walking was much easier there than on the tundra. Along the trail we discovered two tree sparrow nests, both of them having four pale-green, brown-speckled eggs in them. Although these birds are called "tree" sparrows, their nests were on the ground, hidden among tufts of dry grass. Everywhere among the willows we came across ptarmigan scat, indicating there was a healthy population of the birds in the area. We only saw one of them, but he treated us to a good view of his spring plumage, a rich dark brown head and cape over his still white winter coat. We also saw a number of small tiger swallowtail butterflies, dwarfs compared to our swallowtails in the Interior. And we found an old yellow jacket nest, the first one I'd ever come across in the Brooks Range.

At a little after noon we stopped for tea and a snack. To start a fire I used a bundle of old dry stems from bear root. As tinder they were even better than paper. Jen and Cindy rested while I tended the fire and checked out some animal sign on the sand bars. Again, recent wolf and bear tracks were mixed in with those of moose, muskox and caribou. Four Mew gulls cruised overhead one after the other searching for tidbits offered up by the fast flowing river.

After our batteries were recharged we continued down the Sadlerochit River. The gravel bar walking was the best we'd had since the dryas terrace at the beginning of our trek, and we made good time all afternoon. At a little after 5:00, we came to a spot we thought had all of the qualifications of a good campsite: fresh water from the river, piles of dry willow drift for a fire, flat platforms for the tents, and a wonderful view of some high red lichen-encrusted cliffs, where we suspected there might be a pair of nesting gyrfalcons. But on glassing the cliffs with my binocs, I could find neither aeries nor birds.

We had an early dinner, and afterwards I took a little stroll downriver from camp. Right away I found an old Pepsi can and some aluminum foil from a prepared meal package. Hunters from Kaktovik had probably left both behind during a recent spring hunt in the area. It was disappointing to find these castoffs from civilization in the Refuge wilderness.

As I watched a pair of ravens bee-lining across the valley, I noticed a cow moose studying me from the other side of the river. She didn't seem the least bit frightened of me, and when I started walking back toward our tent site she headed in the same direction. I pointed her out to Jen and Cindy, and they told me she had acted the same way when she had ambled by opposite them.

Back in front of our camp again, the cow stopped and ogled us carefully from across the river. She had her hackles up, but otherwise seemed only curious at our presence. It was as if she had never seen humans before. When I whistled at her, rather than flee, she quickly moved to the edge of the river and began fording to our side. The river was boiling with rapids at that point and we hadn't expected her to try to cross. But there she came, her hackles up and long ears back. Just as she reached our shore, though, her ears went forward again, indicating she at least wasn't angry enough to charge. Once on shore, she stopped and watched us, as if searching for something. Her mule ears constantly twitched back and forth and she lifted her nose high in the air to try to smell us better. I told Jen and Cindy that she must have recently lost her calf, probably to a bear, and was looking for it. Somehow, she might have associated us with the incident, thinking her calf was among us. After a long moment of indecision, though, she finally left us, headed downriver in the direction of Sadlerochit Spring.

During my short walkabout I noticed that the main channel of the Sadlerochit swung abruptly back into the steep mountain flank to the north, and I was worried we might not be able to get past the cliff face without some fancy footwork. The next morning we would have the answer, but even if we couldn't cross to the other side of the river to avoid the cliff, the worst we'd have to do is climb up over the mountain and rejoin the river farther downstream.

In the evening, while brushing my teeth, a spotted sandpiper landed next to the water and began pecking for food. It wandered randomly, poking and jabbing for tidbits of larvae and insects, and peeped constantly, probably to keep in touch with its mate who must have been close-by. Before I called it quits for the day, I gathered a bundle of dry wormwood and bear root for fire starter in the morning. This area, too, was rife with recent grizzly diggings to take advantage of the carbohydrates in the bear root. We just hoped they wouldn't come knocking at our door as we slept.

Over breakfast we watched a spectacular aerial display above the red cliffs by a male gyrfalcon. The wind was brisk up there and, wings outstretched, he stood into it for a long time, suddenly taking a steep dive below the cliffs. Then lifting once again in the thermals, he hung above the cliffs, finally shooting down like an arrow and landing on the lip of the rocky precipice. Was he showing off for the female somewhere nearby?

We broke camp an hour earlier than usual, then headed downstream along the cobbled riverbed. Soon, though, the course of the river jogged abruptly back in our direction, forcing us to walk up on the bank again. But the tundra was dry and we trotted right along. As we stooped to admire some budding blue lupine, Cindy pointed at two rusty cans, one an old-style aluminum pop can with tin top and bottom, the other a tin lard container, both probably left behind by spring hunters from Kaktovik many years ago. Who knows, they might have been the same ones who broke their snow machine skis in Sunset Pass. No matter, we buried the garbage and focused on a golden eagle soaring in the thermals above the red cliffs, then made our way across a difficult stretch of bog and willow and continued along the edge of the river.

We finally came to the place where the Sadlerochit bumped into the rocky cliff I had seen the day before. I knew we wouldn't be able to continue following the riverbank around the bend of the mountain, and unless we wanted to ford the river somewhere nearby, we would have to climb up and over the mountain. I left the choice to the women, and they decided they didn't want to press their luck with the swiftly running water. So up we went.

The 600-foot climb wasn't as bad as it looked, and both Jen and Cindy weathered it well. The route took us gradually up and across a south slope studded with wild flowers, including our first forget-me-nots of the trip. We finished the climb along a rocky ridge over a naked saddle, then down to a creek thick with willows, where we built a small fire and warmed up with a pot of hot tea and a snack. Just in time, because as the tea water started to boil, a dark cloud of wind-blown rain sneaked over the hill and forced us into our rain gear.

We still had to hike over another high ridge, but the wind was gusting so hard it blew us easily up the slope. When we crested the top, though, it was blowing at such gale force that it knocked Jen down on the tundra. Then the rain began to pelt us from behind and I knew it was time to search for cover.

Deus ex machina! Not far away there was a deep groove in the tundra and we quickly took refuge in it until the wind and rain let up. When we found a few wild flowers blooming around the edges, including arctic lupine, I told Cindy that in South America the highland peoples had domesticated these legumes to produce much larger edible seeds. Edible, that is, after they were soaked several times in water to rid them of their toxic alkaloids. The rhizomes and leaves of arctic lupine are also edible, but only after they've been cooked, again to liberate the alkaloids. Eaten raw, they cause a drunken stupor, and could be fatal in large quantities. A number of years ago, when a mining engineer discovered a hoard of the large seeds in some ancient lemming burrows in the permafrost, he sent some to the National Museum of Canada to be analyzed. Carbon dating showed them to be more than 10,000 years old. Six of the seeds successfully germinated within 48 hours, and a year later one of the plants flowered and produced seed. A true survivor.

After the rain began to let up, we climbed out of our groove to look for a campsite. We headed down to the Sadlerochit River, where it had looped around the mountain, and found a soft platform for our tents on the thick insulating mosses of another permafrost polygon. Again, we had to use stone hammers to pound the stakes into the subsurface ice. Not far away a handsome brown female northern harrier flew in circles around us, making a fuss about our disturbing her nest, but she finally settled down and returned to brood her eggs in the tundra. A much smaller bird took up the scolding where the harrier left off. It was hidden in the willows, but when its scolding turned to a cheerful *sweet sweet sweet weetaweet*, he gave away his identity as a yellow warbler.

Just as we finished setting up our tents the rain stopped and the sky cleared, allowing us to dry our raingear and packs. Our boots were another matter, and we decided they would probably never dry out completely. Even if the weather turned sunny and clear for a week, there was too much wet tundra in every direction, and the Goretex membrane in the boots couldn't keep up with it.

After resting and reading for a spell, Jen and Cindy prepared dinner while I explored the steep bluff behind our tents. We were afraid we might not be able to skirt the edge of the river the next morning, so I set out to find us a path. Fortunately, the muskoxen had pioneered the way and had worn a deep trail through the willows right next to the water. When I returned to camp I reassured the women that we would not have to climb over another mountain.

By this time the sky was clear and pale blue in every direction and, although our campsite was in shadow, the coastal plain was gloriously sunny. The high clouds to the northeast were like thinly stretched marshmallows, reflecting the evening light back on us, and making our dinnertime almost a magical event.

Before finally turning in for the night, I glassed the other bank of the Sadlerochit River in vain for any sign of the ever-elusive muskoxen, and I wondered where they had gone. Jen and Cindy confessed this was the hardest trek they had ever taken in their lives, but they were good sports about it and looked forward to the next day. Maybe tomorrow we'd see a musk ox.

By early morning it had turned bitterly cold, with a stiff north wind blowing in a thick fog, but I managed to stay warm enough in my sleeping bag by putting on everything I had in my wardrobe. Luckily, I'd brought along my polar fleece, down vest and long johns.

At about 8:00 the wind ceased, but the fog was thicker than pea soup, and I worried that we might not be able to see well enough to continue on to Sadlerochit Spring. In that case, we would use my compass.

After eating, we still had no visibility, so I broke out the compass to give it its first run of the trip. There was no hurry, and we slowly struck camp and set out on the muskox trail I'd found the night before. Not far along the edge of the river, I discovered some jumbo-sized grizzly bear tracks, still so damp on the surface of the rocks that they must have been made less than an hour before we struck camp. Since the tracks were headed in the same direction we were going, the bear must have passed very close to our tents while we were eating breakfast, probably detouring across the face of the bluff behind us. That was enough for us to immediately take out our referee whistles and start blowing them, hard and loud! With the fog thick enough to cut with a knife, we felt the more noise we made the better. We joked that we must have sounded like a referee jamboree.

About a half-mile from our camp, we came upon a large freight sled and three empty plastic fuel barrels in the middle of the tundra, probably abandoned by Kaktovik Inupiat after a recent spring hunt. We thought a possible explanation for leaving them behind was to show they still used the Sadlerochit country as they had in times past.

When we arrived at the spring, we knew our theory must be correct. There was such an abundance of wildlife around the place that it was probably the first hunting destination for Kaktovik hunters when the weather got a little warmer. And what a natural wonder the spring was! It wasn't a hot spring, but the water from inside the mountain was about 10-15 degrees warmer than other water in the area, gushing out in such copious quantities that it formed its own small river, and a micro climate that included plant species normally found much farther south, including wood fern, oak fern, tall fireweed, tall Jacob's ladder, saussurea, and a larkspur I'd never seen before in the Sadlerochits. A whole host of other Arctic species also grew in profusion there, and were much more advanced in growth than I'd seen elsewhere.

The spring flows all winter, undoubtedly the reason the muskoxen frequented the area. Alas, we didn't see them because of the thick fog. I did identify a number of duck species, though, including shovellers, wigeons, and pintails. I wondered about their migration pattern and thought they were among the few ducks that didn't have to wait for the spring thaw in the Sadlerochits. It was probably another reason why the Kaktovik people hunted there at that time of year. Jen and Cindy also reported they saw an American dipper feeding at the edge of the spring where it gushed out of the mountain. At first, I questioned their sighting, but later found out that a pair of them lived there year round due to the permanent open water. The Sadlerochit Spring left us in a state of awe, and we wished we'd stumbled into it the day before. It would have been a magical place to spend the night, and so much warmer.

We continued on our trek west, reckoning by compass through the misty rain and thickening fog, climbing higher on the flank of the mountain to try to find better walking country. The tundra wasn't unbearable, since it was still mostly frozen underneath, but I knew we would find more solid ground higher up, so up we went. For a while we found what we were looking for, some easy going on dryas terrace, then over a long stretch of what appeared to be an ancient formation of limestone pebbles and small shards of broken shale. It was ideal walking on this section, and the women were in excellent spirits. After crossing the second creek, though, things got more difficult, and for a half-mile we had to slog through some serious tussocks. This was a new experience for Jen and Cindy, and having to negotiate them by compass in the fog made it new for me, too.

We made it past the bad tussocks by the time we reached the next creek, and thought it was time to make a fire and have some tea. Although still early in the afternoon, we felt so comfortable there that we decided to pitch our tents for the night. The creek bottom had a good supply of dry willow, guaranteeing we could have an ample fire till we went to bed. Besides cooking our dinner over it, we were also able to dry our boots, insoles and socks. How often did we remark on what a luxury it was to be able to build a fire in such a cold land!

In late afternoon the misty rain stopped, the fog bank lifted, and we could see the Coastal Plain in front of us, along with the Sadlerochit River and the Arctic ice pack. Then ever so slowly the greening flanks of the mountains behind us began to open up, and we found we were exactly where our map and compass put us. Gradually the fog turned to low clouds, allowing us a glimpse of a lone short-eared owl as it fluttered over us like a big moth. We were elated to see blue sky again and chatted cheerfully around the fire while we made dinner. Somehow the subject came up about spreading my ashes in the Refuge. It was in my will, I said, but I hoped it wouldn't be too expensive when the time finally came. Jen said she'd make sure it was done on a backhaul to keep the price down.

After washing my hair and beard, I retired to our tent to surreptitiously watch a Smith's longspur on a nest in the side of the creek bank. Cindy had discovered it earlier, and when we peeked in we found six dark green eggs. Even with our tents only six or seven feet away, the female bird came right back to the nest to incubate the eggs. And there, I presume, she stayed for the rest of the night. I don't really know, because I nodded off at about midnight under a blue sky, with the promise of more of the same in the morning.

And there was, although the clear skies also brought frigid weather. In the early morning I was so cold, even inside my sleeping bag, that I was afraid I might get hypothermia. Finally I zipped Jen's and my bags together to try to warm up. Even so, it took the better part of two hours for me to feel comfortable enough to go back to sleep. It was the coldest I had ever been in a sleeping bag, and I was sure it was because I hadn't been eating enough oil-based foods like peanut butter or dry fish.

By 8:00 I was still dead tired, but when I peered out of the tent I noticed a thick blanket of clouds creeping our direction from the southeast, and I thought we'd better hit the road for Sunset Pass before it started raining. We were all packed up and ready to head out an hour later, and after taking a snap of the longspur nest, we were on our way across the tundra again.

We slogged for a long time over more wet tussock country, with only a few breaks of solid dryas terrace to give us respite. I was in front and alone with my own thoughts, and Jen and Cindy were patiently trudging behind, having a good chat nonetheless. At about noon we reached the end of the tussocks and were crossing a small creek, when I caught some movement on a large snow flush upstream. I glassed the area and saw first, one, two, then three newborn chocolate-colored grizzly cubs cavorting in the snow. Then I spotted the momma bear a short distance away in the willows, methodically digging for roots. She had a dark brown coat and was still totally unaware of our presence. Two of the cubs were running around on the snow, playing tag and jumping on each other and having a good old time. The third was less active and mostly sat near its mother while she searched for food. It was fascinating watching them, but Jen and Cindy wanted to move on to avoid any chance of an encounter with the mother bear. I assured them that as soon as she smelled us, she and her three cubs would be out of there in a flash.

And that's exactly what happened. After we crossed the creek and started up the other bank, the breeze took our scent toward the four bears. I watched with my binoculars as the mother bear lifted her nose to better catch our smell, whirled around, and began bouncing rapidly across the tundra with her cubs in tow. She didn't slow down until she and her family were far up on the mountainside. We were amazed at how high they climbed to avoid us. She had probably been shot at by hunters, I thought, since her association with humans was so negative. Now this fear would be transferred to the cubs, which was as it should be, if they were to stay out of trouble with people visiting the Refuge. The bears finally disappeared behind a high mountain ridge, and we didn't see them again. I told Jen and Cindy it was unusual for grizzlies to have triplets this far north.

On our way over the final ridge before Sunset Pass we came across a wide patch of blooming snow buttercups that, with their shiny yellow petals, were bright and cheery even under cloudy skies. Lavender woolly louseworts were also in full bloom now, as were the fragrant purple Pallas's wallflower. In spite of the cool weather, the wildflowers continued their advance toward what would become in just a few days an explosion of color on the tundra. I was eager for Jen and Cindy to observe this event before we returned to Fairbanks, and was happy to see that it was on its way. Along with the wildflowers, we found more of the black caterpillars that we'd seen crawling across the tundra over the past week. We knew they provided much of the food for tundra birds such as jaegers, plovers and bluethroats, but we wondered which of the butterflies they became.

At last, we rounded the final bend and were back in Sunset Pass again. Just as Cindy yelled, "Yeah, our creek!" I glimpsed something big and blonde and woolly up on a bench across the creek. I pointed, and announced that our blonde buddy was back. From his markings, he was the same bear we had dubbed Blondie a few days earlier. As he rooted around for food, he must have walked near a jaeger nest, because two long-tailed jaegers were dive-bombing him fiercely, going round and round and nailing him each time on his big furry head. I could empathize with him, since I had been treated the same way only a few days before by a pair of jaegers. I watched this little drama unfold through my binoculars, and could see a definite look of harassment on the bear's face as he quickly stepped away from the nest area. Only when he was a safe distance from the jaegers did he resume digging. By then he was about 300 yards away, and since the wind was in our favor he wasn't able to detect us, and we passed him without his even glancing up.

As we approached our old campsite, we were anxious about the condition of our little yellow tent, which we had left standing to protect some of the clothing and equipment we had left behind. With the bear feeding nearby, we weren't sure whether or not the tent would be torn to shreds by curious bruin claws. Even if it had escaped the bear, we wondered if it had withstood the high winds that sometimes whistled through the pass. So when we saw it still standing, and the plastic tubs and bear barrels we had left inside in their original places, we breathed a big sigh of relief.

"But our little creek is gone," Cindy yelled. And indeed it was, as dry as a bone. So was its parent creek, the Itkilyariak, although we found some water in a small pool about 100 yards upriver. We were prepared to move our camp closer to the water, if necessary, but hoped the rain that was coming would replenish the creeks. More than the lack of water, we were concerned that Dirk had not yet returned with Cindy's food. It would be a bummer to have to continue on short rations for the rest of the trip.

It began to sprinkle, so we quickly set up our tents and dived under cover. During what soon became a healthy downpour we napped, then I read my book, *White Waters and Black,* to Jen. Written in the early 1920s, it's a fascinating story about an ill-begotten scientific expedition from La Paz, Bolivia, down through the Amazon jungle. While reading, we heard something squeaking beside the tent. I peaked outside and found two parky squirrels approaching us. We wondered what they were up to, and hoped they weren't after our food. We would have to be vigilant about burning every little tidbit of refuse, because we did not want to encourage them any further. Little did we know what really interested them.

During a lull in the rain, we heard the slow drone of a distant airplane that sounded a lot like Dirk's Beaver. Sure enough, it was Dirk, and after an exploratory swing over the airstrip, he swooped down and gently landed the big bird on the hard terrace in the middle of the valley. When he got out of the plane he apologized for the mix-up with Cindy's food. Somehow he had taken it back to Coldfoot with him after he'd picked up a group of rafters from the Canning River. The food had been offloaded with the rafters' outfit, then flown to Fairbanks, where it was discovered. When the rafters sent it back to Dirk he at first didn't know who it belonged to. But after thinking about it, he finally concluded that it was ours and he should get it to us as soon as possible. He had tried delivering it to our camp two days earlier, but couldn't land because of the high winds. Now he handed it to me packed in three small bear barrels that he said we could hang on to until he came in to get us.

On our way back to the airplane, I asked if he could take us over to the Hulahula River sometime soon, then pick us up after a week. He said there would be no problem and that he could do it in two days. Then he climbed up into the driver's seat, gunned his big Pratt and Whitney engine, and took off into the moody sky.

Right after Dirk left, it started to rain again, but no matter, we had our long lost food back. I remarked to Jen and Cindy that it was like a deus ex machina that he landed just after we returned from our walk around the mountain. Cindy hadn't heard this term before, so I explained it as she opened the bear barrels and began spreading out the food on our tent floor. We couldn't resist the new vittles, and ate our dinner on the spot – cheese and summer sausage on crackers. Finally, some oily food, so we could stay warm at night.

After we finished eating, the rain eased off and I built a fire with some of the dry kindling we had stored in the yellow tent. As I was stoking the flames, a red Piper Cub flew over us a couple of times, checking us out for some reason. Then he flew off up the pass and was gone. I wondered who he was. We drank a hot cup of tea around the fire and chatted until the rain resumed in earnest and we headed for our tents.

Jen and I were determined not to be cold that night, so we zipped our bags together right from the start. Then, while we listened to the rain come down in bucketfuls, we congratulated each other for investing in our new Mountain Hard Wear tent.

Summer Solstice –

It rained till about 5:00 a.m., when the heavy staccato of the raindrops fell off and I thought the storm had ended. Serene silence followed and I went back to sleep. As I nodded off again, the temperature even seemed to be getting a little warmer. At 8:00, when I opened the tent fly, I discovered why. There was an inch of new snow outside, and the tent was covered with it. The protective layer of the snow had warmed up the tent interior considerably. When I got out of the tent, I found the water running in both creeks again. In spite of the snow and dense fog, the ambient temperature seemed fairly warm, probably because there wasn't much moisture left in the air. There was also no wind, not even a faint breeze. Our planned trip up to the Tors, though, would have to be put off till another day. We couldn't see more than 50 feet, and it was still so cool that even the few mountain avens and purple saxifrage that had escaped the snow had closed their petals tight to conserve heat.

I immediately kindled a fire with the dry willow branches I'd put under one of our plastic storage tubs the previous night. Cindy gave me some crumpled pages she had finished reading from Jen's book, *Winter Solstice*, and I used those as fire starter. Then we had coffee and instant oatmeal for breakfast and sat around the welcome flames, hoping for the sky to clear. We also went out on wood gathering forays, both to stay warm through physical activity and to keep the fire replenished while we waited for the fickle fog to lift. Lucky, there were a lot of dead willows in the creek bed.

At times, the sun shone faintly through a thin veil of cloud cover, teasing us with its ghostly presence, then the fog would close down tight on us again. It did this into the afternoon, as we gathered bundle after bundle of dry willows to feed our small fire. Our fireplace consisted of only four rocks, in a more or less rectangular shape, with a portable cooking grill over the middle two. Since it's so small and efficient, I refer to this arrangement as my Indian fireplace. When the breeze began to pick up, I busied myself building a rock wall to act as a windbreak.

I noticed the mother bluethroat was gone from her nest for a long time, so I went over to check on the eggs. There were now eight of them and they felt cool to the touch. I wondered if she had abandoned her nest. There were only two little footprints in the snow at the edge of the nest where she had perched before taking off, and no indication that she had come back even for a short visit. It didn't look good for the success of the brood. We worried the still unborn young would die if she stayed away too long. And where was dad? Finally, at about 2:00 in the afternoon, after almost all of the snow had melted, the female scuttled back into her nest.

By then we felt the need for a short walk, and headed down the Itkilyariak to check on our jaeger friends. The fog had begun to lift and we could see almost a half-mile up and down the valley. The ceiling, at about 500 feet, increased the closer to the coastal plain we walked. When we frightened a female Baird's sandpiper off her nest, she did a pathetic broken-wing act, hunkering down in the tundra, peeping and vibrating and limping and keeping herself the focus of attention. Since it was a cold day, we left the little sandpiper nest alone and continued in the direction of the jaeger nest. Jen and Cindy stopped a prudent distance from the nest while I advanced toward the female. At first, she paid me scant attention, but at the last minute she hopped up and started dive-bombing me with a vengeance. I ran quickly over to the nest, found the same two eggs in it, and hurried back to Jen and Cindy, who were both grinning at me for what they undoubtedly thought was a ludicrous bout of bird bravado. We walked on and found the creek running strong where the previous day it had been bone dry.

On our way back to the tents we followed the creek bed, searching for fossils similar to some I had found in the morning at camp. Those were good high profile specimens and Cindy was particularly interested in them. We had no luck finding any more, but hoped in the days to come to discover their source. While returning, we came across the male Baird's sandpiper standing sentinel not far from the nest, and we also watched a northern harrier cruising across the valley, dropping every now and again to check for voles and lemmings, then sailing onward. As we approached camp, we gathered dry willows to build another fire to make tea and keep us warm while we chatted about the chance of Dirk making it in the next day to pick us up and take us over to the Hulahula River.

After finishing my tea I was still restless, so decided on a walk up the creek to try to find the male bluethroat. I wasn't very far from camp when I spotted four young bull caribou slowly ambling down the east side of the valley, grazing as they went. I never expected them there, and hurried back to point them out to Jen and Cindy, telling them I thought they were probably from the Central Arctic herd, since the Porcupine herd was still too far to the east. The caribou had already smelled our fire and located us by the time I got to camp, regularly glancing in our direction to monitor our intentions. But they didn't seem to be overly wary, I imagined because they had never been hunted by humans. We watched them as they fed on cotton grass, occasionally lifting their gangly hind legs to scratch their heads and shoulders with their crescent-mooned hooves. Finally, when I returned to my ramble up the valley, they hightailed it in the other direction.

During my walkabout I spotted another harrier, swooping toward the creek, searching for prey. I was so intent on watching the hawk that I almost stepped on a rock ptarmigan. It just about scared me out of my britches when it suddenly shot up in front of me. The guttural call these ptarmigan make is a dead ringer for the growl of a grizzly bear and had fooled me many times before. Not far away, several parky squirrels were playing outside their dens, loudly scolding me as I passed them by. With the day beginning to warm up, they seemed to be rising to the surface everywhere. Their Inupiat name, *siksik*, aptly describes their sharp call.

At dinner, I noticed a slight change in the wind direction and wondered whether the fog would soon be gone. Slowly, it rose into the rocky heights, leaving only trailing rags and tatters of what it had been in the morning. These became radiant with light as the evening progressed and the sun came around the mountain, backlighting everything with an alpine glow. While this was happening, a short-eared owl flew over us, "lazily flopping its wings," as Jen put it.

I cracked more willows after dinner so we'd have plenty of dry kindling in the morning, then sat next to the fire to warm my hands. Soon afterward I retired to the tent with Jen. As I wrote my daily notes we again heard the sweet song of the male bluethroat. Sounding at first like a weak robin's warble, it changed to a cricket-like chirp, then to a combination of liquid twitters, whistles and various other calls that I had never heard uttered in such profusion from a single bird. What a lovely song to go to sleep by.

July 22 –

From my journal: *It's 10:00 p.m., and we're sitting by the fire again after a sparkling day in Sunset Pass. Dirk didn't get in at noon like he said he would, and we've resigned ourselves to staying the night here in the Pass. Perhaps tomorrow he'll come in to take us over to the Hulahula River. The fire burns hot and ever so quickly begins to cool because of the poor quality of the willow we're using. There just isn't very much carbon left in most of it. Jen throws on some more wood and the fire burns hot again.*

It's been a good day, though. The fog lifted by 8:30 a.m. and I heard the telltale pop of our small gas can, expanding, indicating the sun was beginning to shine through the clouds. I immediately put on some hot water for tea and oatmeal, then began to help Jen and Cindy dismantle the camp in preparation for Dirk's promised arrival at noon. While we were eating, two young bull caribou passed us to the east, coming fairly close to our tents. I slowly waved my hat and whistled at them to attract them even closer, as I had been taught to do many years earlier while working for the master guide, Hal Waugh. A little later in the morning, as I was glassing the other side of the creek, I spotted two more bull caribou lying in the tundra. One was an older bull with a large rack decked out in fresh velvet, and the other was his younger sidekick. They eventually got up and fed for a while, then slowly ambled along the valley away from the Coastal Plain. Since there was probably still not very much high quality food down there, they had their noses headed for greener pastures. I imagined these bulls, too, were a part of the Central Arctic herd.

As we watched the caribou, a cross fox climbed up the west bank of the creek and began marking everything in sight with its scent glands. The sun's rays reflected rusty red from its front quarters and a rich dark brown from its rear end and long flowing tail.

Our bluethroat was still there, furtively flitting in and out of her nest. Maybe by being away from the nest so much, this was her way of slowing down development of her embryos until the warmer mosquito weather arrived. Arctic nesting birds have uncanny strategies of survival up here.

The sun shone brightly by 11:00 a.m. and the low angle of the light made the mustard-colored glacier avens glow over on the east bank. A merlin dashed by, and as I followed him with my binocs, I noticed yet another grizzly bear heading up the valley in our direction. He was still about three quarters of a mile away, and at first I thought he was Blondie, the well-behaved bear we had run into twice so far. But then I saw he had darker brown rear quarters, and I knew he was a different bear. I ambled toward him for about a quarter mile to get a better view and leave some scent, then after confirming he wasn't Blondie and briefly glassing the jaeger nest with my binocs I doubled back to camp to watch the bear from there. He still hadn't detected us and wandered whimsically across the tundra, digging for food. When he reached the environs of the jaeger nest, though, his nose jetted suddenly into the air, his furry body wheeled around, and he started racing toward the ravine on the east side of the pass. He stopped once, then twice, to look around and sniff the air, then he sprinted on up the ravine and out of sight. Jen and Cindy had never seen anything quite like it, and were amazed at the difference between the behaviors of the different bears. So was I.

Noon came and went, and still no Dirk, so we ate lunch, read and napped for a while. I fixed the rubber bumper on the toe of my boot, which had worn through during our trek around the mountain, then read some more. I was glad my book, White Waters and Black, *was an interesting one. Although it was written in a formal, sardonic style, the author's descriptions of the interactions of the members of the expedition were absolutely hilarious. What's better is that the stories were true. Human behavior under conditions of adversity is so variable, and so fascinating.*

At 6:00, Jen and Cindy and I took an hour's walk over to Weller Creek. We all wished we could have gone up to the tors at the head of the creek, but with Dirk scheduled to arrive, we couldn't stray from camp for very long. Back at camp again, I took a bath in the fast diminishing Itkilyariak Creek, then returned to Weller Creek to take some pictures of the flowers that were now out in force in the area.

At 9:00, we ate dinner, and afterward set up our full camp again. Only Cindy had to put her tent up, however, since we had left ours standing for a possible onslaught of wind and rain.

Now it's 10:30, and while getting ready to retire to our tents, we hear the sweet warble and chirp of the male bluethroat. I try searching for him, but he sings from quite a distance away, and his location varies so much that I finally leave him in peace and walk back to the tent. I wonder why he seems to be all over the place at the same time. Is he a ventriloquist like the blue grouse, and able to project his voice in different directions to baffle would-be predators? Or is he just hyperactive like myself, flitting around from bush to bush in rapid sequence? Eventually I know I'll find the answer, but for now I'm totally baffled. Jen and I also wonder where he spends his time during the day while his mate tends to her nesting duties.

At 11:00 p.m., the sun continues to shine brightly and climbs down along the mountain ridge to the west, heading for the Arctic Ocean. The solstice is now over and the light will begin to diminish from here on in. Almost all evidence of any storm clouds over the high mountains to the south has dissipated. If the snowstorm was the reason why Dirk didn't make it in today, then there shouldn't be any excuse tomorrow.

June 23 –

Again from my journal: (10:00 p.m.) *It's been a stellar day for us, with bright sunshine from morning till night, if one can describe this as night. The sun is rounding the bend from the west again, starting to tiptoe down the ridge and across the Beaufort Sea. Presently, we're watching yet another grizzly bear on the far slope of the mountain to the southwest. This one is light gray, almost white, and we've dubbed him Snowball. We spotted him late this afternoon as we were returning from the hoodoo tors to the west of us. We had waited until noon for Dirk, but when he didn't show we left him a note that we had taken a walk up Weller Creek into the hoodoos and would be back late in the afternoon.*

Once in the hoodoos, we found an almost surreal world of limestone tors encrusted with small fossils. Atop some of the formations were colorful mats of mountain avens, Kamchatka rhododendron, villous cinquefoil and cut-leaf anemone, among others. I also spotted a male gyrfalcon cruising above the rocky cliff on the opposite side of the gorge. That's where I found an aerie with three young in it the last time I was there in 1997. This one was a handsome gray bird, and, who knows, maybe even one of the same falcons I saw back then. Jen and Cindy were really enchanted with the area, and referred to it as a wild garden.

The grizz continues to dig for Hedysarum roots high up on the north slope of the mountain, just above the line of shadow cast by the opposite ridge as the sun bends lower toward the Beaufort Sea. It strikes me that the reason he is digging for roots up there is that they're tastier than the ones down here. There it is still cool and the roots haven't begun to transfer much of their starchy energy into the production of new growth. So that's why he's feeding at such high elevation. Since we started watching him at 3:00 p.m., he's steadily climbed higher and higher.

After getting back to camp, we gathered more dry willow for firewood to add to the large pieces we had picked up along Weller Creek on our way down from the tors. Because it was so warm we didn't need a big fire, but we built a small one to heat up some water for tea and one of our dry Mountain House dinners. For dessert, Cindy and Jen mixed up a hefty pot of instant chocolate pudding, which we scarfed down as soon as it gelled. Yum.

After dessert, a parky squirrel crept into camp and began nibbling at a small patch of ground near our tents. Suddenly we figured it out. It was feeding on residues of salt left where we had urinated during the night. It must have been salt-starved, and took advantage of the only salt source in the neighborhood. I snapped a couple of close-ups of him feeding. Cute.

A little while ago our first robin flew into the area with a loud aggressive warble. He didn't stick around for long, though, and headed south back up the valley. We wondered if he might eventually nest somewhere nearby. The female bluethroat, meanwhile, continued to scuttle in and out of her nest all evening, probably on feeding missions, since her mate didn't seem to help her.

This has been our warmest day yet, and we were able to walk around dressed only in sandals. The sky continues as clear as quartz crystal, and we're hoping we're into one of those long-lasting Arctic high-pressure fronts. We've decided not to wait for Dirk any longer, and to walk northwest of camp over to Marsh Creek for three-days so we can appreciate this run of good weather. Jen and Cindy love our base camp, but are looking forward to moving someplace different for a short spell.

At 11:00 p.m. the male bluethroat begins singing again. What a lovely song. In some ways he reminds me of a mockingbird.

Our day began with the sun so warm in the early morning that we had a hard time sleeping. We were thankful our new tent had a flap that opened in back to allow air circulation.

Two parky squirrels, bickering over rights to nibble next to our tent, awakened us again. Listening to them banter back and forth, we were amazed at the variability of their nibbling vocabulary. Most of it seemed to be a form of high pitched mumbling, but abruptly the decibel level would rise to a shrill squeal or an angry bark. When the squirrels got too close to the edge of the tent, though, I peaked around the corner and shooed them away. I didn't want to tempt the fates by having them nibble on the tent itself.

Breakfast was late, and it took us time to strike camp, but by noon we were on our way down Itkilyariak Creek, headed for Marsh Creek. Right away we ran into six bull caribou, including two with huge racks, resting and grazing on the other side of the creek from where we had found the broken snow machine skis. By now wildflowers were studding the slopes, and as we crossed a saddle leading west from Sunset Pass we found yellow arctic arnica, the dainty alp lily, and weasel snout in full flower. The latter is a purple member of the figwort family, and it is a mystery to me why someone chose to liken the plant to the snout of a weasel. The nodding bell-shaped cassiope was also out in profusion. With their little white bowed heads, they always remind me of a church crowd in the middle of prayer. They're such pretty little flowers, they look like they might have some perfume to them, but on bending down to sniff them, I am always disappointed in their lack of even a hint of fragrance.

As we took a short snack break on the other side of the saddle, we noticed the ubiquitous cotton grass starting to fluff out. Too bad the cows from the Porcupine caribou herd weren't in the area to benefit from the high nutrient value of these plants for their calves. I wondered if large numbers of either of the two caribou herds that used the area would be here in time to take advantage of it. In the miles and miles of coastal plain that stretched in front of us we saw only three small caribou bulls, almost certainly stragglers from the Central Arctic herd.

While crossing the base of a slope jumbled with black-lichened talus, a pair of snow buntings rushed by us, landing on nearby rocks. They were curious and peered at us intently. I stared back at them with my binocs until something else caught my attention. "Oh, oh, we've got another furry visitor," I said.

We watched closely as a light-brown grizzly ambled down the middle of the valley we were in, unwittingly headed straight for us. To avoid him we retreated into the talus, then perched on a patch of mosses and lichens and waited to see what he would do. He hadn't spotted us, and certainly hadn't smelled us, and kept zigzagging in our direction, digging roots as he went. Finally changing direction, he tacked toward the other side of the valley. He was soon engaged in rooting for more food, and while he had his head buried in the tundra we sneaked on by him. He didn't even look up as we passed him about 200 yards away, which I thought was a little strange. At that close range, bears usually catch your strong smell, wheel instantly, and are out of sight within minutes. Not this time, and we watched the big guy until we were long gone ourselves. He was so busy digging while we made our escape that we dubbed him "Bizzy" for the rest of our stay in the Sadlerochits. By now we had seen so many of these bruins that we had to name them to tell them apart.

After another hour of quietly walking along an old caribou trail at the foot of the mountain, we made it to the top of the valley. Then we crossed a wide, heavily tussocked saddle and slogged down toward Marsh Creek.

Instead of a wide, shallow creek bed like that of the Itkilyariak, we found a deep gorge with steep walls. The east side was still packed with snow, which clued us in on the wind direction during the winter months. The creek bottom was heavily braided and strewn with large rocks and willow growth, and as much as I searched with my binoculars, I couldn't find an ideal place to locate our camp. Cindy said the gorge looked "just too daunting" to go down into, so we searched elsewhere for a nice spot in the sun to put up our tents for the next two nights.

It wasn't long until we came across a hidden cranny on the tundra, lying out of reach of the stiff east wind and offering a lovely view of Marsh Creek and Camden Bay to the north. It was also right next to a small tributary of Marsh Creek that would serve as a source of running water. What more could we ask for? And yet there was more. Behind our camp was a tall, rugged volcano-shaped massif that I referred to as "Sisyphus Mountain" because there seemed to be a hunched human figure halfway up its talus slope pushing a huge boulder. Wildflowers shone like miniature suns on the tundra, and a long snow flush on the other side of the creek reflected the sun's rays back on our camp until well past midnight.

At dinner we watched a Say's phoebe play food tag with a pair of wheatears. He was after a caterpillar one of the wheatears held in its beak.

The phoebe chased the wheatear back and forth from bush to bush and rock to rock, but in the end the wheatear managed to hold on to its prize. As I followed their movements, I noticed a redpoll nest in the willows just down-hill from our tents. There were redpolls flitting around it, and one even sat in the nest, but when I climbed down to check it for eggs I found nothing in it but a comfortable bed of feathers. After watching the nest a little longer, I decided that the young had already left home. As everywhere else in Alaska, the redpolls had started their family in the cold weather of early spring, and they were now free from their child raising responsibilities and could enjoy the rest of the summer before heading south of the tree line again. No wonder redpolls are known as the toughest small bird in the north.

Just before calling it quits for the day I heard the raucous cries of young ravens coming from the other side of the ridge above camp. I had heard them earlier and wondered if there was a nest located somewhere on the edge of the gorge. I would check the next morning.

Toward midnight, as we chatted in our sleeping bags, Jen heard what sounded like an airplane approaching overhead. She thought it might be Dirk on his way to Sunset Pass to pick us up, but soon realized it was only a giant bumblebee buzzing just outside the tent. I told her that's what happens when you're waiting for an airplane pick-up. We all got a good laugh out of it anyway.

There was a faint crescent moon hanging in the morning sky when we awoke, and the sun was shining again. It was Jen's birthday, and we hoped for another sparkling day so we could explore some red rock formations we could see downriver. I had heard of red rock like this farther to the west, by the Canning River, but not along Marsh Creek. I thought it might be sandstone, but soon after starting out I found I was mistaken. Only a short distance from camp, while side-hilling down to the creek bottom, we came across some of the stuff and saw that it was heavily oxidized and eroded shale stone, similar to what we had briefly walked on during our way back from Sadlerochit Spring.

We continued along the now much lower east bank of the river, and spotted a golden eagle soaring high above, hunting for parky squirrels with his telescopic vision, and undoubtedly checking us out at the same time. With my binoculars, I reciprocated and focused my own curiosity on him. His mottled brown and white feathers pegged him as a juvenile. Down on the ground we came across an array of tundra birds, including Smith's and Lapland longspurs, wheatears, a Say's phoebe, two pairs of long-tailed jae-gers, a rough-legged hawk and a couple of male yellow wagtails. Since the wagtails were a new species for me, I watched their flight patterns closely as they whistled and flew back and forth above the willows on the edge of

Marsh Creek. I told Jen and Cindy they were among the few North American birds that migrate as far as northern Africa and southern India to spend the winter months. We wondered if they traveled with the bluethroats as they migrated south and west to similar wintering grounds. Speaking of which, not long after we spotted the second wagtail, I heard the telltale sweet warble and chirp of a male bluethroat. He was singing loudly with the same variable repertoire as our bird in Sunset Pass, so I guessed he had a nest nearby. Try as I did, though, I could not locate the bird anywhere, and finally gave up. By then the women were already more than a quarter-mile ahead of me and I had to hurry to catch up to them.

Marsh Creek was much larger than I'd thought, with copious quantities of water flowing between its wide banks. But it was a piece of cake walking on the river bottom because of the dryas terrace that provided such a hard surface. Our friend Andy Keller, in Fairbanks, had told me that it continued like this all the way to Camden Bay on the Beaufort Sea, and I kicked myself for not having planned enough time to take a longer trip in that direction.

When I caught up to Jen and Cindy, they remarked on the explosion of wildflowers everywhere. I told them it was just beginning. The blossoms of a myriad species were now opening by the millions all around us, and the later in the day it got, the more blooms there were. In a day or two the process would be at its height and it would be like walking in the middle of a flower garden. Dryas and rosebay carpeted the riverbanks, and lupine, cassiope, campeon, numerous saxifrages and so many others filled in the gaps. It was a spectacle already beyond words, and I jested with Jen that it was better than a birthday cake with candles.

As we ate our lunch we spotted a small band of caribou, including a cow and a yearling. We wondered if the Porcupine herd had begun to make its way over to the coastal plain, but decided it was still a little early for them, judging from what Dirk had told us when he dropped off our food. Then again, caribou moved quickly when they had a mind to, and it was possible these were part of the vanguard of that herd.

After returning to camp that evening I heard young ravens calling again from the other side of the ridge. My curiosity got the best of me, and when I climbed up to take a look I was sure there was a nest just over the brink of the cliff that commanded the deep gorge. From where I was perched I couldn't see down into the nest, but the high-pitched squawks of the young told me there were three of them, and that they were hungry.

That wasn't all I discovered over there. On my way back from the rim of the canyon, I found myself face to face with two marmots. I couldn't believe it. Never in my wildest imagination did I think there were marmots living this far north. But there they were, poised as though frozen on a tongue of talus, peering at me like they'd never seen humans before. I approached slowly and got to within 40 feet of them when they turned and started back into the cracks of their rocky domain, where I supposed they had young in a den somewhere. I knew they weren't hoary marmots because the color of their fur was too dark. And they didn't whistle at me like hoaries. I later learned they were Alaska marmots, *Marmota broweri*, also called the Brooks Range marmot, because that's where they hole up, literally. In fact, these marmots have one of the most northerly distributions of any marmot in the world. Their den, often underlain by permafrost, is where the female gives birth to six or more young. They usually live in colonies and when winter blows in, all of the colony residents may hibernate together. This begins in September and, incredibly, lasts until May or June, when the melting of snow exposes the ground and reveals food plants. That's one long sleep!

In the early evening a yellow and green Supercub flew over our camp and tipped its wings at us. We wondered who it was, hoping the pilot might stop at Sunset Pass and read our note to Dirk. We still wanted to go over to the Hulahula, if at all possible. There would just be enough time if the weather held off, although a big low pressure system lumbering in our direction from the northwest seemed to be growing in size as we watched. I predicted we'd feel the first drops of rain by morning.

Back in our sleeping bags again and reflecting on the day's events, Jen said she'd had one of the most memorable birthdays ever.

In the morning, when we heard raindrops smacking the ripstop nylon of our new tent, we thought we'd be slogging back to Sunset Pass in a heavy downpour. But in a few minutes the drops stopped and there was silence. Poking my head through the fly, I saw only low clouds scudding above us. Undeterred by a little wet weather, one of our marmot friends was scuttling down the opposite bank of the small creek beside camp. When he scuttled back up again to his home in the talus, I figured it was time for us to sally forth, too, and get ready to return to base camp. We hoped the rain would hold off till we got back, but realized that we were, as always, at the mercy of the elements. Looking up at the sky again, I noticed a rough-legged hawk heading into the Marsh Creek gorge. Wrong thing to do, I thought. A few seconds later, out boiled two angry ravens in fast pursuit of the hawk. When he saw them, he did an immediate about face and sprinted down the creek as fast as his wings could carry him.

We had a quick breakfast, broke down our tents and bid farewell to our little redpoll friends as we prepared to strike camp. We wondered where the redpolls would spend their winter. Were they some of the birds that fed at our feeder in Fairbanks every year when it got cold? Unless they were banded, we would never know. And maybe that's the way things should be, a mystery. Perhaps we don't need to know every detail of the lives of the animals around us.

On the way back to Sunset Pass we found the same caribou trail we'd followed over to Marsh Creek. Located at the edge of the talus slope skirting almost the entire length of mountain fronting the coastal plain, it made for good hiking. Snow buntings and Lapland longspurs birddogged us, hopping from rocky mound to rocky mound as we walked, and jaegers sailed swift and graceful above the tundra searching for insects and birds' eggs. But besides a lone bull caribou resting at the head of a draw and a handsome golden cross fox trotting toward him "with a mission," as Jen put it, the vast greening plain in front of us seemed empty of large mammal life.

The first thing I did on reaching our little yellow cache tent was check the note we'd left for Dirk. Nope, he hadn't been there. Nobody had, in fact, meaning we were on our own till the 29th when Dirk was to pick us up and take us back to Coldfoot. Cindy and Jen informed me that our creeks were dry again, although there was still an ample pool of water upstream. We again talked about moving the campsite nearer to the water, but chose to remain where we'd been because it was closer to the bluethroat nest.

By now we had decided to watch the nest until we left, but when I glassed it with my binoculars I saw nobody was home. Hurrying down to check it out, I found three of her creamy-green eggs had recently been transformed into ugly little hatchlings with oversized heads that hung limp over the other five eggs. Her real work had just begun, I thought. Sure enough, the second I left the nest she was back with something in her mouth for her three young ones. Just as she was making herself comfortable atop her now mixed brood of chicks and eggs, miracle of miracles, who suddenly showed up but our ever elusive father bird, perching about 10 feet away from the nest on a low willow. And what a fanfare of song he brought with him. Starting with a cricket chirp, he changed quickly to a squeaky whistle, slid into a variable twitter, then to a melodious warble, threw in a few buzzes and trills, then went back to his chirp again. It was the most varied birdsong I'd ever heard in Alaska, and reminded me a little of a mockingbird's song.

And what a handsome bird he was – in fact, one of the most colorful I'd ever seen in Alaska, with his orange spotted blue throat patch and black and orange bands separating the blue from his bright white chest. So far, though, he hadn't helped his mate carry any food to the young. By the way he was hanging close to home, he must have known some of the eggs had hatched. He even chased a wheatear round and round the perimeter of the nest, as if to assert his rights to the area, but never an attempt to contribute to the family food coffers.

It started raining about seven and was pouring by eight. When the downpour stopped an hour later we jumped out of our tents, started a fire and prepared another of our Mountain House dinners. This time it was chili, and it tasted pretty good. As we ate, the woolly layer of clouds on the mountain to the south of Weller Creek began to dissolve, revealing something that hadn't been there before. Focusing my binocs, a tiny sliver of light became another grizzly bear, ambling across the eastern flank of the mountain, grubbing for bear root like his cousin a few days before. Grizzlies are experts at differentiating the various stages of growth of bear root, as they also are at distinguishing this plant from its relative, the wild sweet pea, whose roots contain the mildly poisonous alkaloid, swainsonine.

At about 10:30 the rain began in earnest again and we had to retire to our tents. It was time to break out the cards and small cribbage board I'd brought along. Jen had never played before and I was pretty rusty at it, but we managed to have fun with the game till well past midnight.

First thing in the morning, we had a ringside seat to an aggressive interaction between the male bluethroat and what looked like the same wheatear from the previous day. The bluethroat chased the wheatear round and round until finally the wheatear left the scene. What was the bluethroat doing, I wondered. Defending his hunting territory, probably. There were only so many insects to share in this neck of the Arctic, and soon there would be even more mouths to feed. Standing sentinel seemed to be the male's job now, along with providing moral support for his busy mate. Maybe singing was his way of accomplishing both tasks.

When the female left the nest I hurried down to check it out. As I suspected, there was one more hungry mouth wide open, making a total of four live bodies and four still encased in their shells. My hunch was that since the eggs had been laid a day apart, they would hatch a day apart, too.

Back to the male, I noticed that each time the female would make a food foray away from the nest he would chase after her, shadowing her every move, as though he were her personal bodyguard. He stood by while she stabbed her insect quarry and clamped it in her beak, then when she raced back to the nest he raced back with her. But he stopped abruptly about two feet from the nest, sometimes landing on the ground and curiously cocking his head as though wondering what was going on in there. Then he would return to his sentinel duty in the willows, flying a circular route around the nest about 300 feet in diameter, singing as he bounced from perch to perch.

Since there were still low-lying clouds obscuring the Weller Creek Tors, we decided to forgo that area and take our walk south toward the summit of Sunset Pass. We still hadn't explored a couple of the side valleys up there, and we were game for new surprises.

Before starting out I glassed the mountainside to see how our furry friend from the evening before was doing. By now we had decided it was the same white bear we'd seen the previous week and had named Snowball. And, sure enough, he was still in the neighborhood, only a little farther up on the mountain. And still doing some serious digging, which meant he'd be no problem for us as we proceeded through the pass.

Our route again took us by the remains of the old Inupiat camp, then along the creek to where it bent to the east. We wanted to cross over at that point and head for the top of the pass, but the water was too high and too swift, discouraging us from crossing. So we changed trajectory and followed the north bank up into a side valley. Most of the way the ground was flat and hard and densely matted with mountain avens, which made for good walking. When we got near the top of the drainage, though, the terrain got a little rockier and we stopped for lunch. Opposite us was a large stand of willows where I hoped to locate more bluethroats, but as much as I glassed the area and listened for the telltale song, I didn't find any. It looked like the only nesting pair in the pass was our family down below. And although we saw no large animals up there, we did run across a small grasshopper and a tiny slug. We were amazed they were living this far north.

As soon as we got back to camp I went down to check on the jaeger nest. I was hoping to find the eggs hatched before we returned to Fairbanks, but so far they weren't cooperating. And the jaegers were still as aggressive as always, dive bombing me and almost hitting my hat several times before I finally escaped. I never hung around there for long – only a quick sally over to the nest, then back again.

Only moments after reporting the jaeger news to Jen and Cindy it started raining again, and the three of us dove into our tents and sleeping bags until the rain stopped about an hour later. When it looked like the weather might hold we crawled out, kindled a fire and cooked up a double portion of our Mountain House potato-broccoli dinners in a stainless steel pot.

At 10:15, we called it a day. The wind had died and low clouds from the coast were settling in again. By this stage we actually relished the cool windy weather. We had already seen our first mosquitoes and knew that if it got much warmer we would quickly be seeing more of them. The coolness would hold them at bay, and we hoped the wind would keep the coastal fog to a minimum. If those conditions existed in the morning, we'd be able to hike up to the Weller Creek tors again.

When I opened the tent flap in the morning the coastal fog was back with a vengeance. Since we knew we weren't going any-where for a while, we took our merry time getting up. When I finally did stick my head out the tent, I saw that Cindy had beaten me to the punch and started the morning fire for us. I was impressed. She was becoming quite a good camper.

Breakfast was the same as usual, oatmeal, except for multiple cups of coffee, over which we watched the bluethroats while they went about their own morning routine. Again, every time the female would sally forth after insects for her burgeoning family (now with five mouths to feed), the male would shadow her movements, finally following her back to the nest, but never right to the door. He'd only hang around, curiously cocking his head, flying up to an overhanging willow branch, then down again, scurrying in and out of the grass, approaching as close as 12 inches, then darting out into the open to peck at an insect. Was this preliminary to eventually helping his mate feed their growing family, we wondered. Would the cry of eight nestlings prompt him to take action?

By late morning the remainder of the fog lifted and the sun began to shine, so we finished our last cup of coffee and prepared to leave for the Weller Creek tors to try to find the gyrfalcon aerie we'd been searching for the last time we were up there.

The water level in the creeks had gone down, so we had no trouble fording either the Itkilyariaq or Weller Creek. Right away we saw another young golden eagle soaring in the thermals above us. His mottled brown and white markings were a dead ringer for the one we'd seen only a few days earlier near Marsh Creek. He looked like he was having fun, and we were sure he was ogling us with his telescopic vision. Then he swerved westward, and the last we saw of him he was headed toward Marsh Creek.

On glassing the slopes to the south, our furry friend Snowball was nowhere to be seen, and Cindy and Jen felt a lot better, since they still had a huge fear of big bears. But a new fear was looming in their minds. Hordes of mosquitoes would soon be hatching from still water everywhere and swarming to suck our blood. Up until now the cool weather had delayed the inevitable, but on this day whenever the sun came out a small mob of tiny buzzing kamikazes trailed behind us.

Although mosquitoes became more of a topic of our conversation, they still took second fiddle to the extravaganza of wildflowers that blanketed the tundra in every direction. Jen and Cindy had never seen so many wildflowers, perhaps thirty different species of them, blooming all at once. I couldn't resist taking a photo of the two women with their heads in the middle of a cluster of lupine and rhododendrons. "Tundra posies," I dubbed them.

When we got up to the tors, I spotted a male gyrfalcon gliding down from the other side of the small canyon that fell off below us. He cut his glide short and perched on a tall spine of rock opposite from where we had stopped to examine some fossil-filled limestone. As we continued looking for fossils, I heard a sudden commotion over the edge of the cliff we were walking above. Approaching the steep wall from another angle to get a better view, I spotted not only the male gyr sailing above the canyon but the female climbing quickly away from the cliff face. I glassed carefully and found the source of the commotion, three squawking young in a rock cavity tearing at the recently delivered carcass of a ptarmigan. I had found the aerie I'd been searching for. And by the looks of it, the fluffy white and black aerlettes in the nest were hungry.

The bird that seemed to be squawking the most was the smallest and clumsiest of the trio, maybe because he was hungrier than the others. He was in back of the aerie and deferred to his siblings as they tore into the now bloodied white feathers of the ptarmigan. But when the other two chicks had gulped their fill, the youngest bird took his own turn at the meat. After they finished eating, the birds stretched their wings and wobbled all over the narrow confines of their rock ledge. I was amazed at first that none of them plummeted to their death, but as I watched them stumblebum around, I noticed their bottom-heavy pear shape. "Lead bottoms," I smiled, then climbed back up to find Jen and Cindy.

I had to search for a while before locating the women, but finally there they were busily inspecting the fossil rock formation they had discovered during our previous visit to the tors. By their hollow cylindrical shape, I suspected the fossils were crinoids. I had seen them elsewhere and knew they were common in Alaska. They are also ancient, dating from the Ordovician Period, about 500 million years ago. As one of earth's oldest life forms, 600 species of them continue to live in today's oceans. Cindy and Jen were studying them so intently, I thought they might want to take the whole formation home with them. They seemed to be having so much fun that I joined them, carefully examining the different shapes of the fossils with the butt end of my binoculars.

On our way down from the tors we took our time, stopping to enjoy the wildflowers and take pictures of them. We knew this was our last day in the Refuge and wanted to soak up as much of the beauty as we could. We found several new ones in bloom, including nodding pink shooting stars, aka dodecatheon, yellow two-flowered cinquefoils, and large patches of the white-blossomed boykinia, or bear flower, another favorite food of grizzly bears. The brilliant sunshine made these tundra bouquets sparkle. And, as if not to be outdone by the sun, the moon also got into the act, glowing in the late afternoon sky and adding to the mix of light and color.

We were hungry when we got back to camp, so Jen and Cindy started our beef stroganoff and gravy dinner while I took a bath down at the creek, which by now was comfortably warm due to the bright sun and a tepid breeze blowing from the south. It was a good time to clean up before heading back to civilization the next day.

During dinner we continued our bluethroat-watch, as mom foraged for food for their five young and dad stood sentinel by her whenever she left the nest. He still hadn't participated in feeding the chicks, but every once in awhile demonstrated an active curiosity about what was going on inside the little grass cave. Later, as his mate brooded the young and eggs, he flew off down the creek again to chirp and twitter and warble his heart away.

A gigantic thunderhead that had been hanging over Mt. Chamberlin all day finally began to dissipate as we finished dinner. It was the tallest cloud we'd seen over the Brooks Range since arriving two weeks earlier, but by late evening most of it had dissolved into a transparent membrane of white haze. Blue sky was moving in on all sides, and it looked like we might have some good weather for our pick-up the next day.

June 29-30 –

Jen and I were awakened by the stirrings of someone breaking twigs down by the fireplace. When we peered outside the tent we found Cindy already lighting the morning fire and putting water on for tea. She said it was such a lovely morning that she just had to get out and enjoy it. We felt the same way and quickly joined her. Besides, this would be our last day to watch the bluethroats whose nest I checked as soon as I saw the female leave. There were now six hatchlings, the first three having grown quite a bit since we saw them a few days earlier. They had fluffier downy feathers, stronger necks, and their eyes looked like they were ready to pop open at any moment.

At about noon, while Jen and Cindy visited around the fire, I walked down the creek for a couple of miles to see if I could locate any more caribou or bear. I also stopped by the jaeger nest to see how the eggs were doing. They still hadn't hatched, and both jaegers were feisty, as usual, although the mother bird dive-bombed me more earnestly than her mate. This fit the pattern of most other large birds I'd encountered in Alaska. For species like falcons, gulls, terns and jaegers that actively defended their nest, it was the female who did the best job.

As I headed back I watched a rainsquall sprinting in from the west. It missed me completely but had drenched our camp and forced Jen and Cindy to visit inside our tent. I built up the fire again and put on some more water to use up what remained of our hot chocolate. When Jen suggested we eat one of our last two dehydrated meals, I was a little nervous about using most of the rest of the hot food. But since her intuition told her Dirk was going to make it in that evening as planned, I went with that and broke out the package.

Just as we were finishing lunch, dark skies rolled over us again and the rain fell even harder than it had before. There was still blue sky around the tattered edges of the storm, but we were getting a little worried about what we couldn't see off to the west where the squalls were originating. Right after the rain the male bluethroat showed up only a few willows away from the nest and began his repertoire of beautiful song, in celebration, it seemed, of his growing family and the magnificent wilderness that we were all a part of.

If I could have sung a song so wonderful at that moment, I would have too.

In the late afternoon we were chatting around the fire when we heard the slow drone of what sounded like Dirk's Beaver. "But he had said he'd be here in the evening," I mumbled, and grabbed my binocs. Sure enough, it was Dirk's big blue and white clunker. What a lovely sight, seeing it still flying, and him alive. When he hadn't shown up the week before to take us over to the Hulahula River, we seriously wondered if something had happened to him.

After apologizing and explaining that he'd been delayed by a group of rafters who had overshot their pick-up point, and a hiking trio who had begged by Sat-phone to be rescued, we immediately decamped and headed east for the Aichilik River. He had other clients over there, he said, who also needed a lift back to Coldfoot. I told Jen and Cindy we were in luck because the Aichilik lay clear across the Arctic Refuge and we'd be able to see the rest of its coastal plain on the way over.

As we lumbered across the north side of the Sadlerochit Mountains, we retraced the route we had hiked just a week earlier. Ever so quickly we winged over Sadlerochit Spring, now magically mantled in sunlight (but with not a single muskox anywhere in sight), then above the swollen Sadlerochit and Hulahula Rivers. Next came the Okpilak and Jago Rivers, which I had never seen before, followed by an expanse of tussock country that I wouldn't wish on anybody. It didn't seem to bother a band of 50 caribou, though, the first of the Porcupine herd that was now slowly trickling into the coastal plain to take advantage of the blooming cotton grass. This vanguard seemed to be mostly composed of bulls, and we saw no cows with newborn calves. Before leaving for the Brooks Range from Fairbanks, Fran Mauer had told us the herd would probably calve on the Canadian side of the plain. From what Dirk had learned since then, Fran had been right. In any case, it seemed that at least some of the herd was headed for the part of that area coveted by multinational corporations for its possible oil prospects. Shaking my head, I remarked to everyone through my headset on the need to preserve the region for the herd. Even if the caribou didn't use it that summer (and they did, as it turned out), it had been their core calving ground almost every other year. Of course, there were many other species that also needed the area, including countless birds and insects, and for them, too, the coastal plain ought to remain in its natural state.

When we landed at the airstrip next to the Aichilik River, what a surprise and disappointment to see three small tent cities located within a half-mile of each other. Everyone, it seemed, had come here to watch the Porcupine Herd cross the river and head for their favorite feeding ground on the coastal plain. Jen and Cindy commented that we had made the right decision to go to Sunset Pass, where there were no other people and the place felt more like the wilderness it was.

After picking up three backpackers from one of the tent cities, we took off again into the wild not-so-blue yonder, a little anxious about how Dirk was going to avoid the stormy weather he said was between us and Coldfoot.

He first chose a southerly route toward the headwaters of the Kongakut River, dodging thunderheads and lumbering over awesome snow-capped mountains and valleys verdant with the new growth of summer. On many of the south-facing slopes, we could make out bands of Dall sheep, some small ones of rams, others much larger of ewes and lambs, resting or feeding on what we knew were vivid carpets of colorful wildflowers. Then he veered west, heading for Arctic Village, he said, where he would have to leave us for a couple of hours while he flew back to Caribou Pass on the Kongakut River to pick up a rafting party who had to catch a flight to Fairbanks that night.

As we skirted more storm cells and mountain peaks, I recognized many of the features we were flying over. The Kongakut River saddle over to the Sheenjek River slowly slipped under-wing, then zigzagging north, the headwaters of the Hulahula River, finally heading south again down the Chandalar River to Arctic Village.

While waiting for Dirk to return we walked the mile or so into the village with two of the other Coldfoot passengers to take a look at the school there. When we arrived at the scattered complex of red-painted buildings that comprised the school we found some of the older boys playing basketball on the outdoor ball court. We also ran into one of Cindy's next-door neighbors working there, doing summer maintenance work. Small world.

We got back to the airstrip just ahead of a big rainstorm, and when Dirk taxied onto the tarmac a quarter of an hour later, Jen was her usual "Johnny-on-the-spot," urging everyone into immediate action to unload the Beaver and reload it with our own stuff so we could "get the hell out of there before we were caught by the full brunt of the storm." She also wanted to get over to the Coldfoot Cafe before it closed at midnight so we could have a bite to eat. It was touch and go with the weather, though, as we crossed over the many headwater forks of the Chandalar River. The sky was leaden and ominous, and Dirk again had to do some creative dodging back and forth around thunderheads to miss the worst of the huge storm that surrounded us on all sides. But by 11:40 p.m. we were on the final approach to the airport at Coldfoot, touching down just above the heads of two red foxes that had decided to run across the gravel at the last moment.

At 11:50, we jumped into our little Toyota pickup and headed for the local greasy spoon for a late dinner. Dirk and the other two passengers followed us in their own trucks. During our meal, I told Dirk how worried we were about him when he didn't show up on the 22nd, and that it would have made us feel better if he had landed at Sunset Pass to tell us he wouldn't be able to take us over to the Hulahula River. He apologized, and after some coffee we went back to his plane, unloaded our gear into the Toyota, and began the six-hour drive back to Fairbanks.

Post Script: I still wonder what the rest of the story was with our little family of bluethroats. Did the male finally join his mate in catching food and feeding it to the nestlings? I think he did. He was probably just a first-year husband who simply didn't know what was expected of him. It seemed that he was learning as their family grew larger. But I'll never really know, and it will forever remain a mystery. And there's nothing wrong with a mystery, is there.

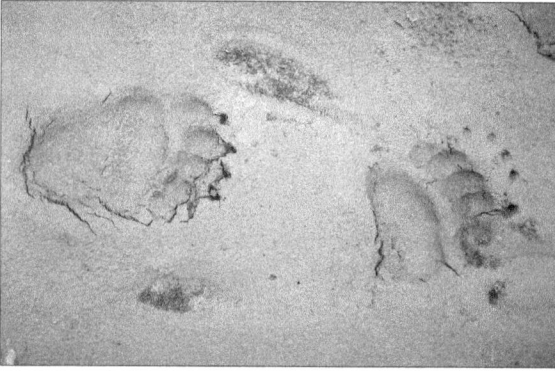

PHOTOS

1. Bluethroat male (USFWS)
2. Grizzly bear tracks
3. Coral fossils

Chapter 5

Caribou Rivers Trek
June 6-July 8, 2002

June 6 –

Finally, after months of talking and a month of planning and preparation, Don Ross and I loaded his 22-foot home-built canoe on top of his little yellow Toyota pick-up, loaded the truck bed full of our camping gear, and left early in the morning from Fairbanks for the village of Circle on the Yukon River. This was to be the longest summer outing both of us had ever taken, and we were anxious to begin.

Muskoxen on Coastal Plain

The Steese Highway was in fair shape as far as Central, but after that it turned into a morass of frost heaves and potholes, slowing us to a crawl almost all the way to Circle. At Birch Creek we stopped in the middle of the bridge for a break and took our first photo of the expedition. The canoe was longer than the pick-up by several feet and seemed precariously perched on top. It was the first time we had looked at the canoe-truck combination critically, and it brought a smile to our faces. Glancing at the water flowing under the bridge, we noticed it was in spate, and it reminded me of the spring in 1999, when I had taken advantage of the high water to float this lovely wild river with my son Steven.

We arrived in Circle at about noon, and while putting the boat in the water and packing it to the brim with our supplies, we struck up a conversation with two Indian fellows, Albert Carrol Jr. and his son, who told us they were related to our friend Richard Carrol in Ft. Yukon. They said they were working on the new lodge being constructed on the riverfront, under the auspices of the Dept. of Commerce. It was being built of logs and looked like it would eventually be a very beautiful structure. Don and I hoped there would be enough tourist traffic to pay the expenses.

After saying goodbye to the Carrols, Don put on his safari desert hat to protect his neck from the sun, started his little 4 stroke Honda 10 h.p. kicker, and away we went. It was the first time I had ridden in his canoe, and it performed far better than I thought. The frame was made of high tensile aluminum, covered with a nylon skin. Only 2 1/2 feet wide, it reminded me of a South American "dugout" canoe, and cut through the swift current of the Yukon River like a charm.

Along the wide expanse of the Yukon we came across large numbers of mergansers, wigeons, furtive Canada geese, and a myriad of Arctic terns that were probably feeding on Shee fish minnows, since the stretch of the Yukon we were on was where our biologist friend Fran Mauer had indicated the Shee fish spawned.

Don stood up in the back to guide the boat through the maze of braids on the river. The water was fairly high, but it was silty, with strong swirls and upwellings, and he wanted to make sure we didn't ground out on a sand or gravel bar. It was a lovely calm day, with high fluffy cumulous clouds crowding a liquid blue sky, and we made the 90 miles down to Ft. Yukon in only five hours, by around 6:00 p.m. When we arrived, there were a few Kwich'in Indian residents chatting on the shore, and one ambled over to warn us to be careful and not leave our boat unattended. So while Don was getting our charter pilot, Kirk Sweetsir's old beater of a pick-up I unloaded the canoe.

When Don got back with the truck he had his friend Heimel Korth with him, along with our third walking partner, Clancy Crawford. Clancy was a teacher from Anchorage, who had flown in to Ft. Yukon that afternoon to join us on our hike across the Brooks Range. Together we loaded the pick-up with our gear and boat and transferred everything over to Kirk's place. Kirk had bought Don Ross's charter business when Don retired in 2000, so we were actually driving Don's old truck over to the house he had sold to Kirk. There we met Kirk's mother Pat, who told us her son was still in the air, but for us to make ourselves at home and she would have dinner ready shortly. While we ate we chatted about our imminent trek from the edge of the Beaufort Sea, across the Arctic Refuge Coastal Plain and the Brooks Range, then down the Sheenjek River to Ft. Yukon. After dinner, the three of us organized our food and gear into piles, one for the Coastal Plain, the second for the mountain crossing, and the third for the trip down the river in my collapsible Alley canoe.

The next day we were up at the crack of dawn, although, since Ft. Yukon is so far north, there is no dawn during the summer. There is 24-hour sunlight. The real reason we were wide awake was because Pat was up early, too, cooking a big breakfast for us of bacon and eggs and fresh fruit before Kirk flew us out to the Coastal Plain. While we were eating, Heimel came over to chat. Not for long, though, because the weather was good, and Kirk planned to take us up to the Jago River as soon as we were ready. In no time, we had everything loaded in the back of his old beater truck, drove out to the airport, stuffed our packs and ourselves into his Cessna 185, cleared for takeoff, and away we went.

Once over the Brooks Range, we were flying above hundreds of rivers and creeks and thousands of snow-capped peaks. En route, Don and Kirk told stories about their predecessor Roger Dowding, who had been killed in a weather-related accident in 1992. Finally, we flew over the high, glacier-studded Romanzof Mountains, then sped down the Aichilik River and over to the delta of the Jago River, our destination. As we did so, we could see large numbers of caribou from the Porcupine herd grazing quietly on each side of the Aichilik, punctuated by a light brown grizzly bear roaming in between. We followed the Jago, with its labyrinth of braided gravel bars, almost all the way to the coastline of the Beaufort Sea, where Kirk found a solid stretch of gravel and sand to set us down on. After some easy small talk about the wonderful weather and the high birth rate of the caribou herd this year, Kirk took off and headed for Arctic Village to pick up another group of clients. We found a good flat spot on the dryas terrace of the east bank of the river, then set up our tents. At first, it was a little awkward getting organized, but we knew it wouldn't take long to get into a routine.

After a cup of tea and a sandwich, sent compliments of Don's wife Kyoko, Don and Clancy and I walked out toward the coast on the tundra. Clancy was a little tired, so he went back to camp early. Then, when the tundra became soggier and soggier the farther inland from the river we slogged, Don and I finally decided it wasn't worth getting our feet any wetter and we, too, trudged back toward the river.

While in the tundra, we spotted a rich variety of birds, including long-tailed and parasitic jaegers, glaucous gulls, white-fronted geese, sandhill cranes, pintails, long-tailed ducks, stilt sandpipers and semipalmated and pectoral sandpipers. Golden plovers, Lapland longspurs, red and red-necked phalaropes, and a rock ptarmigan were also there. We came across a mystery bird, too, a redpoll with a yellow breast, something we later learned was caused when redpolls fed next to the yellow pollen of willow catkins. Most of the birds we encountered were in some form of display mode, especially the longspurs with their evocative tinkling song, as they fluttered skyward, then glided slowly down to the tundra again.

Wildflowers were in bloom everywhere, including wind anemone (from Greek *anemos*, wind), purple mountain saxifrage and black oxytrope. The dainty red catkins of the tiny least willow (*salix rotundifolia*) were so pretty they could have qualified as wildflowers. Farther along, we almost bumped into a cow caribou with its gangly-legged newborn calf; a parky squirrel, recently emerged from its long sleep underground, scolded us with its telltale *sik sik* alert call; and on a tall *nunapik*, the Eskimo name for a raised nubbin of land formed by continuous deposition of organic material over 1000s of years, we found hairy pellets filled with lemming bones burped up there not long ago by a snowy owl.

Don commented on the sparkling skies. Having flown countless times over this area, he reminded Clancy and me that the Coastal Plain was usually socked in with fog as thick as pea soup. From my own experience in 2001, at Sunset Pass in the Sadlerochit Mountains, I didn't expect it to be so sunny, windless and fog-free. In the distance, to the south, not more than 20-30 miles away, we could see both the Sadlerochits and the much higher Romanzof Mountains that we had just flown over. And a real bonus: only three large winter mosquitoes lethargically buzzed around to greet us.

After a rest, I walked upriver to the melting remains of a long snowdrift that had created a pond next to the river. There I spotted a red-throated loon watching the spectacle of several pairs of long-tailed ducks in the middle of a mating frenzy on the river, chasing each other, diving, flying up briefly, diving again and again, spray flying in all directions – expressing for me the frenetic spirit of the Coastal Plain at this time of year. Don pointed out an Arctic fox randomly zigzagging across the tundra as it hunted for voles and lemmings. It was in the middle of its color change and had a black line running up and down its rump. When we arrived back in camp we got a good look at a peregrine falcon cruising overhead, and we wondered if its aerie was far away.

While we were preparing for bed, a herd of muskoxen came into view on the higher east bank of the river, then wandered over to within a hundred feet of our tents, where they began feeding on the dryas and willows. There was one big bull, with a large boss at the base of its horns, and nine cows, but no calves. When the animals crossed an intervening snowdrift, they fell through the snow into a deepwater creek at the edge of the snow, bellowing loudly as they went down. We laughed, but I'm sure it was a rather cool surprise for the animals, in spite of their thick qiviut wool coat. While the big bull fed calmly near our tents, the females bumped and fussed at each other constantly. From inside our tent Don shot some good videotape footage of them. They were still in the neighborhood, slowly ambling toward the Beaufort Sea as I zipped myself into my sleeping bag for the night – not "night" as one usually thinks of it, for there is no night in the Arctic during the summer months, only the perpetual magic light of the solstice sun rolling relentlessly across the northern sky.

When I crawled out of the tent in the morning the muskoxen were gone. Over coffee we wondered why there weren't any newborns, and suspected it might be grizzly bear predation. We'd been told that grizzlies had learned to penetrate the circular defense posture of muskoxen and grab the calves from their mothers. It was a lovely sunny day, though, and the black-striped Arctic fox was back, bouncing around the tundra and willows searching for his morning meal.

After breakfast we broke camp and headed upriver. On top of the snowdrift where I had watched the loon and long-tailed ducks the evening before, we found fresh grizzly bear sign. From its tracks, it looked like it had been heading directly for our tents, then veered back upriver again, probably wary of our man-smell. We figured he was following the spoor of the muskoxen.

Near mid-day, we encountered two snowy owls perched on their respective *nunapiks*. It was nice to see their big, fluffy-white bulbous bodies again after more than ten years. There are a lot of these ancient *nunapiks* on the Coastal Plain, some of them quite tall and rich in vegetation, indicating longtime residence of snowy owls there. On one of these I found a large pellet containing the bones of a parky squirrel, among others stuffed with bones of voles and lemmings.

We continued following the Jago upstream, until at a little after noon we arrived at a cold freshwater creek coming in from the east. It was too deep to hop across in hiking boots, so we changed into our river crossing footgear. Mine were an old pair of neoprene booties my nephew Fox had given me years ago. Opposite this point on the river was a high bluff where we thought we might spot the aerie of the peregrine we saw yesterday. On glassing it carefully, though, we found nothing.

Nine nervous yearling caribou showed up as we walked, and we spotted a pair of semipalmated sandpipers, among many other species of birds. Later, we came across the pathetic remains of a baby muskox, possibly killed by the same grizzly whose tracks we'd found in the morning. We had heard that muskoxen numbers on the Coastal Plain were declining due to grizzly attacks, and this seemed to offer some proof of that. There was nothing anybody could do about it, however. Nature would simply have to run its course until the muskoxen developed strategies to protect themselves. Two golden eagle feathers lying next to the calf's carcass told us these large birds were somewhere in the neighborhood.

We camped just upriver from the dead calf on a flat stretch of dryas terrace. Over a dinner of rehydrated Rice Alfredo, liberally doused with Frank's hot sauce, we chatted about Clancy's high school teaching experience. He had mostly enjoyed it, he said, but recently retired so he could devote himself to his summer adventure guiding business. This was the first walk in many years he had been on where he wasn't working as the guide. With Don, we chatted about his experience in Cuba a couple of years before, when he traveled there with the "Pastors for Peace" emergency relief effort. While in Havana, he attended a conference at which Fidel Castro spoke. He said he was impressed with what he had seen in Cuba, especially with their social, education and health infrastructure.

We talked more after dinner around a small campfire that I'd kindled with dry willow sticks. I'm always amazed at how readily people communicate around a campfire, and I'm convinced it has something to do with our "primal beginnings." In terms of our evolution, humans have spent much more time around a fire than we ever did in a house.

Golden plovers were whistling their incessant *tooleek* as we chatted by the fire. Clancy said they were among his favorite birds. Mine too, I echoed, not only for their handsome colors, but also because of their annual globe trotting behavior. Among birds, they are one of the champion long-distance migrants. Alaskan golden plovers travel in large sweeping flocks to their wintering grounds in South America by first flying southeast across northern Canada where they gorge themselves with crowberries, then to Labrador and Nova Scotia. From there, they travel south directly over the Atlantic Ocean and Brazil, finally to the pampas of Argentina and Bolivia, where they spend the winter months. They return to Alaska over western South America, Central America, the Mississippi Valley and the Canadian Prairie provinces. Altogether, they travel nearly 20,000 miles both ways.

Before calling it quits for the day, we wondered if the fog gathering to the north would envelope us before midnight, and when it would disappear the next morning. Given the nature of the Coastal Plain, it most certainly would eventually reach us, but for now the sun was still shining to the northwest, its rays brightly shimmering on the dancing waters of the Jago River directly in front of us. As the fog advanced, it reminded me of a gray wash of watercolor spreading slowly across a painting. Adding to the canvas, two young bull caribou grazed placidly nearby.

In my tent, while writing in my journal, I inspected a snowy owl feather I'd picked up earlier in the day. I held the fuzzy-edged, black-spotted white feather against the late evening sun and marveled at its artistic qualities. Mother Nature was quite the artist.

The fog did come in that night, totally enveloping the camp in a dark cloak of cold moist air, making it difficult sleeping for me. I finally put on my down jacket, zipped my bag over my head, and slept. Don had no problem, since he'd brought a heavy down bag. I should have done the same.

June 9 was a short day. We walked at the leisurely pace of one mph, and decided to stop early and camp on the Okerokovik River, near its confluence with the Jago. Okerokovik is a corruption of the Inupiat Eskimo, *uqurevik*, meaning "place where blubber is cached." There we came across a mated pair of handsome ruddy turnstones, which I hadn't seen since the spring migration in Hooper Bay more than 20 years earlier. Turnstones, I learned, have some unique traits among sandpipers. Not only do they return to the same nesting sites every year, they mate with the same partners, making them monogamous like ourselves. Both male and female have brood patches, help each other incubate the eggs, and they both tend the young after they leave the nest, although the male does most of the work in this regard.

Since first arriving on the Jago we had been noticing brown cocoons on the ground. On the Okerokovik we noticed even more of them. While investigating one of them more closely, I discovered a black pupa inside, very close to hatching into a butterfly. I wondered which butterfly it would metamorphose into. I guessed maybe the arctic chryxus, which is the species I'd seen most often during my trips to the Arctic.

After pitching our tents, Don and I walked up the river for a half-mile or so, where we saw more caribou, including one newborn, making our total for the day around forty. Later I found turnstones again, two pairs this time, just down the river from our camp. I watched them roll small stones in the riverbed while searching for food, and suspected they were nesting close by, since they were extremely aggressive toward any would-be predators that approached. When jaegers even flew near the area, both pairs of turnstones took off in hot pursuit, routing them every time.

Over another willow fire we chatted about the similarities and differences between Buddhists and Christians, and the connections between humans and animals. It goes without saying, we agreed, that birds and caribou don't have religious beliefs, but neither do they need them to keep them behaving decently in the world. And so with us humans, the wellsprings of our moral behavior don't originate with religion. They go much farther back to our animal origins.

During the night I heard a bird call that was totally unfamiliar to me. Its hollow *whoo whoo whoo whoo* sounded a little like a small foghorn. Then in the early morning I heard it again, repeated over and over not far from the tent. But it was so tantalizing I didn't want to disturb it by searching for it, so I just lay in my sleeping bag listening to it till it finally faded in the distance. It became our mystery bird until a few days later when serendipity turned my Peterson's Field Guide to the page describing the flight display call of the male pectoral sandpiper. Mystery solved.

After breakfast I walked over to check on the turnstones. They were still there, busily turning stones and searching for their morning meal. On the way back, I spotted a male savannah sparrow, with his mustard colored eyebrow and his buzzy song. Above me, two immature golden eagles were cruising at altitude, and much lower a male northern harrier dressed in his handsome white plumage was being chased by an angry turnstone. On a tundra *nunapik*, two long-tailed jaegers were mating. It was now time for them to start laying eggs and go about the serious business of raising their family.

Just before we broke camp, a big brown grizzly showed up, making a beeline for a small herd of caribou, including five newborns. As soon as they got his wind, though, away they went at top speed toward the northeast. Realizing it was fruitless to pursue them, the bear stopped, sat down and started digging for bear root. If he couldn't get himself a caribou, the roots of the *hedysarum alpinum* would have to do.

During our trek up the Okerokovik we saw our first lesser yellow legs of the trip, and my first ever buff-breasted sandpipers, with the male's very different mating behavior – first fluttering above the ground with hanging bright yellow legs, then standing with one wing up in the air, followed by a two-wings-in-the-air display. The male was so intent on this that he allowed me to approach closely enough to take his photo. Surrounding him was a veritable wildflower garden of mountain avens (*Dryas integrifolia*) and Pallas's wallflower (*Erysimum pallasii*), along with glacier avens, purple mountain saxifrage, windflower and northern oxytrope.

After lunch, we found a recently dropped cow antler. It still had fresh blood on the end that had been attached to the head. Since cows lose their antlers right after giving birth to their calves, we knew this cow now had a young one running alongside her.

Once again we camped early, at about 3:00, on the west fork of the Okerokovik. Right away we encountered turnstones, four of them, in action. One was giving chase to a jaeger, and three others were pursuing a pair of gyrfalcons. A while later three buff-breasted sandpipers showed up on the tundra, the male raising one wing then both wings, hoping this display would entice the two females watching nearby to mate with him.

After returning to Fairbanks, I learned more of the details behind the courtship display of buffies, as some people call them. We had inadvertently located our camp next to the lekking site of these long-distance migrants, who travel each year all the way from Argentina to the Coastal Plain to nest and raise their young. Unbeknownst to us, there were probably other competing males not far away showing their own finely marbled underwings to the same females. For it is on the lekking ground that the females examine their potential mates, then select one for copulation. The white flash of underwing lining is apparently what first brings in the females and is the primary focus of their attention. Up to six females may gather around the lekking court of a single male, perhaps swapping notes about the relative qualities of his wing feathers. At first, the male makes almost no sound.

An article by J.P. Myers describes what happens next:

As the females approach, he first hulks over, ruffling his
back feathers and starting a quickened tread. Abruptly he
rears back, thrusting his head up and wings out, keeping his
bill parallel to the ground while marching in place. Only now
does he vocalize, a subtle tic-tic-tic *timed to match the slow*
footsteps taken in place. As a crowning gesture he draws his
neck in and throws his bill back, gazing catatonically toward
the Arctic sky. The females crowd forward, inspecting minute
details of his underwing.

Then one of three things happens. Either the females in concert decide the male is a worthy suitor and they all stay to mate with him, or they
may steal away while he is still in full display to check out the underwing
qualities of another male on an adjoining part of the lek. This is apparently
what happens most, until finally the females make their decision. Frequently,
however, something happens that totally disrupts the best nuptial efforts of
the displaying male. Suddenly a neighboring male may burst down upon his
competitor, mounting and viciously pecking him on neck and head, thereby
breaking up the courtship. The interloper then flies back to his own lekking
territory, followed post haste by all of the female inspectors. There the same
display pattern begins again until it too may be interrupted by the original
male or by yet another competitor lurking nearby. The females move back
and forth from one exhibiting male to another as their wedding parties are
crashed. Finally, at some point, a balance is struck and the females all mate by
turn with the excited male. So it is that at least one male's heroic efforts will
not go unrequited.

Not far from camp another small herd of 25 cow caribou with newborn
calves showed up, the calves capering about on the snow bank, still not very
sociable with each other but having fun running back and forth. One cow had
twins, the larger one nursing mom. Meanwhile, we watched as another calf
nervously searched for its mother, couldn't find her, and kept on going in the
opposite direction of the herd, thus making itself a prime target for roaming
predators. A number of the cows were grazing in its general direction and
finally one of them came down from the knoll it was on to search for the
calf. But it stopped short when it didn't see the calf anymore, and ambled
back up the knoll again. With such an unconcerned mother, and two golden
eagles showing up overhead a few minutes later, the calf didn't have much of
a chance by itself.

I wandered back down the river a hundred yards or so to search for the
turnstones again, and I found three of them, one male with two females. The
male was ruddier than the females, and I wondered if they practiced polygyny.
I saw more aggressive action by these turnstones, too, first against jaeger and

raven intruders, then later in hot pursuit of a male northern harrier. They'd spotted the harrier from more than 200 yards away, then mobbed him with the help of two golden plovers. What a spectacle that was.

Just before bedtime, three more small herds of caribou passed near our camp, all headed southeast. Were they already returning to Canada?

June 11 was overcast, and there was even a light snowfall before we got up in the morning. Another pectoral sandpiper was sounding his foghorn – an apt call for the weather this day. When I walked down to check on the turnstones, I found four of them, two mated pair, but with extremely close nesting territories, it seemed. Were these genetically related birds, or was this some sort of survival strategy? Or both, I wondered. They certainly cooperated closely when chasing predator birds from the neighborhood. Near our tents a pair of buff-breasted sandpipers fed peacefully. They were very handsome birds, indeed, with their creamy buff color, especially when observed through good binoculars, like those my dad had given me before he died. Thanks, Dad.

After breaking camp, we followed the river toward the southeast. In the distance we spotted a small herd of about 40 cows and 30 newborns heading our way, but they soon stopped to feed on the greening tundra. In the riverbed we noticed the willows were getting taller, and we began seeing new species of birds, including willow ptarmigan, with their husky spring call, and tree and fox sparrows singing like virtuoso minstrels. On the water a female canvasback showed up, along with a pair of green-winged teal. We also found the remains of a male bluethroat. It had been recently killed and was missing its head. We wondered if this was because the brain was the most nutritious part of the bird. The first arctic chryxus butterflies began fluttering above the tundra, so it seemed the pupae from the cocoons were completing their long metamorphosis.

We called it a day in late afternoon, and made camp behind a high willow grove on the riverbank. It was a good tent site, since it was out of the wind and on flat, grass-covered ground. A gray-cheeked thrush welcomed us with its characteristic "wolf whistle" song, followed by a handsome male yellow warbler cheerfully singing, "I'm sweet, oh so sweet." While Clancy prepared hot water for our dinners over his camp stove, I busied myself building a fire with some of the large dry willow sticks we found there. Don was checking out a redpoll nest he had just found. Later, as we took our first bites of rehydrated dinner, it started to snow very large flakes. When the snowfall became even heavier, we decided to retire to our respective tents and catch up on our journals. My notation for the day begins: *I am presently inside our green dome tent (or as Don calls it, our "casa verde"), watching the fluffy snowflakes fall and quickly begin to mat the ground with snow cover. We wonder how many inches will be on the ground by morning. No birds are singing now, and we hope things go well for them. At about 8:30 the gray-cheeked thrush starts to sing its fluted cat-call song, and within minutes most of the snow has stopped falling. This seems to be a pattern among birds. Today I learned from Don and Clancy that the compass declination at this point on the Coastal Plain is 32 degrees. That is, the magnetic pole is 32 degrees east of true north.*

We awoke with clearing skies and a medley of bird song, including our gray-cheeked thrush and a fox sparrow. We also heard our first Wilson's snipe winnowing high overhead. What a weird but lovely sound, especially on the Coastal Plain.

As I kindled the fire in the morning, I used some old dry shoots of wild celery I found growing near our tents. It was amazing how the flora were steadily increasing in variety as we got closer to the mountains. Lupine, rhododendron, mountain heather, dryas and blueberry were all beginning to blossom forth. Soon we would have a veritable carpet of wildflowers around us.

On striking camp we came across an old tent ring of rocks once used by the Nunamiut Eskimos during their spring caribou hunts. There was another one nearby, plus some old caribou antlers. Theirs must have been a tough life, even in that pristine wilderness. Of course, they never had any idea of the contemporary meaning of "pristine" or our concept of "wilderness." The land was simply there for subsistence and survival.

A journal entry for the day reads: *We're slowly making our way up the Okerokovik at about six miles per day, according to our map. Another snipe winnowed overhead as we walked, and we soon came across two pair of yellow wagtails. These are an Asian species that, like the wheatear and bluethroat, spend their winters in southern Asia. Speaking of bluethroats, right after spotting the second pair of wagtails, I heard the telltale cricket chirps of a male bluethroat. I quickly found him on a willow, performing his varied repertoire of song. Clancy and Don had not seen or heard bluethroats before, so we stopped for lunch on the spot and watched and listened to him for the better part of an hour. Even his spouse showed up, and he strutted his stuff for her in the air while we watched. His display flight was similar to that of the Lapland longspur and American pipit. And what a beautiful blue and rust necklace he wore.*

As we ambled along the east bank of the river, we saw an increasing number of birds. A pair of harlequins showed up. Both the male and female were still together, signaling that her eggs still had not all been laid. Once that happens and the male has fulfilled his purpose, he bids farewell to his ephemeral mate and heads for the ocean. It's up to her to do all of the incubation and child rearing.

In mid-afternoon, I spotted two more bluethroats. I couldn't believe our good luck to see four bluethroats in one day. We watched the male do a full display, first, flying round and round about a hundred feet above the female, singing non-stop as he flew, chirping, twittering, warbling, buzzing and more. When he finally landed on the ground he chased the female, fanned his rusty tail feathers and quickly mated with her. Then he jumped into the air again and repeated the whole ritual.

We camped just a short ways upriver from the bluethroats. Right across the river we spotted our first upland sandpiper, with his characteristic bubbly whistle. Then, incredibly, a gray jay sailed over our heads and landed on top of a tall willow on the other side of the river. Normally, gray jays are associated with coniferous forest, and this guy was way outside his usual range. There was no forest for more than a hundred miles south of us. He was a true pioneer. We also spotted a pomarine jaeger cruising low over the tundra. Pomarines are the largest of the jaegers and have rounded tail projections twisted ninety degrees to the rest of their body, a characteristic difference from its cousins, the long-tailed and parasitic jaegers.

The day turned out clear with fluffy cumulous clouds in a cerulean blue sky. The conditions made the high Romanzof Mountains to the south appear even closer than they were. And seeing the lower Sadlerochit Mountains over to the west brought back some good memories from the previous summer, when Jen and Cindy and I spent 16 days backpacking in the area. While scanning the horizon to the north we watched the silhouette of a lone cow moose walking resolutely across the tundra toward us, every now and then glancing nervously behind her. Was she worried about a trailing grizzly bear? And had the bear gotten her calf? She finally disappeared over a hummock, heading in the direction of the foothills of the mountains. We wouldn't be moving that resolutely, but by the next day we would be in those foothills too.

From my notes: *Don and I are presently inside the tent looking towards the high snow-mantled Romanzofs. The late night light reflecting from the mountains is particularly pretty now. A snipe is winnowing above us and an upland sandpiper is bubbling on the other side of the river. Rock and willow ptarmigan are laughing at each other and at us, it seems, in their own peculiar way. What a special area, this Coastal Plain.*

June 13 –

Again from my journal: *The fog came in last night at 10:30, but was gone by early this morning before we got up. In spite of the fog, upland sandpipers awakened me several times with their twittering bubble-whistle. This song has been described as "weird and unearthly" by some, but their flight song is even more so. I liken it to the "wolf whistle" of male humans as a pretty female happens by.*

I was still in my bag at 7:00 a.m., but the sun was shining, making it warm in the tent for the first time since the beginning of the walk. It was good to be warm again, but I knew it would be much more interesting outside, so I unzipped the tent, greeted the world, and climbed out. Clancy was already moving around, stoking up his little Whisper Lite stove for coffee and tea water. We chatted awhile, making enough noise to rouse Don, then ate our oatmeal and granola breakfasts.

It was so sunny and warm that we made another cup of tea and visited around a little willow fire I'd made, then just took our time breaking camp. When we were ready to hit the trail again I checked my watch. It was 9:30. Why I even bothered to wear a watch during our trek I couldn't fathom, except that maybe it gave me some artificial notion of structure where there was none. Don didn't wear his watch because he said he wanted to experience only the rhythms of nature. Even with my watch, though, I knew I reveled in these rhythms too.

At mid-morning we came across yet another bluethroat, a male proudly displaying his rust and blue chest to the world, cricket-chirping like there was no tomorrow. Clancy said that as he listened to the call he was transported back to his family's farm in the Midwest, where real crickets chirping were a unique characteristic of the auditory landscape. A short while later, another pair of yellow wagtails presented themselves, the male busily singing his continuous *tsewee tsewee tsewee*, while dancing aerially in a random circle around his territory. As a female watched close by, the male bounced up and down in the air, erratically raising his tail and spreading his wings, trying his hardest to entice the female to stick around. Once he pursued her, probably trying to whisper sweet nothings in her ear, but she would have none of it for now and left. No matter, he kept up his persistently hopeful song and dance, filling the air with music and movement.

During lunch we watched two pairs of harlequins consorting nearby. With their red, white and black mottling, the male is the most colorful of our northern ducks. They are my favorite species of duck, not only because of their vivid colors, but also because of their preference for wild surroundings and white water.

After another rest stop near the mountains, we started walking again. All of a sudden, there was a scruffy pile of light gray fur lying on the riverbed directly ahead of us. We knew it was a wolf, but why so inert and unmoving, we wondered. Was he dead? In a moment we learned he was anything but dead. Slowly, at first, he moved, turned toward us, lethargically got up on all fours, sniffed, bolted a few yards, stopped, turned again to quizzically investigate us for a few seconds, then hightailed it toward the riverbank. There he stopped, probed us with his inquiring eyes, then loped off at a steady gait up the valley till he disappeared from view. We were a little baffled by his behavior, but finally decided he must have been sleeping off a big feed, very possibly on a little caribou.

We set up camp on another flat terrace of mountain dryas. There was very little water running in what was now just a sporadic creek, so we had to go a little farther than usual for our supply of tea water. After our cup of tea, Don and I strolled up the Okerokovik for a mile or so to see what we could see. But we found only a lone cow caribou searching for what we speculated might have been the calf that was now in the belly of the lethargic wolf we'd just seen.

We looked up when we heard the raspy call of a rough-legged hawk, and there he was, perched high above us on one of a stair-stepped series of limestone tors. He was evidently doing sentinel duty near his aerie, because when a golden eagle approached he quickly and resolutely gave chase, forcing the eagle to take a detour around the area. On the ground, we came across our first shooting stars, or what I like to call *dodecatheon* because of the way the scientific name rolls so perfectly off the tip of the tongue.

During dinner I was casually glancing up toward the ridge just behind us when I caught the movement of what at first looked like a rather strangely behaving caribou. On glassing it, however, I saw it was another wolf. He stopped, sat down on the slope, watched us for a while, lay down, got up and indolently ambled around, then lay down again, this time watching caribou slowly but cautiously file by, both above and below him. Some of the caribou stopped and stared at him, almost seeming to taunt him. Finally, he got up and nonchalantly strolled back over the ridge where the caribou had come from. By the wolf's behavior, and the presence of the other wolf we had seen earlier, we figured they had a den somewhere nearby. What a treat – two wolves in the space of only a few hours.

While collecting some drinking water from the creek, I was curious about what the turnstones we'd seen earlier might be eating, so I turned over some of the cobbles to check for larvae. I was amazed at how many there actually were, and could only guess at their myriad species. I'd already seen a couple of caddisflies mating, so knew some of them had to be caddisfly larvae. But there undoubtedly were stonefly, black fly and dragonfly larvae, plus many others. No wonder, there were so many turnstones and other sandpipers on the Coastal Plain. With horror, I tried to imagine what oil development would do to their numbers.

Rain, rain, go away! It started early in the morning and had that certain quality to it that made me think of Noah's ark. At about 8:00, when it seemed the rain might be abating, we got up and ate some breakfast. The river was flowing again, reminding me of the previous year at Sunset Pass, when the same thing happened to Jen and Cindy and me. Just as it seemed the creek was going to dry up, it would rain and the flow of water was replenished.

As soon as we struck camp the clouds rushed in again and the rain resumed, this time accompanied by sleet and snow. By now we were headed for the Aichilik River and, in spite of the rain, decided to follow through with our original plan to walk across the foothills of the mountains. We knew we wouldn't have the view of the Coastal Plain or the Arctic Ocean that we'd hoped for, but who knew what we might see? Since I wanted to avoid the tussocks, I climbed up a ridgeline that started immediately above our camp, and followed it for as far as I could. Don and Clancy took the lower route through the tussocks.

When I neared the top of the ridge, I surprised a large herd of about 500 cows and newborn calves resting. They must have been a part of the herd we'd seen the evening before that had been taunting the wolf. They were extremely skittish, and hightailed it as soon as I loomed into view. As they quickly moved away they made a constant burping noise, which I at first mistook for a covey of willow ptarmigan. The caribou slipped like phantoms down the mountain en masse, reminding me of a river. Don and Clancy met some of them as they were walking 300 feet below me in the tundra, which further spooked the herd, causing them to move east toward the Aichilik.

At this point the ridge line began to peter out, so I carefully climbed down and joined Don and Clancy on the tundra. After crossing a deep gully we found some stable ground at the base of the mountains that turned out to be pretty good for walking. But the rain and sleet made it soaking wet, and when my feet started complaining I knew the Goretex liners of my boots had failed the test. Since I'd paid so much for them and had only worn them for a year, Clancy advised me to send the boots back to REI where I'd purchased them.

We continued to see caribou on all sides of us, and we wished we'd had more of a view to the north, where we were certain there were thousands more of them. But that wasn't to be. Even the bird life was scarce, although we saw a pair of pipits along the way. Clancy told us a little later that he had found their nest, which he said had several eggs in it.

In the early afternoon we reached an overlook above the Aichilik River. The sleet and rain had abated somewhat by then, and through a film of mist and ragged ends of fog we could see aufeis covered the river for miles in both directions. The ice made us feel even colder than we were, so we figured it was time to have lunch. We huddled under the lee of a large rock and ate some peanut butter and crackers along with a Cliff bar. Given the circumstances, those usually boring foods tasted pretty darn good to us.

When we resumed our trek the wind continued to bluster and gust for the next couple of hours. About a mile north of the Aichilik airstrip, in a stand of tall willows, we came across another male bluethroat chirping and warbling and twittering his repertoire of happy song as though his life depended upon it. But as much as I tried, I couldn't find the elusive bird. Since it was so windy, he had hidden deep within the willows, and even with binocs I couldn't pinpoint his location.

On arriving at the airstrip, we found a wealthy old Canadian acquaintance Glen Davis and his adventurer-guide Ken Madsen camped at the north end waiting to be ferried over to the Kongakut River. This wouldn't happen till the next day, they said, so we had the opportunity to visit with them. They were there with Ken's two older daughters, both in their twenties, and a male friend of the daughters. When we first arrived, Ken was taking photos of wild lupine. I told him of our bluethroat encounter just downriver, and soon afterward he and the others took off to try to find him. None of them had ever seen a bluethroat before.

Our charter pilot, Kirk Sweetsir, had dropped some extra food for us at the airstrip, and we found it still intact, except that he had mistakenly put our Sheenjek River food (cheese, tortillas, etc.) in with it. He'd also forgotten to leave the bear barrels upside down, and I found rainwater had entered through the top. No matter, we'd discuss details for the Sheenjek River food drop with Kirk when we saw him the next day.

By late afternoon a welcome sun began to shine through thinning clouds, and we could seriously think about drying out our wet clothes and equipment. My boots were soaked, and I vowed to send them back to REI as soon as I got back to civilization. After taking care of our wet gear, we organized our food resupply, then ate the steak dinner that Don's wife had sent us. As we were eating I watched a pair of pipits feeding near our tents. Earlier I had found their nest with six brown eggs in it.

In the evening I walked up on a high tundra bench to take some pictures of the area. The river valley was wider than I remembered it from the previous year. With low rolling foothills in the foreground, and tall snow-peaked mountains far to the south, it was truly a lovely area. I could now understand why it was a preferred destination for many guided hikes.

As we turned in for the night, the sun and shadow combination on the mountains was almost magical. A mixed herd of about 200 caribou rested or fed on the gently sloping hills of the east side of the river, but most of the animals were young bulls with small black-velvet nubbins of growing antlers. Every now and then a thundering explosion broke the silence of the valley, caused by aufeis sloughing off into the river, still quite high due to the recent rains. We were hoping that by the time we got to the Leffingwell River the water level on the Aichilik would be down enough to be able to cross to the other side and continue our hike up the Leffingwell.

During breakfast the next morning a herd of about 500 cows and calves nonchalantly ambled north behind us, and across the river another mixed herd of the same number of young bulls and cows casually fed on the tundra. Suddenly, many of these animals started moving quickly upriver. I glassed the area to see why. Two dark brown grizzly bears slowly lumbered along the other side of the Aichilik. They weren't the least bit concerned about us, probably because they were already well fed on bearroot and newborn calves.

Ken Madsen had told us that both Kirk Sweetsir and another pilot, Dirk Nickisch from Coyote Air, were going to fly in to the Aichilik strip sometime around noon, so we decided to stick around till they came by in order to give Kirk instructions about our cheese and tortillas, which were supposed to have been a part of our Sheenjek drop.

Dirk came in first to take Ken and his crew over to the Kongakut River in two loads. Then when Kirk finally buzzed in, I kiddingly pointed out his error with the cheese and torts, and gave him his new instructions. He assured us the food would be back in his freezer by evening, and that its next stop would be the Sheenjek River the day before we arrived there. A thunderstorm was threatening, so we picked up stakes and headed for our next camp, located about two miles upriver.

The farther up the river we walked, the more aufeis there was, which Don thought might be due to the late springs and cool summers of both 2000 and 2001. We wondered if it would be the same this year. For the sake of the birds and caribou, we hoped not, since both had suffered population declines those years.

Speaking of caribou, we now spied more than a thousand of them spread out on the rounded flanks of the hills across the river, the most we had seen so far. Near where we planned to camp we also spotted nine Dall sheep grazing on the new spring green of the mountain slopes. And wildflowers were in bloom everywhere, including white mountain avens, wind anemones, Arctic poppies and the ever-redolent Kamchatka rhododendrons.

We arrived at our tent perch overlooking the river just in time to escape a gully-washing downpour that dumped buckets of rain on our tents. As the drops fell, the constant booming of huge chunks of aufeis breaking off into the river heightened the thunderous effect of the storm. And the pelting rain on my tent poignantly reminded me of how inadequate my waterproofing job had been back in Fairbanks. Thanks to Clancy's Aquaseal, however, I was able to reseal most of the stitching at the troublesome base of the tent. But the storm didn't last long. After an hour we were back outside again. And when a pair of red-breasted mergansers flew by below us, I asked Don if there were fish in the river. He said he'd seen people catch Arctic char and grayling in it, so that probably explained their presence there.

During dinner we heard a couple of robins scolding each other, then later a male robin singing a little off-key. Probably the males had just arrived and were setting up nesting territories. I remarked to Don and Clancy that I'd sing off-key like that, too, if it had been a year since I'd last sung my spring song.

While glassing what Clancy referred to as the "sensual" landscape of rounded hills on the other side of the ice-mantled river, we estimated there were as many as 10,000 caribou roaming and feeding and resting in the tundra. We wondered where they'd come from. The light from the evening sun made them stand out from their surroundings more than usual, but surely they couldn't all have been there before. Any way you cut it, there were more than I had ever seen before, yet it was only a fraction of the number in the Porcupine herd that these were a part of. Don referred to them as a herd of porkies, and said we had the best seats in the house for viewing them. He was right, and we watched them until late into the white night.

Father's Day –

According to Clancy, in the past there had been a gyrfalcon aerie on one of the rocky precipices just upriver. After breaking camp we checked it out and, although there were plenty of old sticks and streams of white guano spilling down the cliff face, indicating much use of the nest by ravens in previous years, there was no evidence of recent use by gyrfalcons. Ravens are notoriously messy with their guano. Gyrs and other falcons are not.

Not far from the old aerie we came to where the river crashed into a rock face and forced us to make a choice between fording the rushing water or climbing to the top of the precipice and going down the other side. As much as we tried, we could not find a good place to ford the deep racing channels of the Aichilik, now in spate because of the rains. So we decided to hump the 800 feet up to where we could circumvent the steep cliffs, then gradually wend our way back down again to the river. During our climb we surprised a small herd of caribou, also on its way to the top, and a number of Dall sheep ewes and lambs, which we suspected were part of the same small flock we had seen the day before grazing and eating mineral salts near the old raven nest.

While climbing down the other side of the mountain we spotted a male horned lark perched on a rock and surrounded by a wonderland of wildflowers, including Arctic poppies, cinquefoil, lupine, arnica and the aromatic moss campion. Once at the bottom, we were visited by a Say's phoebe, then a small flock of cliff swallows that was beginning to nest on the side of the rock precipice facing the Aichilik and, according to Clancy, were probably the farthest north colony of these swallows in the U.S.

After lunch, as we hoofed it over the tundra toward the Aichilik River, we encountered a large number of nesting Smith's longspurs. One of the nests we found had four buff-colored eggs in it, and the sweet twittering song of the males could be heard all around us. These birds were on the Alaska Bird

Watch list because of their rapidly dwindling numbers, so I was amazed to see so many of them. Nearby, as we approached a high bank of the river, we were surprised by a female merlin that suddenly flew up in front of us. Since these falcons often nest on the ground, she had probably been brooding her eggs.

In the same location we met many mixed herds of caribou, one of which I attracted so close with my waving-hat trick that I was able to get a couple of fairly good photos of them. There were still thousands of caribou on the opposite side of the river, most randomly grazing, some lying down, and a few small herds straying onto patches of aufeis to stand in the cool aura of the ice. It was truly an awesome sight. When a large contingent of the animals began moving quickly north, I glassed around to see what had disturbed them. My hunch was a bear and, sure enough, a big grizzly soon came into view, nonchalantly crossing the aufeis. When he reached the flowing river itself he carefully selected a shallow route across some riffles, even lifting his stomach to avoid getting his fur too wet. We all laughed because it seemed such a human thing to do. When he approached the high bank where we were perched about 200 yards away, he glanced in our direction and stopped to stare at us. Then he continued up the bank where he stopped again, stared intently at us for about a minute, then suddenly wheeled in the opposite direction and lumbered off, periodically glancing behind him as he marched north. While Don taped him with his video camera, he guessed he had been shot at by hunters, who often flew into the area in August.

All afternoon caribou were our constant companions. When we finally made camp they were still on all sides of us, along with a small flock of 13 Dall sheep ewes and lambs. We set up our tents on the edge of a stand of tall willows, not far from an old wolf den. A small creek flowed in front of us, and except for a few mosquitoes it was an ideal location. Unfortunately, by dinner a rainsquall began to blow through the valley and we had to eat our stir-fry with cold splats of water on our bowls and noses. When the rain splats grew more intense we decided to do our teeth and batten down the hatches. It was time to write in our journals and do some reading. This would be the first time we'd have to use the mosquito fly at night. There weren't many of the little buggers, but enough to be a nuisance while we slept.

Just before calling it quits, I opened up my Father's Day card from Jen. It said that, "Because you're my husband, I wanted to give you something really special and out of the ordinary for Father's Day.... so for 24 hours I'll let you be right." She added, "Actually for the next three weeks or until you get home. Love, Jen."

June 17 was another rigorous day. After waking up at 4:30 a.m. to a snowy landscape, we ate breakfast and checked out the now defunct wolf den, which proved ample enough for a large human, myself, to back down into. We also took some photos of the hundreds of bull caribou feeding in the area, now surrounded by a snowscape that highlighted their antlered forms.

We decamped at about 9:00, and slowly hiked through the shallow snow up a westward trending branch of the Aichilik, finally fording a braided part of the swollen river. At first, we thought we might be able to cross a stretch of aufeis that from a distance appeared to completely bridge the river, but by the time we got to the bridge it had collapsed and we had to doff our boots and socks and ford the braid in our sandals and booties. The water was frigid and deep, but we knew this crossing was trivial compared to what we would have to do farther up the main channel of the Aichilik. It would be deeper yet when we crossed the main channel later to get over to the Leffingwell Fork of the river and follow it up to Bathtub Ridge. It had started to drizzle and sleet again, so we had our work cut out for us.

We stopped for lunch in the lee of a rocky cliff, and it was then that Clancy informed us that he wouldn't be able to go on. He said that his bad knee was feeling terrible, and it would be better if we went on without him. He would slowly make his way back to the Aichilik airstrip and wait for either Dirk or Kirk to fly in to pick up their other passengers. He had eight days of food left, so he wasn't worried about starving to death, he said. After trading us one of his pots and giving us his extra supply of gourmet coffee and tea, we each gave him a big hug and again hit the trail. I felt bad for him, not only because he really wanted to finish the trip with us, but also because he admitted his bad knee represented a watershed in his life, that is, no more long trips such as this one!

By now the river had turned into a maze of shallow braids, and Don and I decided to try our luck fording them. Again we changed footgear, and in sleet and snow began wending our way carefully across the cold silty waters of the Aichilik. Clancy stood on the bank watching us until we reached the east shore of the river. We could only imagine what he was thinking.

Since the Leffingwell Fork lay on the other side of a high pass just to the north of where we forded the river, we dried our feet and pulled our socks and boots back on, in preparation for our climb to the top of the pass. I glassed one final time through the trailing tendrils of falling snow to try to see what Clancy was up to. I could just make out the blurry form of his tent, which he had probably erected so he could further rest his knee before going back to the airstrip.

Just around the bend from where we changed back into our boots, we ran into a large herd of caribou resting and grazing at the base of the mountain pass. We estimated their numbers to be at least two thousand, but there were probably a lot more. After sneaking up on some of the closer ones and taking their photos, we plodded up the mountain and over the snowy saddle of the tussock-studded pass. We were preceded on all sides by uncountable hundreds of caribou, most of them cows and newborn calves, suspicious of our intentions. It was good to see so many newborns, which would begin to make up for the disastrous losses of the past two years. There were also numerous yearlings and some older bulls, all in their own separate herds.

We rested awhile on the other side of the saddle and watched a curious cross fox watching us. He didn't seem very concerned about us and soon went on his way. We did the same and slowly descended the other side of the slope. The tussocks weren't as bad on the downside of the pass as they were on the upside, but the snow made them slippery and we both took tumbles more than once on the slog down. About halfway to the bottom we found some recent caribou afterbirth and thought of the fox again.

Finally on the Leffingwell Fork, we located a good campsite on a dryas bench and pitched our tents. We had wet feet and were tuckered out, but managed to gather enough dry willow sticks for a small fire to cook dinner. We would have to cook over a wood fire from now on, since Clancy took his gas stove with him. I had sent my own stove over to the Sheenjek with Kirk.

The evening sun was trying to shine through the thick cloud cover, but it was reluctant to stay out, keeping the ambient temperature only in the high 30s. It had hovered around the freezing point all day, which made me glad I'd brought my heavy clothes with me. The silver lining in this, however, was that it would delay the mosquito hatch.

From my notes: *We've retired to our tent a little early because of the cool weather. At the head of the valley the sun is shining strongly, and we're hoping that tomorrow will bring warmer weather. As I write in my journal, I can see caribou on the opposite bank of the river. A robin hopping around near the front of the tent brings back familiar memories, as does a white-crowned sparrow singing his song, "Don't want to go to school no more!"*

This was our first morning without Clancy, and we missed him. While cooking breakfast over a smoky willow fire we watched masses of caribou streaming through the saddle of our soggy pass of the day before. At first, we wondered why they were moving so quickly, but soon discovered the reason when a big brown grizzly bear came into view, marching over the top not more than 100 yards behind the nearest caribou. It was quite a sight to see what looked like rivers of animals crossing the mountain flank.

After striking camp we headed upriver along the west bank of the Leffingwell Fork, named after an explorer who spent ten seasons roaming the area. He was so infatuated with the region he used his own resources to return time after time to explore the wonders that exist here. My young trekking buddy, Andrew Benedetti, once told me that Leffingwell was a distant relative.

The walking was so good on the dryas terrace of the west bank that I thought my boots might have a chance to dry out. We were in high spirits as we started, and a Wilson's snipe winnowing above us added to our euphoria. Legions of caribou stretching for as far as the eye could see in every direction completed the picture, with cows and newborns, young bulls, and older bulls all in their own almost exclusive herds. By now, the newborn calves were big and strong enough to be able to cavort back and forth as fast as their sprangly long legs would carry them. It was funny watching them through my binoculars.

Everywhere we turned there were surprises waiting for us, including wildflowers like larkspur that I had only seen once before over at the Sadlerochit Spring, in 2001. It still hadn't flowered, but by the crowfoot shape of its leaves I knew what it was. There were so many rhododendrons in bloom that they made the place smell like a perfume parlor. Our first wandering tattlers were tattling along the edges of the river, and while eating lunch on a knoll above a frothy cluster of rapids we watched one of these fascinating birds repeatedly chase a spotted sandpiper away from its feeding territory. Tattlers are much larger sandpipers, and their call is a sweet liquid toodle that seems to accompany them everywhere, hence their name.

As Don and I walked south, we noticed the caribou, especially the cows and calves, were beginning to move in a northerly direction downstream toward the coast. There were more large bulls in the area too, but these didn't seem to be going anywhere. Don said the cows and calves would soon be on their way back over to the Kongakut and Clarence Rivers, and finally to Canada where they originally came from. The others would eventually follow later in the summer. None of the caribou were in big hurry, though, and Don thought it was probably because there still weren't many bugs around due to the cooler temperatures. Mosquitoes, botflies and warble flies don't do well in cold weather, so they're less of a problem for the caribou then. But when it warms up, the insects become a real scourge, botflies lodging in the animals' noses to lay their eggs and warble flies laying theirs in the upper legs and abdomens of the poor creatures. Mosquitoes by the hundreds and thousands meanwhile suck their blood on every square inch of exposed hide they can find. Don and I were glad we were there during the cooler weather.

In the afternoon, we came across a small colony of upland sandpipers, with their short chortling calls. I flushed one of them from its nest, which I searched for only briefly because I didn't want to keep the bird away too long. I had stumbled on them before in the tundra and found they laid four speckled buff-colored eggs in the shape of a cross. Smith's longspurs twittered sweetly from the tops of nearby tussocks, dropping and hiding among them when we approached too close.

We set up camp above the river where we could see huge numbers of caribou, mostly cows and calves, sashaying back and forth across the mountain slopes, moving according to their search for food and the constant threat of danger as the scent of predators wafted up and down the valley. After dinner, we watched another mixed herd of more than 2000 animals ambling along the mountain flank above our tent.

While watching the caribou, there was a sudden flurry of wings above us as a northern shrike chased a redpoll up the river. The two birds went round and round in the sky, twisting and turning, pirouetting and somersaulting, as the smaller bird tried to outmaneuver the much larger shrike. It was incredible how the shrike shadowed the redpoll's every move, following on its tail even as it dived into the willows on the other side of the river. I imagine it caught the bird because neither of them flew out of the willows. The mini drama certainly set off an alarm among the redpoll population near our campsite because it took them about 15 minutes to settle down again.

On glassing across the river, I noticed a cow caribou running along the riverbank, first up, then back down, over and over again. Sometimes she would jump up abruptly as though spooked by something unseen. We thought she might have botflies or warble flies chasing her, but it seemed too cool for that. And all the other caribou remained still as she went through these antics. We could only guess as to why she was doing this. As Don said, "Caribou are such goofy animals sometimes."

In the evening we were inside the tent writing in our journals when yet another large herd of several thousand caribou slowly crossed the tundra just behind our tent. The bulls and yearlings came so close that we could hear their ankle tendons clicking, and their loud burping and grunting sounded like a cacophony of barnyard animals. They smelled the part, too. With my binoculars I could even see the warble fly welts on their sides. The cows and newborn calves kept their distance from us, and some of the cows still looked a little thin, their ribs showing through their summer coat. They were earnestly feeding on avens and other forbs in their path. We watched them for almost two hours, until they finally disappeared from view.

After breaking camp the next morning it rained for a couple of hours, so hard that we had to hunker down under the convenient ledge of a small cliff. It was a good opportunity to ogle caribou, though, and we noticed for the first time that almost all of the several hundred we could see out there were bulls. They were skittish, probably because some of their recent associations with humans had been as targets for Indian hunting rifles, near Old Crow or Arctic Village. Like the cows and calves, they were heading in a northerly direction, which meant they too might be starting their return migration to Canada.

The hiking conditions were pretty good as we wended our way up the valley, the easiest part being over two patches of aufeis on the river. One of these was almost a half-mile long, and we found that by walking on the darker portions of the ice, covered by fine particles of sand, we had our best footing. These patches of aufeis were quite thick, possibly because they hadn't fully melted during the past two cool summers.

We had two surprise encounters with grizzlies that day, one a blondie patrolling the opposite side of the Leffingwell, and the other a dark brown bear on our side. As we stood and watched him, the second bear sat down on his haunches on the talus slope above us and peered in our direction for several minutes. Then he turned, slowly climbed up the mountain and disappeared over an adjoining ridge. It was curious that he decided to take the most difficult escape route, but it was possible that he, too, had been shot at by hunters.

Among the birds we came across were a pair of psychedelically colored harlequin ducks that whizzed by me at shoulder level as I prepared dinner by our anemic fire on the river's edge. There were also several Smith's longspurs, a few pipits, and a pair of wandering tattlers hunting at the edge of what was now just a large creek, repeating over and over again their telltale tootling whistle. That was suddenly accompanied by another sound.

From my notes: *We had just finished dinner and were listening to a wandering tattler when a loud staccato noise abruptly alerted us to a small herd of about 60 bull caribou gazing intently up the mountainside. They were all watching a large boulder come crashing down the steep slope, making such a frightful noise that at first I thought it might roll right on top of us. It stopped short, however, and the caribou continued on their way north.*

June 20 –

What a day this one! From my journal: *It's 3:00 p.m., on the cusp of the summer solstice, and it's blowing a snowstorm the like I've never experienced at this time of year. We had to stop and bivouac to get out of the terrible force of the wind and snow, and there are already three inches of snow on the ground.*

When we first started walking in the morning, the weather wasn't actually that bad. Through light rain we watched a few bull caribou passing north on both sides of the river. One of them had antlers with such a flat profile they reminded us of a moose rack. Just after the snow storm slammed into us from the north I came across a pipit feeding a little like a dipper, both along the edge of the creek and in the water itself. It had little choice, though, since by then the surrounding land was almost completely mantled in snow.

At 9:40 p.m., we're still bivouacked, now in about six inches of snow, and it's so cold my pen will barely write. This cool weather is really going to set back the birds. But maybe it'll squeeze all of the moisture out of the air and clear the skies by morning. On popping my head out of the tent, I even once saw some blue sky through the racing clouds, so just maybe.... For the moment, however, it's back to snow, hard flakes against the tent making a loud staccato whackety whack sound, and a strong wind still noisily flapping the tent fly, in spite of our attempts to secure it tightly to the ground.

Another glance out of the tent, and the blowing snow has subsided enough for me to make out two caribou bulls hunkered down not more than two hundred yards up the valley, waiting out the storm as we are. I also catch a glimpse of a raven taking advantage of the lull to wing its way closer to wherever it was headed earlier.

A cursory study of our topo map tells us only that we are at approximately 3600 feet elevation, which would partly explain why it's so cold, and why I'm inside my sleeping bag and wearing every last stitch of clothing I brought along with me on this trip.

Summer Solstice –

In the early morning when I opened the tent flap and peered out at the world there was snow for as far as the eye could see, with drifts of eight inches around our tent. The ambient temperature was 25 degrees, but with clear skies and a sparkling sun, it wouldn't be long till the snow started to melt. We hoped sooner than later, because we had to begin our climb toward the high pass that would eventually take us back into the Aichilik River Valley.

First, though, we had to eat breakfast, which we were actually able to cook over a fire because of the dry willow sticks we'd stashed in our packs the day before. As we spooned down our last bites of warm granola, Don pointed at several strings of caribou feeding on the snowy slopes below Bathtub Ridge on the other side of the valley. Although he wore his desert safari hat, he had to squint in the blinding sunlight. Shaking his head, he remarked that he was glad he'd brought that hat along. With his pale white skin, it might literally be a lifesaver.

Then off we went under a pellucid blue sky over a mountain landscape that can only be described as a winter wonderland. But after walking for about a quarter mile up toward the basin of Bathtub Ridge, we discovered we were on the wrong branch of the Leffingwell. Somehow, during the height of the storm the day before, we had completely missed the mouth of the west fork and had continued up the main fork. We remembered that we had eaten lunch at its mouth, but thought it was premature to be there yet.

So we double-checked our compass against the map, and decided we'd best cut across country through the deep snow to recoup our loss. It was slippery, sometimes dangerously so, as we climbed up, then down, the mountain into the drainage we should have started up the previous day. At one point we came to a slope covered with fine talus with an angle of repose of about 65 degrees. I escalatored down with no trouble, but was worried about Don. I watched him carefully as he made his way to the bottom, indicating the trail I had taken and how I had done it.

After rechecking our map, we took another shortcut, finally ending up on the tributary we planned to take all the way to the top. As we slowly and surely wound our way along the thread of black water creek, the snow-shrouded mountains fell off behind us. Everywhere, despite the elevation, the rhythm of bird life was returning to normal. White-crowned sparrows were singing again, as were pipits and even a few tattlers. Glancing back down the valley, the whole range was beginning to open up, looking more like a colossal bank of cumulous clouds than the mountains they were. With most of them now below us, I felt like I was walking on air. It wasn't air, though. It was very slippery snow, and as the valley narrowed we decided to walk up the middle of the creek bed where most of the snow had already melted. It wasn't as dangerous walking in the water itself because there was less chance we'd chuck our knees in a snow-filled hole or slip on a snowy rock. There was still comparatively little melt water running downstream, due to the cooler temperatures toward the summit of the pass, and our feet actually stayed fairly dry.

Near the top, I stopped to wait for Don. The scintillating trickle of creek was so inviting I shed my pack and took a cold, and I mean cold, drink of water. I was still so hot and sweaty that I also doffed most of my clothes and washed my hair and bathed my perspiration-drenched body. Then I rinsed out my T-shirt. I knew it wouldn't take long for the bright sun to dry it on the back of my pack.

Looking at our map, we were convinced that after reaching the end of the creek and the 5000 foot saddle of the pass, we would be home free, and it would be clear sailing from there all the way down to the Aichilik River. Not so. When we were at the top, we saw that we still had a long way to go until we could even think about descending. After a snack, though, we were ready to hit the trail again, and four times we climbed down about 200 feet, then back up 200 feet to the summit of yet another saddle, until finally we reached a point where the slope peeled off and we knew it was all downhill from there on.

It was a hard slog across those saddles, but there were some wonderful rewards. The view, for one. Although the mountain crags above us were stern and rugged, down below they were sensuously beautiful in their continuous blanket of snow. Another was the mated pair of Baird's sandpipers standing stoically in a shallow dribble of runoff, waiting for the snow to melt in the alpine tundra so they could get back to the serious business of nesting. And then at the verge of the last of the four summits there was a snow bunting, flitting from snowdrift to snowdrift, eyeing us with as much curiosity as we did him. Tough birds, I thought, even if they were designed for northern living.

During our descent we were glad the sun had melted the snow on the rocks. It would have been treacherous otherwise. In any case, the route was extremely arduous, and Don and I soon realized we had chosen about the most difficult passage possible through the mountains. We wondered if even Leffingwell, who had explored so much of the eastern Brooks Range, had taken this trail. Often some of the openings in the rocky draw were only a couple of yards wide, and we had to thread our way carefully through them, always mindful not to slip on the slimy cobbles studding the edges of the running water. Gradually the creek widened, however, and conditions improved. By mid-afternoon we were cheered when we found our first forget-me-nots peeking through some melting snow. Arctic poppies showed up in profusion, and we were really heartened when we saw an immature American dipper, still showing its light belly feathers, hunting for fly larvae in the middle of the creek. About halfway down the valley we also began to hear wandering tattlers whistling on both sides of the stream, which was music to our ears after so much silence in the high pass.

A patch of kiwi-green moss in a little backwater prompted me to stop and take some photos. I hadn't seen moss glowing so brightly in many years. Don followed suit with his new video camera and took some close-up footage of the unique moss. It was a good break and prepared us for the detour we were forced to take a few minutes later when we were dead-ended by a 30-foot waterfall. There was no way around it but up, a long way up, then across a very steep half-mile or more of talus-studded mountainside. Thankfully, we discovered a good sheep trail that traversed the mountain and took us down to exactly where we wanted to camp on the Aichilik River. There we found a flat platform for our tent near plenty of tall dry willows, then built a fire for some tea and dinner. It would be our first hot meal in 48 hours, since we had missed dinner the previous evening because of the snowstorm.

While eating, I noticed tracks in the snow on the mountain slope on the other bank of the river. Judging by their sizes and shapes, they were made by a variety of animals, ranging from weasels, parky squirrels and voles, to foxes, bears and moose. I shook my head and remarked to Don what a marvel it was that these critters could survive in the Brooks Range all year round, in spite of such a difficult climate.

The past 36 hours had been difficult for us, too. But as Don declared, "It proves that when the going gets tough, the tough get going."

Saturday the 22nd was a shorter day, but no less rigorous. While studying the map over our Spartan granola breakfast we could see we would have to continue down the main branch of the Aichilik, then cross to its middle fork and follow it south, up and over another pass that would finally get us closer to our destination. But between our camp and the middle fork was a series of steep bluffs abutting both banks of the river. If we wanted to avoid multiple fording back and forth we would have to climb up the mountainside and find a way across there.

We were lucky because soon after starting our climb in the morning, we found a well-traveled animal trail about 300 feet above the river that we were able to follow all the way to the middle fork. On both sides of us towered the blocky, cream-colored limestone mountains, for which this area was famous, and wildflowers like forget-me-nots and fragrant rock jasmine and rosebay grew in profusion up and down the south-facing slopes of our route.

About a half-mile along the trail we spotted a white wolf standing on the other side of a deep ravine. When he saw us approaching he headed up the mountain and disappeared around a rocky promontory. We thought we wouldn't see him again, but suddenly there he was, peeking at us from above the rocks. He seemed to be as curious about us as we were of him, and when we sat down to watch him through my binocs, he did so, too, then moved on from perch to perch along the ridge line of the ravine, trying to get a better view of us. Each time he stopped he serenaded us with a repertoire of howls and yipping, and ululating like I had never heard before. We figured there must be a den somewhere nearby and that he was a young sentinel wolf announcing to the rest of the pack that we were in the neighborhood. His ululations were amazingly varied, but there was one constant refrain that probably meant, "Men in the neighborhood, beware!" When we finally moved on, he paralleled us for a long time, about 100 yards above our own trail, howling and yipping all the way. His howls echoed weirdly across the valley. I tried to imitate them, but Don told me I sounded more like an owl than a wolf.

Farther on we came across a pair of shrikes trying to catch a young parky squirrel. They chased it from willow thicket to willow thicket, but each time they dove at it the little guy ducked under a pile of dead wood. I had never seen these birds work cooperatively before, and it was one more lesson for me.

After crossing the Aichilik to its middle fork, we again followed caribou and sheep trails both on the river bottom and on the slopes when we were confronted by steep cliffs and didn't want to ford the river. Wading across the main Aichilik to get to the middle fork had been frigidly cold and dangerously swift, so the fewer fords there were, the better. One final crossing of the middle fork was necessary, though, when we were stopped by high bluffs with perilously steep talus slopes above them. Even the caribou didn't take the high road here, but walked right through the deep rushing water. So we bit the bullet, removed our boots and forded the cold river water to the west bank, where we picked up a well-traveled caribou trail. There we surprised seven large bulls at such close quarters that we were able to snap some good photos of them. We also spotted three small Dall sheep rams feeding above the east bank of the river. They were losing their winter coats and looked a little scruffy, much like we did, I imagine.

By now we were ready to camp. According to our map we had only walked 4½ miles, but the valley we were in had opened up to give us a spectacular view of the surrounding mountains, including several high limestone peaks that reminded Don of cathedrals. For this reason he dubbed the place Cathedral Peaks Camp. Since we still had a 2600-foot grind to the top of the pass before heading down toward the Kongakut River, we figured we needed a shorter day to rest for this next major effort.

From my journal: *There are four young rams feeding opposite our camp right now. I just got back from a short walkabout up the river to check out a narrow spot in the canyon where there are cliffs on both sides and just barely enough room for us to skinny through to the other side and thus avoid having to climb above it. Once again, the animal trails told the story. If they could make it, so could we, was my constant refrain. During the walk I found my first four-petalled gentian (Gentiana propinqua) of the trip, with its many small blue tubular flowers.*

I'm watching a female harlequin swim deftly down the rapids in front of our camp, hunting for whatever she can find. She takes the whitewater like I might do it in a canoe or kayak. Then she flies back upriver and starts down again. There's no male with her, so that means she has laid her eggs and he has split for the ocean. The eggs are not yet at a critical incubation stage, so she can take the time to indulge her appetite. Later, she may not be able to do this.

Don hiked in another direction, and is still not back. Oh, oh, he just walked up behind me. I saw his reflection in my glasses. He told me he managed to cross the river and then climb the ridge to where he had a spectacular view of the three pinnacled, stair-stepped limestone mountains that he named the camp after. He likes to name every camp after one of its distinctive features. I've never done that, but it has merit as a mnemonic device.

The sky is back to blue again, with fluffy cumulous clouds moving rapidly in from the south. There's a ring around the sun, and I wonder what that means. Probably even warmer weather, I hope. It's warmer already, and it's the first time we've been able to sit outside like this in the evening since the beginning of our trip.

It rained off and on in the early morning. By the looks of the ominous clouds toward the pass, we thought we might even encounter snow up there. As it turned out, most of the hike through the pass was straightforward. In fact, it was the best walking yet, and some of the best I'd ever had in the Brooks Range, but the elevation gain of 2600 feet made it a challenge with our heavy packs. Even so, by following well-traveled caribou trails we made it to the summit by noon. We surprised a blond grizzly lumbering down toward us, but he was a polite bear who hightailed it up the talus slope to avoid us. He was also a handsome one, with a thick woolly coat and a small dark brown spot on his hump. Soon afterward, we bumped into a pair of bull caribou that seemed to be spooked about something, possibly by the bear's scent, and bypassed us at a run down the other bank of the creek.

There was only patchy snow in the barren saddle of the pass, and perfectly quiet except for the sweet tinkling song of a couple of male Lapland longspurs. We stopped to eat behind a small rise studded with large boulders. It was just enough protection to keep the steady southwest wind at bay. While munching our nuts and crackers, we noticed the swiftly moving clouds were mixed with smoke from a forest fire somewhere to the south. Haze filled the air, blurring what might have been majestic vistas in every direction.

When we started down the other side of the pass the winds were blowing even harder, and other than the myriad of black, lichen-studded rocks, the whole area looked like it had been scoured clean by an alpine glacier only recently melted into the mountain. Farther down, the wind abated a little and the walking got much better. At one point, the going was so easy it reminded me of the Aichilik side we had just come up, and we made such good time I thought we might even get as far as the west fork of the Kongakut River before dinner. That was not to be, however. Early in the afternoon, Don told me one of his legs was really starting to bother him and that he needed to stop and camp as soon as we found a decent spot to put up our tent. Otherwise, he didn't think he'd be able to go on the next day. His old battered LL Bean boots had been chafing his shins, especially his left one, and it was making it very painful to walk.

Good fortune found us a flat place near the river to set up the tent, and I built a fire to brew us some tea. Between mouthfuls of hot tea I advised Don jokingly that a successful walk required three important things: boots, boots and boots – good ones! We also chatted about some of our unusual botanical findings of the day. One of them was golden saxifrage, which I hadn't seen in a long time, and the other was a subspecies of alpine arnica that I had never encountered before and dubbed woolly arnica because of the hairy neck warmer it had wrapped around its budding yellow flowers. The botanical term to describe this is "pubescent," and I wondered if the word's root was the same as that for "pubic." A curiosity from the mammal world was a dark race of the parky squirrel, apparently found only in the Brooks Range.

We knew we'd eventually run into them, and the next day we did. Mosquitoes! It was only after we finally started up the west fork of the Kongakut that a few of the beasties began trailing us. In the morning it had been too cool for them as we slogged the rest of the way down from the pass under a heavy cloud cover.

Don's leg was feeling much better, though, since wrapping it with two of my Ace bandages, and we made good time on the caribou trails that seemed to abound everywhere. He took the low road next to the creek and I took the high road on the mountainside, and we met to eat lunch just above the confluence of the two forks of the Kongakut. There we compared notes on the wildlife we encountered. We'd both seen a lone golden eagle soaring high in the upper valley, and then eight young bull caribou grazing on the other side of the creek about halfway to the confluence.

After starting up the west fork, the caribou trails were like highways, and the walking conditions were so good that by the end of the day we made it almost to the head of our last pass over to the Sheenjek River drainage. We had covered close to ten miles, our longest day yet.

My journal reads: *We're now camped at the head of the west fork of the Kongakut River in a broad amphitheater and poised to climb our last of five passes, cross the Continental Divide and head down to the Sheenjek. All water from the top of this Divide flows either south and west to the Yukon River and Bering Sea or back the way we came to the Kongakut River and the Arctic Ocean. The amphitheater we're in is impressive, with its jagged mountain peaks punctuated by patches of snow left over from the snowstorm that slammed into us over on the Leffingwell. But there is no sign of animals anywhere.*

Although we're a little bushed from our long day of walking, we've just finished a double-sized beef stroganoff dinner and feel quite stuffed and happy. The sun is shining and its warmth keeps us outside near our small willow fire, chatting and writing up our notes of the day. One of mine is about a dead snowy owl I came across earlier in the afternoon on the upper part of the west fork. Nearest I could tell, it had been killed and eaten to the last little tidbit of meat sometime during midwinter by a super hungry wolf. Only its skull, neck and backbone were left, along with a spray of snow-white feathers that were strewn across the tundra. There is a nesting pair of tattlers across the creek from our camp. At first, both birds were a little upset about our presence, but they eventually got used to us and carried on with their daily chores.

June 25 –

Today is a special day from my journal: *Happy Birthday, Jen. Last year at this time we were tussock-jumping in the Sadlerochits.*

We're finally on the Sheenjek River, camped on a gravel bar to avoid the mosies, which have been pretty bad today. Within 200 feet of our tent is a small stand of white spruce, which also means we're now at tree line. Sort of exciting to be here after all of our hard work.

Our day started under a wonderful blue sky, and we easily climbed over the last of our five passes. In the saddle we found more of what I call woolly arnica. But most of them were in full golden bloom and had less wool around their necks. These alpine arnica are truly that, alpine, and grow in very moist high mountain passes. We also found a few Ross's avens (Geum rossii), another handsome yellow alpine wildflower. They seem to prefer drier slopes, though.

The passage down the valley to the Sheenjek turned out to be difficult walking in its mid section and we had to constantly cross the creek, back and forth, and climb up and down the slopes on each side, always following the caribou and sheep trails. 'If they can do it, we can do it,' I kept telling Don. We got some relief from the tough going when two gray-crowned rosy finches surprised us by the creek. They were a particularly orange race, so orange that I thought at first glance they were robins. I hadn't seen rosy finches since my solo walk in the Kongakut back in 1986. Like Say's phoebes and chickadees, they are friendly birds and don't seem bothered by our presence. Don had never seen them before.

About halfway down the creek we had to follow high caribou trails to avoid steep precipices and rocky canyons. Then gradually we descended along these trails to the creek bottom and traced them to the Sheenjek Valley. I recognized the country there because three summers ago I had walked it with Andrew Benedetti and Dan Hatfield. Near the mouth of the creek, perched high on the mountain flank, we spied 11 Dall sheep – six ewes, two lambs and three large rams – our first "charismatic megafauna" since yesterday morning.

On the tundra wetland paralleling the Sheenjek River we came across another colony of nesting upland sandpipers, and in the small stand of spruce we saw a northern shrike and a gray jay, both very similar looking birds with very dissimilar behavior. At the edge of the riverbed in the willows were two Say's phoebes, and a robin was singing joyously as we searched for a place to put our tent on a gravel bar of the Sheenjek.

Suddenly, Don pointed across the river where a big chocolate brown grizzly bear was digging in the riverbed for roots. A few moments later I spotted a lighter bear slowly descending the mountain on the talus slope above the first one. We watched with bated breath as the second griz came closer and closer, studying the chocolate bear, then finally joining it in its foraging for bearroot. They must have been siblings to get along so well. The last time I'd seen anything like that was on the Porcupine River with Fran Mauer when two huge bears approached our camp and we had to stand close together with two other people and make enough noise to frighten them off. We watched our Sheenjek bears for more than an hour as they tore up the ground after roots and contended patiently with a pesky raven that noisily tormented them while they ate. Only after we started bathing our smelly bodies in the river did they begin to amble off and finally disappear around the bend. 'Maybe they didn't like our naked white skin,' I wondered to Don. 'Or our smell,' he rejoined.

So, it's been another full day. We should be at Double Mountain and our canoe in two days.

For the better part of the next morning we walked in perfectly photogenic weather, with tall thunderheads mushrooming into the deep blue vault of the Arctic sky. We kept mostly to the cobbled riverbed until the bending river forced us up on the bank, then across an expansive outwash made by a long drainage originating in the Davidson Mountains to the east.

A couple of times we followed a caribou trail through small stands of white spruce. There we encountered two bear rubbing trees, one of which was torn to pieces by the bruins that had used it. Both spruce trunks were loaded with copious amounts of brown and blond grizzly fur.

Somewhere along the route we got off on the wrong trail, because we ended up in a tangle of willows that reminded us of thick jungle. It took us an eternity to bushwhack our way through, and just as we emerged on the other side we spotted Kirk Sweetsir's Cessna 185 buzzing downriver from the headwaters of the Sheenjek. We hoofed it out to an open gravel bar and waved at him as he sped low over the river toward our drop-off point opposite Double Mountain. When he saw us he did a 360-degree turn, slowed, descended to almost treetop level and waved back at us. He smiled, then regained elevation and continued down to the airstrip, located about ten miles away. We could see our canoe stuffed in the cargo hold, so we knew he was on his way to make the drop.

Not far from the willows, while crossing a broad meadow of dry wetland, we encountered our first lesser yellowlegs. There were several of them, and during a short snack break a mated pair of these tall sandpipers came over and perched on a mound, then paraded noisily over a heap of boulders directly in front of us. In the same wetland we came across two pair of semipalmated sandpipers. Almost stepping on one of their nests, I bent down and snapped a quiet photo of their four brown eggs. As with other sandpiper species, the eggs were arranged in the shape of a cross in a shallow scrape on the ground. The tapered ends of the eggs all faced inward so they wouldn't roll out, and for more effective brooding by both parents.

When the meanders of the river forced us up on the bank, we discovered we were in alder country. Surprisingly we had not encountered alders until now. As I was examining their dark green leaves, Don pointed toward the tundra at a lone bull caribou grazing there. He soon saw us, and remained peering at us for the longest time before finally wandering off upriver. We ruminated about the possible reasons why some caribou are mavericks, and on their relative chances for a long life. Much like humans, I thought.

While watching the caribou, Don spotted yet another grizzly about 300 yards inland. It was a fairly small cinnamon and silver-haired bear, and he was digging for roots in the tundra. There was a stiff breeze blowing, and every time it caught his fur, it whimsically flounced up and down, exposing the rich silver color of his inner coat. Because of the favorable direction of the wind we were tempted to watch him longer, but remembering the anecdotes we'd heard about the foul nature of small bears we decided to move on.

In late afternoon, when we spotted a fast-moving thunderstorm heading in our direction, we quickly found a flat spot on the bank beside a long stretch of aufeis, set up the tent, and dived inside to escape the rain. Peering out the tent door, we had a spectacular view of the river and its thick aufeis, especially after the storm began to ebb down the valley.

As we ate our rehydrated chicken teriyaki dinner next to the aufeis, our first pair of arctic terns drifted over the twisting trail of the river through the ice with their deliberate wing beats, much like those of jaegers. A red-breasted merganser sped by on his way upriver, and overhead an immature golden eagle soared in the thermals, trying to avoid the aggressive onslaught of a pair of angry northern shrikes.

Later I wrote in my journal: *It's evening, and we're sitting on a wooded knoll overlooking a colossal shelf of aufeis not more than three miles upriver from the Double Mountain airstrip. Our camp is about 300 yards directly below the knoll, and Double Mountain is just on the other side of the river. The tail end of a rainsquall is racing down the valley, leaving us with tattered clouds mixed with patches of blue sky. The play of light and shadow on the aufeis and mountain is worthy of a poem, but I resist and continue with the day's notes. I wouldn't have resisted a few years ago, but I don't write poetry much anymore. Realizing that, I feel a twinge of regret. Maybe I have writer's block. Maybe I fear it won't be appreciated. I really should begin to write poetry again.*

With my binoculars, I can just barely see our food drop and canoe in the distance at the end of the airstrip, where Kirk had dropped it late this morning. We hoped that when he returned to Ft. Yukon he phoned our wives to tell them we were okay.

Ever since we set up camp, the aufeis (as thick as ten feet just a few yards in front of our tent) has been calving regularly, with a crashing roar that reminds me of my raft trip down the Copper River two summers ago when we were camped only a mile upriver from the gigantic Child's Glacier. From its immense face the glacier calved into the river every 15-30 minutes with a resounding boom that sounded like rolling thunder, so it made for a terrible night's sleep! I wonder what it'll be like here tonight?

In the morning, before heading for the airstrip where Kirk had dropped our canoe and food, we figured we had two choices getting there: easy walking on the aufeis for a short distance, then slogging through a half-mile of tussocks and wetland till we reached higher ground downriver; or climbing up the mountain from the get-go to try to avoid most of the tussocks. Since trudging through the wetland would have been sheer hell with heavy packs, we chose to climb the flank of the mountain and dodge the tussocks. Once we got to a good viewpoint above the river, we saw we had made the right decision.

As we started out, I spotted a pair of bohemian waxwings cavorting in the treetops. They were the first waxwings I had ever seen so deep in the Brooks Range. Then I flushed a female mallard from her nest. On closer inspection, I found six beige eggs in it. Farther along we ran into more upland sandpipers and lesser yellowlegs. The simple presence of these birds, even the sassy yellowlegs, blunted the edge of the hard climb up the mountain.

When we finally made it to the airstrip, we found everything intact. Sitting down on the two heavy-duty rectangular aluminum food containers that Clancy had loaned us, we surveyed our surroundings. There was much more aufeis than I remembered from the last time I was in the neighborhood with Andrew Benedetti. If it melted as swiftly as the ice we were camped by last night (and that was so fast I barely recognized the same spot in the morning), it would soon be gone. But we wondered about the condition of the aufeis downriver.

My attention was taken by a semipalmated plover nervously flitting around us with moth-like wing beats. The tiny bird probably had a nest somewhere nearby, so we quickly ate lunch, transferred our gear down to the river-bank and began assembling my collapsible Ally canoe. It was then I noticed the river had changed its course. The main channel was now several hundred yards to the west, and where we were next to the riverbank there was only a shallow backwater in which to launch and float our canoe. We had no choice, however, and loaded everything on board and disembarked.

We had to line for the first quarter-mile, but eventually we found a deeper part of the main channel where we could begin paddling. The river braided a lot at the outset, but the water level was high and we had no trouble negotiating the shallower braids. About three or four miles downriver we stopped to check out an 80 acre Native allotment, recently put up for sale by Robert Solomon, from Ft. Yukon. It was actually owned by Robert's aging mother Hanna, who lived in Fairbanks, and was the only private in-holding along the Sheenjek River. If it were sold for purposes of building a hunting lodge, as advertised by the realtor, it would compromise the designated Wilderness it was located in. After inspecting it, though, we decided they would have a problem selling the land for their asking price of 150,000 dollars, because most of the allotment was a wetland. Still, what a paradox. Right after Robert was presented with the Goldman Award for environmental activism in Washington, D.C. (along with 25,000 dollars), he put the allotment up for sale! (The Solomon family later decided to take the land off the "auction block," and it reverted to its original status.)

After floating for another mile or two, Don announced that he was too tuckered out from the morning's climb to go any farther, so we decided to look for a place to camp. We soon found a good flat spot for the tent on the riverbank, gathered some dry wood for a fire, and put on some tea water. A quesadilla dinner followed, using the spinach tortillas and Frank's hot sauce that were part of our food drop. What a tasty change from the dry meals of the past two weeks.

My last thoughts, as noted in my journal, before nodding off were of some of the wildflowers we saw that day: *Pink plumes blooming on the tundra. Boykinia (bear flower) on the mountainsides just now sending out small white blossoms. Death camas starting to flower along the river, along with yellow northern paintbrush, dwarf fireweed, fragrant wild sweet pea, and all the vetches and bear root. Spring in the Arctic Refuge. Lovely, lovely, lovely.*

June 28 –

From my journal: *We're presently camped on Kuirzinjik Lake – the Lobo Lake of Murie fame. We just finished a hard-earned dinner of quesadillas and soup. "Hard-earned" because we started out this morning in a miserable downpour and paddled against the wind almost all day, with only two hours of respite soon after we set out. The consolation was that the rain stopped completely at about 10 a.m. and, although it remained unusually cool, the sun even showed its bright and shiny face a few times. For the first two hours we paddled through the broken twists and turns of aufeis that I was convinced had not been there five summers ago when Andrew and I floated the Sheenjek. Both Don and I think that with the recent cool summers the aufeis may not melt completely here either, leading to an accumulation of ice in the river bed. We joked that maybe these were the first signs of glaciation of the area.*

Our first stop of the day was at Last Lake, now called Ambrosevajun Lake (meaning "Ambrose's Lake" in Kwich'in) on the maps. We wanted to check out a landing strip there that Don knew had been used by hunters in the fall. It was still completely covered in aufeis, so we couldn't make out the condition of the airstrip, but there was ample evidence back on the riverbank that hunters had been around, since they had left so much of their garbage there. "An annual problem," Don admitted.

Then it was down the river again. Almost immediately we encountered a cow and calf moose on the left bank. They had been resting, but as soon as they saw us they were up on all fours and bolted into the willows. On the other side of the river we stopped to climb a knoll to check our bearings. We reckoned we were nearing the Muries' Lobo Lake where we wanted to do some exploration. From the top, we spied the Old Woman Hills just a few miles downriver and, since our map showed Lobo Lake on the north side of the hills, we knew we weren't far away.

An hour later we were paddling into Lobo Lake. The river was so high that it allowed us to access the lake through a small outlet slough opposite the Old Woman Hills. Several years before, floodwaters had scoured out this slough and drained the lake to a shallow shadow of itself. But now things were different and we simply took a gentle turn and followed the current directly into the flooded lake. While searching for a dry place to set up our tent we could see why the Muries chose this particular lake over others to camp on in the spring of 1956. Besides being deep enough at the time to land a float-plane on, it had a wonderful setting in the mountains. If the number of birds on the lake when we arrived was any indication, it also must have had a large population of waterfowl. We certainly saw plenty of them during the first few hours we were there, including red-breasted mergansers, lesser scaup, northern shovelers, mallards, black scoters, American wigeons, green-winged teal, long-tailed ducks, and a pair of tundra swans flying directly over us during dinner.

Again from the journal: *Tonight I can hear the eerie wailing of a pair of Pacific loons on a nearby lake. They're joined soon after by the rhythmic winnowing of a snipe directly above our tent, reminding me of Mardy Murie's mention of the snipe over Lobo Lake in her famous book, Two in the Far North. Yes, little wonder why the Muries selected this lovely place for their three-month sojourn of study on the Sheenjek River. For the Muries, it was also the spirit of this wilderness that stirred them to push for the creation of the Arctic National Wildlife Range. It evidently captured the imagination of the Eisenhower administration, for in December of 1960 the Range was officially established by then Secretary of Interior Seton.*

One of the wildflowers that adds to the spirit of this place is the dwarf bog rosemary, which I find everywhere I walk on the damp tundra. It's hard to believe this pretty little plant (Andromeda polifolia), with its pendulous pink flower, is poisonous. In fact, andromedatoxin, a common toxin of the heath family, was first isolated from bog rosemary. It causes low blood pressure, breathing difficulties and intestinal upsets. The botanist Linnaeus named the genus after the mythological Ethiopian princess, Andromeda, the daughter of Cassiopeia and Cepheus, who, according to the Greek myth, was rescued from a sea monster and then married by Perseus. Linnaeus wrote that this plant "is always fixed on some turfy hillock in the midst of the swamps, as Andromeda herself was chained to a rock in the sea, which bathed her feet as the fresh water does the roots of the plant."

It's still very cool out, but the big bonus is that the lake is virtually mosquito-free tonight.

As I opened the tent flap in the morning, I noticed the water level of the lake was higher than it was the night before. It was now quite close to the entrance of the tent, and when I scanned its surface I spotted four tundra swans on the other side of the lake, slowly drifting toward us. I whispered for Don to wait a minute and moved back into the shadows of the tent, my camera at the ready. Within 15 minutes the swans were only about a 100 feet from us, so close we could clearly see their tannin-stained heads and necks. They remained there for nearly a half-hour, barking back and forth to each other, and even after we got out of the tent they hung around, probably wondering what we were. We decided they were just curious teenagers looking for a thrill.

While gathering kindling near our tent for our breakfast fire, I discovered a fresh digging of bear root with the roots newly exposed. I asked Don if he'd done the excavating. Negative, he said. Then I remembered the bumping noise around the food chests that I'd heard in the wee hours of the morning. Had this been an uninvited ursine visitor? If it was, it was a close call, and we were glad Clancy had loaned us his metal food containers.

While eating our granola we watched a pair of savannah sparrows approaching to feed their young in a nearby ground nest. With extreme caution, they patiently waited in the tops of the willows, then closed in, nervously flitting from limb to limb, until finally jumping down to feed their ravenous gape-mouthed chicks. I glanced at Don and pointed at my granola, "Bird feed, Don, bird feed."

Before continuing downriver we paddled around Lobo Lake, exploring its shoreline for any remains of the camp the Muries had set up in the 1950s. A walk on the east side revealed an old Indian fall hunting camp. Only the rotting log base and rusting iron stove remained of what had probably been a canvas wall tent. At one time the camp had a raised cache and an underground cold storage. We guessed the people who had built it were Arctic Village (Chandalar) Kwich'in. But we found no evidence of the Muries' camp anywhere. We decided their operation had been on the east shore, and had been superseded by the Indian camp. Judging by the garbage left around the old wall tent, the Indians had been much less careful campers than the Muries.

While canoeing I glassed the many birds on the lake, and spotted six new species, including a white-fronted goose, Pacific loon, Bonaparte's gull, Arctic terns, a pair of rusty blackbirds, and a small flock of bank swallows skimming gracefully across its tranquil surface.

From Lobo Lake we moved downriver a mile or so to Old Woman Creek, where we found some beaver cuttings and a couple of porcupines, along with a ton of mosquitoes. Our most intriguing find was an old Kwich'in grave at the top of the highest of a cluster of hills named Old Woman Hills. It was a traditional burial, marked by four arrowhead-shaped spruce posts, one at each corner. The wooden posts were wizened, gray with age and weather, each leaning in its own direction at crazy angles to the hill. On exploring the remaining dozen or more hilltops, we found large flat rocks placed on the ground in rectangular patterns, as though they outlined other graves. In some cases, very large boulders had been placed in the middle of the rectangles, possibly to keep predators from digging up the bodies. On one hilltop I also found an ancient hammer stone and a stone flake. The hills would have been an excellent overlook for hunters in the old days, where they fashioned their tools while watching for moose or migrating caribou heading in their direction. We wondered for how many millennia those ancient hunters had used the area in their eternal quest for their elusive quarry – and to fish for salmon, too, since salmon spawned as far upriver as Lobo Lake. The name Sheenjek, in fact, means Salmon River.

About mid-afternoon we finished our reconnaissance of the Old Woman Hills and paddled a few more miles on the river. We soon found a good level spot for our tent on a small gravel island, and there we made an early camp. First thing after setting up our tent, I took advantage of the sunny weather and washed my hair and socks in the now receding water of the river. I then made a small fire for a mug of tea and our broccoli soup supper.

Just after dinner the wind died and the mosquitoes resurfaced to become their usual annoying selves. So we retreated to the tent to write in our journals, that is, until we heard the loud splashing of a large animal walking in the river, maybe even crossing toward our gravel island. As we slowly eased out of the tent and moved closer to the source of the splashing noise, we hoped it wasn't a bear. But it turned out to be just a lone cow moose, who stopped in her tracks on the other side of the river when she heard us approaching. We thought we were being so quiet in our movements, but apparently not so, because when we glimpsed her through the willows she had her big mule ears and long Roman snout facing squarely in our direction, then nimbly jumped up on the bank and disappeared.

When we got back to the tent, we discovered we had left the fly open in our excitement. So, before continuing with our journals, we had to snuff out the lives of about 50 mosies that had taken advantage of our brief absence from the scene. We wouldn't repeat that.

Last notes: *A male snipe is winnowing its weird quavering 'call,' (the sound made by the vibration of a stiff feather on both sides of its tail) directly above us as we resume our writing. It winnows as I read my book, and winnows when I close my eyes, and winnows as I fall asleep...........*

After checking our measuring stick at the edge of the water, I found the river had gone down almost 12 inches overnight. It was still high, though, and running with a strong current. As we finished breakfast, serious rain clouds seemed to be headed our way, so we struck camp and hit the trail a little earlier than usual.

The river was faster with more rapids than I remembered from my earlier trip down the Sheenjek. Right after starting out we encountered our first white-winged scoters and an early-bird beaver. Then, around a steep bend, a young bull moose suddenly jumped from the left bank into the water and we had to back-paddle hard to keep from bumping into him. He looked as surprised as we were, and after swimming a few yards through the deep water, he turned around and swam back toward the left bank where he'd been resting. We wondered what might have happened if he had been a she with a young calf. But there was no time to pursue that thought because our attention was taken by other critters, like the osprey that flapped over the river in front of us with a fish in his mouth, followed by a bald eagle. We were now far enough down the river where these huge birds could find enough fish to sustain themselves. An old regular, a golden eagle, soared high above in the moody sky, and there were gray-cheeked thrushes, a Harlan's hawk, and small bands of curious Bohemian waxwings that twittered at us as they flew back and forth across the river when we came into sight.

We left the last high mountains behind in early afternoon. Only a few brawny hills remained before we planned to launch into the flat country the next day. We camped close to the east fork of the Sheenjek, and as we prepared our dinner we could hear a slate-colored junco and a myrtle warbler singing to celebrate what had turned out to be a glorious day. Twice, I also heard the harsh, *burry rreeBeea* of alder flycatchers.

Finally, just before calling it a day, we heard the telltale call of a hermit thrush. And what a wonderful fluting voice it had. First, a long, deep introductory note. Next, a note not quite as long with a slightly higher pitch. Then finally, a trill so high and thin I wondered if I really heard it at all. Some have described the song as: *Oh, holy holy,– ah, purity purity,– eeh, sweetly sweetly.* In 1865, Walt Whitman wrote of the hermit thrush in a poem remembering the recently assassinated Abraham Lincoln. He felt the bird's song had a heartbreaking purity that perfectly expressed his sorrow at the president's death. He wrote:

> *Solitary the thrush,*
> *The hermit withdrawn to himself,*
> *Avoiding the settlements,*
> *Sings by himself a song,*
> *Song of the bleeding throat,*
> *Death's outlet song of life....*

July 1 –

I awakened to a myrtle warbler singing this morning. It was nothing like the pure notes of the hermit thrush the night before, but in their songs very few birds compare to thrushes.

The level of the river was down eight inches, but the current was still rushing along, and we made good time paddling in the morning. The afternoon was another matter. Right around noon the wind began to pick up steam, and before long it was blowing with a vengeance. Don said it often kicked up like that along this particular stretch because the course of the river valley aligned with the direction of the prevailing winds, thus creating a funnel effect.

Just downriver from the east fork of the Sheenjek we pulled ashore and Don led me along a trail he remembered from when he had flown into the area in 1999 to an old trapping camp belonging to our friend Heimel Korth. Heimel had left behind a raised log cache, the log frame of his winter canvas tent, and at least a cord of firewood. We also found a children's book entitled, *The Man Who Ate Car Tires*. According to Don, Heimel, his wife Edna, and their two daughters had stayed there only from September to March, when they decided to return to their cabin, 30 miles to the east, on the Colleen River. He hadn't had much luck trapping wolves on the Sheenjek, Don said, and it was pretty cold living in the frame tent, so they moved.

We saw no large animals all day, only the tracks in the sand whenever we landed to take a break on shore. We knew full well, though, that many eyes watched us as we drifted like phantoms down the river. It was often a topic of conversation in the canoe or around the campfire – about the unseen lives and interactions of our four-legged relatives, and of the general state of nature since we humans became dominant on the planet. We both agreed that it wasn't a pretty picture in most places, which for us underlined the need to preserve the small amount of wilderness there was left on earth. Although we were still in the designated Wilderness portion of the Refuge, we realized we would be crossing the invisible line into a less-protected category of land the next morning, so we savored every drop of our experience in the Wilderness and let it soak deep into our consciousness.

For me, much of this experience included birds and wildflowers. And from the time we pushed off in the morning there were plenty of these. We came across three more ospreys, including one standing in its nest on the top of a small white spruce. The wind was careening through the forest, making the tree sway back and forth, and the osprey looked like it was doing some sort of aerial dance on its nest. Our curious waxwing friends greeted us again and again at every turn in the river; we met our first common mergansers on this side of the mountains; and a pair of red-throated loons raced over us, looking like they were flying "upside down." While we were stopped for lunch on a gravel bar, both orange-crowned and yellow warblers, and ruby-crowned kinglets serenaded us from both banks of the river. And as icing on our cake, a myriad of colorful wildflowers abounded on all sides of us. Some of these included merckia, Siberian aster, starwort, fragrant prickly rose and the prayerful yellow Drummond's avens. Dwarf fireweed were also blooming in profusion, converting the gravel bars to long pink bouquets.

The day wasn't without its challenges, however. A combination of fast water, high winds, sweepers and narrow braided channels tuckered us out, so that by late afternoon we were ready to call it a day. We stopped to make camp on another of the Sheenjeks's welcome sand and gravel bars, where there was plenty of wood for a dinner fire and a stiff breeze to keep the mosquitoes at bay. We were even able to write in our journals around the fire right up until bedtime.

It rained a few drops while we slept, and when we crawled out of our tent in the morning there was still low overcast threatening more rain. But it was a false alarm, and as soon as I finished lighting the breakfast fire the sky cleared and the sun shimmered and bounced across the rippling surface of the river. We even escaped the wind for part of the morning, although soon after crossing the Refuge Wilderness boundary at Monument Creek the wind came back with a punch.

Just before noon we arrived at the Koness River, where the water was running black and clear, a nice contrast to the murkiness of the Sheenjek. Don's friend, Richard Hayden, had a cabin about a half-mile downriver, and we planned to drop by to see what condition it was in. I had visited the cabin in 1998 with Andrew Benedetti and wasn't impressed with the way Richard had left it. Unfortunately, this time it was just about as bad, with Blazo cans piled helter skelter, and junk everywhere. There was a big hole in his roof and another in the side of the cabin, where porcupines had chewed through. It didn't take much to imagine what the place looked like inside because it smelled like porcupine crap. About the only "improvements" were a blue tarp on part of the roof and a Tundra Ski-do snow machine parked directly across the front door. Don knew Richard well enough to say that "he didn't run a very tight ship," and we both wondered why the U.S. Fish and Wildlife Service continued to grant him a permit to use the place.

Before heading down the river again we ate some lunch on a gravel bar, away from the mess of the cabin. There weren't as many rapids in the afternoon, but the water was still running swiftly, with spruce sweepers and drift logs lying in wait on both sides of the now heavily braided channel. The wind, blowing constantly in our teeth, made it even more challenging for us. But Don was a virtuoso bowman, and with his special steering stroke (a slow prying motion with his paddle blade almost straight ahead and parallel to the bow) we got through the tight situations with no problem.

In mid-afternoon, we "rounded the bend" on our topo map and began to paddle eastward. The wind now blew at our backs, and the braided river consolidated into one channel and straightened out for a while, making it easier to paddle. At about the same time, I discovered that by sitting on Don's food bucket behind my seat I could stretch my legs and relieve the pressure on my knees, which were really killing me. When I put on my boots to warm my cold feet I kidded Don that I was ready to go for another three hours. But he said he was bushed and wanted to call it a day, so we found a good gravel bar with a sandy platform for the tent and enough dry willows for a fire, and made camp.

As we drank our tea, we rehashed some of the day's sightings, or lack of them. We hadn't seen a single moose, and we thought it might be because of the lack of browse in the area. There was no evidence of large scale forest fire anywhere, and the entire river basin seemed to be composed of climax white and black spruce. We came across more beaver, though, and an array of different birds, including Harlan's hawks, a goshawk, and a pair of red-throated loons that delighted us with their characteristic burping call. We also saw many herring gulls. In fact, the river seemed to belong to those gulls. Every half-mile or so they would attack us, and once dropped a whitewash bomb on both of us. It was so perfectly on target I was reminded of the old ditty about the "Birdy, birdy flying so high, dropping whitewash in my eye. But I'm a good boy, I shan't cry. I'm just glad that cows don't fly!" Herring gulls are as pesky and noisy as lesser yellowlegs any day.

My last note of the day: *Looks like another low-pressure front is moving in our direction. By morning we'll know if there's any rain attached to it. We're camped just outside the Refuge boundary. Only a few high hills lie off to our west, and by mid-day tomorrow we should be in the Yukon Flats.*

Sure enough, in the early morning we did get some rain. But by the time we were up and out of the tent we could see a broad belt of blue sky over the western hills, and it looked like it was going to be another good day for paddling.

I had no problem lighting our breakfast fire, since I had stashed some dry twigs under a piece of plastic, and in no time we had eaten our bowls of oatmeal and were on our way again. Although the river had fallen another 4-5 inches, it still had plenty of current, so we quickly left the high hills to the west behind us and began our last leg of the trip through the Flats to the Porcupine River.

There were fewer braids now, but more sweepers and logjams to contend with, so we always had to be on our guard. Finally, early in the afternoon, all the braids of the river came together into one main channel, meaning fewer worries about logs and sweepers, and an easier time paddling. The wind also cooperated and made it one of our calmest days yet.

At about 1:00 we watched a low hill to the north called Outlook Point disappear from view. From then on we wouldn't have any physical landmarks to tell where we were, so we'd have to go by the shape and direction of the loops and bends on our topo map to reckon our approximate location. But Outlook Point told us we were now well into the Yukon Flats Wildlife Refuge, and only about three days from our destination, Ft. Yukon.

It was another day without a single sighting of a large animal, and we encountered only a few beaver in the early morning and later in the afternoon. But there was a large diversity of birds, including more burping red-throated loons, our friendly twittering waxwings, tiny alder flycatchers snatching flies right over our heads, Swainson's thrushes calling softly on the forest floor, and northern waterthrushes boldly proclaiming the day in the willows at the edge of the river. We also heard the lovely high-pitched wheezing of two varied thrushes dueling at the top of opposite spruce trees. And down below I could just barely make out the distinctive sewing machine-like song of a blackpoll warbler.

The most memorable wildlife encounter of the day was a clash between an Arctic tern and a pair of herring gulls. The tern was defending his nesting turf from the gulls and viciously pursued the gulls, even jabbing them in the rear end several times with his dagger-like bill. The gulls were twice his size, but deftly outmaneuvered and outgunned by the tern, and left the area post haste.

Prickly roses were blooming everywhere along the river, and their fragrance matched that of the wild rhododendron and sweet pea we had come across farther upriver. We had missed the rose bloom in Fairbanks, but we certainly caught it on the lower Sheenjek along with the blossoming of the bluebells. These two species of wildflower bloom simultaneously and I think, more than any other wildflowers, are symbolic of the Interior. I love to see them blossom forth in early spring, and as I age I drink deeper than ever of their wonderful pink color and lovely smell.

My journal again: *It's about 9 p.m., and one of several rainsqualls has just passed over us. We're listening to the lovely chorus of bird song after the storm, and recognize among the many species the killy, killy, killy, of an American kestrel, as it repeatedly flies over our tent. No wonder one of the common names of this little falcon is killy hawk. It's another new one for our trip list, as is the ruffed grouse, which we can hear drumming across the river. What a nice ending to another great day.*

It was such a beautiful sunny morning I couldn't resist getting up a little earlier than usual to build a small fire for some tea water and listen to the bird songs that were everywhere around us. An alder flycatcher particularly caught my attention, with his buzzy *rreeBeea* or *three beers,* a little like a short form of the olive-sided flycatcher, which my dad always described as *quick, three beers.*

After a breakfast of my hearty river pancakes, we broke camp and started paddling in the now much slower current. There were few braids this day, but we quickly found the trail of the river to be different from the one on our topo. Over the years there had been so many new channels cut by the spring floods that it was almost impossible to follow the route marked on the map. We took a number of these new channels, which often turned out to be shortcuts through the maze of the lower river. One of them was probably a mile long, and quite narrow and swift in places. The logjam that Andrew Benedetti and I encountered on the lower river in 1998 didn't turn out to be as much of a labyrinth as I remembered, and Don and I easily made it through to the other end.

By early afternoon the river consolidated again into one major channel, and was slower moving, making us paddle a little deeper but also allowing us to appreciate the bird life much more. In addition to all of the old regulars like Canada geese, killy hawks, and countless Arctic terns diving earnestly for minnows up and down the river shallows, we encountered three Pacific loons. I mentioned to Don that I'd never seen these loons on the river before, and maybe they were there for the same reason the terns were. While reading about them once, I told him, I'd learned they were one of the best divers of all the diving birds, and had been known to dive as deep as 240 feet. They could remain underwater for at least five minutes and swim for hundreds of yards without surfacing for air.

Not long after seeing the loons, Don silently raised his arm and pointed off the bow toward the right bank. There, a dark brown grizzly bear was poised to jump into the deep water. We slowed down and watched him while he made up his mind. It was overcast, with low light on the river, and the bear must not have been able to see us because he suddenly made the plunge and started swimming for the other bank. By then I had my camera out and fired away several times as he swam in front of our bow, slowly climbed out on the other shore, then stood up on his hind legs to get a better view of us. As soon as he figured out who we were he dropped back down, moved farther up on the bank, turned around one final time to check us out, then disappeared into the willows. It all took no more than five minutes.

After our sterling morning, the weather changed to mostly cloudy and cool. Only for about an hour in the afternoon was there enough cheery sunshine to allow me to take off my polar fleece and paddle in my T-shirt. It was then I noticed the moose flies, and realized this was the first time we had seen them since the beginning of our trip. I remembered the last time I was down the river with Andrew the moose flies had plagued us terribly from the first day we started at Double Mountain. But the weather had been warmer then. This year it was cooler than usual and the flies didn't show. Only over the last day or two had the water finally begun to warm up enough for us to take a bath and wash our hair without shivering.

Towards the end of the day on the lower river we discovered a few old clearings made decades earlier for fishing and hunting camps by people from Ft. Yukon or Old Crow. By the way the spruce had begun to grow back, it appeared the sites hadn't been occupied for many years. We chatted about how the river might have been in those days when it was peopled with Indians who only led a subsistence way of life. It would have been so much more interesting to float then.

July 5 was to be our last day on the Sheenjek.

As soon as we crawled out of the tent we checked the river level and found it had gone down about five more inches. But there was still plenty of current and, despite the long bends and meanders, we made it to the Porcupine by early afternoon. It rained all morning, and if it hadn't been for the many birds along this stretch, it would have been less interesting. We added three new species here, including a pair of belted kingfishers hovering over the river in quest of small fish, two female buffleheads, and a mob of 25 Bonaparte's gulls on a gravel bar that we thought might have been unsuccessful nesters because of the cool spring weather. About our cutest bird sighting so far was of a female tern with its chick trying to nestle awkwardly under her wing to keep warm, having a little trouble at first because of its large size, but after pushing a little harder it finally succeeded.

Near the mouth of the Sheenjek we came across an immature bald eagle perched on top of a lone cottonwood. The cottonwood was higher than the surrounding willows, but not by much. This was truly a luxuriant jungle of some of the tallest willows I'd ever laid eyes on. They seemed to thrive in this extensive wetland. But one species of tree that didn't thrive on the Sheenjek was the paper birch. As much as we searched, we didn't see a single birch tree, even on the highest banks. Only when we started down the Porcupine did we begin to encounter them.

While still on the Sheenjek, we came across our first white mosquitoes, the same species that had surprised Andrew and me in 1998. When I reported it to Richard Carrol in Ft. Yukon that summer, I remembered him telling us that it was their new brand of mosquito. It was indeed. It was almost diaphanous, and even acted differently, barely making any noise with its fluttering wings as it stealthily sneaked up on an exposed patch of arm or neck and zapped us. Its injectant was so effective that we almost never felt its probing proboscis. Only after it had sucked us dry and flown away with a bulb of our blood in its body, did we begin to feel the itchy reaction.

By noon it stopped raining, which made the rest of the trip down the Sheenjek more enjoyable. The sun wasn't shining yet, but the prickly roses and spirea blooming along both banks of the river, made up for the lack of sunshine. Each time we floated close to either bank I detected the mildest fragrance of rose. It wasn't as strong as rhododendron or sweet pea, but it was there nonetheless, and I breathed long and deep to catch its full effect.

When we were finally out on the Porcupine, we found high water levels there, too. The current moved us along so swiftly that we were down to the lower mouth of the Black (Tranjik) River in only three hours. At that point we were ready to call it another day and pulled ashore on a lovely buff-colored gravel bar like the ones I remembered from previous trips on the Porcupine. The sun was out by then, and we took our time putting up the tent and building the fire. We knew it would be our last night on the river, so we savored these final rituals, including the heating of our tea water and the preparation of our dinner. We'd saved some tortillas and cheese for this occasion and, with a pot of creamy broccoli soup, we relished each bite to the fullest.

My journal: *It's 8:30, and I'm writing these notes in some glorious evening sunshine. A semipalmated plover is scurrying around on the sand and gravel catching small flies that scoot back and forth across the ground in the cool breeze. The frenetic little bird once approached so close I could almost have reached out and touched him. I was amazed at how fast his tiny legs moved as he chased the flies. I hear sandhill cranes trumpeting in the distance. It's the first time since the Coastal Plain. A nice note to go to sleep on. Goodnight.*

We awoke to an overcast sky and spits of rain, but by the time we'd finished our breakfast the clouds were thinning and it looked like an auspicious beginning to another day on the river. It was to be our last day on the Porcupine and when our paddles hit the water we hoped to be in Ft. Yukon around noon. The water level was up three more inches, making the current a little stronger, and at first we sailed briskly downstream. But when we rounded a wide, loopy bend a gale-force wind struck us so hard that we had to dig deep and fast to make any headway. Only when we eased into the leeward stretch of the bend were we able to relax a little. But it wasn't long till we were again facing into the teeth of the storm and we had to paddle for all we were worth against the silty wind-tossed waters of the big river. Even the ravens struggled as they coursed across the river to try to find respite in the tall trees.

With such a fierce wind it was not a good day to watch for bird life, or any other form of wildlife either. On the gravel bars we only came across grounded flocks of adult terns without chicks, although there may have been a few young hiding somewhere out of the wind, behind the sparse willows on the islands.

We began to relax when we recognized the small sandy opening to the slough that would finally take us the rest of the way to Ft. Yukon. It was on the left bank and we headed straight for it, lest the current sweep us past its mouth and make us fight our way back upstream again.

Once inside its entrance, what a dramatic contrast there was between the stormy waters of the river and the peaceful black surface of the slough. Here, too, the water level was high and we had no trouble finding our way to a good take-out spot near Ft. Yukon. While I disassembled the canoe and organized our gear, Don walked into town and borrowed his old car from Kirk. Since the car was small, it was a challenge cramming everything into it, but we were soon driving back along the dusty road to Kirk's place. His mother Pat was there to welcome us, and Kirk himself arrived soon after to offer us a well-appreciated beer. They invited us to shower up, then partake of a fine hot chili dinner with all the trimmings, including ice cream for dessert, quite a change from our fare on the trail. And as friends do when they get together after a long hiatus, we chatted on and on till almost midnight.

In the morning after a hearty breakfast, Don and I made preparations to head back up the Yukon River to Circle where we had started our odyssey. Although it was windy when we pushed off into the wide silty river, the wind was at our backs and the sun was shining gloriously, both signs that seemed to bode well for us.

Since the start of our trip more than a month before, the level of the river had gone way down, exposing many sand and gravel bars and at times making for some tricky maneuvering. We would often hit shallow water and have to cut the engine and paddle to deeper water where we could again start upriver. Once, when we were completely bottomed out, crosswinds made it so difficult for us that we had a frustrating time getting back into deep water. But persistence paid off and after 15 minutes of frantic paddling we were back on the trail. Only twenty miles out of Ft. Yukon we came across several large fish wheels turning slowly in the current, but we only encountered two boats all day long. And it was a long day, especially for Don, who had to hold the kicker handle for almost ten hours.

Whenever I'm on the Yukon River, I'm struck by the amount of country where there are no people. It's probably one of the only rivers left on earth where this is the case, and Don and I were privileged to be able to experience it. But such a large river doesn't allow for much birding. We only came across a few bank swallows and gulls, although there were still a lot of terns feeding in the same general location we'd seen them on the way down from Circle, probably in association with the sheefish spawning grounds. Don and I both agreed that the Yukon would be a tedious river to canoe all the way to the mouth, because of its impersonal character, and with so few birds and large mammals or wildflowers like those we saw on the Sheenjek. We wondered if the many Germans and Japanese who floated it in canoes thought about it this way. Probably not, since they were mostly products of urban living and still not fully in tune with the smaller details of nature.

Early in the evening there was a massive mushroom thunderhead forming in the western sky, and when the sun disappeared behind the tall cumulous clouds its rays fanned out like a thousand spotlights in every direction. I wished I'd had a few shots left in my camera.

Close to midnight we still hadn't made it to Circle, so we stopped to camp at a spot that only recently had seen the retreat of high water from the sand and gravel. It wasn't a pretty place, with the chaos of driftwood, pools of water, wet mud and sand, and rocks and broken trees everywhere. But we were bushed and needed some sleep, so found the driest patch of sand we could, cleared the stones and debris away, and put up our tent and crawled inside. Finally it was warm enough for me to sleep in my bag without my polar fleece on.

July 8 turned out to be another blue-sky day – fitting, we felt, for the last one of our trip. After breakfast we set out to cover the remaining 15 miles of the river to Circle. Don still had to be on his guard as he guided his long canoe up the river, but the water was deeper now in the braided channels and there was no wind, so within an hour and a half we were landing the dugout at the boat ramp in Circle. An hour later we had all of our gear offloaded and packed in Don's little yellow truck, the canoe securely tied on top, and we were homeward bound for Fairbanks.

The gravel road hadn't changed any, with potholes, washboard, and soft mud for almost its entire length, but sitting side by side in the relative quiet of the truck cab gave us a chance to talk about some of our experiences over the past month. There was the wild land that we trekked and floated through, the staggering numbers of caribou that brushed shoulders with us for so long in the mountains, and the astounding variety and amount of loquacious birdlife and blooming wildflowers everywhere in the Arctic Refuge. There were the huge wide-open chambers of sky, the clear air, as yet unsullied by the engines of the juggernaut, and the pure water of the creeks and rivers flowing endlessly on both sides of the Continental Divide. And there was the simple motion of the trek itself, step by step through the mists of the Coastal Plain, across the tundra of wet polygons and mountain saddles, deep and plodding through the snow of the pass near Bathtub Ridge, treading like mountain sheep along their high narrow trails, and tiptoeing bootless and barelegged in the frigid fords of rushing torrents. I glanced over at Don, who was still wearing his safari desert hat, and whistled, "Whew, Don, what a helluva trip we just had!"

PHOTOS

1. Caribou along Leffingwell River
2. Tundra swans at Lobo Lake
3. Grizzly bear on Sheenjek River

Chapter 6

Spring Creek to Marsh Fork
June 11-June 23, 2003

We had such a great adventure in the Sadlerochit Mountains in 2001 that Jen and I decided to do another Arctic Wildlife Refuge trek, but this time in the Marsh Fork area on the west side of the Refuge. After studying maps and talking to friends we asked our Coyote Air pilot, Dirk Nickisch, if he could drop us off to the north of Arctic Village on a tributary of the Junjek River called Spring Creek. From there we would walk over Carter Pass, then hike down an unnamed tributary to the Marsh Fork of the Canning River. We invited our Fairbanks friends, Phil and Jean Wildfang, and their son James, a geologist who was champing at the bit to get into the Refuge to study its amazing structures. I had worked with Phil closely on the Northern Environmental Center Board of Directors, and Jen and I had socialized with him and his wife Jean on a regular basis. So we knew they would be compatible on an outing like this.

Marsh Fork aufeis

On June 11 (Wednesday), Phil and Jean and their son met us just outside Fairbanks in Fox, and from there we drove in two vehicles up the Dalton Highway to Coldfoot. It was a route Jen and I had taken two summers earlier with Cindy Wentworth on our way to the Sadlerochit Mountains in the Arctic Refuge. While crossing the Yukon River bridge we could see the big muddy river was in spate and hoped the downriver villages would escape most of the high water.

Once in Coldfoot we drove over to the airstrip to see if our charter pilot Dirk Nickisch was home. We found him busy working on his airplane, getting things ready for our early morning flight into the Refuge. He invited us to a beer and showed us his new addition, a small office he said his wife Danielle had built last summer. She hadn't arrived yet, but would soon be coming up from Fairbanks with their two kids.

After finishing our beers, we drove down to the edge of the Koyukuk River to camp. Jen and I put up our Mountain Hardwear tent, then built a small fire and had a bite to eat. Phil took his family over to the greasy spoon in Coldfoot to have a hamburger there, and after they returned we chatted around the fire until midnight, when we decided to call it quits. Seven in the morning would come quickly, and we wanted a good sleep before heading into the wilds of the Refuge.

What a lovely clear day it was when Jen and I opened the flap to our tent – hardly a cloud in the sky, the rushing sound of the Koyukuk River beside us, and brawny mountains all around. But I knew this wouldn't hold a candle to what was to come. Our friend, Fran Mauer, had told us the Marsh Fork area had some of the prettiest scenery in the Refuge, and we were looking forward to it.

When we got to Dirk's place he was just about ready to go. So we piled all of our gear next to his de Havilland Beaver and waited for him to give us the signal to start loading it on board. It only took fifteen minutes to neatly pack both our gear and ourselves in the plane, and by 8:30 Dirk was revving his big nine piston radial engine in preparation for takeoff.

The Beaver took off easily into the blue sky from the ample runway and banked in a northeasterly direction toward our destination on Spring Creek. At first, we flew over State land where four wheelers had pierced the wild country in every direction with a web of stiletto trails, but soon we came to the border of the Arctic National Wildlife Refuge and the incursions by man's motors ended and true wilderness began. The Beaver is not a fast airplane, lumbering along like an airborne turtle, but it is tried and true, with a safety record that matches that of the DC-3 and Boeing 747. So with perfect confidence we lumbered for another hour, across the drainages of the North and Middle forks of the Chandalar River, over the Wind River valley, and into the Junjik River country, where I asked Dirk about the possibility of canoeing down this river to the Chandalar and Yukon Rivers. He said it would be a good float, so I filed that one away for next year.

Finally, after skimming across the spine of yet another range of sawtoothed mountains, we were in the Spring Creek drainage, ready to begin our descent. First, Dirk flew over the high bench he planned to land on, to scope out any possible changes in the surface from last year, then ever so slowly he curved around and carefully brought us down on the flat dryas terrace that served as our airstrip here. With barely a bounce we touched the ground and glided to a halt in less than 200 feet. The Beaver wasn't called a Short Take Off and Landing (STOL) craft for nothing.

As Dirk roared back into the sky we waved goodbye, then began searching for a place to put our tents. The Spring Creek valley we were in was so ruggedly beautiful and the weather so perfect that we decided to camp close to where we'd landed and do some exploring in the surrounding mountains. It didn't take long to find a good camping spot that fulfilled all of the requirements. Located on a low bench of well-drained soil next to a rushet of clear water, still harboring some of last winter's ice, the area was abloom with a white carpet of mountain avens. Since avens are a member of the rose family, I commented that we would be sleeping on a bed of roses. Directly in front of us was a blanket of aufeis extending for hundreds of yards up and down the river valley.

After erecting the tents and eating a short brunch, we decided to climb a small mountain to the east of camp. Following a long ridge, we stopped often to identify the wildflowers already beginning to paint the landscape with rich colors. We also came across several tiny willows on the mountain: least (*rotundifolia*), netleaf (*reticulata*), and skeleton-leaf (*phlebophylla*). Every time I find *phlebophylla* I am so amazed at how small it is that I gratuitously point out to everyone within hearing range that it is the tiniest tree on the planet, its catkin almost twice as large as its stem.

As soon as Dirk's Beaver had disappeared down the valley, we began to notice the birds in the area. Even before our hike up the mountain, we heard tree sparrows, redpolls, and a robin singing their sweet spring songs. Almost next door to our tents a loquacious wandering tattler tootled along the edge of the creek, busily poking the shallows for food. During our climb we spotted a violet green swallow dancing in the thermals, and a pair of wheatears nesting in a sheltered nook just below the top of the mountain. The swallow was a surprise, and a first sighting for me of a violet green in the Brooks Range.

Except for birds, that afternoon we saw only one other animal denizen of the tundra. A colony of parky squirrels had set up camp even before us not more than 150 yards from our tents, which caused us some concern for our food supply as we were climbing on the mountain. We took the chance, though. Since there were no trees or high grass between the colony and our camp, we figured the parkies probably wouldn't want to expose themselves for that long an exploratory journey into what was for them the great unknown. But if they'd had even an inkling there was food available, they might have ventured forth.

During our climb up and down the mountain James explained the visual geology of the area to us. He pointed out associated formations of limonite, garretite, hematite and magmatite, all iron oxides that we found together on our side of the valley and that we could see continuing on the other side as well. He also gave us a detailed explanation of the folding limestone strata, ubiquitous in every direction, showing us the fault lines where the limestone articulated with pulverized shales and slates that also contained some very colorful iron oxides. He said that most of what we saw was of early Mesozoic age, ca. 265 million years B.P., although some could be from the late Paleozoic, ca. 300 million years B.P. We had an especially good view of it all from our perch on top of the mountain. From there we could also see a long way up the valley, where we were headed the next day. It looked like fascinating country and we were eager to start trekking in it.

When we got back to camp we had a small snack, then Phil, James and I did some exploring on the aufeis opposite camp. Neither of them had ever walked on such an extensive ice formation before, and they marveled at the fascinating phenomena associated with the ice, such as the small mounds and ridges of powdered lime that were scattered everywhere on the surface. These were the result of windblown limestone from the surrounding mountains that had been washed around by melt water. We picked some up with our fingertips and tasted it. Yup, limestone. Then there were the felt leaf willows (*Salix alaxensis*) leafing out and blooming right through the ice. The darker color of their branches had absorbed the sun's rays, melting a tunnel almost all the way to the base of the tree. Tough plants, those.

We followed the creek as it meandered through the aufeis, sometimes disappearing under it, then suddenly appearing again. A green-winged teal sprinted by, headed downstream. Then my eyes fastened on something I'd never seen before, a little hobbit-hut of a nest made of interwoven mosses and grasses sitting neatly on a ledge almost halfway up a low cliff face on the other side of the creek. About a foot in diameter, it had an arched opening near the bottom. Phil likened it to an igloo. Not far away were the owners, two American dippers, known to some as water ouzels. One of them, perhaps the male, had just fed the other, then quickly fluttered off. The second bird remained perched on the ledge next to its hobbit-hut, but flew away when we approached a little closer. Soon the first bird returned with a small larva in his mouth, but his mate wasn't there. So he waited on the ledge for her to come back. We quickly took our cue and retreated. After supper I returned alone to watch the male approach the nest and call in a sweet voice as if beckoning his mate to come out. No one responded, though, and the bird finally flew off. While I watched the dipper, a wandering tattler quietly sat down on the cobbles right beside me. I soon realized it was a female on her nest and silently slinked away.

After the others retired, I sat around our little fire, taking in the lovely evening and writing in my journal. The white sun was still shining brightly to the northwest, getting ready to begin its slow roll across the midnight sky. A few clouds were developing above the valley to the north, but rain didn't seem to be in the cards, and I looked forward to the surprises that awaited us the next day.

Friday the 13th, a good luck day for us, full of wildflowers, birds, fascinating geology, sunny weather and great camaraderie. It couldn't get any better.

Our plan was to walk up the valley for a few miles and make camp just close enough to Carter Pass to be able to hike the next day over the pass, then down to the confluence of the headwaters with one of the main tributaries of the Marsh Fork. Since Dirk had flown most of our food over to the Marsh Fork airstrip on the 12th, our packs were fairly light and we could enjoy this part of the trek.

While breaking camp we were serenaded by a white-crowned sparrow singing, "don't wanna go to school no more!" These little birds are always present in summer in the Brooks Range, and their sweet song follows us everywhere. Before leaving the area, though, I wanted Jen and Jean to see the dipper nest we'd found the day before, so we headed over there. They were impressed that a bird as dainty as the dipper could build such an elaborate and unique nest. After taking a couple of photos, we continued on up the wide valley, following the dryas terrace bench on the east side of the creek. These terraces are one of the reasons why I love hiking in the Brooks Range. They are like walking on a lawn carpeted with wildflowers.

We said goodbye to our last stunted, wind-blown spruce, aka krumholtz spruce, and soon came to the broad expanse of aufeis that we'd seen from the summit of the mountain we'd climbed the day before. Since the temperature had dropped below freezing in the early morning, we found it easier walking on top of the ice than along the soggy bank. We carefully wended our way across it, hopping over narrow rivulets of sparkling melt water, and walking around some of the deeper clefts left by fast flowing streams on the surface. By the end of the summer all of this ice would melt and the fresh water would find its way, first to the Junjek River, then the Chandalar and Yukon Rivers, and finally to the Bering Sea, a long way to flow. While crossing, I showed Jen and Jean the thermal holes bored in the ice by greening willow stems and dead leaves blown there by high winds during winter.

After leaving the ice I spotted a pair of semipalmated plovers calling their telltale rapidfire *too-ee, too-ee, too-ee.* I showed James what they looked like in my bird guide, since he had said he wanted to learn more about the birds and flowers on this trip. He reciprocated by describing the history of the predominantly limestone mountains surrounding us. Calling these formations flatirons because of their unique shape, he said this was due to differential faulting, uplift and erosion. After he pointed out the geological pattern, I could see what he meant about the tectonic pushing force originating from the south. The lead edges of the flatirons all pointed toward the south.

We ate a brief snack, then took a shortcut across a broad outwash plain, where I flushed a gray-crowned rosy finch from its nest. Located in a thick clump of dry grass, the nest had seven dark brown eggs in it. It was the first rosy finch nest I'd ever found. I showed it to Jen, took a photo, then quickly left the scene. We didn't want to interrupt this friendly little bird's incubation routine for too long. Then it was over to the other bank, on what by now was a bone-dry creek bed. I was astonished to learn later that this was because of the nature of the tectonic uplift from south to north that James described to us earlier in the day. The surface water percolated underground, following the porous limestone strata from the south to the north side of the Continental Divide! Finding no water in the creek was worrisome, so, although it was still early, when we encountered two small pools of clear water next to some flat ground for our tents, plus a plentiful supply of wood, we doffed our packs and made camp. Besides, after already checking our topo map, we knew we were close enough to Carter Pass to make it the next day over and down to where we thought we might camp then.

In mid-afternoon, Phil and his family and I hiked up the flood plain we were on and climbed a low saddle to see what lay in store for us toward Carter Pass. We also got a good view of the rugged limestone mountains that lay to the west of us. At one point James dropped behind to examine and collect a *foraminifera* fossil and some calcite crystal, which he showed us when he caught up. On the saddle he found a formation of fractured shale that he explained was evidence of what he called a fault junction, where the shale had slipped away from the underlying limestone.

While examining the shale and other rock, we chatted about a book I was reading titled, *The Eternal Frontier*, by Tim Flannery, an Australian ecological historian. His chapter on the asteroid that smashed into the earth 65 million years ago, causing the extinction of the dinosaurs and most other forms of life in North America, was fascinating. It hit at the north edge of Yucatan, forming was is referred to now as the Chicxulub Crater, 180 km. in diameter, and releasing the equivalent of 100 megatons of high explosive, a hundred times the amount needed to cause a global catastrophe. This information wasn't new to James, but most of it was for the others and me.

On our way down we came across a pair of American pipits in nuptial mode. The male flew over the female like a skipping butterfly, all the while sweetly singing his heart out. I was happy to see them because this area was scarce in the wildlife department. There was plenty of fossil wildlife, however, and when I looked closely at the rocks I found them studded with evidence that this mountain range had at one time been under a vast ocean. Now the ocean is located to the north of the range. And this change didn't happen overnight, or even in thousands of years, but in tens and hundreds of millions of years. Thinking about rocks in that way is sort of like a slap on the forehead, and a little humbling.

Back at camp, I found Jen reading in the tent. There were no mosquitoes, so the fly was open. Time for dinner, I told her, and we gathered some willow sticks for a small fire and heated up some water for one of our beef stroganoff freeze-dried meals. We never eat prepared food like this at home, but in camp it really hits the spot.

We chatted around the fire for a while about the state of the far away world, and about some of our own more interesting sightings of the day, then when the sun slid behind the mountain and we started to cool off, I washed my socks, brushed my teeth and retired to the tent to write in my journal and read Tim Flannery's book.

We awoke to another scintillating day, although when I went over to fill our pots with fresh water, I found that almost all of the water in the pools was either frozen or had disappeared. The only explanation we could conjure up was that the underlayer of ice holding the water had thawed, allowing the pools to drain. The same thing had happened to me once before a few summers earlier on the Kongakut with Andrew Benedetti and Dan Hatfield, except then no water remained in the pools and we had to do without our morning coffee. At least this time there was enough water remaining to allow us to make coffee and fill our Nalgene bottles. Over our coffee and granola breakfast we chatted about the mess our "Present resident" Bush (aka Shrub) was making of the country. Every day he seemed to do something to unravel the social and environmental fabric of the nation. We only hoped that post war Iraq would turn sour for him, and he would slide far enough into the abyss to lose the next election.

Then it was onward and upward to Carter Pass, named after a prospector who apparently wandered these mountains searching for the noble metal gold and, thankfully, never found it here. Not far from camp we ran into a pair of horned larks. They were in the middle of their mating frenzy, so paid us little heed. The male's flight song is a little like that of the Lapland longspur, and filled the air with sweet tinkling and chirping that flowed on and on like a mountain stream.

At the head of Spring Creek we came across a small lake, where James hoped to find a few fish. It looked a little shallow, but he tried his hand anyway, while we took a lazy break in the mid-day sun. Scanning the area for birds, I found a pair of semipalmated plovers and another pair of horned larks. There were no ducks in the lake, something that should have tipped us off as to why James was having no luck catching any fish. It didn't take long for him to figure it out, though, and within a half-hour we were on our way again.

Less than an hour later we summited Carter Pass and started down the other side. We rested near the top for a few minutes to glass the area with our binocs and to check our map. James reported that we were at 3800 feet elevation and on the rim of the Continental Divide, meaning that all water flowing south eventually ended up in the Bering Sea and all water flowing north ran into the Arctic Ocean. Glassing to the north, we could see a frozen lake just down from the pass that looked rather interesting.

And interesting it was. It was covered with candle ice except along the sloping edges, where the ice had pulled away from the shoreline and exposed the frigid black water. The patterns created by the separation were quite beautiful and I took some snapshots of them. While composing the shots I began to notice bird activity, a lot of it. There were several species of birds, all busy feeding on something very small. When I peered down at the ice I found scores of tiny stonefly larvae, called naiads, trying to make their way from the open water up the sloping shore ice to land. Who knows why they were doing this, unless they were getting ready to metamorphose into adults. It didn't matter anyway, since most of them didn't make it past the hunger of the birds.

Semipalmated sandpipers, pectoral sandpipers, American pipits, and semipalmated plovers were cashing in on the bonanza food supply before spilling north into the warmer valleys and Coastal Plain, where they would begin nesting. One pair of semipalmated sandpipers had apparently decided to make the alpine lake their home, however, because the male was scurrying around on shore doing his one-wing-in-the-air nuptial dance in front of the female who patiently watched nearby. It reminded me of the dance performed by a buff-breasted sandpiper I came across on the Okerokovik River the previous summer. I told Jen and the others to continue walking while I watched this windfall of birds a little longer. I had a feeling it might turn out to be the most birds I would see in one place for the whole trip.

I caught up to the others just above a small gorge we had to cross to be able to go on down the valley. It would have been impossible to follow the west side of the gorge because its talus slopes were too steep. The east bank with its gentle tundra-covered slopes was the obvious route to follow and we searched for the best trail across the gorge. I was the first to the other side because I found a way up an almost vertical snow bank. Luckily, the snow was still stable enough to take my weight. After everyone was up we parked ourselves for lunch on a lovely patch of tundra just above a partly hidden waterfall. Even though the bank was fairly high and steep at this point, my curiosity got the better of me and I found a way down to the waterfall. What a reward when I clambered over the rocky creek bottom and into a vault-like enclosure to get a better look at it. On each side of the vault was a fascinating series of tortuous limestone striations and many examples of cobbled coral. I could see James was totally captivated by the area, too, because he climbed up the steeper west side of the gorge to investigate the geology there.

Continuing down the creek, Jen spotted five ewes and two lambs grazing on the south-facing slopes on our right. With the recent melting of the snow and increasing intensity of the sun, the slopes were just starting to green up, and we imagined these first tastes of new growth were quite savory for them. They were our first Dall sheep so far, and we advanced toward them to get a better view, but they quickly spooked and soon vanished behind a high ridge above us.

Since the limestone banks of the gorge were even more vertical the farther we hiked downstream, there was no way to actually walk in the creek itself. This meant we had to cross four extremely steep side gullies ("bivots," James called them), if we were to continue toward our destination. One of them was so difficult that I decided to carry Jen's pack up the incline myself. It was then I discovered her pack was lighter than mine! The final leg of the day took us along a narrow rocky sheep trail for a half-mile until we reached the bottom of the creek. There we had to take our boots off to ford the fast-flowing current. It was our first cold-water crossing and went without a hitch, except that while reaching for my little electronic camera to snap a photo of James wading the stream I dropped it on a rock. And, KAPUT! That was the end of the camera. I tried fixing it, but the electronic mechanism had been damaged beyond my ability to repair it.

As I examined the camera, an adult dipper landed just downstream from me and daintily began tiptoeing under the rushet of water flowing around him. I was so mesmerized by the little bird that I forgot about my problem. What an appropriate time for him to show up. He revived my spirits almost completely.

When I caught up with the others they had already doffed their packs and were preparing to make camp on a grassy meadow overlooking the creek. It was our loveliest campsite so far. We were hungry, and as soon as Jen and I set up our tent we joined the others in gathering dry willows for a cooking fire. We put on a large pot of water, and it wasn't long till we were busily eating another of our Mountain House freeze-dried dinners.

Our immediate biological needs taken care of, Phil, James and I explored downriver to try to find a good ford back across the creek. Scoping with my binoculars, I saw that in 200 yards or so there was a confluence of this creek with another larger one coming in from the east. We knew it would be easier to cross higher than lower, so we mentally marked a good spot for the next morning. During the walk James explained more of the geology of the area, and we also saw our first mew gulls on their own exploration mission in search of food. James wondered if they were finding fish. If they were, he said, maybe he would have a chance to use some of the flies he had made especially for this trip. Phil and I both hoped he would, too.

When we returned to camp we reported our findings to Jen and Jean, then continued gossiping late into the white night. One of our favorite subjects was the quality of light in the Arctic, especially toward midnight. I was still thinking about it after I turned in and wrote in my journal: *The midnight sun is beginning to crawl across the northern cleft in the valley where we're camped on one of the tributaries of the Marsh Fork of the Canning River. It is shining so brightly I can feel its warmth on my face. I never cease to be amazed at this midnight sun of ours. I think it's one of the reasons why I return to the Refuge at this time of year.*

When it finally disappeared from sight behind the mountains, it was almost one o'clock in the morning. The wavy edges of the creamy gray clouds above the distant peaks glowed from the backlight and made me think of wildflowers.

I awoke to the echoes of a wandering tattler sweetly chortling along the edges of the creek. Just below our tent the creek tumbled through a pocket-sized limestone canyon, hence the echoes. I was the first to awaken and went down to the creek to watch the tattler. While I was at it, I checked the little stick that I'd placed at the water's edge the night before to see how the creek level was doing. It had gone down, which I half expected at this time of year, since things usually freeze at night, thereby contributing less moisture to the creeks. It was good luck for us because we were planning to do at least two crossings today.

When I got back to camp, there was still nobody out and about, so I walked over to a small limestone boulder in the middle of our meadow and pondered it awhile. Who knows how long it had been there, but with all of its encrustations of lichens and mosses, it was so fascinating I felt I should write the outline of a poem about it. Here is its finished form:

On the Marsh Fork

I awoke early to a wandering tattler's call,
and left my tent
to explore this ancient Arctic limestone canyon
that we're in now
on the Marsh Fork of the Canning River.

It was there
I caught shafts of light
echoing bright
from a block of white rock
hunching conspicuous and
alone
in the middle of our campsite meadow.

Approaching the rock,
I could see it had
tumbled down
under a more ancient sun
from its lofty aerie above,
crashing as it toppled
end over end,
sounding like a booming cannon

above the silver ribbon of river below.

But now it is silent,
and,
fractured by time and weather,
it has grown old in the meadow,
but handsome
with its spreading crusts
of black and orange and lemon-yellow lichens
and its mantle of mosses
sprinkled with sprigs of tiny willows
sprouting nascent yellow catkins,
and sere blades of last year's grasses
mingled with green spears of new ones
pushing towards the sun.

Wildflowers,
snow-petaled mountain avens and
blue-tinted white anemones,
poke through the mosses and lichens
rhythmically bobbing their heads
back and forth
in the early morning canyon breezes.

Atop the rock
a bleached and broken parky squirrel bone
perches alone,
abandoned by a snowy owl
or hungry fox,
themselves once perched
on the limestone pedestal,
as they tore at bloody meat and gristle,
scarce sustenance
for yet another day
here in the Arctic.

Dead leaves on other willows
just now waking to spring
trace outward from the chalky rock
and cross deep animal trails
made by sheep and caribou
and grizzly bear
on their way to who knows where
up and down this craggy canyon.

Soon,
like them,
we, too, will follow these trails
in search of the mystery
that lies
just around the next bend.

As we finished breakfast I heard the metallic buzzy *dzeet* of a dipper in the canyon, so we all grabbed our binoculars and watched him as he bobbed and dipped and swam in and out of the water, searching for his own breakfast. I explored up and down the creek in quest of the dipper's nest, but try as I might I couldn't locate it. I did find some interesting geological strata, however, including ancient coral reefs that James said were a part of the Lisburne Formation. At 1500 feet thick, the Lisburne represents one healthy span of cosmic time – certainly a lot healthier than it is on Earth today. I wondered how our own human-caused sediments would look a few million years hence.

While I ogled the fossils of the coral reefs, who should wander by again but my little dipper friend. Constantly teetering and bobbing up and down, he scurried back and forth at the edge of the creek, in and out of the water, sometimes almost totally submerged, kicking up the bottom for insects and their larvae. He was the dull gray color of the wet stones, save for the constantly flicking white nictitating membrane (third eyelid) around his eyes, used to protect them from dirt particles suspended in the water.

With our first mosquitoes trailing behind us, we broke camp at mid-morning and walked downriver for about a mile, where we forded the creek, then trekked east up a large tributary of the Marsh Fork. After crossing the two main braids of this branch of the river, we rested for a while on a patch of tundra studded with wildflowers, and decided we liked the spot so much that we'd camp there the night. We pitched our tents in a veritable garden of fragrant wildflowers, including Lapland rosebay, sweet pea, rock jasmine and moss campion.

After some lunch we hiked for several hours upriver to explore the valley. Our map indicated that if we had walked to its headwaters, we would have crested a saddle that led down to another tributary of the Junjik River called Water Creek. Search as we did, we found scant evidence for recent use of the valley by large mammals. We only ran across a single lower mandible from a Dall sheep lamb on the top of a high bluff overlooking our camp, possibly brought there by a golden eagle that had scavenged it from wolves. The area was definitely not rich in browse, although I did find a plant I'd never seen before, Jordal's oxytrope (*Oxytropis jordalii*).

On our way back to camp we had our first hard rain shower, and even a little hail. But we hadn't seen the end of the rain. Just as we finished preparing dinner, we had to run for cover, bowls of soup in hand, to our tents to escape a gully washer, hitting us so suddenly and with such stiff winds, that we had to put our backs to our tents from the inside to prevent them from collapsing. It was one of the hardest winds I'd ever experienced in the Brooks Range. Thankfully, the storm lasted only a half-hour. Even so, after a short nap, when I checked the water level of the river next to our fireplace on the gravel bar, I found the fire pit almost totally submerged, so hurriedly rescued our cooking gear for fear the river would rise even more and float everything away. I wondered how the water level would be the next day when we would again have to ford the river, this time at the confluence with the Marsh Fork. Since the sky was beginning to clear, maybe it wouldn't be so bad.

After rescuing our kitchen gear I was wide-awake enough to write in my journal without first taking a short nap. I noted that pipits, horned larks, tattlers, redpolls, robins and willow ptarmigan seemed to be the bird species nesting in this drainage. The birding highlight of the day was a male American pipit doing his mating display, marching back and forth in front of the female with his two wings bent at the elbows. When he flew high in the air, he reminded me of the horned lark we'd watched on the other side of Carter Pass. He tinkled and chirped and warbled to his heart's content, and I imagine he hoped also to his mate's heart's content.

June 16 –

From my journal: *We're now camped at the Marsh Fork of the Canning River. And what a breathtaking place it is. Fran Mauer and Don Ross said it would be. Now we see for ourselves what they meant. With craggy, yellow limestone mountains to our south, east and west, and gray, sensually rounded mountains to our north, this is the most stunningly scenic spot I've seen yet in the Brooks Range. And there are lots of birds here to boot. After seeing almost no birds all day, finally we spotted not only our old regulars, but also a couple of new species, including an upland sandpiper and a golden eagle. As I glassed the eagle with my binocs, soaring over the limestone crags to the east, I wondered if he had an aerie somewhere nearby.*

We may not have encountered many birds while trekking downriver, but we did see our fair share of Dall sheep – three bands of them, all ewes and lambs. One band numbered 14 ewes and 10 lambs, an excellent success ratio for lambs, it seemed, probably due to the warm spring. We also saw a few scattered rams sitting off by themselves, watching us amble across the aufeis below them.

About half of our route downstream was on top of aufeis, making it much easier than hiking over the river cobbles, my least favorite walking. At first, Jen felt a little leery about traveling on the ice, especially after hearing loud thunderclaps in the distance that seemed to originate from the middle of the aufeis. When I explained the noise actually came from huge (sometimes 8-10 feet thick) chunks of ice breaking off next to the river and falling into the flowing water, she began to relax and eventually got used to the sound.

We only had to make two river crossings, one right off the bat after striking camp in the morning, and the second just before we got to the confluence with the Marsh Fork. The water was frigid on our bare feet and legs, and when James heard us moan loudly he ventured downriver on top of the ice to see if he could find a shallower ford so he wouldn't have to take off his boots.

At one point he disappeared behind a high wall of aufeis, and Jean began to worry about him. Eventually he came back into view, though, and joined us, saying his search had paid off. He'd found a heavily braided part of the river where he was able to light-foot it across the shallow water with his boots on. As we were looking for a good ford near the confluence a rainsquall caught us, and we all hunkered down by the riverbank for a few minutes while the storm spent its fury. It didn't hold a candle, though, to the hellbender that had blasted our tents the previous night, and we were soon on our way again.

After a cold-water crossing to the east side of the river, we walked onto a wide gravel plain strewn at one end with gigantic limestone boulders that had toppled down the mountain countless millenia ago. Like the rock in my poem, they too were studded with colorful lichens, mosses and other plants. At the north end of the plain were two small Cessna aircraft, one of them taxiing for take-off. When it was in the air I recognized it as Don Ross's old 185, now owned by Kirk Sweetsir, who must have just finished chartering someone in here. We waved as he buzzed overhead, and he tipped his wings at us.

We soon learned the other Cessna belonged to a Swiss couple, Felix and Salomé Egolf, who worked for Swissair as pilot and attendant. They said they were on vacation for a couple of weeks and flying around northern Alaska. They would be here only till the next day. We chatted with them for a while, then headed for a stand of tall willows, in search of a campsite with upwelling spring water that our friend Clancy Crawford had told us about back in Fairbanks.

It didn't take long to find the place, and we quickly set up our tents on a flat bench beside the springs. The next order of business was to collect some dry willows, build a small fire and begin dinner. We were famished and, since we now had tortillas and cheese from our resupply, I made quesadillas for everyone.

Before our digestive juices overtook our muscle function, James and I climbed halfway to the top of the craggy limestone mountain just south of camp to check out a dark concave geological formation. On the way up we found a lot of Dall sheep sign, including a few perches in the sun, where they had recently taken a siesta. What great views the sheep had in every direction, especially to the west up the Marsh Fork. By 8:00 p.m. the westering sun painted the myriad braids and streams of the river melted platinum. It also exaggerated the visual effect of many of the folds and faults of the surrounding mountains, which James said were a part of the Lisburne Formation.

On our way back down the ridge, James told me about his recent career as a geological consultant for the Ute Indian people in Utah. He said that Indian tribes in the Lower 48 had a lot of Federal money to do geological and environmental studies on their tribal lands. Since the money was authorized under the 1975 Indian Self-determination Act, it was fairly easy to apply for by the tribes.

We stopped by for a short visit with our Swiss neighbors, still parked on the edge of the airstrip, and just sitting down at their portable table to eat a meat and potato dinner. Felix said he had prepared the potatoes under the embers of a fire he had built near his plane. The night before they had celebrated Salomé's birthday with a candlelight dinner, he told us.

Just before turning in for the night we suddenly heard several loud blasts of a foghorn coming from the direction of Felix's Cessna. Phil and James hurried over to find out what the problem was. They soon returned and reported that Felix had used a foghorn he'd brought from Switzerland to scare off a bear, which he said he had glimpsed over by the river. Reflecting on that for a moment, I mentioned to the others that his camp was almost a quarter of a mile away from the river. Hmmm!

By now we were all wide awake, so after re-stoking the fire and fortifying ourselves with some Yukon Jack that Phil had brought along, we gossiped into the long white night. As the sun turned and wheeled across the Arctic sky, shooting rays of light through the Kongakut Valley, we watched the slow motion play of mountain shadows on the striated slopes behind us. By midnight, those steep slopes were a pastiche of golden browns and mellow greens, grays and heathers, so that I felt almost mesmerized by the place and remarked that this was indeed the magical spot that Fran had told us about, although we could have done without the foghorn!

Jen said she had a hard time sleeping because she was worried about bears, probably because of Felix's foghorn the past evening. As it turned out, we weren't finished with Felix, for as we were eating our breakfast, who should fly over but Felix and Salomé. I guess he wanted to say goodbye, so he buzzed us at almost willow-top level. Once was fine, but he didn't leave it at that. He banked and did a tight "Sky King" turn, then buzzed us a second time, making it evident that he didn't understand the concept of "wilderness solitude."

We decided to break camp and head east to get as far away from the airstrip as possible, so we could have some real solitude. Just as we started out, Jen discovered a wandering tattler's nest. While crossing the creek beside our campsite she flushed the momma tattler from the nest and found her four handsome brown-blotched blue eggs nestled among the dark gray cobblestones. We took a quick look at them, and I pointed out how they had been placed in the nest scrape on the ground with the narrow ends of their oval shape all facing toward the middle, probably because that made it easier for the mother bird to brood them.

While Phil and James took the high road in the dry tundra, Jen, Jean and I decided to try our luck through the willows. It was the wrong move. We soon found ourselves walking in a wetland, and a slippery one at that because of all the moss-covered rocks we had to negotiate. Once, while crossing a small creek, Jen tripped and fell on her hands and knees. She got up immediately without a peep and continued on as though nothing had happened, not even looking down at her wet pants. What a trouper, I thought. She and Jean then set off for the higher drier tundra while I went down to a small lake to check out the bird life there. What a bonanza I found: a Wilson's snipe, semipalmated and Baird's sandpipers, a pair of semipalmated plovers, and a small flock of cliff swallows, part of one of the farthest north nesting colonies in Alaska.

By the time I was ready to continue my trudge across the wetland, the others were out of sight. Finally, I spied them resting on a distant ridge and decided to take a short cut to intercept them. The short cut turned out better than I thought, and I got to our rendezvous river crossing before they did. Then it was a long march up through tundra tussocks to a low saddle, where James and I had spotted a small pothole lake from our mountain vantage point the evening before. There we rested while Phil repaired one of the metal pins on his ancient pack. He had loaned his new pack to James and tried to save some money by using his old one on this trip. As Phil worked on his pin, I glassed the lake and found a fox sparrow in the willows and another tattler, tattling along the shoreline. Just as he finished his repair job a rainsquall caught us and we had to don our rain gear. But it only lasted a few minutes, and we hit the trail again.

Right away we started down one of the most fascinating limestone rock canyons I'd ever seen in the Refuge. Its walls were perpendicular on both sides and about 200 feet high. It reminded me of a canyon out of the Southwest, except for the boggy tundra down the middle. Sometimes the bog turned into shallow ponds, which when they abutted the canyon walls required us to wade. Our feet became sopping wet, but we had no choice and plodded on through the water.

While eating our afternoon snack beside one of the ponds, I caught a glimpse of our first marmot near the top of the north wall. Since Jen and I had already seen this species of marmot during our 2001 trip into the Sadlerochits, we knew it was a *Marmota broweri*, aka Alaska marmot. These are smaller and browner than the hoary marmots found in the Interior, and they don't whistle like hoaries do. On the north wall of the canyon I also noticed what looked like a cave with a lot of interesting vegetation at its mouth. Wondering why the plants were so much greener than elsewhere, my curiosity finally got the best of me and I was soon on my way up the slope to check it out.

When I reached the entrance, I discovered the reason why it looked so lush there. Everywhere, forget-me-nots, larkspur and many other wildflowers grew in cheerful abundance, because inside and immediately outside the cave there was at least half a ton of sheep droppings, probably left behind by Dall sheep hiding from thunderstorms, or in winter, during some of the hellacious snowstorms they have in these mountains. While I was investigating the inner part of the cave, which was about 12 feet deep, a pair of Say's phoebes suddenly showed up and began flying in and out of the cave. I suspected they had a nest somewhere nearby, and when I squinted my eyes and peered closely along the shadowy backside of the cave I found it.

What a nest it was. Located on a small ledge toward the cave roof, it was not one nest but two, this year's effort neatly nestled on top of last year's. Made of winter Dall sheep hair, downy ptarmigan feathers and muskox quiviut, the nest contained six perfectly white eggs. While peeking into the nest, both parent birds fluttered close by my head like big moths, their bills clicking nervously a mile a minute. I vacated the area quickly after glancing at the eggs, lest I disturb the birds too much. As I left I had both thumbs up to the others on the canyon floor watching me with their binoculars – my first Say's phoebe nest, ever!

Before going down, I wandered out to the edge of an overlook above the canyon, where I found more lush green vegetation surrounded by small piles of sheep turds. When I noticed the grass and wildflowers were bent to the ground all around me, I figured a flock of sheep had recently bedded down here. As at the cave entrance, vivid blue forget-me-nots seemed to be the most abundant wildflower in bloom. I thought they must be a tasty tidbit indeed for the sheep to eat so many that the plants would later grow and flourish wherever the animals left their droppings.

We continued on, and again we were forced to wade through an even deeper and larger pond that stretched from one side of the canyon to the other. Fortunately the water was only up to our knees and we didn't have to swim, because there was no other way to get to the other edge of the pond. The water was warm, so warm that I couldn't resist taking a short swim. I shed my clothes except for my shorts, walked into the water and took the plunge – not once but twice, because it was the warmest water I had ever experienced in the Arctic. Even better, the floor of the lake was as soft as baby skin on the bottoms of my feet. Opening my eyes underwater I could see why. The entire lake floor was carpeted in moss. What a delight. I yelled over to Phil and Jean to join me, but Phil only smiled and took my picture.

It wasn't long after my swim that we found Jen and James on the other side of a dry creek, checking out the possibilities of the bank for a good place to put our tents. Since the bank was a dryas terrace, it was a perfect campsite. Not far away there was a small seep of water, and enough dry willows for a cooking fire. While setting up the tents, Phil spotted some young rams slowly walking across the mountain slope opposite us. They glanced in our direction every now and then as they poked along, but otherwise didn't seem to be worried about our presence. Then, as I was building the dinner fire, Jean pointed at a golden eagle that had just hopped off its perch on the cliff line above us. When it caught a thermal and began spiraling upward, it called several times, reminding me of a red fox barking. It kept soaring, round and round, until it was only a speck, then drifted away to the west. Phil was amazed, and I had to admit that it was an awesome spectacle. Scanning the cliffs, I soon found the aerie with the female sitting in it. During dinner I was watching the cliffs out of the corner of my eye, when suddenly she leapt from the edge of the nest, and with a few quick wing beats caught an updraft and away she went into the wild blue yonder.

From our chat about the awesome behavior of eagles, we drifted back to some of the other highlights of the day. Phil and James both had the gift of the gab and found scores of topics to pull out of their hats. I told Phil that he reminded me of Jen's dad, Joe, who seemed to be able to talk forever about the most mundane things.

As in every setting where there are grizzly bears, campfire talk drifts in the direction of bruin encounters. When we headed out in the morning we found a lot of diggings close to our camp, where grizzlies had been scratching for their favorite spring plant food, bear root. This fanned the flames of bear fear that Jean and Jen had from the first day of the trip. I assured them they didn't have to worry anymore, though, because the plants of these roots were starting to flower, thus causing the roots to lose their tasty flavor, and since they were slower to mature higher up on the mountain, that's where most of the bears would be now. This allayed their worries enough to allow them to eventually get to sleep.

Meanwhile, as we chatted around the fire, the ragtag clouds that had been with us earlier in the day finally disappeared and the sky returned to blue again. It also turned cooler, and we were already at 3500 feet of elevation. We were glad we had brought our warm sleeping bags. And we always remembered the relationship between weather and mosquitoes. Even during the middle of the day there were still very few of the little buggers about, so we were all in favor of the cooler temperatures sticking around.

June 18 –

From my journal: *As I write this in my tent at night, a squall is pelleting our tents with raindrops. But I sure can't complain about today's weather, including the strong breeze that kept the first crop of kamikaze mosies at bay all day long. I wonder if the amphitheater we are in has anything to do with the advanced state of the mosies here. Tomorrow would tell. We're presently camped on the edge of a low saddle, between a tributary of the Marsh Fork and the broad valley of the Marsh Fork itself. We have an awesome view of the valley, with all of its aufeis and braids and sun-glistening meanders. And of the sensually rounded western mountains beyond, that, according to James, are mostly composed of shales and slates instead of limestone like the ones to our south. In fact, directly behind us is a gigantic massif of limestone that reminds me of flying buttresses or a huge coxcomb, "that even sings to us in the wind," waxed*

Phil. I listened closely, and I could hear something that reminded me too of singing, which brought back memories of the Maya temples at Palenque, Yucatan, that were built with so-called coxcombs on top to make the temples sing in the wind.

We trekked about four miles this day. The only mammal we saw besides Dall sheep was a little lemming near our morning camp. As we ate breakfast, he scooted back and forth along the bank of the dry creek, where we had camped the previous night. Stopping momentarily to stare at us with his big brown eyes, he reminded me of a pica. Keeping an eye on the female eagle, we watched her lift off from her giant nest once the sun had moved into a position where it could keep the eggs sufficiently warm without her. We encountered the sheep later in the morning down the creek a mile or so. They were a mixed band of 22 ewes and lambs, with one young ram crossing from north to south along a ridge to a rocky promontory above us. Their wary behavior told me that over the course of their collective lives they had probably encountered hunters in the area.

After ogling the sheep, we looked at our map and found a medium-sized lake to the west that James wanted to check out for fish. I told the others it might be advisable to take a shortcut across the north flank of the mountain to bypass any tussocks there might be lower down. So James and I took off according to plan. But at some point there was a communication breakdown because when I stopped to wait for the others on a viewpoint overlooking the lake nobody showed. While James went on ahead, I continued to wait. Finally, I glassed around with my binoculars and saw them heading down the creek bed for just the place I suggested we avoid. Well, I would intercept them, I thought, and quickly saddled up and fast-stepped toward the lake.

We finally met near the east end of the lake, but Phil was a little miffed at me for what he thought were unclear instructions. Even though I felt I had explained myself fairly well back on the river without giving outright orders to follow me, I apologized. After all, I was the expedition leader.

Meanwhile, James tried his luck with his fly rod. But after an hour he still hadn't gotten a single bite, so we decided that either there were no fish in the lake, or they just weren't biting. I took the opportunity to glass for birds, and added four new ones to our trip list, including a white-winged scoter, two greater scaup, a savannah sparrow, and a raven, whose raucous calls told me its nest must be located somewhere in the craggy flutes of the high mountain buttresses above us. Earlier in the day I had also bumped into a couple of northern shrikes just down the creek from our previous campsite. After watching them for a while, I decided they were a mother bird with one of her recently fledged young. She was angry at our intrusion and her calls sounded like a mix between a mad catbird and a bell-croaking raven. I'd never heard the second call before. The fluffy young shrike was perched innocently on a willow branch near its mother, not uttering a word.

From the lake we moved another quarter-mile or so to the edge of the saddle overlooking the wide Marsh Fork valley. After setting up our tents, James and I climbed to the top of a low, eroded hill to the north of camp. At the summit he explained that it was part of a shale-slate formation that struck east and west. He said that these mountains were more rounded because shale doesn't hold up to weather as well as limestone. On the way down, I found two new wildflowers for the trip, cut-leaf anemone and pink plumes. James and I had somehow missed Phil, who had started up the same hill earlier. As we were reaching the top we could see him just walking into camp below.

When we returned we all cooked a light dinner over our gas stove, then retired to our tents to escape some rain coming in from the south. By midnight the rain had stopped and the tattered clouds were moving off to the west. I watched the sun do its roll again, and as it passed across the north end of the Marsh Fork valley it reflected a vivid yellow light from the limestone ramparts above us. The effect was stunning and I missed my camera to capture the memory. It was too late to awaken Phil for his camera, so I had to let that one go. Maybe tomorrow night at base camp....

Looking down on the Marsh Fork in the early morning, the aufeis reminded me of scattered clouds over the river. With the sun's light now shining directly on the mountains on the west side of the valley, I could see a limestone formation that I hadn't noticed the day before. Its strata bounced and twisted all over the place until finally they dived under the sensual hills of shale and slate and disappeared. It was one of the most dramatic displays of ancient geology I'd seen in these mountains. When I showed it to James he was awed by it too.

It was to be another sparkling sunny day. So far the weather had cooperated with us every morning. Raindrops had pelted our tents some evenings, and often in the very early morning, but by breakfast the rain was gone and we were back to perfect. This morning was even better when a pair of my favorite flycatchers, Say's phoebes, flew in to hunt for bugs in the nearby willows. They took turns fluttering down from their perches to catch unwary flying insects, carrying their prizes back to the willows to eat. I suspected these birds had a nest in a small cave somewhere in the limestone ramparts just south of camp. This big amphitheater seemed to have a lot of phoebes, maybe because of the way it warmed up during the day, causing an early hatch of mosquitoes and other insects.

But it still had not warmed up very much where we were. The morning was quite cool, and that actually delighted us, since it meant fewer mosquitoes while striking camp and departing downslope to the river. Once we started walking in the wide valley itself, the wind took care of any of the pesky buggers that made it that far.

Our route followed the river plain south toward our base camp at the airstrip, and most of the way it was pretty good walking, give or take a few challenging sections of cobblestones. We saw a lot of wildlife. Right off the bat we spotted nine ewes and three lambs grazing on the flank of the mountain to our east. While Jen and the others walked ahead, I stayed behind to watch a turf battle between a pipit and a parky squirrel. The parky had stumbled on the pipit's nest in the tundra and poked its nose into the nest cavity while the mother bird was home. She didn't appreciate that one bit and fluttered and pecked the squirrel so hard that finally the little guy retreated. But the pipit wasn't taking any chances and kept fluttering right behind him so he wouldn't change his mind. When the pipit turned and flew back to her nest and the parky stopped to glance over his shoulder, he had such a sheepish expression on his face that it reminded me of a kid caught red-handed with the goods. I wondered if he would try his luck again when the mother bird was off the nest.

By then I was far behind the others, and when I caught up to Phil, he reported that he had seen an Arctic tern. It was flying over the open water, he said, and he could tell it was a tern by the way it flew, with its snappy wing beats. It turned out to be the only tern we saw during the entire trip. Shortly afterward, I flushed a Smith's longspur from its nest. This bird was a lucky find, I told the others, since their numbers had declined so much they were now on the Audubon Watch List. I remarked that it was sad that so many bird species were beginning to disappear from our skies. And they agreed that we humans were the cause, with our highways and fast cars, our communications towers, high-rise buildings, pet cats, suburban sprawl and much more. Where would it all stop?

Among the highlights of our meanders up the river was a lovely gravel island meadow, mantled in Lapland rosebay, so redolent with fragrance we could smell it long before we saw it. This was followed shortly by our crossing of a patch of aufeis that I thought would be our best bet to get from one bank of the river to the other. The women were at first doubtful because of the high water under the ice and the rapid rate at which the bright sun was melting it. But I took the lead to show them it was safe, and once on the other side we were ready to continue walking again. But not before Phil picked up some candle ice in his bare hands and let it fall to the ground. As it fell, he smiled broadly and shouted, "Diamonds, diamonds!" He used to have fun doing that when he was a kid, he said, although it wasn't with ice. During a snack break, toward the end of our walk on the river, Jen spotted an unusual cobble lying next to where she was perched. She picked it up and found it had a fossil fish embedded in it. When James looked at it he thought it might be fairly old, like maybe 300 million years old, he guessed. He was so intrigued by the fossil that Jen gave it to him. On stowing it in his backpack, he said he'd take it home with him to give him some perspective when he needed it.

We arrived back at our base camp at the springs in mid-afternoon, and I immediately gathered some dry willows and built a fire for some tea and hot chocolate. While we sipped our drinks around the fire Phil and James and I had an animated discussion about whether or not the U.S. was an ideal system for other nations of the world to emulate. Phil maintained it was, but James and I took another point of view, arguing that it depended on their social and cultural histories. One of the major problems with many leaders in the U.S. was that they didn't understand the historical realities of other countries outside of our tradition. An important reason for this, I thought, was that they had never resided in those countries. For them to have even a basic grasp of the mindset of foreigners, I felt it was necessary to spend at least a couple of years living abroad.

In the evening I showed James the mother wandering tattler and her nest scrape with its four beautiful blue, oversized eggs. When I first pointed her out he had difficulty spotting her on the nest because of her camouflage coloration. She looked almost exactly like one of the dark cobblestones that surrounded her on all sides. His amazement was mine. I don't think he had ever seen anything quite like her before. So much do we take these birds for granted!

Then I bushwhacked through the willows to the river, where I flushed a pair of pectoral sandpipers. The female had been on her nest, but I didn't stop to check it out and continued walking. En route I found tracks in the sand of both a snowshoe hare and a lynx that was probably in hot pursuit. Although I had been told that both of these animals lived on the north side of the Continental Divide, it was the first time I had ever run across evidence of them this far north.

From my journal: *As I write late into the bright night, I have been sitting in front of our tent watching the mountains change while the sun's yellow light crawls once again across the rugged outline of their limestone face. I spot a golden eagle soaring high and fast above a snow-splotched ridge, making a beeline in the direction of its aerie. Down on the ground, the tattler is still sitting placidly on her nest among the gray stones as though she were one of them herself. A few mosquitoes are now buzzing around me, but only a few. It's still pretty cool out, in spite of the dazzling sunlight. I wish I could have this beauty around me forever.*

We stuck close to base camp the next day and only took an exploratory hike up a short tributary of the Marsh Fork that lay a mile to the east of us. It was a narrow, steep valley and scattered with large cobblestones, making for slow progress. So we hiked just a couple of miles up it to another drainage entering from the south, then climbed a high knoll of gnarly rock where we had a good view in every direction. We ate lunch there and glassed the area for any form of large mammal life. Nothing, probably because there were such slim pickings. By the looks of the old grizzly diggings we found, the few bear that had passed through had only paused briefly to unearth a little bear root, then kept padding up the valley and over to the Chandalar River. They would have starved here.

On my way down from the knoll I discovered a chunk of limestone that I decided had to be an ancient coral pedestal. There was very little coral left on the base rock, but it was easy to see where maybe 300 million years ago the polyps had been fastened to it, but over time had broken off. After confirming my Keim theory, James eyed the rock with such avid curiosity that I gave it to him to take home. The valley was loaded with large chunks of eroded coral, and other fossils, too, including one Jean picked up that James said was a gastropod of some sort. He guessed it was only about 280 million years old. What poignant reminders of our own insignificant timeline on planet Earth.

While climbing out of the small drainage on the trail back to base camp, I stopped by the lake where I'd found so many birds a few days before. I wasn't disappointed this time either. There was a herring gull and nine teenage Canada geese, floating placidly in the middle of the lake. It was no surprise seeing the gull, but the geese were a surprise, as was a female red-necked phalarope skulking among the sedges. I knew she was a female because of her bright breeding colors, for among phalaropes there is a reversal of sex roles and plumage. The male has the drab coloration, since he is in charge of both incubating the eggs and raising the chicks until they're old enough to fly. The female may lay eggs in more than one nest, meaning she has at least two mates. I watched the female phalarope do her "swim and spin" act, which is their characteristic mode of feeding. They spin like tops on the surface of the water, kicking up the bottom sediments and causing any food items to rise to where they can easily snatch and eat them. Phalaropes are able to float on the water because of their dense breast plumage.

While crossing the creek next to base camp, I accidently flushed the tattler from her nest, so I took the opportunity to snap a quick photo of her brown-splotched teal-blue eggs. The eggs were quite large so that the chicks could mature enough inside to leave the nest as soon as they hatched. But the color I had a hard time figuring out. The blue was simply too bright to have camouflage value when the female was off the nest. On the other hand, she blended in so well with the surrounding cobblestones that she could quietly remain brooding even as a fox padded by right next to her. She moved for me only when I nearly stepped on her. But suppose she did tiptoe away from the nest to feed every once in awhile, how was she to quickly relocate her eggs? Keim theory supposes the color helps. It's a question of tradeoffs made for survival.

On my way back to camp I did a pond check for mosquito larvae. At higher elevations, where more direct sunlight warmed the small pothole tundra ponds, the larvae were just about ready to hatch. But lower down, where we were and the water was cooler, there was still no sign of them. The women were especially glad to hear that.

Jen was brewing some tea when I sat down around the fire, and she smiled when I told her about my pond check. She had been busy doing some painting, this time of arctic poppies and willows. It was very nice work, as were the others she had done during the trip. She is really quite a good artist.

Over dinner we chatted about the need to lock up wilderness areas like the Arctic Refuge, to keep them from the clutches of the multinationals. Once they get ahold of them, they despoil them and prevent future generations from experiencing what they were like in their original form. We also planned our next day's hike up toward the headwaters of the Marsh Fork. We had three days left and thought we'd spend them there.

Before turning in for the night, I pointed out to Phil where the wandering tattler was patiently brooding her eggs. The bird was so well camouflaged that even with binoculars he had a hard time finding her, until finally a slight movement of her head gave her away. If Phil had been a fox, I doubt she would have moved at all.

Summer solstice, and we awakened to another sparkling day in paradise. Although there was a ring around the sun the night before, indicating the possible approach of some weather, nothing happened. So, we took our time over breakfast, casually broke camp, and just as casually ambled over to the creek we had followed down from Carter Pass. We were headed along the main branch of the Marsh Fork, which we planned to follow upstream for a few miles, and then establish another base camp from where we would explore some more. There had been so little rain we had no problem finding a shallow place to cross, so we changed into our sandals and forded the cold water to the other side. Just before crossing, I spotted a gray jay in a rare copse of stunted cottonwood trees. The jay was our first for the trip, and I made a note to check out the cottonwoods after we returned from our hike upriver.

Farther up the Marsh Fork, we ran into another new bird for our trip, a rock ptarmigan, who gave us its characteristic warning growl as it fluttered off. Phil was impressed with the loudness of its growl, and I told him a few stories about running into them as I blithely rounded a blind bend somewhere. Each time, their alarm call sounded so much like an angry bear that it scared the daylights out of me. Since this bird was mottled all over in grayish-brown and white, it was a male. The female, which is almost totally brown at this time of year, was probably nearby on her nest.

For most of the route along the river we hiked on dryas terrace, making for easy walking. A myriad of old caribou trails made it even better. As we followed the interweaving pattern of tracks, we couldn't help but wonder which caribou herd had etched them into the shallow tundra. We didn't think it could be the Porcupine herd because we were too far west. How about the Central Arctic herd? Probably. But there was no way to know. Which is okay by me. There have got to be mysteries.

After pitching our tents on an expanse of flat dryas terrace, Phil and I took off in different directions to see what we could see. I climbed up the north slope of the mountain behind us to get a good view of both the Marsh Fork and the steep canyon of a tributary flowing in from the south. And what a view it was. The rock strata on the other side of the canyon had so many twists and folds in it that it looked like a roller coaster. I found more fossils, too. Most of them were simple crinoids, but one was a very nice bivalve. Not far from camp there were recent grizzly tracks angling up the mountain. I wondered what he was after, bear root, or.... I soon found out when I rounded a bend and glanced up the slope. A lone Dall ram was poking along up there, about 200 yards away, feeding in a little cranny filled with grasses and wildflowers. I ducked down, moved back a ways, then quietly started up the mountain again, thinking maybe I could get a little closer to him.

A few minutes later I spotted Phil coming across a low ridge in my direction. He yelled a greeting, but I motioned for him to be quiet and pointed toward the ram, who was still out of sight for both of us. When Phil caught up, we both stalked the ivory white animal from a grassy slope about 100 yards above where he was grazing, then rested on our bellies and watched him for an hour. He was so oblivious to our presence that he kicked a wallow in the side of the fine scree and lay down for a bask in the sun. A few times he looked hard in our direction, but finally relaxed and even turned his back to us. Shortly afterward we left him none the wiser, not wanting to disturb his peace and quiet. Besides, we hoped we'd see him again the next day.

Before returning to camp, we climbed higher on the mountain to get a view to the east. Following a wide ridge, composed of ancient shattered shale, we reached a vantage point where we could almost see into the drainage leading up to Carter Pass. The southern slope gradually tilted toward the north, then dived into the earth when it came to the Marsh Fork, indicating the presence of a major fault. The ridge was awash with green vegetation all the way to the top, telling us it was probably a favorite grazing spot for Dall sheep. There were none then, though, so we headed down to camp, chatting about how good it felt to be on the mountain, and how we were among the few lucky men our age who could still climb like this.

Jen and Jean were in camp when we got back, and we recounted our serendipitous sheep discovery to them over a mug of tea they had brewed. When James returned, we had dinner and compared notes on our outings. He had gone up the same mountain behind camp and had run across a shale formation similar to the one Phil and I followed on top. We were curious about what it was, so he looked it up on his geological map. At first, he thought it might have been a part of the Siksikpak Formation, which dated back to the Pennsylvanian-Mississippian Period, about 400 million B.P. He changed his mind, though, and dated it to only 65-70,000 years ago, because it lay above the much older limestone deposits that were ca. 300 million years old. When he wondered about the name Siksikpak, I told him it was an Inupiat Eskimo name that meant big parky squirrel. *Siksik* was the sound the critter made, and *pak* meant simply "big."

When I mentioned finding the recent bear tracks on the mountainside, the women again looked a little unnerved. But I reminded them of the bear dung we had seen in the morning on our way up the valley, and how it had been totally filled with plant fiber, which meant the bears were eating plenty of bear root. And where was the tasty bear root now? High up on the mountainsides, so no worries.

Before zipping up the tent fly for the night, I did another weather check. All was well, it seemed. The low-pressure system that began to form in the early evening was now dissipating, and the second ring around the sun in 24 hours had disappeared completely. The six herring gulls cruising above the river earlier were still there, possibly searching for Arctic char, although I wondered about that. A tattler wandered by along the river's edge close to our fireplace, and I watched it for a few moments before finally saying goodnight to the remarkable world outside.

June 22 was yet another magnificent day. After breakfast the five of us climbed up the steep south-trending canyon that Phil and I had seen the day before. It was a challenging hike, because of the large cobblestones scattered everywhere, and the many creek crossings we had to make. I suggested walking along the slope of the mountain, but didn't get any takers, so we stayed down below. Only a few hundred yards into the canyon Jen and I spotted five large rams feeding in the same verdant cul-de-sac where Phil and I had spotted the single ram the previous day. Then, on glassing the other side of the canyon to the west, we counted eight smaller rams. We pointed them out to Phil and Jean, since James had already headed up the mountain to check a rock outcropping he thought looked interesting. He would probably run into the five sheep on his way up, they said. Sure enough, not long afterward we saw the rams retreating quickly to the south along one of their trails. They had either spotted James, or caught his scent, and weren't taking any chances.

We ate lunch on a small knoll above where the canyon narrowed to just a keyhole. Jen and Jean where fascinated with the keyhole, so after lunch they walked up into it a ways farther while Phil rested, and I scrambled up the mountain to see if I could locate the five rams we'd spotted earlier. I found more fossils several hundred feet up, including some bivalves and trilobites. I hadn't run across trilobites before. While examining them, I watched Jen and Jean picking their way back down the thread of canyon they had just gone up. Then I found a game trail and angled over toward where we'd last seen the sheep. In spite of a lot of sharp limestone talus, I managed to get high enough to locate a sixth ram bedded down below me. I watched him for a few minutes and then started up a steep ridge to find his buddies. Suddenly, there they were above me on a rocky crag, at first glaring at me, then turning and fleeing up the ridge. Darn! I wasn't high enough. I carefully climbed after them for a short distance, then thought better of it and caught a sheep trail across the talus that ended at a water seep. I was thirsty and a little winded, so took another break there. Far below I could see the tiny ant-like figures of Jen and the others as they slowly wended their way down the sinuous course of the creek, hopping across it every now and then, always picking their trail with care through the myriad cobblestones.

At that point I too had to choose my trail carefully, because of the broken nature of the slope. Several hundred feet above where Phil and I had seen the lone ram the day before, I came across a sheep perch. Located on the edge of another ridge, it was carpeted with forget-me-nots and Jacob's ladders, both with sky-blue flowers that somehow made this rugged environment friendlier. While pausing for a few minutes to catch my breath, I glassed the big ram below me. He was still resting peacefully on the brink of a limestone crag, peering in my direction. He knew I was there, but he didn't seem too concerned. By the full curl of his horns and his nonchalant behavior, I guessed him to be the alpha male of the band.

After scrabbling over more broken limestone, I breathed a sigh of relief when I finally came to a rounded ridgeline of shattered shale talus. I followed it up, then down again, into a small catchment basin where the sheep had dug large holes in search of minerals, which explained the popularity of the area for the rams. On a south-facing slope I discovered a species of dandelion I hadn't seen before, *Taraxacum phymatocarpum*. I later learned this species is found only in the far north and on the Seward Peninsula.

Once I've climbed so high on a mountain, I hate to go down, especially in gorgeous weather, but the others were probably wondering where I was, so I headed back. Midway, I saw what looked like an orange tent located on an incline just above the river and about 300 yards downstream from our own camp. We hadn't seen it the day before as we walked upriver, and I wondered if we had some new neighbors.

It turned out the tent was unoccupied. All the evidence pointed to its abandonment the year before by a pair of hunters, who had left behind everything but their packs and sleeping bags. Even their sandals were inside the tent, along with a fall, 2002, issue of a hunting magazine and a still-unread cowboy novel. The tent smelled like death warmed over, and at first I thought I might find a dead human inside. But it was only a lemming that had managed to find its way in and couldn't find its way out again. Next to the river

I found the remains of the hunters' food supply, strewn in every direction by a grizzly bear that had discovered the camp either in autumn or early spring. Their plastic food bowls were a part of the scattered remains.

I dismantled the tent, which had been pretty badly damaged by the wind and winter snows, and placed it down by the river where we could pick it up and take it back to the airstrip the next day. I then gathered the garbage and returned it to camp for burning. While feeding it into the fire we had fun theorizing about what had happened to the hunters. Maybe they'd been spooked by a bear and abandoned ship for that reason. Only later did we learn from our pilot, Dirk, that the previous autumn there had been an early heavy snowfall, and a guide named Hendricks had radioed his sheep hunters to leave their camp and head downriver for the Marsh Fork airstrip where he would take them out. The shameful part of it was that Hendricks never returned to collect his Eureka tent or clean up the camp. Dirk told us that this was common practice for some guides.

Dinner was beef stew with mashed potatoes, and we were all hungry after a long day's hike. As we ate, we watched the herring gulls as they cruised up and down the river, hovering and swooping to the river's edge to catch some sort of insect larvae, we finally decided. Our tattler showed up again, tweedling sweetly as it earnestly picked among the stones for its own food. Around the campfire I mused to the others about how fascinating it would be to see through the eyes of birds, as they caught and gobbled down their favorite foods.

Our last morning on the Marsh Fork was warm, with clear skies for as far as we could see in every direction – an auspicious day for Dirk to make it in to pick us up. But first we had to get back to the airstrip.

There was no hurry, though, since Dirk wouldn't be there until later in the afternoon, so we took our time over breakfast and enjoyed our last granola meal in the Arctic Refuge, which we probably wouldn't see again till the next spring. Then we struck camp and walked downstream, stopping briefly to pick up the smelly remains of the hunters' tent. Retracing our steps along the dryas terrace, we followed the same deep caribou ruts we'd used coming up. Again, we wondered about the animals that had once ambled through there in such huge numbers as to leave these well-worn trails. Above the mountain peaks on the north side of the river three herring gulls were drifting in the upwelling air currents caused by the bright sunlight on the south-facing slopes. It seemed they were lollygagging, too. Since we had time to kill, whenever we stopped for a break I wandered off to photograph the many species of wildflowers in bloom, especially rhododendrons, sweet pea and northern yellow oxytrope that offered a profusion of fragrance and color everywhere we walked. Dwarf fireweed was beginning to do the same, and tucked between all of these were sprays of yellow arnica, red shooting stars and miniature grass of parnassus that added even more beauty to our surroundings. We had come here at the right time, no doubt about that. While scanning a wide meadow carpeted with rhododendrons, I spied one plant that stood out from all of the others. Instead of the usual magenta color of the flowers, every bloom on this shrub was as white as snow. I had never found an albino rhododendron before.

After crossing the by-now even lower and warmer tributary creek separating us from the airstrip, we set up our tent in the shade of some large willows, ate a hot beef stroganoff lunch, and waited for Dirk. Knowing it wouldn't be for a couple of hours till he zoomed overhead, I moseyed over to the river where I'd seen the small copse of cottonwood three days before. I found about thirty of what are also known as balsam poplar nestled among the willows. Some of the poplars were tall and leafy enough to even offer some shade, which I felt my poor skin really needed. In spite of wearing gloves, the backs of my hands had suffered from the relentless sun and they were dark brown and almost as dry as parchment. They were also dirty, as was the rest of my body, so when I found a warm pool of water at the edge of the river I shed my clothes and took a welcome bath.

I still had plenty of time, so I wandered back over the river cobbles, searching for small fragments of coral to take home with me. I thought my grandkids and our next-door neighbor's kids might like a pocket-sized piece of geology from the Arctic Refuge. There was certainly a lot of it to choose from, and in just a few minutes I had four river-worn stones that were perfect examples of the 300-million-year-old coral formations found in this part of the Brooks Range. Glancing up, I noticed a large band of about 40 ewes and lambs grazing on the mountainside just across the Marsh Fork. With the continued greening of the slopes, they would quickly put on weight, which they would need to successfully cope with the coming winter.

Only a few minutes after returning to camp, Dirk buzzed over, a full hour ahead of schedule. While the Beaver came in for a noisy landing, we quickly dismantled the tent and stuffed our packs with the kitchen gear and food we had gotten out for lunch. Then, it seemed in an eye blink, we were taking off, beelining up the Marsh Fork toward Coldfoot, which lay about an hour to the west. Since the sky was crystal clear, Dirk flew us over the higher mountains to the north, where we were able to peer into drainages and mountain passes we had never seen before. He told us of many other great walks we could take some day along rivers like the Ivishak, Wind and Ribidan that we still hadn't experienced firsthand.

Perhaps one day we would.

PHOTOS

1. Frank by aufeis igloo
2. Phil and Jean at Marsh Fork
3. Frank and Jen on aufeis

Chapter 7

Music Men on Birch Creek
July, 2003

July 23 (Wednesday) –

After traveling up the Steese Highway to the put-in parking lot at milepost 94, and unloading the canoes and gear, my brother Dave and Fairbanks friend Andy Keller drove the two cars down to the take-out parking lot at milepost 140. Meanwhile, Dave's partner Barbara and I organized our gear so it would be ready to go when Dave and Andy returned. Shuttles always take a while, but sometimes they're more dependable than hitchhiking back to your vehicle at the end of the line. Barb and I had everything squared away within an hour, then chatted for a few minutes with four Norwegians who had just gotten off the

4:00 a.m. sunrise over Birch Creek

river. They said they had been lucky with high water and didn't have to line their canoes at all, especially here on the upper portion of the river. After the Norwegians departed, Barb and I took a walk along the Steese Highway until Dave and Andy returned. It was a stellar day, with a bluebird sky and billowing white candy-floss clouds, and we were anxious to start paddling. When two thrush-sized birds suddenly flew over our heads I thought they looked familiar. Whipping my binoculars up, I identified them as Townsend's solitaires. Their eye rings and wing patches were dead giveaways. Barb said she'd never seen solitaires before. I told her these gentle thrushes weren't seen much by anyone in Alaska during the summer, since they seemed to prefer nesting in the remotest nooks and crannies of the state's forests.

We were on the river by 4:00 and, although we got off to a pretty good start, the water was so low that we were forced to line just about as much as we were able to paddle. Talk about scratches on the bottom of the canoes! But the hulls were made of tough material (Kevlar on the borrowed Old Town, and Royalex on my Mad River), so few worries there. Thankfully, it was a sparkling clear day, and just being on this Wild and Scenic River energized our bodies and spirits. Not long after we set out, I saw my first Harlan's hawk of the summer soaring over the river, effortlessly following the whimsical eddies of the late afternoon thermals. Just watching this dark northern variation of the Red-tailed hawk gave me goose bumps.

Finally, after much hard work, we reached the Harrington Fork, where some additional water flowed into Birch Creek, allowing us to float more often than line. By 9:00 we were ready to camp, and after building a little cooking fire and eating a tasty supper of quesadillas and fresh lettuce from my garden, we called it quits for the day and retired to our tents. Dave and Barb were weary but in good spirits, as were Andy and I. Andy was particularly high about being on the river for the first time, and joked constantly, especially with Dave.

I slept well until 5:00 a.m., then only fitfully with worries about low water and the possibility of having to do more lining, especially on the lower reaches of the river. Little did I imagine what was in store for us toward the end of the trip. I finally dozed off, and dreamed of flying backwards high into the air above my pursuers, who were trying to arrest me for being a terrorist.

Our camp was located opposite a dark green meadow of sedges and juncus, and the night before I had commented that we'd probably see at least one moose there before we left the next morning. Sure enough, when I opened the flap of our tent I spotted a brawny bull moose languidly munching on the lush vegetation. His antlers were at least five feet wide. It was nice to see there were still a few big ones around like that. Nearby, an alder flycatcher was calling its telltale *three beers!* And, yes, he was singing in the alders. Higher up in the birch I could also hear a western wood peewee. To my ear, his call sounds more like *wee-pee* than *pee-wee*. While listening to these songs I ambled down to the river's edge to check its level. The little stick I had placed there the previous evening was two inches above the water line, indicating a steady lowering of the river. Seeing this, we found ourselves hoping for rain. Rarely do I wish for rain on a trip like this. But lining is not easy on either the canoes or passengers.

Dave and the others were somewhat the worse for wear from the lining we did the day before, but after a hearty breakfast of my special river pancakes everyone felt up to another day of travel, and we were on the river again by mid-morning. The day began with a pellucid sky, like the water we were paddling on, but as the river miles went by, high clouds began to form, making it look like we might get some rain, after all.

We stopped at a little after noon on a gravel bar for some soup that Barb cooked up. In it she mixed miso (a soybean product), seaweed, carrots, noodles and some of Andy's dried mushrooms. Delicious, and a first for me. Just before leaving, Barb found some blueberry bushes under a stand of willows. They were full of berries ripe for the picking, and we all pitched in to gather enough of them for our next morning's pancakes. How unlikely to find them so near the water's edge.

By now, there was a fair amount of water in the river, and we were able to float long distances without lining. Only at some of the more difficult rapids were we forced to line around them. At Clum's Fork we gained a lot of additional water, making for much easier paddling, although the rapids were larger, too, keeping us on our toes whenever we heard their loud splashing in the distance.

On the stretches of calm water I kept my eyes peeled for birds. I wasn't disappointed. Red-breasted mergansers and common goldeneyes were busy escorting their young to hiding spots under the banks, several small flocks of curious Bohemian waxwings flew over, and a merlin complained in a tall spruce. High above us three Harlan's hawks and two bald eagles soared in the updrafts, and in the willows on both sides of the river Wilson's and yellow warblers competed in song with the strident calls of northern waterthrushes.

Finally, we came to the dogleg turn in the river that I'd been talking about all day as a great place to camp. It was a little early, but since everyone seemed ready to call it a day, we did. The gravel bar on the left bank of the river had all the qualities of a great camp site: splashing black water, firewood, sand to perch the tents on, a few large stones to use for our fire ring, wildflowers, and singing birds.

We fried quesadillas again for supper, this time with some dried refried beans that Andy had brought with him. It was early, so we chatted around the fire and did some exploring near camp. On the gravel bed of the river, Andy and I found some elegant hawk's beard (*Crispa elegans*), a wildflower that looks like a diminutive dandelion. It has basal leaves with numerous lemon-yellow petals, and up close is truly an elegant flower, although I think its close cousin, the dwarf hawk's beard (*Crispa nana*), is even showier.

Every time I'm on a river I check out the treasure trove of cobblestones laid down over the eons by its flooding waters. This river was no exception, and on the gravel bar we found a lot of Birch Creek schist granites mixed with pink and white quartz, ground smooth by the relentless motion of the river over hundreds of millions of years.

We went to sleep with the lovely sound of splashing water in our ears, and because there was now plenty of water in the river, I slept like a log.

July 25, my brother Dave's 59th birthday.

Happy Birthday, David.

When we crawled out of our tents we were greeted by a curious family of Bohemian waxwings, perched in the top of a tall cottonwood just in back of camp. They were calling in a high-pitched twitter, sounding a little like they were singing Dave a Happy Birthday song. So we three humans joined in and sang him Happy Birthday, too. Andy went even further and slapsticked his own version of the song, which went something like, "Happy birthday, happy birthday, happy birthday, David Keim, happy happy birthday to you." Then I cooked up a couple of big blueberry pancakes for him over the fire, which he said made his morning.

As lovely as the place was, with its splashing rapids and deep pool of black water in front of us, we finally had to leave it in mid-morning. We were in no hurry, even though it looked like some big thunderheads were moving in at the higher elevations upriver. But where we were it was still sunny and warm, with only a stiff breeze beginning to build up behind us. "Better wind than mosies," Dave reminded us. Besides, the direction of the wind was downstream, so no problem.

In late morning we came to the first of three major rapids that we would have to line or portage, depending on the amount of water feeding their frenzy. The first two we lined with little problem, but the third one, called Shotgun Rapids, which coursed through a small canyon confined by rock cliffs, we had to study really hard before lining. At first, I thought using the right bank would be better, but the hydraulics seemed even more auspicious on the other side, so we decided to try it along the left bank. It was the right decision, although there was one point were Andy and I could have lost our canoe when the stern rope broke as I was slowly feeding the canoe over a churning ledge of water. Thankfully, Andy held on to the bow rope, and the canoe bounced like a big bubble across the surface of the frothing water, coming to rest exactly where we wanted it. A lot of excitement for a couple of seconds, but we both learned something from that encounter. I used the same technique with Dave, as we lined the Mad River canoe through the same difficult spot. This time, though, it worked like an orchestrated dance. On my mark, Dave released the stern rope, and within five seconds the canoe dropped below the ledge, bubbled over the top of the foaming rapid and, with me tugging on the bow rope, swung easily into the rocky backwater where I was awaiting it.

Before starting to line, we met a German couple who had come through the night before. They were both wearing hip boots, and I couldn't help mentioning to Dave and Andy how cumbersome they must be compared to our Teva sandals. We saw them again, just downriver from the canyon where we put in for lunch, but they took off before we had a chance to chat with them.

We were happy to be past the canyon without incident, since the last time I was through here with my son Steven, we had overturned and lost some of our kitchen gear while attempting to run the rapids. It was the ledge that got us then, and I had to do some fast swimming in very cold water to retrieve many of the items that I had failed to secure to the boat. What a bummer that was, and if it weren't for Steven's lighter and a quick warming fire, I would have had a severe case of hypothermia.

On the gravel bar where we took out for lunch we found a bountiful supply of flat stones that demanded to be used in a stone-skipping contest. The objective was to skip them clear across the river, and we all joined in with great enthusiasm and laughter. Even Barb participated, for the first time since she was a young girl, she said. This was the first time, too, that she had ever been on a wild river, and it was evident she was excited. For almost her entire adult life she had been occupied with raising her five children, so she hadn't had time for the fun she was having now. She's a spunky woman, and Dave is lucky to have her.

Down the river again, this time through some fascinating geology along the riverbanks. The metamorphic strata of Birch Creek schist were everywhere. They angled up and down in every direction, overthrusting sister strata, then sinuously twisting and bending back on themselves like enormous brown and white snakes. They were very ancient, too: Precambrian, dating more than 600 million years B.P. According to a geology paper I did many years ago, Birch Creek schist is composed mostly of quartzite, quartzite schist, quartz-mica schist, mica schist, and feldspathic and chloritic schists, which translates into a lot of old rock.

In late afternoon, we floated through a section of the river where there had been a recent forest fire. I remembered the burn from the last time I was through with Steven in 1997. It had occurred just the year before. By now, the succession of trees and flowers, intermixed with the gray pick-up-stick pattern of fallen trunks, made the burned area quite beautiful. Angled sunlight shining on magenta fireweed, and the new green of young birch climbing up the mountainsides, caused intense contrast and magnified the already vivid colors of these plants. Thick stands of sedges and juncus and burnet undulated in the wind along the shores of the river, and in the alders and willows western wood pewees and alder flycatchers were still voicing their territorial songs. Back of the higher banks in the tops of the white spruce I could hear the *clankety-clank* flight calls of white-winged crossbills, as well as the lovely fluting of varied thrushes.

Just on the other side of the burn we passed the Germans, who had decided to call it a day and make camp. We continued on to Harrison Creek, where we stopped to watch a small bull moose feeding downriver along the opposite bank. Meanwhile, I boiled some water over a small fire for a mug of tea. Since the sun was out and the day warm, Andy and Dave decided to take a short swim and wash up. It was still too breezy for me to think about swimming, so I remained by the fire to chat with Barb. Pointing at the flattened pillow-shaped clouds in the sky, I guessed there might be some rainy weather beginning to move into the area.

Shortly after getting back on the river again, we came to an abrupt turn with some high cliffs. When we heard the plaintiff warning calls of two peregrine falcons, I suspected they had an aerie nearby. I glassed the cliffs with my binocs, and finally located it in a small crevasse toward the top of the cliff. I couldn't see the young, but I knew they were there because of the fuss the adults were making. On the cliff face, about five feet above the water level, I noticed a lot of defunct cliff swallow nests, but absolutely no swallows. In fact, the only small bird we saw in the immediate area was a warbler, skulking in the trees next to the river. The peregrines were eating themselves out of house and home, I thought.

At about 7:00 we stopped to camp on a large gravel island that had all the amenities: firewood, sandy beach, wildflowers, singing birds, drinking water and bushes for Barb to hide behind. After Dave leveled a sand platform with his paddle and set up his tent, I helped him fix the zipper on the mosquito fly. It needed some soap so it would zip more easily. That taken care of, I had to quickly prepare our quesadilla, beans and rice dinner, so we wouldn't be eating in the rain that we could see marching steadily down the valley. The drops started pelting us when we had just half-finished eating, but we simply donned our rain gear and continued with the program. The quesadillas turned out a little wet, but no matter, they were delicious anyway, as they always are when camping.

It turned out to be only a small storm cell, lasting just 20 minutes, so we didn't get very wet. When it was all over it left a double rainbow in its wake, ending right next to us at the near edge of the river. It was the first time in our lives the hypothetical pot of gold was within arm's reach, that is, almost, because we never did find it. Dave agreed that, even without the pot of gold, it was the best birthday present ever.

As I brushed my teeth next to the river, I watched the waxwings veering and lurching back and forth, hunting the myriad insects that came out after the rain. At least they found their pot of gold.

We awakened to light rain and, although it made breakfast a little more difficult, it could have been much worse if we had been farther upriver where the storm clouds were more ominous and the rain appeared a lot heavier. In any case, that's what we brought the granola for.

We were on the river by mid-morning. It was still sprinkling, but after three gorgeous days, who was going to complain about a little rain. Besides, things look different when they are wet, and often their colors are more vivid. That was certainly the case with the rock cliffs we passed. The russet color of their quartz-schist strata stood out like cockscombs, and Andy commented again and again on the crazy zigzag patterns of the bedding planes. The glaucous-green of the Alaska sage plant growing on the cliff talus was also richer, as was that of the caribou lichen.

Right off the bat, we bumped into two more peregrine aeries on bends in the river where there were high rocky precipices. The parent birds aggressively swooped down and shrilly warned us not to tarry and to keep on paddling down the river. As we passed under the cliffs, I again noticed the conspicuous absence of cliff swallows, the air space around their mud-daubed nests being eerily motionless and silent. Only a single adult flew erratically overhead, knowing if it didn't, it would instantly be in the peregrine's stew pot.

By noon the sun was shining bright and hot, and the high hills surrounding us reflected a patchwork quilt of light greens and grays. It was an interesting year for the Interior's forest, since most of the aspen leaves had turned gray from the action of a tiny parasitic white moth called the leaf miner. Its almost microscopic larvae eat through the middle layer of the leaf, forming a maze of looping trails that look much like the meandering of a river. The leaves don't die or shrivel, but take on a gray cast, distinguishing the aspen from other deciduous trees not affected by the parasite. The color change is actually quite pretty. It's the first time I'd ever seen this phenomenon.

Along a wide bend in the river we floated past a stretch of bank with a veritable garden of wildflowers, including dwarf fireweed, wild rhubarb, blueberries and boykinia (bear flower). I asked everyone which of those plants they'd like to have with dinner, since they were all edible, although boykinia is preferred by bears. Barb said her choice would be some ripe blueberries for dessert. That was my preference, too, I told her, because the others are most edible when they're young. Then, ever so fleetingly, the garden of flowers and wild colors was just a memory, although I hoped for Barb's sake we would find more blueberries downriver.

Early in the afternoon the wind began picking up, sometimes gusting at 15 or 20 mph, making it tricky to negotiate some of the larger rapids. At one point, Andy and I ran the canoe up on a big turtle back and teeter-tottered there for an anxious ten seconds until we were finally pushed off by a combination of the strong current and the careful shifting of our weight in the canoe. Dave told us later that, aside from our being in danger of a dramatic capsize, it was actually quite funny watching us seesaw back and forth on the rock. A few moments later we almost went over again as we were forced into a hairpin turn on a narrow stretch after a shallow, rocky set of rapids. Dave and Barb didn't smile then because they came to the bitter edge of doing exactly the same thing. We knew it was time to take a break and have some lunch.

For the next couple of hours after lunch the river kept us on our toes with its many sets of challenging rapids. Only once did we come close to spilling, but this time our anxiety was instantly substituted with curiosity when a peregrine falcon flew directly over us. It wasn't noisy like the others, though, and I decided either the male hadn't found a mate or for some reason the aerie wasn't successful.

Midway through this spate of rapids we came across the largest tributary of Birch Creek yet. Called South Fork, I remembered it well from the misadventure my son Steven and I had had on the river several summers before. It was there that he and I had stopped to eat our dinner of quesadillas. We had lost all of our kitchen utensils to Davy Jones' locker when the canoe capsized at the big rapids upriver, and we had to improvise by using thin flat rocks to heat up our tortillas and cheese. We had to admit, though, that those were the best quesadillas we had ever tasted.

By late afternoon the high winds were making it difficult for us to paddle on the stretches of river that opened to the west. At the same time, we couldn't help but marvel at the amazing variety of clouds scudding across the sky from that direction. Some were billowy and thick, with trailing glaucous-gray edges, while others were thin and linear and totally white. Still others were filmy and feather-like. They all seemed to be spinning off a huge low-pressure system that lost most of its power by the time it got to our side of the mountains. If that was the case, I thought, we had better be careful about rising water levels that night.

While rounding a big bend we heard the cry of what I thought was a Harlan's hawk. But when I saw it soaring above us, its color reminded me of a light phase red-tail. Then I noticed its dark wrist patches and changed my call to rough-leg. It was our first one of the trip, although the mountain habitat had been perfect for them since the beginning.

By now, though, the mountains were quickly diminishing in size and we could see the end of the line where they finally petered out and the flat lands began to take over. This meant that soon the river would start to slow down and we would be paddling a lot more. Already we were past the last of the red-ochre cliffs, where we'd spotted yet another unaggressive peregrine falcon that had probably had the same bum luck as the one we'd seen earlier. Then we came to our final big rapids, where both Dave and I stood up as we threaded our canoes through the labyrinth of rocks and frothing water. Andy had started calling Dave "the gondolier" because of his habit of standing while he bobbed through the rapids – quite a skill for a guy who sometimes doubted his ability to make it all the way down the river without dumping. But I never lost confidence in him. Ever since we were teenagers he had been my best canoeing partner.

I could see our last low mountain coming up to the north and figured it was time to think about putting in for the night if we wanted some pretty scenery to look at. The sun was still shining and, with the wind blowing unabated, its rays cast a whimsical light on the mountainside mosaic of birch and aspen. As we rounded a long heavily cobbled bend of the river, a female pintail duck raced overhead, followed closely by a small frolicking flock of waxwings that curiously tipped their heads to check us out. There were birds here, I thought. Maybe this would be a good camping spot for the night. Andy and I went ashore to see if there was any sand among the cobbles to put our tents on. Sure enough, just a hundred yards down from where we landed we found two patches of the all-important stuff. They were small, but they would do the trick. There was plenty of firewood, too, and, best of all, a small copse of willows put us right on the edge of the wind so that we wouldn't have to worry about mosquitoes or other insects of their ilk.

While Dave and Andy put up the tents, Barb and I prepared dinner. Our menu this time included vegetable noodle soup and grilled cheese sandwiches, which was something different from our usual fare. Since both Andy and I were amateur botanists, some of our dinnertime chat around the fire included a couple of the new wildflowers we'd come across that afternoon, Alaska sage, and thoroughwax. The latter was the only member of the wild carrot family, *Apiaceae*, with yellow umbels, the umbrella-shaped flower heads of the many species in this family. I mentioned that where I used to teach in the Lower Yukon Delta, the Yup'ik Eskimo people included at least two of those species, wild celery and cow parsnip, in their subsistence diet. But there was one species they shunned because it was so highly toxic, the water hemlock. Sometimes children had eaten it by mistake and died.

We also talked about the old cabin we'd found just down from South Fork. It was built of spruce logs with a sod roof and had apparently been an old trapping cabin. Its roof was beginning to cave in on one side because of the weight of the spruce trees growing in the sod on top. Like all abandoned cabins, the interior smelled like ancient must, and I didn't linger long inside. And also, like most abandoned cabins, there was a lot of garbage strewn around, both inside and outside. Andy found an old hammer he thought he could use, so he snagged it and threw it in the canoe. He is a firm believer in the three R's: Reduce, Reuse, Recycle. So am I, and I grabbed a small roll of electrical tape that had been slightly chewn by a bear.

After dinner, we took a short stroll downriver as far as we dared. Because there were so many mosquitoes around, Dave especially did not want to venture close to the willows and alders. As it was, our CO_2 and body warmth attracted a small multitude of them, and Dave started running to avoid the wicked thrust of their thirsty proboscises. As he ran, he yelled, "Run, swat, kill, kill! The only good mosy is a dead mosy!" "But," I reminded him, "what would the warblers and flycatchers do without them? Like the alder flycatcher that's calling 'three cheers!' right behind our camp? Or the ospreys that just flew over? Even they depend on them indirectly, since they catch fish that eat mosies and their larvae. And think of all those blueberries and cranberries that count on them for pollination!" "Okay, Okay," he rejoined, "but I still love to kill them!"

Since it was early, we built up the fire to ward off any pesky mosquitoes that happened to penetrate our natural wind baffle, and continued our campfire banter. Andy, Dave and Barb, all being musically inclined, sang some old favorites of theirs from the 60s, 70s and 80s. I had never learned the lyrics of those songs the way they had, and was amazed they remembered them so well. I was also aware that I probably would never experience this combination of personalities and musical talent again, so I listened closely as I watched the skies getting moodier, and wondered aloud if we would have more rain by morning. I thought we would.

I was right. The wind really picked up in the early morning, and even rolled over one of our canoes. The skies were completely overcast when I went down to turn the canoe back on its side, and the level of the water had risen two inches. Not long after I got back in my bag it started to rain, and did so off and on until about 8 a.m.

When the rain finally stopped we made breakfast, broke camp and headed downriver. Before stepping into the canoe I glanced at the little stick I had poked in at the edge of the river the night before. It was almost submerged, which meant the water level had gone up four inches since I'd checked it earlier. The rains that had fallen upriver in the mountains were just beginning to reach us down below. We wondered how much more the water would rise by the time we took out two days hence.

Almost as soon as we started paddling, a young cow moose stepped out into the river and crossed in front of us. She was in a hurry, and without even a glance backwards at us soon disappeared into the willows.

With the increased water flow the current kept up a speedy pace and our canoes pushed steadily away from the high hills into the flat lands to the northeast. It wasn't long until the hills were far behind us, and the only relief was a ridgeline that paralleled us to our right. There were rainsqualls all around us, but none of them hit us head on. It seemed like every time we'd don our raincoats, a few minutes later we'd have to take them off again.

Once we were away from the hills, we bumped into more and more swallows. But these were bank swallows, drabber cousins of the cliff swallows we'd seen upriver. Bank swallows make their nest holes in the sides of high banks to escape predators, although on one stretch of the river we saw where a bear had been ambling along and easily reached his paws up to dig out the eggs or young birds in the holes. Rudyard Kipling's "Nature raw in tooth and claw," came to mind. In spite of their bad luck here, the swallows in the air seemed to be relaxed, not having to worry about diving peregrines in the immediate neighborhood like their upriver kin.

On the stone-scattered shore directly below one swallow colony, we suddenly came upon a pair of wandering tattlers, shorebirds I had never seen before along Birch Creek. I wondered where their young were hiding, and guessed they were probably hunkered down somewhere nearby. With their camouflaged feathers, they were dead ringers for cobblestones, and you'd have to almost step on one to see it.

In late morning we came across a new channel the river had carved sometime over the past couple of years. Although I normally didn't venture into these channels because of some bad luck I'd had with them in the past, I took a gamble on this one. The old channel bent steeply to the left and had some dangerous sweepers in it, but the new one ran straight and seemed clear of obstructions. With the current moving so quickly, we had to make an instant decision.

Our choice of the new channel almost proved our undoing. What looked to be a clear opening to the left of a big root system was actually blocked underwater with the tapered top of a skinned spruce tree. We hit it head on, almost tipping into the river. We were able to keep the canoe upright, though, and slowly but surely slipped along the length of the tree-top, and finally over its tip, and escaped getting wet. We immediately went ashore and hurried upriver to warn Dave and Barb. Fortunately, they still hadn't rounded the bend and we were able to motion them over to the old channel. They had to do some slick maneuvering, but the gondolier and his partner came through with flying colors.

Continuing on down the river, a northern harrier followed us, cruising overhead for whatever small rodents he might find along the banks. He peeled off just as we surprised another cow moose feeding on her own favorite fare of diamond leaf willow (*Salix planifolia*). The current was still strong and we were able to creep right up on her before she finally saw us and beat it back into the bushes. I wondered aloud to Andy if the heavy willow diet of moose helped prevent body aches and pains. We both thought it was possible, since the leaves and bark contained salicylic acid, the main chemical ingredient in aspirin.

In spite of the fast water, the west wind was stronger than ever, and when the river looped back in that direction we had a heck of a time making any progress. By early afternoon we were ready for lunch anyway, so we put in to have a bite to eat. As usual, I had bagels liberally smeared with peanut butter, while Dave and Barb ate a soy paste called miso, which they heavily sprinkled with garlic. I tried some of their miso, and it was actually quite tasty. As we ate, Andy sang more songs from his younger days. He'd started doing this the evening before around the campfire, and today every time we floated side by side with Dave and Barb he pulled one after the other of these songs out of his hat, caroling to his heart's content. We were amazed at his repertoire, and his memory. Dave and Barb knew many of them, but Andy seemed to remember them all.

Back on the river again, Andy kept on singing, to keep Barb awake, he said, because she hadn't gotten much sleep the night before due to her thin sleeping bag. She hadn't expected the nights to be so cool. When Dave spotted another chum salmon in the river, that jolted her awake for a while, but her alertness was only temporary. Finally she had a chance to rest when we pulled over so that Andy and I could climb a slumping bluff to reconnoiter our location on the flats. Since there were so few landmarks on the lower river, this was our first opportunity all day to pull out our maps and compass to seriously study our position. We could see Ketchum Dome to the west, and there was a reflection off what was probably a metal roof in the Circle Hot Springs area, so we figured we must be closer than we'd originally thought to our take-out. On top of the bluff we found a beautiful specimen of strawberry spinach, known by the scientific name of *Chenopodium capitatum*. It's a member of the goosefoot family, and is closely related to lambsquarters and its domesticated Andean cousin, quinoa. Its brilliant red fruit is sweet and may be eaten raw, or used for jelly and syrup. Its leaves are also edible, tasting a lot like domestic spinach.

Just before stopping for the night we heard our first yellow-shafted flicker. Initially, I thought it might be a Wilson's snipe, but I listened more closely and decided that the repeated high-pitched bark was made by a flicker. Besides, snipes only do their territorial barking in the spring of the year.

It was time for dinner and sleep, so we took out on a wide stretch of gravel with a couple of tiers of sandy banks, just in case the water began to rise and we had to move higher up later on. Right away Dave and I set up his tent, while Barb and Andy cooked dinner. Barb put together a dish she called falafel (a mixture of yoghurt, cilantro and lamb in pita bread), and Andy prepared a special rice and seaweed meal. We were hungry and looked forward to sharing food and stories around the campfire.

While eating, Dave told us his story about a black bear encounter he'd had while working on the TAPS oil pipeline project in 1976. He was standing outside a company commuter bus when a medium-sized blackie ambled up to him and sniffed his shoe. Dave stood his ground, then reached down and gently fondled its mouth to check it out. When the bear stood up, eyeball to eyeball with him, Dave said it looked like it was standing there kind of wobbly, so he put his hand out for the bear to rest its paw on, and he could feel the sharpness of its toenails. Then Dave reached up and touched the bear's nose, feeling the wetness of its nostrils. Finally, its curiosity sated, the bear dropped down onto all fours again and ambled back into the woods. The people in the bus were so totally blown away by this that they thought Dave was insane. He lost his job over it, he said, although he later got it back after filing a grievance with the State.

In the spirit of storytelling, I recounted one of my tales about a curious second year grizzly cub that spotted me while I was hiking alone on the Kongakut River in the northeastern part of the Brooks Range. He was with his mother and another cub, and for some reason started heading in my direction. Thankfully, he was diverted by a parky squirrel, which he immediately tore after and began digging for in the tundra so feverishly that he completely forgot about me. Chunks of sod were flying in every direction, and I was tempted to watch the drama to its conclusion. On second thought, I didn't want to push my luck with mama bear, so I quickly hotfooted out of there.

Our bear stories were added to by more of Andy's songs, which he retrieved from a memory bank that never quit. Dave provided music with his mouth organ and, once started, the songs flowed from theme to theme for more than an hour. There was a synergy there that went on and on. That is, until I suggested a short walk down the river. Even with the good music, I needed to stretch my legs. So, stretch our legs we did, and while doing so discovered a few differences in the beach compared to others we had camped on. The cobbles were now much smaller, and there were more black manganese nodules than before. At first, I thought the black stones might be basalt, but knew better when I knocked off flakes that showed absolutely no conchoidal fracture. There were also more spotted sandpipers than we'd seen on the upper river. Their characteristic spotted chests, *pweet pweet pweet pweet* call, and ubiquitous presence at the water's edge make them easy to tell apart from other sandpipers during the summer months.

It began to shower after we returned to our tents, continuing off and on until about 10:30, when the sun finally broke through to the northwest of us, shining so brightly that I had to leave the tent to check it out. What an awesome sight – the birch trees across the river luminous with yellow light, scudding clouds to the southeast backlit by the setting sun, black spruce behind us silhouetted against the clearing skies, and in the north the dissolving clouds reflecting zesty pinks and peaches. There was no word in English strong enough to describe the scene, so we didn't even try. We simply watched and marveled.

In a half-hour or so the wind had died and a few mosquitoes buzzed at our door. When I finished my journal notes and finally closed my eyes to sleep, I heard the sound of a beaver working in the river. I wondered if his diligence was a message about higher water to come, and I told myself to wake up in a couple of hours to check the water level.

I awakened at 1:30 a.m. to find the river level had gone up more than 12 inches since putting my stick in at nine the previous evening, and it seemed to be rising as I watched. I yelled for Dave and Andy to help me move the canoes and gear up next to the tents, just in case. Before closing my eyes again I set my internal alarm for 3:00 a.m. On schedule, I awoke to find the water had come up 12 more inches, and that in only one and a half hours! I decided it was time to break camp, build a fire and wait on the highest bank for enough light to proceed safely down the river. By now, there were some very hefty trees complete with their root systems lumbering dangerously along in the fast current, and we wanted to make dead sure that when we finally put in we didn't get close to them.

By 4:00 a.m. we were gathered around our fire drinking hot cups of chocolate. The water continued to rise as we gulped. Inch by inch it crept around our canoes, and we decided that when they started to bob in the water we would launch. It wouldn't be long. Meanwhile, we sipped our hot drinks and watched the sunrise. Beginning as a pink blush on the northeast horizon, the sky became brighter and more orange as the sun came closer and closer to the silhouetted spruce trees. When it finally edged the forest rim it was wrapped in wispy gray clouds, except on one side, where there was an opening in the sky. Bright golden rays stretched out on all sides of the opening, suggesting a king's crown.

As the sun continued to rise, so did the river. It crept higher and higher on our canoes, gained more momentum and grew fuller of woody flotsam and bubbly rafts of tannic suds, formed by the huge volumes of water flowing into the river from both tundra and forest. None of us had ever seen anything like it. We were a little nervous, to say the least. Even so, Dave managed to play his harmonica while Andy sang more of his repertoire of songs from the 60s and 70s. When Dave put his harmonica away, Barbara asked what our strategy would be on the river. "Just try to stay ahead of the trees," I told them, "and remember that you can paddle, they can't!"

After a nervous laugh, we jumped into our now-bobbing canoes and shoved off downriver. It was 5:30, with at least enough light to distinguish the low profile of the floating logs from the silty cream color of the running water. But with the dark curtain of tall trees standing on both banks of the river, there was still a great deal of shadow, making it difficult to see all possible combinations of danger that might result in catastrophe for either of our canoes.

Once, as Andy and I paddled cautiously in the widening river, weaving our way among the by now wall-to-wall carpet of logs lumbering along in the quickening current, we were almost capsized by a spruce trunk floating about 40 feet ahead of us. We thought nothing of it at first, but suddenly we heard a loud crashing noise off to our left. The giant, tentacled root system of the tree was snatched and held by a huge tangle of big sweepers hanging from the bank, instantly causing the partly submerged trunk to whip back at us. When the tree abruptly lifted up in the water and raced through the air it sounded like a jet plane screaming down for a strafing run. If we had been two feet closer we'd have been thumped and dumped into the crowded muddy river. As it was, in the blink of an eye we hit the scalped top ten feet of the tree, slid at an angle along its thin leading edge, and finally floated over its naked tip. It was a close call, and Andy knew it better than I did because he was in the bow. We were both speechless and didn't say anything until Dave yelled from behind us, "Holy shit, France, that one almost got you!" I could only mumble, "Yeah, no kidding!" When he and Barbara caught up, he half-jokingly remarked, "'Davy Jones' locker' almost took you down, France! Again!"

Shortly afterward, we found ourselves rapidly approaching what appeared to be a giant raft of floating trees. Taking immediate evasive action, we realized at once that it was a logjam. And not just any logjam! The water level had gone up so much that the logs were all beginning to move downriver at the same time, scraping and grinding the gravel bottom as they went. I had never heard or seen anything like this before. Only by hard paddling did we manage to avoid it before the pile of logs broke up completely and blocked the river. If that had happened, we would have had a much more dangerous situation to contend with. Lady luck was with us, and we got around it, but it was a stern reminder of the incredible power of moving water.

Something else I had never seen before was the swiftness of the river in the lowlands. Normally the current flowed at about three to four mph here, but ever since we'd launched in the morning we were traveling at almost 10 mph. If we kept up this pace, we would be off the river in two or three hours. Slowly but surely, though, the speed of the muddy waters began to slacken and before long we were moving at about five mph.

As we rounded a bend we saw what looked like a large rubber raft in the middle of the river. Quickly approaching it, we could see that the blue and yellow hulk was overturned, and that it was stuck in a logjam at the head of a small island. I wondered aloud if it would be worth salvaging. Only when we floated right next to it did we see the raft was in near perfect condition. Instantly we made the decision to pull over on the left side of the island to make an attempt to pry it off the logjam.

After securing our canoe and jostling our way through a forest of thick willows, we reached the head of the island and surveyed the situation. The raft had flipped over on its side and was tethered to the jumble of logs by a long, blue synthetic strap that had somehow jammed among them, thereby keeping it from floating down the river. We judged the distance to the edge of the logjam to be about 25 feet, and almost abandoned the project when I stuck a long pole through a narrow crack in the logs to measure the depth of the water. There didn't seem to be any bottom, but when I tentatively stepped out onto the raft of logs it was totally stable. The current had packed the mix of tree trunks, roots and other debris so tightly that there was little danger we would fall through. So, knife in one hand and pole in the other, I scrabbled out to the side of the raft, cut the synthetic strap, and pushed and shoved with the pole for all I was worth, until the raft finally freed itself and began floating down the river.

We then jumped off the logjam and raced back through the willows to the canoe. As we peeled off into the current, we could see the raft floating past Dave and Barbara, who were still waiting for us in a backwater close to the end of the island. I yelled for them to help us catch the raft so we could shepherd it the rest of the way down to the take-out. It was easy enough to corral, but not so easy to control on the swollen river. I felt a little like a cowboy trying to round up a cavorting calf. Prodded by our paddles, the raft would first scud over to one side of the river, then back to the other, then float calmly for a while in the mainstream. Suddenly, a breath of wind would push it toward shore and it would get hung up on a sweeper. When that happened it took skill and effort to pry it loose and coax it back into the mainstream again.

While Andy and I were playing cowboy with the raft, Dave and Barbara were far in front of us searching for the take-out. On a straightaway, just after we heard the telltale rattling call of our first belted kingfisher, Dave was yelling from somewhere up ahead that they had found the take-out trail. We quickly bumped and prodded the raft ashore with our canoe and paddles till finally we were home free.

The rest was easy, made even easier because the water level was flush with the trail. Unloading the canoes, transporting them and the raft into the parking lot, deflating the raft, and organizing our gear took all of a half-hour. Then Andy and I took off in his vehicle for the put-in to get my Toyota Four Runner. When we arrived at the headwaters parking lot, Birch

Creek was flowing higher and muddier than I'd ever seen it. Three hours after we had left Dave and Barbara behind at the take-out, we were back to pick up the boats and gear. In the space of just those three hours the level of the river had gone up another foot and was encroaching on the trail to the parking lot. And it continued to rise as we watched. We thought of the Germans we had passed three days before, and hoped they were okay.

PHOTOS

1. Approaching Shotgun Rapids
2. Shooting lower Shotgun Rapids
3. Arctic arnica studding hillside after recent forest fire

Chapter 8

Canning River Journal
June 25 to July 5, 2004

June 26 –
In the early morning, fog had crept up from the Beaufort Sea coast along the Marsh Fork of the Canning River where I was camped, and I wondered if this would prevent my friends from making it in from Coldfoot on their Coyote Air charter. The fog dissipated by about 8:00 a.m., just in time for a big rainsquall to begin pushing in from the north. Again I wondered about my friends, but the storm broke up, too, even before it reached my camp. So I gathered some dry willows for a fire, ate breakfast, drank a cup of tea, and then read a few more pages of Loren Eiseley's book, *The Immense Journey*.

We finally begin our float

Kirk Sweetsir had dropped me off the day before at the Marsh Fork airstrip after I had helped my friend Clancy Crawford guide four bird watchers for several days on the Coastal Plain of the Arctic National Wildlife Refuge. Kirk was flying two of Clancy's clients back to Ft. Yukon, so I tagged along as far as the Marsh Fork. I planned to meet five friends farther downriver, so after Kirk dropped me off, I hiked eight miles down to what was known as the "bench strip." Their charter pilot, Dirk Nickisch, would land them here, and together we would float down to the Coastal Plain in a raft and inflatable kayak. At the end of the trip, Dirk would pick us up somewhere on the Coastal Plain and fly us back to civilization.

It was midmorning when Dirk finally flew over, his Beaver lumbering slowly above the airstrip. But he didn't land and just kept on heading downriver. He soon returned, however, and when I waved he banked his plane and started his descent. He touched down with a few bumps, backtracked to where I was waiting, and quickly came to a stop. He then revved his engine to turn the plane into the wind, cut the power and jumped out of the cockpit. In a matter of minutes my friends were on the ground. Phil Wildfang and Fran Mauer were first, followed by Phil's wife, Jean, Fran's wife Yoriko, and Ritchie Musik. While we unloaded the packs and food, Dirk explained that during his first flyover he hadn't seen me and thought I'd walked down to the next airstrip.

After a half-hour, Dirk was back in the air again with the pledge he'd be here the next day with the rest of our load, including the raft, inflatable kayak, and other personal things that had been left behind in Coldfoot. I wondered why some of these items weren't on the airplane this trip, but didn't say anything. I was just glad to see that everyone had arrived safely and none the worse for wear. After a few deep breaths, it was time to haul personal gear down to the campsite on the river, set up our tents and get organized until Dirk returned with the boats and tackle.

Just as the others finished setting up their tents, it started to rain. Not hard, but we had to wear our raincoats as we ate our lunch and chatted about the gear snafu in Coldfoot. Apparently many personal items were left behind, because final preparations had been inadequate and people had brought too much stuff. Phil and Fran grinned and said I should have been present in Fairbanks for a gear shakedown. "Easier said than done, guys," I grinned back. "I was having fun bird watching on the Coastal Plain."

There was still a lot of day left after lunch, so I proposed a hike to the top of the mountain behind camp, to take a look at the surrounding area and our route downriver. We took our time on the way up because of Ritchie's bad knees, identifying plants and flowers as we climbed to a ridge that would eventually take us to the summit. Fran's wife, Yoriko, especially enjoyed seeing the flowers, and refamiliarizing herself with their names and smells. Some that we came across were boykinia (bearflower), two-flowered cinquefoil, spotted and thyme-leaved saxifrages, saussurea and bog rosemary.

While climbing with Yoriko and Ritchie, I told them a little about bog rosemary (*Andromeda polifolia*) – how, like so many other members of the Heath family, it contains the toxic compound andromedotoxin, which lowers blood pressure and causes breathing difficulty and intestinal upsets. And about how the famous Swedish naturalist Linnaeus had named the genus after the mythological Ethiopian princess, Andromeda, the daughter of Cassiopeia and Cepheus in Greek mythology, who was rescued from a sea monster and then married by Perseus. Consulting my plant guide, I read that Linnaeus had written that the plant was "always fixed on some turfy hillock in the midst of the swamps, as Andromeda herself was chained to a rock in the sea, which bathed her feet as the fresh water does the roots of the plant." It sounded to us like Linnaeus was very much the romantic.

Close to the top of the mountain, Fran and I stopped to watch a pair of Smith's longspurs flitting across the tundra. The male landed near us and sang his sweet warbling song, which went something like, *swee-tew weetee-teetew, weechew*. With his orange-buff colored breast and black and white mottled face triangle, he was a handsome bird.

Once on top, we could see all the way south to the main Marsh Fork strip, where Phil, his wife Jean, their son James and my wife Jen and I had explored so much the previous year. Phil pointed out the nearby mountain that he, James and I had climbed. The huge patch of aufeis that I had passed on my way to the bench strip was directly below us, and we had a good view of where the river had forced itself through the ice in deeply carved clefts during the spring melt. I recounted to Fran and Phil how, the day before, a grizzly bear had surprised me on that same stretch of ice as I was soaking my feet during a lunch break. We all wondered how the three fields of aufeis farther downriver would be when we came to them. For now, though, we just enjoyed the breathtaking view and the lovely weather.

We didn't stay long on top because of the stiff cool breeze, and when Ritchie and Yoriko caught up to us we headed back down toward the river. About halfway to the bottom we stopped and sat awhile above a meadow of yellow wildflowers called Lessing's and alpine arnica. I told the others of the poisonous quality of these flowers, too. Like rosemary, they should never be eaten, although the roots and flowers of the European species, Arnica montana, are still used to make ointments for external application in the treatment of bruises, sprains and swollen feet.

Once back at camp we heated up some tea water, then prepared dinner. We were hungry after climbing the mountain. During our meal, conversation rambled on and on, ranging from President "Shrub's" war in Iraq, and his abysmal environmental excesses, to the screw up with the raft. For the latter, I accepted part of the blame, since my original written instructions to Dirk, regarding transport of the raft to Coldfoot, were not as explicit as they might have been. As a result, somewhere along the line there was a misunderstanding.

Just before calling it quits in my tent for the night, I heard the distant cry of an upland sandpiper somewhere in the tundra. The rapid rippling trill of its flight call, followed by a long, slow, breathy whistle, *whrreee wheeeyee-ww*, a lot like that of a drawn out wolf whistle, made me forget our logistical bad luck, and I dropped off to sleep.

But I didn't sleep very well. Every few hours I woke up, thinking about the raft botch-up, blaming myself, trying to think of a back-up plan acceptable to everyone, in case Dirk never showed with the raft.

After breakfast we chatted idly under a hot sun, wondering if the unusually warm weather was why we weren't seeing the number of sheep we did last year. Glassing in every direction, we saw only a few ewes and lambs, scattered here and there on the flanks and ridges of the mountains. Soon I grew weary because of my missed sleep, and I went to my tent and napped till late morning.

We had just finished lunch and I was headed out for a walk with Fran and Phil when who should show up but Dirk. Hallelujah, I thought, maybe he's got the rest of our equipment. As we hurried toward where he had stopped his plane, engine still running, we watched him quickly unload a large bin resembling the plastic container I had put the raft in. Then, without even a wave of recognition, he jumped back into the pilot's seat, gunned the motor and took off right beside us, his head straight forward and an angry frown on his face. We glanced at each other quizzically and wondered what the hell that was all about.

Approaching the bin, we could see it was indeed the wayward raft. Dirk told us the day before that he had mistakenly left it in Arctic Village, so we presumed he was angry for having to make an extra trip there to pick it up. But we figured it had been his logistical mix-up in the first place, so why the sour grapes? We were quickly cooling toward Dirk, and just hoped he'd follow through with delivering the inflatable, along with the paddles and some of the other things still missing. So be it, we grabbed the ropes surrounding the bulky container, hefted it across the tundra, down the steep bank, then across a quarter-mile of wide gravel riverbed to a place I had checked out in the morning, where the water was running fast and deep. It was here I thought we could stage to finally start our float down the river.

Then it was back to our walk. I wanted to take a look at three small stands of cottonwood trees (aka balsam poplar) that I had noticed from the top of the mountain. They were located in the alluvial fan made by a creek issuing from one of the valleys on the east side of the Marsh Fork. I thought just possibly there might be some gray-headed chickadees nesting there. It would depend on how old the trees were, since these birds were cavity nesters, needing a tree with a hole large enough to lay their eggs in.

To get to the cottonwoods we had to wade through a thick willow jungle, punctuated every now and then by an open stretch of gravel outwash, deposited by the creek during periods of high water. We checked first one grove of trees, then another. Nothing. We had almost given up, and were pushing our way through the willow thicket toward the third stand of cottonwood, when I heard what I thought sounded like a chickadee. But it wasn't like either of the calls I was familiar with in the Interior. It was slower, more deliberate and lower pitched than those of both the boreal and black-capped chickadees. It sounded an awful lot like the call of the gray-headed chickadee I had listened to on Leonard Peyton's songbird CD before leaving Fairbanks.

I called the bird the way my dad had taught me when I was young (a sound known as "spishing" to birdwatchers), and right away, there it was in the willows, poking around for insect tidbits, maybe to feed its young at this time of June. I glassed it to inspect its topknot and face, comparing it to the pictures of the chickadees in my bird guide. It did, in fact, have a grayer cap than any of the boreals I'd ever seen, and its white cheek patch was larger than that of the boreal or black-cap. Finally, I thought, after hearing so much about this bird for so long, and dearly wanting to see it in my lifetime, I was now observing it up close and personal. When I spished again, it came down right in front of me, ogling me as though I might have something to offer it. Then another chickadee, probably its mate, began calling nearby. It didn't show itself, but its slow and easy spish was identical to the one I was trailing through the willows.

I followed the first bird for as far as I could without totally alienating Fran and Phil with my enthusiasm. It was hot in that breezeless jungle, and they soon headed out into the open. Reluctantly, I followed, listening closely as I pushed the last willows away from my face. *Tsiti ti ti jeew...jeew jeew.* Then it stopped, and that was the last I heard its call. My friends were waiting.

The chickadees weren't the only birds we saw in that thicket of willows and cottonwoods. We also came across a pair of yellow warblers, some robins, a gray jay and a tree sparrow. And when we were finally out on the breezy tundra again, there was another pair of Smith's longspurs, flitting and bouncing in the wind and rattling and clicking back and forth the way they do, like ventriloquists, so that I had a hard time keeping track of them.

Not far from where we spotted the longspurs, I was checking out some tundra wildflowers when I glimpsed something gray in a small cavity in the mosses and lichens. I bent down and peered closer. I couldn't believe my eyes. I motioned for Fran and Phil to come over and take a look at the first yellow jacket nest I had ever found in the Arctic. Fran, who had done research in the Refuge for more than twenty years, said it was a first for him too. We wondered if this was one more indication of climate change.

During our walk back from the cottonwoods we discovered a crystal clear, sandy-bottomed pool of water about five feet deep. Ideal for bathing, I thought, although a little cold. I needed a bath badly, so I disrobed and walked in up to my waist. The water was frigid, but the sun was out and it was a warm afternoon. I had brought along my shampoo, and liberally doused my hair and beard and let the suds do the job for the rest of my body. What a pleasure to have clean hair again. I submerged to rinse, and afterward stood in the sun to let the breeze air-dry my skin. It didn't take long to dry off, then I dressed and returned to camp, where everyone was chatting around the fire, wondering when Dirk was going to come in with the remainder of our gear.

After a tasty dinner of cheese-filled tortillas, I helped Yoriko identify some plants she had gathered. One, dwarf hawk's beard (*Crepis nana*), was just beginning to bloom on the gravel bed of the river, the niche it prefers in the Arctic because of the good drainage the dry gravel offers. It is probably the most symmetrical plant in the north, growing in a perfect circle, and when all of its yellow dandelion-like flowers are in bloom it resembles a miniature sun. Everywhere we looked there were hundreds of these tiny dwarf suns shining at us among the white cobbles.

The evening continued sunny and hot. Even the birds seemed to be affected by the heat, since they weren't singing as they usually did in the later hours of the day. A dark-plumaged young gray jay that flew over camp looked way overdressed for all this heat, and I sympathized with him. So far, I hadn't needed any of the warm clothes I'd brought with me almost a week and a half ago. When it was finally time for bed, there were six people who were very happy to retire under the cover of their tents.

A gain we waited all day for Dirk. He had told us on Saturday (June 26) that he would be in no later than Sunday with three other floaters, and that he would bring in the rest of our gear then. But he never showed. Maybe today, we hoped.

The morning was intensely sunny and sizzling hot, and to protect ourselves from its glaring rays we built a makeshift sun break with our ground tarps. This was the only shade in the area, except down in the cottonwood groves we had visited the day before, but since we felt we had to stay near camp in case Dirk flew in with our stuff, the ground tarps would have to do for now. As we whiled away the morning with tales of past expeditions to the Arctic, complaints about the Bush administration's treatment of the environment, and personal stories from bygone times, we became more and more impatient with Dirk. In anticipation of his imminent arrival, we decided to ferry all of our extra supplies over to the river's edge where we had placed the raft.

We told more stories, quoted ridiculous "Bushisms" (foot-in-the-mouth mistakes made by President Bush), and even repeated some gossip from Fairbanks. Every once in awhile I dodged the chatter and headed for the river to do some birding, or to glass for mountain sheep. But I found not a single sheep on the mountainsides. They were probably all hiding from the sun in their favorite cave or on the shady side of the mountain. If I were a sheep, I'd be there too. The breeze had started to kick up and it was now more comfortable out on the gravel bar. There I found a loquacious white-crowned sparrow, then a pair of semipalmated plovers doing their broken-wing act, indicating they had a nest with eggs nearby.

We were still anticipating Dirk's arrival, so I built a small kitchen fire and cooked up an early dinner of chile and beans for everyone. We were hoping to get on the river before the day was out. Alas, though we often believed we heard the telltale deep-throated resonance of the Beaver, it always turned out to be a false alarm. Finally, at about eight o'clock, we gave up and wrote the day off as a lesson in patience and sociability.

By midnight we had all turned in, and I was just about to nod off when I heard the echo of that deep-throated resonance again. This time, though, it grew louder and louder, so I quickly got dressed, jumped out of the tent and announced to everyone that our pilot had finally arrived. Then I hurried up to the airstrip with Phil and Fran close on my heels.

Dirk appeared on the ragged edge of exhaustion, so we didn't mention that we had been waiting for him for the last two days. He apologized for being late, and to make matters worse, he said he had accidently unloaded Yoriko's life preserver and some of her food at the upper strip with the fellows he had dropped there, and had to fly back to get it for us. By the time he returned an hour later he was looking even more miserable, and when I explained to him that because of the delay we wouldn't be able to float all the way to the Coastal Plain, he did only a half-hearted job of explaining where we could take out early on the river. He simply pointed to a big bend on his large-scale topo map three-quarters of the way down the main branch of the Canning River, saying we would have no trouble spotting a wide gravel bar there where we could take out and wait for him. If need be, we could spruce up the strip by removing any large cobbles and filling in the bumps so he could land more easily. With his index finger pointing so generally at the map, we had the distinct feeling that we might have a little difficulty finding the spot.

No matter, we decided we'd cross that bridge when we came to it, so after watching Dirk's Beaver ponderously bounce off the airstrip into the warm air, we carried all of our gear back to camp. Then we celebrated by drinking some of Phil's Arctic elixir, a mixture of Yukon Jack and Irish Creme. The breeze was down, and the mosquitoes were beginning to flock in our direction, but with the buzz of the elixir we barely noticed them. The tasty brew also heightened the magical effects of the midnight sun as it ignited the mountain behind us with a golden alpenglow. To cap it off, an upland sandpiper whistled plaintively on the tundra.

Launch day. We were up and at 'em by seven, ate a quick breakfast, broke camp and started hauling our stuff down to the raft. As soon as I dropped my own gear by the river I made sure all of the dry bags were secure, then began inflating the raft with my new hand pump. It was a real improvement over my foot pump and made the task so much easier. Fran finished the job while I hoofed it back to camp to carry the last dry bags to the raft. Since Phil and Jean were taking first crack at the inflatable canoe, they blew it up, then tied on some of their equipment. It would only take a small load, and since the canoe was a self-bailing model everything had to be totally waterproof.

Almost all of our gear and supplies had to be stowed on top of a pair of cargo nets that we installed carefully at both ends of the raft. We could not allow the load to sag onto the floor of the raft, so there would be a minimum of abrasion on its vinyl skin when we hit bottom. The vinyl was tough, but not indestructible. With all of the food we had brought along, it looked like we might be overloaded, and when we finished packing we had just enough room for our legs.

Finally, at just shy of noon, we were ready to launch – a long preparation time, to say the least. But it paid off, and we began sailing smoothly down a sparkling clearwater river. The current moved right along, and where there were shallows we got out to line and push the raft over to the next section of deep water. No problem, this was all a part of the adventure and, after so much inactivity the day before, we were happy to put our bodies to work.

We stopped for lunch about two hours down the river at Porcupine Creek and, while we were at it, searched some of the balsam poplar groves for more gray-headed chickadees. After our good luck at the bench strip, I thought we should check out as many as we could of the other stands of these trees along the river. So Fran and Ritchie and I tramped across damp meadows of mosses and sedges and cotton grasses to a long line of poplars that we thought might have a nesting pair of chickadees in them. As much as we peered and probed, though, we saw no more of these coveted birds. But we did find a cottonwood stout enough to serve as a bear-rubbing tree. With grizzly hair up and down its wrinkled and battered trunk, it also had telltale tooth gouges at the height of the standing bear's nose. I had seen this many times before and always got a kick out of imagining the bear, as he stood scratching his back and butt, and then, in his ecstasy, turning his head, grabbing the tree hard in his jaws and ripping it to shreds. If I were a bear, I guess I might do the same.

Back on the river again, we saw our first Arctic terns, a pair of them, cruising above the surface of the shallows. We wondered what they might be looking for. Could there be small fish in the river? Fran said char came up this high to spawn every year, and these may be the result of last year's spawn. But maybe they were also hunting for insect larvae in the water like the two spotted sandpipers that were teetering and bobbing along the shoreline. The spotties were our first on the river, as was the Say's phoebe that flew directly over us.

From Porcupine Creek we encountered some nice stretches of fast water, and we made good time on the river. We also passed under some colossal mountain massifs composed of gnarled and twisted layers of chalky limestone and dark gray slate. We were fascinated with the difference in vegetation on these various rock types. Whereas slopes composed predominantly of slate had a great deal of vegetation growing on them, those made up mostly of limestone had very little of anything green on them. It probably had a great deal to do with pH balance, i.e., whether the soil formed was acidic or basic. Most vegetation in the Brooks Range, it seems, prefers acidic soils.

In mid-afternoon the wind started picking up from downstream, and it was soon so strong that we weren't able to make any headway. So we decided to call it quits for the day on a silty gravel bar – not the best place on the river to camp, but we had little choice. After locating my tent on some unstable silt, I was forced to move it to firmer, stonier ground because, as the strong wind blew through my tent, it covered everything with fine sand and grit. I was a much happier camper on the pebbles, and my Thermarest air mattress took care of any small bumps.

It was Ritchie's turn to cook, so we combined our food and came up with a meat and noodle stew, which we chased with some wine Phil had brought along for the crew.

The day was still young when we finished our meal, so Fran and I ambled a short ways up the alluvial fan behind our camp to a small rock outcropping. From there we had a great view of the valley, and could even see a couple of large bull caribou downriver, crossing a wide stretch of aufeis. This was the aufeis we had wondered about earlier. Could we get through it, or would we have to portage over it? We decided that we'd cross that bridge when we came to it. Then we walked back down the outwash to a spot where the water from the side canyon exited from under the cobbles, forming a wide green wetland studded in cottongrass (*Eriophorum scheuchzeri*). It was also buzzing with thousands of mosquitoes, even with the stiff breeze, so we retreated to the openness of the outwash where the wind blew more robustly. Before we did, though, we checked out a least sandpiper foraging on the edge of the wetland along with a pair of spotties busily doing the same. These birds probably had nests nearby.

That night around the campfire we watched the sun slide behind the mountains to the northwest, leaving us in the wake of their dark shadows. Normally that would cool the air to the point where I would feel like retiring for the night, but not this time. The warm air and flaxen light of the setting sun on the cathedral mountain to our east kept me up in a constant state of awe. Only when the sun had westered all the way around the peaks behind us with no promise of further light on the opposite mountains did I finally go to my tent.

I was up at six, made a small breakfast fire and put some water on the grate for tea and oatmeal. It was another cloudless day, although I can't say "clear" because there was a thin layer of smoke drifting lazily up and down the valley for as far as we could see in all directions. We figured it had to be coming from large fires in the Interior, and wondered what the flying conditions were like there.

We suspected it would be windy again later in the day, so we launched early to take advantage of the calm sailing conditions on the river. We were still a little green in our packing and securing procedures on the raft, but we managed to get everything together by nine o'clock and pushed off into the sparkling water of the Marsh Fork, eager to see what lay in store for us around the next bend. That's what made these river trips so interesting. We never knew what we would encounter, even a hundred yards from our camp.

When we got to the first stretch of aufeis that Fran and I had spotted during our hike, Yoriko was a little worried that we couldn't see the river opening at first. She joked nervously about it being a "bad sign," in reference to Phil's play on her words a couple days before about something being a bad sign, as in a bad omen of things to come. But there was no need to worry because the channel soon came into view, showing us that our way was completely clear. Since Ritchie had never actually stepped on aufeis before, I suggested we stop to let her try it out for size. While we were at it, we checked out some of the willows poking their pollen-coated catkins through the surface of the ice. They had absorbed the sun's light and transformed it to heat enough to melt a tube of ice around them. Other things on the ice, like wind-blown twigs and leaves and feathers, had done much the same. Now they were artistically embedded within the ice in a shallow depression of clear water the same shape as the object itself. There were also small ridges of calcium dust, blown down from the limestone mountains by fierce winter winds and deposited on the ice. That was something new for everyone but Fran and me.

Just upriver from the third expanse of aufeis, the river narrowed and picked up speed, which again was a source of worry for Yoriko. "Bad sign," she said. But the aufeis came and went with no difficulty. It was when we were suddenly confronted with a long string of boulder fields that we grew really concerned. We were kept busy for the next hour carefully picking our way through a maze of giant rocks and swirling water. In the shallower sections we frequently had to jump out and line the raft around the large turtlebacks. But when the water was too deep or too swift, we had to leave our fate to the vagaries of the flowing current, ram the boulders, then bounce and spin round and round until we could paddle ourselves forward again. Finally, after one arduously long rock garden we stopped for lunch.

In the middle of our munching Fran took out his topo map and we tried reckoning where we were. According to the contours on both sides of the river, we had made good enough progress to take out early and do some mountain climbing. And only a mile downriver there was a mountain that looked like it might do the trick. It had a gradual slope and a bench midway to the top – ideal for sheep, and we hoped to see some up there. Now to find a good campsite.

It didn't take long to locate what we were searching for on the left bank of the river. Flat and paved with small pebbles, it was also roomy enough for all of our tents, and not far from some high willows for privacy. We immediately set up camp, grabbed some snacks and water and headed up the mountain. Ritchie said her knees were bothering her too much to go with us, so she stayed behind "to hold down the fort."

The going was steep but interesting, since the slate composition of the slope meant there was a lot of vegetation with many species of new wildflowers we hadn't seen yet, including tall larkspur, which I mentioned to Yoriko is inedible to most wildlife when it is still young because of the toxic alkaloid it contains called aconitine. But as the plant develops the poison in it diminishes considerably, and by the time the fruits mature it is quite edible to wild animals, although not to humans, I emphasized. Farther up the slope we found the dark green shield fern where it grew among settled talus and in small shaded rocky crevices. Because of its scientific name, *Dryopteris fragrans*, I thought it might have a smell, but when I checked I wasn't able to detect any fragrance. I read in my guidebook later that only when they're young do the ferns have a sickly sweet smell to them

Continuing on up, we crossed a series of thick limestone strata, with predictably less vegetation on them. They appeared almost sterile in some areas, fitting the pattern I'd seen everywhere else in the Brooks Range. This didn't seem to bother the grasshoppers we found mating on them, though. Or the Dall sheep that had made their trails through them, leading to resting places in the slatier parts of the slope near the top. Although we saw no sheep in the area, there was recent evidence they'd been this way, especially in the form of fresh droppings, thousands of them, surrounding the shallow depressions of their beds. With all of this organic matter, there were wildflowers like cinquefoils and forget-me-nots growing everywhere around the edges of the beds. While sitting on top of the mountain, I could imagine the sheep lying there, heads and curled horns erect, blissfully chewing their cud, reaching down every few minutes to nip off the little blue blossoms of the forget-me-nots. As they chewed they would peer down at the river far below, probably watching us as we began our steep ascent, then moving off when we got too close for comfort.

As we climbed back down the mountain through the talus, I found the concentric webs of scores of orb weaving spiders. I'd seen some of these on the way up, but I hadn't noticed the long gossamer threads of the orbs, some of them stretching for ten feet among the rocks of the talus slope. In these Arctic alpine areas, where food is comparatively scarce, spiders have to be resourceful in their quest for survival. By the number of their webs, these spiders seem to have survived particularly well. With all the pipits bouncing around the rocks, I marveled at how the spiders did it, since they are a favorite food of these mountain birds.

Finally back at camp again, Ritchie was there to meet us. She said she had climbed a little ways up the slope and had seen what looked like a canyon just downriver. We told her that while on top we saw the canyon too, but couldn't tell whether there were any serious rapids or boulder fields in it. We'd just have to find out what lay in wait for us in the morning. When she asked me about a strange rose-purple colored flower with a sickle-shaped seedpod lying flat on the gravel bar near our tents, I told her it was a wild pea called Nootka milk vetch. According to my plant guide, its scientific moniker was *Astragalus nutzotinensis*. The genus name comes from the Greek word *astragalos*, meaning "neck bone," because of the resemblance of the seedpod to the shape of the vertebra in the back of our neck.

After dinner, while walking downriver with Phil and Fran to explore some big rapids that promised to give us a few thrills the next day, they chatted about their days in the military, as I glassed for birds. Two red-breasted mergansers I spotted were both males and were either non-breeders or their mates had already started incubating the eggs and they found themselves feeling like sore thumbs and swam off to find other company. When I returned to camp and checked my bird guide I found that, as with harlequin duck males, the responsibility of male mergansers toward future generations ends abruptly at copulation.

Writing in my journal late into the white night, I could hear the liquid dweedling call of a tattler wandering along the edge of the shore. It was a pleasant ending to a lovely day.

I was awake earlier than usual, worried about the increasing smoke in the air. I'd never seen smoke like this in the Refuge north of the Brooks Range, and I wondered how much worse it would get. Smoke has always bothered me, partly because I was almost asphyxiated by smoke while fighting a forest fire on the Kobuk River in June, 1971.

After breakfast we struck camp and prepared to launch our boats. Each morning I inflated the raft enough to where it was firm again and would carry the heavy weight we had to load on it. Always, after taking out of the river the previous day, I released a little air so the sun's heat wouldn't overinflate it. The cool of the night deflated the raft, so by morning it was flaccid and needed the extra air. I also inflated the canoe, since I was going to try it out for the first time. Phil volunteered to take my position in the stern of the raft while I took his in the stern of the canoe. Jean would remain in the bow of the canoe.

Fran told us that this morning would probably be a sleeper, since the map showed no major rapids or sudden drops in elevation. But he turned out to be mistaken. The river was actually quite swift, with a lot of drop toward the main Canning River. There were even some class 2+ rapids to give us a little excitement. And the lovely "gin clear" water, as Phil described it, was always with us. Phil's descriptor was one I didn't particularly like because of its reference to alcohol in a wilderness setting. My own use of words might be more like "crystal clear," or "diaphanous," or "gossamer."

When we reached the canyon we'd seen the day before from the mountain, we stopped for about a half-hour to see if we could spot any falcons or eagles nesting on the cliffs. I thought we'd find at least one gyrfalcon, since the cliffs were ideal for aeries. Fran located an old eagle nest, and we did spot one very svelte adult golden eagle, but no mate. Once, I thought I heard the bawling of a young falcon from somewhere high in the rocks, but then decided I was hearing things, so focused my attention on a pair of Say's phoebes flying in and out of a crack in the opposite wall of the canyon. They undoubtedly had young there, and I remembered the phoebe nest I'd found the previous year in a shallow cave near the upper Marsh Fork. It had five perfectly white eggs in it, since camouflage color was not necessary for eggs in perpetual shade. Amazing, evolution!

Continuing on down the river, we spotted the freshwater spring that we'd marked on Fran's topo map. After beaching our rafts on the left bank we walked toward the spring, forded the large stream that issued from below it, and stood in awe before what looked like a waterfall, the way it fell from its source on the slope of the mountain, tumbling in noisy rushing rivulets down to the river. The mosses and other plants growing in the midst of the running water were a vivid forest green, contrasted with the much lighter vegetation on both sides of the spring. A gorgeous array of wildflowers was growing there, mostly yellow-petaled groundsel, but also sky-blue Jacob's ladders and a few small saxifrages – a true artist's palette.

Above the spring, about 150 feet from where we were standing, was a copse of balsam poplar with the greenest leaves I'd ever seen on trees in the Arctic. I also thought I heard a scolding dipper somewhere, but the cacophony of the falling water drowned out the sound of the bird and I couldn't find it. If there was a dipper, I knew there must be a nest nearby, but as much as I searched, I could only come up with an old derelict nest. All that was left was an empty crescent-shaped hollow made of moss. It must have been abandoned as too accessible to predators. (A friend who had floated the Marsh Fork a week before us told me later that the new nest was just around the corner on a cliff closer to the river.) While fording the stream again on our way back to the raft, I spotted a small seven-inch grayling darting for cover under the stream bank. "So, there are grayling here," I commented to Fran. "And Arctic char, too," he rejoined.

Onward, this time over some fun rapids. I really liked the way the inflatable canoe bobbed like a bubble on the water, yet it tracked almost as well as my Ally canoe. Two things I didn't like were its small carrying capacity and the way it was always wet in the stern because of its self-bailing feature. It was a good stable canoe in big rapids, but the Ally was much better in calmer water.

After lunch we stopped to visit with a young couple, Tim and Kathy, and their four-year old son. They were rafting, too, and had camped for the night where we met them. He was an emergency room doctor, she a therapist, and they lived in Anchorage. We chatted about the beauty of the river and the wilderness it was a part of, and that naturally led to a discussion of Wilderness Watch, one of the environmental organizations we three men belonged to. Since Fran was the Fairbanks Chapter representative, he did most of the talking. By the end of our chat they promised to join the organization as soon as they got back to civilization. When I mentioned the grayling we'd seen at the spring, the doc said he had caught a char back at the canyon and eaten it for dinner, which made me wonder how many other floaters had fished for char or grayling. Fish are few and grow slowly in the Arctic, and it doesn't take much to put a dent in their numbers.

In mid-afternoon a wind from the north came up, forcing us to paddle downriver harder than we wanted to at that time of day, so we stopped to camp on a sunny gravel bar next to a clearwater stream called Salsbury Creek. After setting up my tent, I thought I might climb the mountain behind camp, but by then the wind had died and it was just too hot, so I decided to take a bath in the creek instead. I'd found a deep hole of sparkling water with a sandy bottom far enough away from camp for some privacy. Although it was cold, under the hot sun the water was invigorating, and I really enjoyed bathing in this special place where I most likely would never bath again for the rest of my life.

After some late afternoon tea we all felt lively enough to take a short ramble upriver along the now-dry gravel bars. On these we found three new wildflowers, including small grass of parnassus. Since the scientific name for this plant is *Parnassia kotzebuei*, it must have first been discovered by the scientist aboard the ship of the Russian explorer, Kotzebue. We also came across scores of dwarf hawks-beard, now in bloom, although they looked a little thirsty because of the extreme dry weather we were having. Yoriko referred to the hawks-beard as "pincushion," because they reminded her of real pincushions, a natural analogy for the seamstress she was.

On our walk we saw a few wandering tattlers poking along the shoreline for small insects and their larvae, and a pair of terns diving successfully for either char or grayling smolt. Two mew gulls cruised above the river in their constant quest for food, and we could hear an upland sandpiper whistling from the tundra where it probably had a nest. I reflected on how much motion and color and melodious music these little birds, and so many others, give to this otherwise quiet landscape.

Back at the tents, Yoriko showed me a small red mite she'd found crawling up the side of her mosquito fly. She'd never seen anything like it and wondered if it might be dangerous. I told her mites were related to spiders, and that they weren't harmful except to much smaller critters. I looked it up in my guide later and read that this species, named the red freshwater mite, dropped its eggs randomly in the water of ponds and slow-flowing streams or sloughs. After hatching, the larvae crept or swam to aquatic invertebrates, mostly insects, on which they attached themselves as external parasites. In that case, I imagined the sandpipers we'd been seeing ate quite a lot of them.

After dinner, we chatted around the fire until the red sun disappeared behind smoky mountains. By this time the next day we would probably be on the main branch of the Canning, and we hoped the smoke would be gone.

The smoke did not disappear, and that night was the hottest one I had ever experienced in the Refuge. I couldn't even close my sleeping bag until about 3 a.m. A warm southerly breeze blew most of the night, which was exactly the opposite of the normal pattern. Things were certainly changing in the Brooks Range, and I was worried about the consequences for glaciers, river levels in mid-summer, permafrost, the polar ice cap, and for all the animals that needed cold weather to survive in the Arctic.

We were on the river again by mid-morning, and this time Ritchie was with me in the canoe as the bowman. We were in the lead, and right away spotted a couple of male harlequin ducks racing up the middle of the river. They were probably already on their way south and west, since they were no doubt finished with their mating duties. For the harlequin male, these duties end early because after the female lays her eggs the rest is up to her. He and his buddies simply fly off into the smoky sunset, eventually ending up on the northwest coast of Canada and the U.S.

Before taking off downriver, I had mentioned to everyone that when we arrived at a point just above the confluence of the Marsh Fork and the Canning we would have to pull out on the right bank and climb a hill to glass the braided delta for a channel with enough water in it to carry us through with a minimum of lining. While we were doing this, Fran spotted a herd of muskoxen grazing about a mile to our east, and he suggested a short cross-country walk to try to get a better view of them. We were all for it, so quickly changed into our boots and started hoofing it across the tundra. We soon discovered that one advantage to climate change was that the tundra was much drier and easier to walk on, and it only took us about a half-hour to get to a rock outcrop near where the muskoxen were feeding and napping.

We quietly sneaked up the backside of a small rock tor of tilted slate, and glassed the bulky animals from our hiding place. They were all napping except a lone female standing sentinel for the herd. From afar, it looked like a tundra meadow with big brown grassy tussocks scattered randomly on top. Within an hour, though, the "tussocks" were all back on their feet again, grazing nonchalantly on the grasses, small shrubs and wildflowers. We counted a dozen of them, including a big bull with his huge sickle-shaped horns and his harem of eleven cows. They reminded me of the muskoxen I had seen with Don and Clancy on the Jago River two years earlier. Then, there were eleven of them, and they had marched right up to our tents, fed for about a half-hour, then ambled northward toward the coast.

These we were watching had a tattered appearance because of the condition of their fur. In spring, muskoxen get rid of most of their inner wool, called qiviut, by rubbing their bodies on any available surface. Wherever I've seen muskoxen, I've found their qiviut hanging all over the willows and alders in the area. Qiviut is one of the finest animal furs in the world, and is used by the Yup'ik Eskimo women on Nunivak Island to knit expensive scarves, hats and other items, which are sold to tourists.

The big brawny animals soon began fading into a thick stand of nearby willows. Feeling it might be our fault, we decided to leave them in peace and headed back to the boats. Not far from our hiding place, I dallied to examine a thyme-leaved saxifrage (*Saxifraga serpyllifolia*), with its five mustard-colored petals, growing on the gravelly slope. It had been a long time since I'd seen one of these.

Halfway to the river, I stopped to glass a northern shrike that had settled on a small willow to watch us march across the tundra. Somewhere in the neighborhood I suspected his mate was brooding eggs on a nest. I would have ogled him longer, but I was too hot and sweaty and could only think of getting to the boats, shucking my clothes and jumping in the cold water of the river. Which is exactly what I did. Arriving at the landing about ten minutes ahead of the rest of the crew, I quickly peeled off all of my clothes and took the plunge. Whooee, what deliciously cold water! I pushed out into the current and let it take me until I was totally refreshed. Then I swam to shore and jumped back into my clothes, just in time, before Phil and Jean rounded the bend. "I knew that's what you were hurrying for," Jean smiled.

When everyone had returned to the boats, we ate lunch on top of a promontory overlooking the river, and then climbed the rocky slope to search for a good channel that would accommodate the raft all the way to the main fork of the Canning. Our route through the delta turned out to be a piece of cake. Neither our canoe nor the raft had any difficulty finding enough water. When we finally entered the main Canning we noticed that the color of the water had changed. No longer did it have the pellucid quality of the river we'd just been on. It was evident the water from the larger river was influenced by glaciers at its headwaters, for it was a silty, opaque color that didn't even look drinkable.

Phil wanted to do some fishing before going any farther, so after stopping at the confluence, he adjusted my telescopic fishing rod and started casting into the clear water of the Marsh Fork. It didn't take long for a grayling to snag the Mepps hook, and Phil gently reeled the fish in. For a grayling it was a pretty big fish, about 15 inches long, with the typical wide flaring dorsal fin of its species. Since we had plenty of food and no need for the meat, he released the fish and cast his line back into the flowing water, hoping for another bite. He repeated the action with the fluid motion of an experienced fisherman, and we could see he was in his element. As for me, I didn't really enjoy catching fish unless I was hungry. It seemed too much like playing with the animal, with the real danger of irreparably harming it. That big grayling turned out to be the only gullible one in there, though, because Phil caught no more of them and after another half-hour called it quits.

Then it was down the silty water of the Canning to try to find a place to camp. Almost as soon as we were back on the river a breeze from the north kicked up again. We hoped it would begin to clear the smoke out of the valley, since we presumed the smoke had come in from the Interior to the south. But as the wind grew in strength, the smoke only became thicker. What was causing this strange phenomenon, we wondered, and how much worse would it get?

Our attention suddenly focused on a lone bull caribou, running at full bore toward us. We pulled over on the other side of the river when we saw him racing around, shaking his head and twitching his body like he had gone completely mad. Fran said he was desperately trying to keep ahead of warble and bott flies, so they wouldn't lay their eggs on him. Bott flies deposit their eggs in the animal's nose, and when the larvae hatch they can cause serious breathing problems for the caribou. Warble flies lay their eggs on the legs of the caribou, and when they hatch the larvae migrate under the skin up to the caribou's back, where they encyst and continue to grow. Both flies remain in their host until the next spring, when they turn into adults and fly away. Warbles emerge through holes they poke in the skin, leaving a heavily pock-marked hide. It was no wonder the caribou we were watching was acting so weirdly.

As Ritchie and I were rounding a bend in the river we heard an excited voice behind us. I looked back and saw Phil pointing over toward the willows on shore. I couldn't see anything, but when he got a little closer he asked us if we'd seen the muskox in the bushes. Neither of us had, we told him. And I had a good excuse, I said, because I was focusing on a grove of cottonwoods in the distance where I was certain there would be gray-headed chickadees. Oh, well.

In late afternoon we drifted by Tim and Kathy's tent, which they had located on a gravel bar just below a high knoll. We could see their three silhouettes on top of the knoll, and we imagined they were up there to get away from the mosquitoes that, in spite of the wind, were out in force wherever there were a few bushes. It wasn't long after we spotted the young family that we too put ashore, except we landed on the windward side of the knoll so we wouldn't have to deal with the ubiquitous mosies. It was another fine campsite, and we quickly made ourselves at home there.

After dinner I went for a walk along the gravel bar, where I spooked the same bull caribou we'd seen earlier in the afternoon. He was still shaking his head and vibrating his body, trying to get rid of just one fly. Poor devil! He came to within a hundred feet of me, so close that I could see the fly chasing him. Then he ran off upriver toward camp, where I hoped the others would see him.

Even though I was only wearing sandals, the top of the knoll looked too tempting. Earlier, while studying Fran's topo map, I'd noticed a large lake behind the hill. I thought it might have some ducks or geese on it and I couldn't wait until the next day to satisfy my curiosity. So I struck off up the tundra slope, and when I reached the summit, glassed the lake to see what I could see. Surprisingly, there was nothing moving out there except the rippling of the surface from the incessant north wind, although I did hear the wailing of a Pacific loon from somewhere at the end of the lake, probably hiding in the grass, I thought.

When I returned to camp, I asked the others if they'd seen the caribou I'd spooked in their direction. They hadn't, but wanted to try to find it. So we headed back to where I'd watched the poor animal frenetically trying to rid himself of the fly. We had no luck locating it, though, and with the breeze beginning to abate, the mosies started to swarm. It was time to turn around.

I reached camp first and found a least sandpiper with four furry chicks scurrying among the tents. It was uncanny how those little guys disappeared so quickly. When I took my eyes off them just for an instant, they were gone. And, try as I might, I couldn't find them. I waited, and waited, until finally I saw a tiny movement under the lower edge of a large cobblestone about 20 feet away. I glassed it to make sure it was one of the baby birds, then crept ever so cautiously toward its hiding place. Once, when I fleetingly took my eyes off it I had a hard time finding it again. It was that well camouflaged.

I waited for the rest of our crew to walk into camp before I bent down and scooped the baby bird into my right hand and showed it to them. By its size, it looked like it had hatched and left the nest only hours earlier. It had a cute little bill, stubby wings, and its fuzzy buff-yellow feathers were mottled with faint brown streaks and spots, altogether an exquisite blend of color and pattern for hiding on the sand and gravel bars along the river.

After everyone had taken a gander at the baby sandpiper, I took it back to the same cobblestone where I'd found it. While I was holding the little guy in my hand he didn't move a muscle, but the moment I released him he was all energy and scurried over to the parent bird who was waiting on the sidelines. When they met they both peeped once, then sprinted off toward the cover of the riverbank.

The mosies were starting to get pretty bad, so I headed for the river, brushed my teeth, then went to my tent. Behind the protection of a closed fly I could watch in peace and quiet as the Arctic terns incessantly hovered and dove for small minnows and larvae in the slower currents of the river. It was to their high-pitched staccato cries and the sweet tweedling of a pair of tattlers that I picked up my book, *The Immense Journey*, by Loren Eiesley and started reading again. Out of the corner of my eye the circling sun was a deep smoky red, and a flicker of worry stopped me on the page. How would Eiesley interpret this emotion, I wondered. Probably as part of human evolution, when smoke and fire were a valid source of concern for all animal species.

Everyone was eager to climb the knoll near camp to check out the lake I'd spotted the evening before. Since there was now a healthy breeze blowing from the south to keep the mosquitoes down, we slogged up the spongy tundra slope to the top, where we sat for a while to absorb our surroundings. The face of the lake was textured with the fitful movement of wind, so it was hard to see if there were any ducks or loons. Even when we heard the burping of a red-throated loon, we couldn't find it. And only at the leeward end of the lake could we see the telltale evidence of fish hitting the surface. Phil wished he'd brought along the fishing rod to do some casting there before heading back to camp, but it was at the boats, so the fish would have to remain a mystery.

Someone had told Fran before our trip that there was an active wolf den not far downriver, under some bluffs near a tributary called Plunge Creek. We didn't want to disturb the wolves, but we were interested in at least seeing them from afar. So after floating a few miles to where we thought they might be, we beached the boats and climbed a high bank to glass the bluffs on the other side of the river. Having no luck there, we continued floating to another higher overlook where we had a better view of the bluffs. We then ambled back upriver along the edge of the bank for a quarter mile or so and sat on the tundra to eat our lunch and watch for movement in the willows below the bluffs. After more than an hour of scanning and probing every square inch of the surrounding country, we saw no wolves. We did, however, discover a shadowy hollow in the distance that looked like a den. Whether it was the one we were after, we'll never know because we didn't remain long enough to see any action. The adult wolves might have left the pups in the den to nap while they ventured out to hunt, or for some reason they had abandoned the den altogether. Another mystery.

When we'd awakened in the morning the skies were still smoky, and they didn't improve the later it got in the day. In fact, it seemed by midday the smoke was even thicker, which was totally contrary to what we expected. Usually, when the day gets warmer the air rises and takes any smoke higher into the mountains. But there was so much smoke now that particles of fine ash were beginning to sift down on us, and the visibility was only about a quarter of a mile. It worried us that Dirk might have to fly in these conditions, or perhaps not be able to fly at all for days. A lot of "what-ifs" were whirling around in our heads, when suddenly we heard Dirk's Beaver lumbering down the valley at tree-top level. In spite of the molasses-thick smoke everywhere, he was trying his luck to fly under the worst of it to retrieve an important customer at the take-out strip on the Canning River Delta. He was to pick up Senator Harkin from Iowa there, a Senator who so far had voted on our side of the Arctic Refuge issue. It was important that he have a good experience on the Refuge, and part of this meant no delays in his schedule. In any case, we were heartened to see Dirk flying, since we were scheduled to be picked up the next day.

Right after Dirk flew over we watched a moose cow and her calf, running for all they were worth along the far shore toward Plunge Creek. And they kept going, stretching their long legs out over the gravel, turning up the creek, then abruptly disappearing into the willows. I glassed in all directions to see if there was a bear or wolves chasing them but came up with nothing. The others couldn't spot anything either, so we could only guess that maybe there was a predator lurking somewhere nearby and just not revealing its presence, or that a remnant smell of wolves or bear made them so spooky.

It was time to move downriver again, so we pushed off, with Phil and Jean back in the canoe and the rest of us in the big rubber bubble. Right away we spotted six harlequin ducks, two males and four females, resting on a gravel bar. The presence of the females told me they were probably first-year non-nesters, just getting to know each other for next year's mating game. Unlike most other species of ducks, harlequins don't nest until they're two years old. The striking variegated color pattern of the males, preference for the wildest landscapes for nesting, and their daring underwater foraging strategies near the brink of waterfalls and in turbulent rapids make them my favorite duck species.

When we left the high bluffs of the Canning we knew we were close to our take-out spot where Dirk had instructed us to find a long enough gravel bar for him to land on. Not knowing what lay farther downriver, we pulled ashore on a wide bar that seemed like it might do the trick. After securing the boats, we scattered in all directions, searching for any indication that this spot had ever been used by Dirk in the past as a landing strip. An hour and a half later we all met again at the boats and reported our findings. Nothing, except a few tattered pieces of survey tape on a couple of willows, found about a quarter mile in from the river and not likely to be the convenient landing that Dirk had told us about. So we simply hedged our bets and made camp right where we had taken out. We figured that even if there were a better gravel bar farther downriver, we could make this one work by removing some of the larger cobbles and filling the shallow swales with gravel and sand. The bar was certainly long enough. The only problem was that it was next to the river, and if the water level rose any higher Dirk would be landing in it.

We set up our tents for what we thought might be our last night on the river. Then I gathered some dry willow sticks, broke them into kindling-size pieces, and built a small cookfire. Soon I had some river water boiling and brewed us a late afternoon cup of tea. Meanwhile, Ritchie began preparing dinner with one of her big packages of Mountain House chicken. Yoriko also shared some of her home-dried mushrooms and cheese with Mexican chipotle sauce. After such a treat we voted Yoriko the best chef in camp and assigned her to cook for all of us from then on. She thanked us and hoped Dirk would make it in the next morning. For dessert, we celebrated with the last few drops of Phil's Arctic elixir, which were delicious to, yes, the last drop.

Phil and Fran entertained us after dinner with some hilarious stories from their army days when they were conscripts in Germany. Secretly I was glad I had never been in the military and opted instead for the Peace Corps, where I felt I served my country and myself much better. I don't think I could ever have operated in an atmosphere in which the emphasis was always on killing your enemy. Granted, joining the military has probably helped discipline and educate a lot of young Americans, but the experience has also destroyed or severely disoriented too many of them.

In the evening I collapsed the inflatable canoe and cleaned and folded it for backhauling to Coldfoot by Dirk. Then Yoriko asked me to identify a wildflower she'd found growing in the gravel not far from her tent. "Merckia," I told her, "in the Caryophyllaceae family, I think." And when I got out my guide, sure enough, I had remembered the family correctly. "My memory's not as bad as I thought," I continued, "at least not with wildflower names."

While brushing my teeth down at the river, I listened to the flow of the water. With all the worrisome smoke in the air, the sound gave me some soothing relief, at least till I closed the tent flap for the night and began to write in my journal. It reads: *As I write this in my sleeping bag, the smoke is so thick I can smell it, and I'm worried about Dirk making it in tomorrow under the smoke the way he did this morning. Or whether he should even try. But there's absolutely nothing I can do about the smoke, so I'm focusing on the bubbly warbling of a couple of male robins vying for their respective territories, and on the constant white noise of the river purling by just a few yards from my tent. I confess, though, with all the smoke in the air, I'm having a hard time concentrating on the beauty of this place.*

By the morning of the 4th I was exhausted. Worry about the smoke had kept me awake almost all night, and I didn't get more than three hours of real sleep. But I crawled out of the tent at 7:30 anyway so that I could be with the others for breakfast and prepare for Dirk's hypothetical arrival later in the morning. Not that we really expected him. The smoke was still as thick as mud and we knew it would be suicide to try to fly through it. But we spruced up the runway for him a little more, marked the edges with rocks, and set up a makeshift wind flag with one of Phil's old red undershirts. While we did this, Phil and Fran chatted about their military days again. They remembered story after interminably funny story, until it got a little too much for me and I wandered away. I know that's how it is with a threesome, especially when two of the guys have more in common with each other, and the third one becomes the "odd man out." No matter. I had other things I could do.

I ambled downriver again to check out our little airstrip, and to see if the river level had come up. When the wind suddenly died, the mosies came out in force, reminding me of why we were all so eager for Dirk to arrive. But I marveled there weren't more of them, and guessed it was because there hadn't been much rain over the past few weeks. Most of the small potholes where the mosquito larvae swarmed had probably dried up prematurely and the hatch wasn't as large as usual. Their time would finally come, though, and they would be out in fists and hordes.

As I strolled back to the tents a Pacific loon flew overhead, racing low and away from what appeared to be an approaching storm to the west. I couldn't really tell because of the thick smoke, but before I reached camp raindrops began pelting me. I remembered I hadn't put the rain fly back on my tent, so picked up my pace. Good that I did because within 15 minutes all hell broke loose, and Ritchie and I dove for cover in my tent to escape the most violent thunderstorm I'd ever seen in the Brooks Range. It hit us full bore, and we weren't prepared for it because the dark clouds had been so completely obscured by the smoke. Suddenly, we heard rolls of thunder and felt the wind and rain as it pummeled our tent harder and harder. Flashes of lightning were at first just dim reminders of the thunder in the distance, but the closer the eye of the storm came, and the more smoke the torrential rain knocked out of the air, the brighter the lightning was. The thunder was especially daunting, echoing back and forth in the valleys on both sides of the Canning River. It was like being deep inside a long cavernous tunnel as the downpour steamrollered through the mountains. The force of the wind and rain became so severe that Ritchie and I had to prop ourselves against the windward side of the tent to keep from blowing away.

The fury of the storm lasted for about an hour, but as with all furies in the Arctic this one quickly sailed off into the distance. When we peered out from under the rain fly it looked like half of the smoke had been knocked out of the air and it gave us renewed hope that Dirk might make it in, at least by tomorrow morning. The strong west wind that continued buffeting us during our dinner pushed and dragged away even more of the smoke, so that our spirits were high enough for us to hope that maybe Dirk would try to make it in by midnight. Then, we wondered, how could he know what the conditions were like on the Canning? And it could be the smoke was still impossibly bad over in Coldfoot. Too many maybes. Only time would tell what would happen.

So Phil and Fran told more military stories, and when they began to run out, even I recounted a few stories of my own. The one they enjoyed the most was about my appendicitis attack in Marshall in 1998, when Guy Sandlin tried flying me into Bethel one September morning at 5:00 a.m., but was stymied by bad weather and had to take me first to the small village of Napaskiak, where nobody was awake, then to the clinic in the neighboring village of Kasigluk, where I stayed for three hours until my appendicitis burst at 10:00 a.m. Guy then tried Bethel again, was repulsed again by low visibility, and finally flew me up the Kuskokwim River to Aniak. In spite of an ambulance at the airport and a fancy clinic, they weren't able to do anything for me there either, so I managed to convince the Aniak ticket agent for Yute Airlines that I wasn't going to die on their plane while in the air and got on their flight to Anchorage. Next, thanks to help from my cousin Janet, I caught a flight to Fairbanks where Jennifer picked me up and took me to the emergency room at the hospital.

As we chatted on into the night, clouds the color of tarnished pewter began rolling in from the coast and rainy weather seemed to be in the offing for us again, so we decided to call it quits and headed for our tents. I told Ritchie not to worry about putting her tent up. She could bunk in mine, if she wanted, so it wouldn't be necessary to break two tents down if Dirk rolled in first thing in the morning.

July 5 –

Thanks to a codeine pill that Jen had given me before leaving Fairbanks, I slept better than the previous night. But I suffered the consequences for most of the next day, with nausea, a splitting headache, sore back, and no appetite! I'd forgotten I was allergic to codeine, and should have remembered that I'd had to discontinue the use of the drug after my appendicitis operation in the hospital.

In spite of my bad headache, I was able to help Phil and Fran with our makeshift airstrip. The water level had come up during the night about six inches and had flooded the river side of the runway, so that we had to widen it a bit on its other side. The weather was a little doubtful in the early morning, with a lot of high overcast and ragged shards of gray clouds hanging against the mountains, and we were skeptical that Dirk would even try coming in. Later, when the clouds began to lift, our spirits did the same. But by noon there was still no sign of him and the weather started to deteriorate again. Phil announced that he didn't have much hope Dirk would arrive now. Fran said he wasn't so sure. I had mixed feelings because I had seen Dirk fly in much worse weather. When it began raining, though, I was more sympathetic with Phil, so I bee-lined for the tent to try to get some relief for my head. The codeine pill was still having its effects on me and, if it weren't for a couple of interesting bird sightings, I would have retired to my tent earlier.

The first sighting was of a Merlin, casually cruising down the river and suddenly being assailed by an Arctic tern that gave him no mercy. It was like the tern pounced on him, trying to stab him again and again with his dagger beak. The Merlin took evasive action, but each time he did the tern was on him like a cat, pow, pow, pow, aiming for his head, until finally they both reached an invisible line on the river and the tern veered off and winged his way back up toward our camp. As if that weren't enough, when a golden eagle soared too low, the tern and his mate shot skyward like two arrows straight for the eagle. Incredibly, they caught him and gave him such a pounding that the eagle folded his giant wings and plummeted to escape the ire of the terns. Then, when they caught up to him again, he tucked his wings and dove even faster and much farther, finally leaving the terns in the dust. Whew! This was electric stuff and awoke me from my zombie-like state, at least while it lasted.

Just as I was nodding off in the tent, what did I hear but the familiar deep-throated sound of Dirk's Beaver, a long way up the valley at first, but steadily closing in. I quickly put my boots and raingear back on, grabbed my daypack and popped out of my tent in time to see Dirk passing directly overhead so he could scope out our airstrip. He must have approved because on the next go-around he landed with a big bounce and a dip and a few splashes in the shallow water at the edge of the river, then he turned and taxied back to where we were camped. Meanwhile, we quickly collapsed our sopping wet tents, stuffed them in their bags, then hefted them and our packs over to the plane. Fran and I deflated the raft, folded and tied it up and lugged it over to the pile to go out with Dirk the next day. After loading everything we were taking with us on board, Dirk helped me clean up the fireplace and throw the carbonized rocks randomly over the gravel bar.

On Dirk's signal, we all piled into the airplane, buckled our seat belts and put on our earphones. He turned over his engine, revved it to make sure it sounded okay, then gunned it with his brake on. At full throttle he released the brake and we roared down the gravel bar. More splashes, the muted grating noise of coarse gravel on tundra tires, another dip and a bounce, and we were in the air speeding above the slow moving Canning River. Then the airplane banked and began heading back up the valley toward the rain we thought would have prevented Dirk from making it in. These same tattered clouds and scudding rain that only an hour earlier we had looked at with a jaundiced eye we now saw with new lenses, and I heard the expression "breathtaking beauty" issue from the mouth of at least one person.

Two hours later we were in Coldfoot again, busily unloading the airplane and paying our bill. I apologized to Dirk for any misunderstanding over the raft, then we jumped in our vehicles and headed for Fairbanks. About halfway home we had a memorable encounter with a pair of adult whimbrels that challenged us on the road. We stopped the cars, and the tall spindly sandpipers just stood there, boldly facing us in the middle of the road, not willing to give an inch. We suspected they had a family nearby and, sure enough, when we stepped out to check, we found a couple of the gangly young in the grass at the edge of the highway. What a fitting end to our trip.

PHOTOS

1. Unhappy campers waiting under a blazing Arctic sun
2. Caribou running to escape flies
3. Smoky sun on lower Canning River

Chapter 9

A Good Crew Ivishak River to the Marsh Fork
June 5-17, 2009

Jen and I were excited about this trek. We had planned it during the winter with our friends, Keith Echolmeyer and Susan Campbell. Keith's brain tumor seemed to be doing better and we thought it might be a good opportunity to take him out to some of his favorite country in the Arctic National Wildlife Refuge in the Brooks Range. When we spread out

Dennis and Sue fording Ivishak River with Jen

a map of the Refuge on his kitchen table and asked him where he'd like to go, he said the Ivishak River – to hike from there over to the Marsh Fork of the Canning River. A mutual friend of ours, Stan Justice, was interested in going with us. He had been a Peace Corps Volunteer in Nepal back in the early 1970s, so I thought he would be a good fit. Two old teaching friends, Dennis and Sue Lenssen, who had taught with us in the Lower Yukon village of Marshall, also wanted to go, so with two full planes, that would be our limit.

From then on it was plan, plan some more, then pack, so we could make it from where we put down on the upper Ivishak River, with backpacks weighing no more than 60 pounds each, over about 40 miles of rough country to an airstrip on the Marsh Fork. We also had to arrange with Dirk Nickisch, owner of Coyote Air Charter, to set aside a couple of dates in June to taxi us in and out of the Brooks Range. Keith and Susan chose to fly with Kirk Sweetsir, owner of Yukon Air, so they made their own charter arrangements. Since Dennis and Sue had never done a trek like this before, we asked them to join us in Fairbanks on June 3 so we could help them get organized.

We were ready to go by the evening of June 4.

June 5 –

Stan had volunteered his Toyota van to ferry us from Fairbanks up the Dalton Highway to Coldfoot, where Dirk flew out of during the summer. Jen and I and the Lenssens were crammed inside along with our heavy backpacks. It was a tight fit and the road was long, but the crew was a good one and we had fun visiting about the Peace Corps and about old times teaching together in the Lower Yukon Delta. We stopped for a lunch break at the Yukon River Bridge and ate down by the river. Watching the perpetual eddying motion of the Yukon reminded us of our teaching days, far downriver in the village of Marshall.

Seven hours after leaving Fairbanks we were in Coldfoot. Dirk and his wife Daniél and their two kids were home when we arrived and we briefly stopped by their place at the airport to confirm our charter with them in the morning up to the Ivishak River. We told them that Keith and Susan would be flying with Kirk Sweetsir out of Fort Yukon and would meet us on the river the same afternoon. Then we drove up the road a few miles to the BLM campground and, after a late dinner of quesadillas and refried beans, spent part of the night listening to the soft whisper of light rain on our tent.

Over at Dirk's at 8:00 in the morning, he told us the videocams monitoring the passes showed rain and fog, so he put us on a weather hold. But a couple of hours later the ceiling lifted and we were good to go. It was an even tighter fit than Stan's van, but we managed to sardine everybody and their packs into Dirk's blue and white Beaver, and a few minutes later we were roaring off the gravel airstrip and heading north over the muddy, swollen headwaters of the Koyukuk River. And it wasn't the only river that was swollen. Through the bubble window of the Beaver we could see that the headwaters of the Chandalar, Wind and Junjik Rivers were also high with spring runoff. I had never floated these rivers and wondered how they would compare to those I had.

While crossing the pass from the Junjik into the Ivishak River drainage the weather turned a little sour with a discontinuous layer of cloud, and when we landed at the upper bench strip above the Ivishak River, we immediately donned our raingear. It wasn't long after Dirk disappeared into what was quickly becoming only a thin veil of misty rain that we found a campsite down in the willows and made a warming fire with birch bark I had gathered in Fairbanks and some small willow sticks that made a snapping noise when I broke them, indicating they were still quite dry on the inside. As we finished our lunch the rain stopped and we set up our tents.

Then it was time for Stan and me to do some local reconnaissance. He went in one direction and I in another. After heading south and crossing a creek rushing with melt water, I climbed a high knoll to search for a possible ford across the Ivishak. I spotted a heavily braided part of the river about a mile up toward the pass and decided it might be the place to attempt a crossing the next day. I also heard the singing of many birds, including a Say's phoebe, Tree- and White-crowned sparrows, Wandering tattler, and the signature drawn-out wolf-whistle of the Upland plover. I spotted three lone Dall sheep rams feeding on the now-sunny south-facing slopes to the west, which I reported to the others when I got back to camp. Stan said he had discovered a Horned lark's nest on the bluff above camp, with four chicks and one greenish-brown egg in it. Dennis asked us if what he was seeing around camp were wolf and caribou tracks. Yes, and some of them had probably passed through only yesterday, we told him.

Dennis has an intense interest in geology, and while sitting on the bluff above camp we chatted about the limestone and shale-slate formations surrounding us on all sides. The weathered and craggy Lisburne limestone was especially ancient, probably close to 300 million years old, I told him. When I glanced behind us, I pointed out something a little younger, with wings, a Horned lark strutting over the greening tundra, hunting for food, probably for the same young in the nest Stan had found. Later we watched a Smith's longspur involved in the same quest during this short Arctic nesting season, when birds have to frenetically take advantage of the fleeting availability of food to feed and fatten their families before leaving in late July or August on their migration south to warmer climes.

While drinking some tea over our small willow fire we heard the familiar drone of Kirk Sweetsir's Cessna 185. We quickly climbed up the bank to watch Kirk buzz the flat area where Dirk had landed us. There were two passengers in the plane, who waved at us as Kirk brought the small plane around to make his approach to the makeshift airstrip. With a couple of minor bounces he quickly braked, then swung around with a deep-throated roar and taxied over to where we were waiting. After the engine shut down and the three-tined prop came to a complete stop, Kirk opened his door and jumped out on the hard tundra below. Then Keith Echolmeyer and Susan Campbell stepped down and we greeted them like long lost friends. Kirk handed them their packs and chatted with us for a while, then ferried his 185 back up the strip a ways, put the pedal to the metal, roared up into the wind, circled in a wide arc, tilted his wings and disappeared into the misty headwaters of the Ivishak Valley.

After setting up their tent, Keith and Susan joined us around the campfire for dinner and some hot chocolate with Bailey's. As the shadows of evening lengthened, the weather improved until the sky was silver-blue with few clouds. We watched the sun begin to wheel across the mountains to the north, reminding us that we were indeed in the Arctic, and that there would be white light shining on us all night, reflecting the first hints of green on the tundra and sparkles of color from the first blooming wildflowers. Commenting to Jen that this was an unforgiving kind of paradise, we called it quits at 11, brushed our teeth and zipped ourselves into our sleeping bags.

I awoke at six to raindrops and heavy mist rolling up the valley from the Coastal Plain – something we half-expected. As we'd also expected, the light rain stopped at seven, and I got up to make a small willow fire and heat some water for coffee for Jen and me. I roused everyone else with a, "Water's hot!" and they soon greeted us around the smoky fire and ate a hearty breakfast before making preparations for moving upriver in our quest for a shallow ford across the Ivishak. The water had gone down somewhat overnight because of the cool temperatures, but we knew it would rise again by mid-afternoon, so we would have to find a place to cross as soon as we came to a good ford.

The ford I thought might work the day before didn't, so we continued walking up the west bank of the river. It was not an easy route, with a lot of ups and downs, since the river abutted the bluffs in many places, making it impossible to walk in the riverbed itself. It was especially difficult for Keith, and at one point he lost his balance and fell and cut his hand. When Stan confided in me that Keith's equilibrium was off a little because of his brain tumor, we agreed to keep a closer eye on him from then on. After watching him lose his balance again on the brink of one of the high bluffs next to the river, I drew him aside and asked him to please stay away from the margins of the cliffs. He smiled and nodded, later allowing Stan to carry his pack across the face of a talus slope on the edge of the river. The current was especially strong there, so we all breathed a sigh of relief when we reached the other side.

Two steep uphill grinds were hard on everyone, but finally by mid-afternoon we were on a flat, hard surface again, and at the next creek we decided to call it quits for the day and camp. Not only did we have good clear water in the creek, but there was also plenty of firewood and tall willows to protect us from the strong wind coming down the valley. There was quite a menagerie of birds in the area, too. Already we had seen three Common mergansers and a Barrow's goldeneye on the river, and a Northern shrike was screeching at us on the top of a willow just in back of our tents.

A nap was in order after we were settled, then some hot tea brewed over a willow fire, which I shared with Jen, by then so tuckered out she thought she might not eat dinner. Meanwhile, Stan went off to reconnoiter the river, and Dennis, Keith, Susan and I soon did the same up the mountainside behind us. Dennis peeled off to check out a black slate formation, so the three of us continued farther up the slope to get a good view of the valley, trying to locate a good ford across the Ivishak. Studying the area with my binoculars, I thought I found one about a half-mile from camp, where the river braided heavily, but

Keith was doubtful. When Stan joined us later on the mountain, he thought we should at least check it out the next day. He also showed us a small bear skull he'd found with worn and broken teeth, indicating it was from an old bear that we guessed might have been killed by a younger bear.

Back at camp, we found Jen and Sue visiting around the fire over hot chocolate. Jen had eaten some dinner and now felt much better. Dennis got back after we did with his find, a handful of wet slate from a shallow cave in the limestone, where Dall sheep had sheltered and wildflowers were growing in soil made fertile with their abundant droppings. As he explained the geological history of the slate formation he found, my attention was taken by a large gray shorebird called a Wandering tattler that tootled by us on the shoreline, searching for insect larvae. Above us a Golden eagle soared, probably checking us out with his telescopic vision. I wondered if he could see the carpet of wildflowers in our camp, especially some of the more colorful ones, such as moss campion, alpine azalea and purple mountain saxifrage. I wished I had their eyes.

I stayed up for a while, watching the sun flicker lambent light from the surface of the creek in front of our tent, then at last crawled into my sleeping bag and closed my eyes to the sound of bubbling water flowing through my head.

The smell of smoke from the morning fire roused everyone from their slumbers, and slowly but surely they trickled in to sit and visit. Jen and I were already drinking our coffee when Stan ambled over, then the Lenssens, and finally Keith and Susan. The main topic of conversation was the possible ford we'd seen the previous evening, and we were all eager to try our luck crossing there, even though the river had only gone down one inch according to the stick we had placed at the edge of the water before going to bed.

We were packed up by mid-morning and quickly covered the half-mile or so to the potential crossing. The silty water was moving swiftly, but there were plenty of braids that told us this was a promising place to at least attempt making our ford. I volunteered to be the pioneer, put on my sandals, and carefully picked my way across the first half of the river. It turned out to be a piece of cake, and I made the point by walking back to shore with my pack on. After a short conference, everyone decided to try it, too. Stan and I helped Keith across, then we led the others across in shifts. By the time I was finished, my feet were as cold as ice. The second half of the braids proved easier to ford because there were more of them and the water was shallower and slower. We were happy to have crossed without incident, although Keith was sad he wasn't able to do it completely on his own, as he had done in the past. Jen and I were particularly relieved, since we had organized the trip and felt responsible for everyone's safety.

With our boots back on, we jostled our way through a thick stand of willows, then climbed a small knob that afforded us a better view of our route across the river. There we all audibly relaxed, and over a snack marveled at how we had crossed so easily. Dennis pointed out a phalanx of limestone flat-irons that marched across the upper slopes of the mountains paralleling the river. It was good to have him along to give some names and meaning to the geology we were encountering. Stan, meanwhile, got his topo map out, and we studied it to determine which way we would go on the next phase of our hike over to the Marsh Fork. After talking to Keith, we had already decided not to try to approach the Marsh Fork from the headwaters of the Ivishak, because of the difficulty of the crossing over the pass. He had done it several years earlier and advised against it. So, it would be up the tributary creek that flowed into the Ivishak where we were, then a climb across the tundra at the base of the north side of the range paralleling the Marsh Fork.

On the trail again, while wending our way up the creek we flushed a Willow ptarmigan from her nest and quickly counted 10 brown eggs. When Sue found a little white flower that she thought was a forget-me-not, I asked her to bend down and smell it. It was powerfully fragrant for such a tiny jewel, and I told her its common name was rock jasmine. No wonder it's called that, she said. When Dennis approached I pointed at a close clump of fuzzy mustard yellow flowers called glacier avens. There were scores of them tracking up the side of the hill, and their ragged leaves reflected the sun like little green mirrors. They were one of the first plants to bloom in these mountains, and like so many other Arctic wildflowers would only be around for another week or two, depending on elevation, which was one of the reasons I loved walking in the Brooks Range in June, along with all the bird song.

Following an animal trail up the creek, we stumbled into a bull moose with his antlers in full velvet. He was as surprised to see us as we were to see him, and stood bug-eyed, watching us until we were quite close. Then he hightailed it up a clearwater stream and disappeared into the brush. He wasn't the only animal we saw there. While eating lunch a little farther along the creek we spotted seven Dall sheep, all ewes without lambs, prompting us to wonder whether bad spring storms had been hard on the young lambs, or if wolves or bear had eaten them. We would never know. We also watched a pair of Willow ptarmigan that seemed to be in the middle of their mating game. When we first sat down to eat, the ptarmigan stood side by side, but soon the male began slowly strutting away from the female. It was then I decided to play a little game with the male and clucked loudly, *ko peck, ko peck, ko peck, ko peck*, imitating as closely as possible the male's mating call. It had its desired effect. The male quickly strutted back to the female's side and stood there possessively, guarding her from any possible competitor, which apparently he thought I was. We all got a kick out of that.

Farther upstream, Stan discovered two stands of balsam poplar on the south-facing part of a bluff. We wondered aloud if there might be Gray-headed chickadees nesting among them, since they prefer poplar for their cavity nests, probably because of their larger size and softer wood. We spotted a second shrike, and heard a spate of Gray-cheeked thrushes with their characteristic fluted wolf-whistle calls. While I had my eyes and ears in the air listening to the thrushes, Jen found a perfect ammonite fossil in the riverbed. Right beside it was a lovely round cluster of lilac-pink flowers called Pallas' wallflower. Those were our best finds of the day, and I took photos of both of them before moving on.

While climbing up and across a stretch of tundra we discovered recent caribou and porcupine kills, probably by hungry wolves. We figured the caribou had come from the Central Arctic herd, which because of its increasing size was wandering farther and farther east. Not far from there we came across a spot flat enough to place our tents. It was time to camp once again. There was no firewood, but there was good sweet water in a little stream flowing nearby, and we had a great view of the surrounding country, including the flatirons on the other side of the Ivishak River, near where we had camped the previous night.

Over dinner, Jen and I visited with the Lenssens and Keith and Susan, while Stan climbed the hill to the south to see what he could see. His girlfriend, Aporn, wasn't able to come on this trip with him, and he was sort of the "odd man out." He is generally a very quiet, thoughtful person, a great birder and a good friend of Keith, so we were glad to have him along. Since he brought the topo map, we left much of the route up to him, although every night all the men would study it and agree on a general plan.

When we climbed into our tent that night the Arctic sky was a clear pale blue, and from the high tundra where we were camped we had an unimpeded view of the sun slowly arcing across the mountains to the north. It was the first time since our trip into the Sadlerochits in 2001 that we'd had such an opportunity. And that wasn't all. An Upland sandpiper serenaded us with his plaintive "cat-call" whistle until finally I fell asleep and heard and saw no more.

We awoke to another familiar sound, the wheezy buzz of mosquitoes flying lazily around our tent. Not many, but enough to make us wonder if this was going to be an early year for them. We hoped not, and breakfast was made more palatable by our sighting of ten Dall sheep ewes on the opposite mountain. Again, none of them had lambs.

Right after striking camp we were confronted head-on by our second big challenge of the trip, skirting the edge of a deep chasm, where Stan and

I felt more comfortable helping Jen and Sue Lenssen ferry their packs across the precipitous slope. Then it was quickly down to the creek bottom and up another long steep grind to the top of a saddle, near a little pothole pond where some of us doffed our clothes and took a chilly but refreshing swim. "Just what the doctor ordered," I sighed, as I stepped into the tannin-stained water, and exactly what I needed before tackling our next challenge, and what would probably be the toughest climb of the trek. The tundra foothill country here was wrinkled with canyon after myriad canyon, tracing down from the fractured limestone mountains paralleling the Marsh Fork of the Canning River that lay just on the other side. We ate our lunch by the pond, then saddled up, followed a caribou trail down into the maw of an even steeper gorge, and began our grueling step-by-step clamber up the opposite slope.

I carried Jen's pack up the mountain first because it was lighter, then went back down for mine. Stan took Sue's up first, then returned for his. Stan is a very strong climber, and I wished I were his age again. Catching Jen on my way back up, we continued to the top together. She was a little weepy that she couldn't keep up, but by the time she joined the others she was her old in-charge self again. When we found everyone, they were almost at the highest point, and Keith had kindly taken Jen's pack the remaining distance before going ahead to reconnoiter the area for a possible camping spot. He reported that he'd come across a good one just on the other edge of the summit, so we all transferred over there and with the greatest pleasure set up our tents and napped for an hour before having dinner.

While eating, we kept a close eye on a huge nimbus storm cell to the west that was circling nearer and nearer to our camp. When it finally started to spit rain we battened down the hatches and headed inside for the night. In spite of the pitter-patter of the raindrops on the tent, I could hear the sweet buzzy trill of our first Smith's longspur singing from a low willow not far away. A raven croaked somewhere to the north in the direction of Porcupine Lake. Listening carefully as I wrote in my journal, I just barely caught the subdued cricket-like buzz of a Savannah sparrow. And finally, there was the melancholy whistle of the Upland sandpiper again to put me to sleep and haunt my dreams.

It rained off and on almost all night and into the early morning, but stopped right on schedule at eight, so we could eat our breakfast in the open, then chitchat with Stan over his topo map about the day's route. Since the scale of our map was six miles to the inch, we couldn't really tell what sort of terrain we would be walking on, but the route we chose near the base of the mountains turned out to be close to ideal, with few tussocks (which we jokingly referred to as "Wattheads," after Ronald Reagan's incompetent and dishonest Secretary of Interior, James Watt), a lot of finely fractured shale and slate, and old caribou trails that had probably been used by these long-legged animals for untold thousands of years. We figured that by now they must know the best trail across the tundra, so we followed their lead. And once again they were right, and we made good time over some potentially rough country. The weather helped. Although there was heavy overcast with rain on all sides of us, a serendipitous bubble of fair weather floated in the same direction we were going and we remained dry all day.

The caribou trails took us on an up and down roller coaster ride through parky squirrel country. Parkies, aka Arctic ground squirrels, were everywhere, standing sentinel at their den holes watching our every move and barking their telltale high-pitched "sik sik!" Ogling them with my binoculars, I could see their little noses twitching a mile a minute, trying to decide what we were and whether we were dangerous or not. I wondered if they also smelled the Kamchatka rhododendron surrounding us. At this stage in the Arctic spring, the fragrance of their bright pink flowers trumped every other smell in the tundra, and I couldn't help bending down even with my heavy load to fill my nostrils with their delightful perfume. But there were also other wildflowers, among them, white bell-like cassiope, growing in clumps in the deeper tundra, and glacier avens, marching whimsically up the north-facing slopes and reflecting the sun's light on the backside of their green leaves and yellow petals.

Maintaining our elevation around a tall knoll, we climbed over a saddle, then sat down out of the wind and ate our lunch. From our perch, Mt. Annette and Porcupine Lake were directly north of us, and we could make out our destination for the day, the keyhole pass through the mountains to the Marsh Fork of the Canning River. Jen mentioned she was having a good day and felt much stronger. So did the others. On rigorous trips like this one, it usually takes three or four days for most people to feel comfortable with the ups and downs of bushwhacking on irregular tundra trails, but eventually it happens, and they begin to really enjoy the walking from that point on. I like to think of it as the moment of total engagement between my body and mind and the wild land I'm walking on.

Then it was down the mountain again on another old caribou trail to a small creek, where we found our first shooting stars, diminutive pink wildflowers that look a little like their namesake, with the scientific moniker, *Dodecatheon frigidum*, that rolls right off the tip of your tongue, making it easy to remember. As I pointed out these little jewels to Dennis, I spotted a Smith's longspur nest with four smoky-gray spotted eggs in it. I knew the instant the female heard us approaching and jumped off the nest that she was now skulking somewhere in the interstices of the tundra waiting for us to leave, which we did post haste, so as not to interrupt the incubation of the eggs. The Smith's longspur, I told him, was not any old bird. Like its cousin the Lapland longspur, it has an elongated hind claw, but unlike it and all other Alaskan songbirds I was familiar with, it is polygynandrous in the sense that each female breeds with two or three males for a single clutch of eggs, at the same time that each male breeds with two or more females. The males are not territorial, and compete for fertilizations by breeding with females frequently in order to displace sperm from other males. What's more, over a period of one week in June, a female will breed over 350 times on average, one of the highest rates of any bird. So, Dennis, those little smoky-gray eggs were genetically very special indeed.

While continuing on ahead with Stan and Jen, Stan commented to Jen about my stride, which he referred to as "chi walking." He described it as moving with my arms and upper body totally relaxed so that my legs could use all the energy they needed to power me up and down and across the hills. It was an observation I'd never heard before, and said to Jen that it probably applied to Stan's stride, too. Jen also told me she'd had an interesting chat with Keith about his and Susan's early days and their wedding. We were all getting to know each other better, as people do on treks like these. It seemed that so far we were a good crew, with everyone attentive to everyone else's needs, and with respect for each other's opinions, and the necessity for consensus in nearly everything we did. Would that all trips were so congenial.

Stan was in the lead most of the time, but I often joined him, as did Keith and Susan. Keith even forged ahead of the pack at times to scout the tundra for the best route. I was amazed at how nimble he was, in spite of his brain tumor and periodic bouts of dizziness. He wasn't the super athlete he used to be, but he was still extremely strong, and robustly determined. Once he was so far ahead of us that we wondered where he had gone. But he finally showed up after going to the top of a knoll to see what the country looked like to the east of us. Dennis also kept up quite well. Since his wife, Sue, was a little woman, suffering from lower back problems, he was carrying part of her load. By now, though, his pack was lighter, he was stronger, and determination was written all over his face to stay up with us so he could visit about what he was most interested in, the geology of the Brooks Range. While chatting about the origins of Mt. Annette opposite us, he pointed out a long tongue of mountainside that had slumped all the way down to the valley floor within the past year or two. He referred to the phenomenon as solifluction, and guessed it was probably the result of climate change. Global warming was happening fastest in the Arctic, and this was one more indication of the effects it was having in the Brooks Range.

Our attention was still focused on the mud slump when Stan pointed at the western flank of the mountain. Ogling it with my binoculars, I saw five big bull caribou with huge antlers in full velvet. They were just taking it easy, three of them grazing desultorily, and two lying on the tundra chewing their cud. When someone asked if caribou were like cattle in this way, I told them they were. Just like cows, deer, horses and sheep, after eating for an hour or so, they have to rest and ruminate, or chew their cud, to further process their food.

Later I learned the rest of the story. As with all ruminants, caribou stomachs are divided into four chambers, each playing a different part in breaking down and absorbing nutrition from the rough vegetation they eat. Because they don't chew before swallowing, a lot of undigested food accumulates in their first stomach, called the rumen. After the rumen is full, bacteria there begin breaking down the plant material. Then the food is regurgitated in small amounts called cud that the caribou chews into pulp with its molars. It is then swallowed again, but this time the food bypasses the rumen and goes into the second and third chambers. The fourth chamber is a lot like our own stomach, and is where nutrients are absorbed and sent into the bloodstream.

Late in the afternoon we came to a small ravine that, according to Stan's map, led straight south through a keyhole pass in the mountains to the Marsh Fork. One of the options we were considering was crossing the saddle over the pass, then dropping down into the valley of the Marsh Fork. But this would hinge on the condition of the river and how high its waters were, since at times we might have to cross it to reach our destination. We decided that we would do a reconnaissance the next day to the overlook on the other side of the pass to check it out with our binoculars. So the closer we camped to the saddle, the better poised we would be to do this. But we still wanted to stay below the limit of the willows to be able to access dry wood and have a campfire. That would be important, because Jen and Sue were ready for a break from walking, and the fire would keep them warm while we were gone. After cooking with our gas stoves for the past two nights, it would also be a nice change to cook over a fire again.

We found the ideal spot not far from where we deliberated over the map. There was enough flat ground for all the tents, dry willows for firewood, fresh flowing water from the creek, and a lovely view of the Porcupine Valley to the north. In the clear weather we could even see all the way over to the Marsh Fork Valley to the east. I recognized some of the landmarks there, including the mountain face just north of the airstrip, and I reckoned it was approximately eight miles to where we would have to cross the river to the other side. A pair of Wandering tattlers, hunting and pecking along the edge of the creek, welcomed us to the campsite.

After setting up our tent, Jen and I were bushed, so we napped for an hour before joining the others around the fire for dinner. There was already hot water on, so I poured a mug of tea for us, then used some of the rest in a package of Mountain House pasta primavera. It would only take 15 minutes for the dry food to steep and reconstitute into a fairly tasty meal. These dinners are so much better than they used to be, light to carry in a pack, plus easy to prepare, so we mostly used them. Stan and Keith and Susan preferred their own food concoctions, though, which they had prepared at home before the trip. After eating, we chatted for an hour over a nip of Jack Daniels about our plans the next day and sundry other things, then Jen and I retired for the night.

Jen and I were up at 7:00 to make a small fire and heat up some water for coffee and a long overdue hair wash. A couple of hours later five of us set off up the narrow ravine to take a look at the Marsh Fork on the other side of the pass. Jen and Sue stayed behind to rest.

Stan led the way and soon left the rest of us behind. Keith and Susan and I were interested in what Dennis had to say about the geology in the ravine, so we stayed with him. As we wended our way like exploring snails through the slot canyon, he explained the ancient interactions of the limestone and slate formations while I identified the wild plants that made their ephemeral homes there. At one point I found a nice example of exfoliating coral that he said might be as much as 300 million years old. We both put a small sample of it in our packs.

On the downward side of the saddle, while looking into the valley of the Marsh Fork, we watched Stan disappear to the bottom to scope out the condition of the river. With my binoculars I could see the river was too high and dangerous to cross, but he wanted an up-close view, so he morphed into a mountain goat and went down. During a snack and chat about one of Keith's previous hikes down the Marsh Fork, he told us how treacherous his crossing had been over the pass from the Ivishak to the Marsh Fork and emphasized how much better our present route was, especially under the circumstances.

We decided to return to camp without waiting for Stan, since we knew he would catch us quickly once he was back up from the river. At the top of the saddle again, Susan pointed at a Gray-crowned rosy finch on the ground, earnestly feeding on seeds from a pile of detritus made by some small rodent under the snow during the winter. I stayed behind to watch for a while and to take pictures of him eating. As usual with these friendly finches, this little guy wasn't afraid of me at all and kept on feeding in spite of my close curiosity.

I was still within earshot of the rest of the troupe when I discovered something I thought everyone might be interested in, and I called them back to take a look see. I pointed at a long double line of deep tracks in the tundra that detoured around a large boulder. I asked them what they thought it was. Keith smiled furtively and said, "a very ancient grizzly bear trail." He was right on. You could plainly see where for hundreds, if not thousands of years, if the boulder had been there that long, grizzlies passing over this saddle from the Marsh Fork to the Porcupine Valley had deliberately placed their pads alternately for about a hundred yards to get around the huge rock. There was nothing whimsical about the trail, and when we got back to camp it was still a topic of conversation around the campfire. We wondered what possessed bears to do that. Was it a conscious decision they made to follow in the footsteps of previous bears? Was it something that made them feel less lonely in this wilderness, where a wandering solo bear might tend to feel that way? Bears are intelligent animals, after all, and we don't know much about their brains. Then again, we humans like to anthropomorphize everything, and maybe we were just talking through our hats.

After a late lunch we four men took off in different directions to explore our own interests. Mine was birds, and when I heard a couple of male Smith's longspurs singing their high-pitched sweet warbles, I followed them to watch their skulking behavior in the tundra. While I was in the neighborhood I climbed to the top of the hill to check out a route for the next morning. Finding a good one, I placed a caribou antler on a little bare knoll so we could use it as a guide when we first started out. Looking across the ravine, I could make out a long thin thread of trail at the base of the mountain, leading into the canyon we were in earlier in the day. My bet was that a lot of caribou used that route to travel back and forth between the two main valleys. But where were the caribou now? I could only see the five over on the flank of Annette Mountain. Since they belonged to the Central Arctic herd, more of the animals had to be somewhere nearby, and since they were highly mobile animals, we might see some yet.

By the time I returned to camp, the others were also back. Stan and Keith said they had heard a wolf howling in the distance, and Dennis brought back more rock samples to share with us. Most of them were limestone, but there was one that was composed of a dozen or so small dark polygons of what looked like shale or slate, each polygon surrounded by white calcite. Over dinner we chatted about these rock specimens as well as our respective travels in South America, and about the gourmet meals we were going to prepare once we got back to civilization. We were getting a little tired of our camp meals, it seemed. But this was something that almost predictably happened every time we went out for long periods. No matter the group we were with, about 4-5 days into the trip the topic of gourmet food would come up. Maybe the food drop Kirk Sweetsir had made over on the Marsh Fork airstrip would help allay this hunger. We'd be there in two more days, and it would be interesting to see what was awaiting us in the bear barrels.

Then we men all went off in our separate directions again, although I shortly caught up to Keith to show him where the Smith's longspurs were that I'd seen in the afternoon. When I found a handsome male skulking among the tussocks, it was a trick keeping up with him to get a good look at him. One moment he was peeping at us over the top of some cotton grass, the next he was in escape mode strutting through the interstices of the tundra. He finally tired of the game of hide-and-seek and with a loud staccato rattle, abruptly took off into the breeze, veered and flew away in the opposite direction. He had accomplished his purpose, though, to lead us astray from one of his mate's nests. We heard two other singing males, and hoped there were an equal number of females sitting on eggs somewhere nearby. When we returned to camp, we heard our resident pair of tattlers tattling to each other as they foraged for food along the margins of the creek. What were they saying, I wondered, but knew their language was as arcane as every other bird's and would forever remain an enigma to me. As it should be. Mysteries are good for us humans.

The sky was almost a robin's egg blue when we struck camp in the morning, and remained so for the rest of the day. Scaling the steep bank on the opposite side of our camp to the caribou antler I'd placed there the afternoon before, we continued our climb to the elevation we needed to escape the tussocks below, then follow the harder ground that is normally found at the base of the mountains above the valley. And what an imposing valley it was, vastly wide, crosscutting four smaller ones that originated in what mountain climbers call cirques. I had read somewhere that this area had not been glaciated during the Pleistocene, but the cirques seemed to tell a different story, casting doubt in the minds of both Dennis and me.

Not long after we started out, Stan discovered an American pipit's nest with six brown eggs in it, one of them on top of the other five to make it easier for the small female to brood such a large number of eggs. The big question was whether there would be enough food for the adults to feed so many mouths once the eggs hatched. The young would be in the nest for two weeks, and their parents would feed them for another two weeks after fledging, then they would have to fatten up by themselves for their long migration south. So where would all the food come from? The answer was, of course, all around us. In spite of being frigidly cold for more than eight months, the Arctic is a bonanza of insects for about 2½ months, just at the right time to feed huge numbers of songbirds, such as pipits. With climate change, this window of opportunity has been averaging longer, resulting in the increase of many bird populations. Once they start migrating, and they finally get to their wintering grounds down south, is where their problems begin.

Climate change was a topic of discussion again when we spotted a cow moose resting just across the valley from us on the flank of a mountain. With the warmer summers had come taller and healthier willows, especially their favorites, diamond-leaf (*Salix pulchra*) and felt-leaf (*Salix alaxensis*) that grew in the valley bottoms, attracting more and more moose into the area. This moose was probably perched up there so she could see any approaching grizzly bears or wolves. Since she didn't have a calf with her, we thought maybe she'd lost it to one of those hungry predators.

We stopped for lunch at the bottom of the first major ravine that crosscut our route. Later, while exploring, we found some puzzling rock specimens scattered helter-skelter in the creek bed. Dennis and Keith were instant scientists, inspecting them closely, trying to figure out what they were. Stan, and the women and I even got into the act. There were scores of large, butterscotch-colored, egg-shaped nodules that when cracked open had what looked like yolks of fractured black slate with the fracture lines filled with rusty calcite or silica. They were quite beautiful, especially when splashed with water. Stan walked upriver and found what he thought was their source – an outflow of rock and gravelly soil spilling into the west bank of the creek. Dennis guessed they may have been formed in two or three phases – first, the inner nodules by what he referred to as "silicon polarity" in the ooze of the sea floor, then surrounded by a ferrous clay that hardened through pressure and heat. After tectonic uplift, they might have rolled down a river and become rounded into their present egg shape. We knew this was only what Keith called a SWAG, or Stupid Wild-Assed Guess, but we had to start somewhere.

After an hour we got going again toward a small lake we had spotted in the distance, where we thought we might make camp. Along the trail we spotted a lone bull caribou and twenty Dall sheep ewes, again none with lambs, across the valley on the flank of another mountain. The ewes looked unusually skinny now that they had lost most of their hair, but with the greening of the plant world everywhere, we knew they would fatten up in time to be ready for next winter's freeze. We also stumbled on yet another pipit nest, this one also having five eggs on the bottom with one piled on top. I wondered what a jaeger would do if it happened to discover the nest. Would this sixth egg become sacrificial, allowing the others to survive?

What great walking it was on this stretch of our trek. As long as we stayed fairly high on the flank of the mountain, we found the same finely fractured shale-slate that gave us the firm footing we had in the morning. Before we knew it, we discovered a fairly flat platform above the lake, where we could erect our tents and settle in for another night of rest and relaxation. Dennis was really tired, and as soon as he set up their tent dove inside for a well-deserved rest. I remember the furrowed smile on his face just before he disappeared into the tent, and his words, "I'm completely bushed, but I'll see you guys later for tea after I recharge my engine." Meanwhile Stan, Keith and I gathered some dry willows for a fire, and it wasn't long till we had boiling water for tea and hot chocolate. We were hungry, so we also prepared our evening meals and ate them straight away.

During dinner I noticed Stan eyeing the gray-talused mountain, where we had earlier spotted the twenty Dall sheep. I knew what he was think-ing, and, sure enough, as soon as he finished eating he grabbed his daypack and headed across the valley and up a narrow gully leading to the top of the mountain. I followed him shortly afterward, but had no intention of going all the way to the top. I was more interested in finding the animal trails about halfway up and following them over to where the sheep had been focusing most of their attention. The fine talus made for fairly solid climbing, but when I reached the sheep trails I used them, since they were even firmer and more stable. Their firmness was probably because of their constant use over centu-ries as main highways by sheep, and perhaps a few caribou. But why were they there in the first place? I soon found out. At first, I thought it might have been because of a salt lick where sheep came to eat the mineralized dirt, thereby gaining salts they needed for complete nutrition. But my hunch was wrong. It turned out to be a resting area, where scores of sheep had dug out little platforms in the talus on which they could perch and watch the world below them for signs of approaching danger. They were safe there because if a bear or wolf did decide to try their luck, all the sheep would have to do is scale the talus on well-defined trails to the rock precipices above. Human hunters had long figured that strategy out, however, and would climb above the sheep and into the rocks themselves to hunt them from above. I did it myself when I was younger and had a yen for Dall sheep meat.

After exploring a number of these ephemeral sheep perches, I followed the main trail east to just above the lake, where I stepped off into the fine talus and jumped down the mountain (something I call "escalatoring") for about 400 feet to a heavily used vertical animal trail leading directly to the edge of the lake. I had to skid to an abrupt halt about halfway down, though, to take some photos of a wide spray of the brightest blue forget-me-nots I'd seen in many years. When I started down again I noticed that three ewes just above the lake were watching me. They were uneasy and didn't want to take any chances, so bolted instantly back up the mountain. Part of their uneasiness might have been due to the other humans on the opposite shore of the lake. Dennis and Sue were there, trying their luck at fishing, and Keith and Susan were nearby admiring the candle ice almost totally covering the lake. Winter was just fading here, giving us another hint of perhaps why none of the ewes so far had young. The winter had been a harsh one for reproduction, so the ewes would have to try again the next year. I'm amazed that any animals at all are able to raise young in such a severe environment, but they do, and quite well in terms of the big picture and the law of the survival of the fittest.

With those thoughts in mind, I strolled back to camp across the tundra to see how Jen was doing. When Dennis and Sue returned empty-handed without fish, I told them there might be cisco white fish in the lake, but they would probably have to cast their lure for a long time to catch one. A decade ago, on the upper Sheenjek River when I was hungry for protein after two weeks of hiking across the Brooks Range, I had tossed my lure for three hours into a lake teeming with white fish until finally I snagged one and cooked and ate it on the spot with my two hiking companions. But for now they would have to settle for some chocolate pudding that Jen and I had concocted. Keith and Susan joined us next and described the wonderful clinking sounds of billions of spicules of candle ice, sounding like thousands of fine wine glasses, continuously saluting the Refuge wilderness we were in. Stan was the last to roll in to visit around the fire, and told us of the Golden eagle he had spotted soaring above the mountain, and of the Gray-crowned rosy finch and Wheatear he had seen up there. He reminded me of the mountain goat I had been when I was his age.

Just before caching it in for the night, Susan told Jen and me this had been Keith's best day yet. He was speaking much better, his balance had improved, and he felt on top of the world. He was having such a great time, she said, and thanked us for inviting them along.

After a convivial breakfast chat about Stan's climb the day before, and Dennis's renewed fishing efforts in the morning, we broke camp again and headed for the confluence of the south and west branches of the Marsh Fork. I hiked with Dennis for a part of the morning and he explained more about "silicon polarity," the mechanism he thought responsible for forming the stone eggs we came across the day before. He called them "butterscotch nodules," and again said that the inner nodule had probably been formed through silicon being attracted to itself inside the clay ooze matrix of the ocean floor. It sounded a lot like the explanation a geologist friend once gave me for the formation of a concretion except that the nucleus was the result of accumulation of silicon or other minerals around a dead sea plant or creature, and it was based on pH imbalance. Since Nature loves pH balance, he said, more basic minerals accrue around acidic substances until there is a balance. As we chatted, I counted polka dots of Dall sheep all over the flank of the mountain we were on, thirty-three of them by our final tally as we approached the ridge overlooking the river below.

We stopped for a break on the ridge, then, while climbing down to the river, Keith and I tried to locate an Upland sandpiper we'd heard from up there. We never found the bird, but did spot an airplane parked across the river on the Marsh Fork airstrip. It was an awfully familiar-looking Cessna 185, I thought, and when I caught up to Jennifer and let her glass it with my binoculars, we both agreed that we had seen it before. But who might it be?

By the time the rest of us were down to the river and getting ready to cross, Stan was already on the other side. But, no matter, the water was now fairly shallow and we were able to ford without a hitch. Even Keith had no problem. This was another good day for him and, according to his habit, he walked right across with his boots on. Since his boots had no Gore-Tex waterproof lining in them, the water squished out quickly when he resumed walking. Susan did the same. They both thought it was safer and warmer to cross with boots on, and the boots would dry soon enough anyway. Watching Keith cross, Jen and I could see that his balance had improved markedly, and that he walked with the stride of a caribou as he used to. And he chatted with much more fluency. It was good for him to be out here in the wilds again.

After setting up our tents on the east side of the south fork, Keith and Stan and I ambled across the wide alluvial fan the airstrip was on to look for the bear barrels, which had been dropped off there a week earlier by Kirk after leaving Keith and Susan with us on the Ivishak. We found them at the north end of the airstrip, along with a Swiss couple, whom Jen and I had met there back in June, 2006. Felix and Salomé had flown in the day before in their Cessna 185, and were planning to remain until the next day. It was her birthday, and they wanted to celebrate it on the Marsh Fork, as they had done now for several years, including the last time we'd seen them. Felix recognized me right away, and also remembered Jen. What a small world, I told them. They were busy setting up a mosquito-proof shelter for the celebration and, since they had spotted a blonde grizzly across the airstrip only an hour before, they were planning to erect an electric bear fence around the shelter. They had done the same thing the previous night around their tent and airplane, which they had located about 300 yards down the airstrip. As we were leaving with our bear barrels, they gave us three Swiss Toblerone chocolate bars to share with the others. They also invited us back that evening to help celebrate Salomé's birthday.

During dinner at our own campsite, I proposed that we sing Happy Birthday to Salomé when we went over later in the evening. Dennis offered to play his harmonica for instrumental accompaniment, and it turned out to be a delightful surprise for Salomé and Felix, and fun for us, too. While we sang, Felix recorded us with his video camera and said he'd put it on the Internet for us to see later. Then, after some chitchat and the gift of a Fairbanks newspaper to us, we left them in peace and walked back to our tents.

We settled down by the campfire for a while and chatted about a caribou calf Susan said she'd seen crossing the river, although when I glassed in that direction with my binoculars I only saw a cow caribou, probably its mother, grazing on the other bank. We wondered what had happened to the calf. Stan and I also gave our report on our walk over to a small grove of balsam poplars that I'd been keeping track of for the past few years. This was the fourth time I'd been through there, and each time I had made it a point to check on this stand of trees. It seemed that they were as healthy as ever, with even more little ones popping up everywhere. Like aspen, they propagate mostly by their roots. "Who knows," I said, "with the changing climate, in a hundred years there may be a forest of them here."

As I washed up and brushed my teeth at the river, the lens-like clouds that had crowded the pale blue sky earlier were now becoming wispier and looking more like feathers. Up the Marsh Fork to the west, though, a general overcast darkened the sky and seemed to be moving in our direction. Would we have rain by morning, I wondered. The later it got the more certain I was that it would rain. But, no worries, an Upland sandpiper was bubbling at us in the distance, and for now that's all that mattered.

It did rain during the night, and it continued overcast in the morning, so Jen and I took our time getting up and out of the tent. When I heard Canada geese honking at us, that was enough for me and I grabbed my binoculars and crawled outside. I was too late to catch the honkers, but in time for the warmth of a morning fire kindled by Susan, using her YWCA method, which she described as whittling a dry stick into small ears, placing it and others, along with strips of dry wood shavings, on a fire platform, then lighting it with a wooden match. I told her the same method had worked for me, although these days I always brought along a small bag of wafer-thin birch bark strips gathered from my woods back in Fairbanks.

Later in the morning, Dennis, Keith, Susan and I hiked over to a small lake about a quarter mile to the northeast of camp. Every time I had walked over there in the past, I had been surprised by something interesting. This time it was a pair of Baird's sandpipers, three Red-necked phalaropes (possibly a nesting threesome), a female Common goldeneye, a male Red-breasted merganser, and a half-dozen or so Cliff swallows cavorting over the lake itself. These birds were part of what was thought to be the northernmost colony of Cliff swallows in the U.S., nesting on the cliffs just to the southeast of the lake. We were headed that direction and continued seeing them as we climbed over a high tundra ridge carpeted in wildflowers, then down to a small cobbled creek bed that we followed toward its headwaters in a narrow canyon surrounded on both sides by steep dark mountains. It was the same canyon my friends the Wildfangs and I had ventured up five years earlier. Right away we spotted nine ewes and three tiny newborn lambs. They were the first lambs we'd seen so far, and their moms weren't taking any chances, ushering them lickety-split up the mountain slope to a shallow cave, where they waited for us to pass by.

While watching the sheep, Dennis pointed at something else on the other side of the canyon. Moving his hand slowly, he outlined two immense excruciating twists and turns in the limestone strata immediately above us, where he theorized there had been so much pressure exerted by the earth that the strata had buckled under itself several times. He was really excited, and took photos of it to take home to try to convince his "intellectually dysfunctional, born-again, Rush Limbaugh-bleating cousin that he was completely disoriented in his thinking about evolution." While perched atop a low ridge, we ate our lunch and watched four rams hightail it high up the mountain slope, convincing us that at some time in the past, using the airstrip as a base of operations, hunters had shot at them.

While returning to camp in a light drizzle, we came by way of an extensive patch of aufeis so Dennis could experience what it was like for the first time in his life. Keith explained to him that it was seasonal ice formed during the winter from tundra runoff and overflow, and would soon melt. We pointed out to him many of the fascinating aspects of aufeis, including how willows that had been completely surrounded by the ice in winter formed little tubules of melt water around their main stems and branches in spring, the result of the sun's heat being absorbed by the dark bark. Most of the willows even had flowering catkins dangling from them. Anything dark on the surface of the ice had melted a hole in it for the same reason. We found caribou dung, leaves and other wind-blown detritus that had impressed themselves several inches deep into the aufeis. But piles of lime dust, swept down from the mountain slopes by high winds, had the opposite effect. Since it was light in color, it formed little ridges of unthawed ice that were more stable and easier to walk on than the rest of the aufeis, especially in the heat of the afternoon. At the edge of the ice next to the river, where it had melted because of the action of the running water, Keith pointed with his walking stick at the candle ice. The millions and billions of tiny vertical tubes in the ice funneled the sun's rays straight to the bottom, hence contributing to the growth of vegetation there. It does the same, he said, on both freshwater and seawater, causing immense blooms of algae to grow on the bottom of the ice, thus offering a huge food source for smaller creatures such as crustaceans. And on it went up the food chain. The question I posed afterward was what would happen to this important food chain with the increased melting of the Bering and Beaufort sea ice due to climate warming?

Changing the subject, I asked everyone to bend down at the edge of the aufeis and listen to the magical sound of the melting ice underneath. This was something I was made aware of three years before by a soundscape ecologist named Bernie Krause, who was doing a study of all of the sounds associated with the area around Timber Lake, located only fifty or sixty miles southwest of where we were standing. After digitally recording the melt drops, he put earphones on me and let me listen to the feedback. I was just short of awestruck, as I was later when I listened to other sounds he'd recorded from an island in the middle of the lake.

Jen and Sue were sitting around the fire when we arrived back in camp, but Stan was on a walkabout somewhere up the South Fork with his Fairbanks friend Anna and her one-year old baby Rosie, who had been dropped off in the afternoon by Kirk Sweetsir. Jen said she and Sue had helped Anna carry all of her gear over to one of our old camping spots in the willows near a freshwater spring. It was raining when they flew in, so they also helped set up her tent.

We were hungry, so quickly prepared some supper, in spite of a light drizzle that darkened the sky. Later, though, as we sipped our after-dinner cups of hot chocolate, the clouds lifted almost miraculously and it turned into a glorious blue-sky evening. Across the river we counted forty ewes grazing on the shoulder of the mountain we had crossed the day before. Once again, there were no lambs with them, striking me as rather odd. Suddenly, a few of the sheep bolted and started racing for some nearby rock cliffs. Almost instantly the entire flock followed them up the mountain to safe haven on the cliffs. But as much as I scanned the area for a wolf or bear, I couldn't find the source of their fear. It was palpably there, though, and I wondered if it was related to the dearth of this year's crop of lambs.

Just as this drama was unfolding, Felix and Salomé showed up. They had come over with an offering of some extra gas for our little cook stoves. We had mentioned we were a little low on the precious stuff, and they had much more than they needed for this trip. In the morning they said they were headed for Sunset Pass in the Sadlerochit Mountains, then back to Fairbanks and Switzerland, so they were short-timers here. While they were still chatting with us, Stan returned from his walkabout, reporting that he had not found any ice "pingos" up the South Fork. I told him we were going back up there again in a couple of days, and I would find him one then. Although there was a lot of new snow on the mountains everywhere, it looked like we would have some stellar weather during our last three days on the Marsh Fork, and we planned to use the time fully.

June 15 –

"It was a pretty walk today," Jen said, just before putting in her earplugs and saying goodnight.

In the morning, we decided this would be a good day to head for the limestone canyon that Jen and I had visited several years earlier with the Wildfangs and their son, James. We thought Dennis, especially, would be interested in the geology over there. Keith and Susan also started out with us, but Stan stayed back in camp to walk again with Anna and her baby Rosie. While skirting the little lake, where we had seen the pair of sandpipers the day before, Keith and I went down to its shore to make sure they were Baird's sandpipers. Sure enough, the wings were longer than the tail, a clincher for the Baird's. Satisfied, we caught up with the others, climbed the broad ridge north of the lake, then followed it for a quarter-mile to where we thought the creek would be shallow enough to ford. We stopped to rest where we found a recent sheep kill, probably by wolves, yet another reminder of how tough it is for Dall sheep in the Arctic. There we parted with Susan and Keith, since he said he was feeling dizzy and better head back to camp.

Reluctantly, we said goodbye and began descending to the creek to try to find a crossing. About halfway down I heard a loud nattering in the willows, and noticed several robin-sized birds fluttering about. I stopped in my tracks and glassed them with my binoculars. "Well, look at that," I said, "a family of Northern shrikes!" A pair of adults was busy feeding three fledglings perched together in a tall willow not far below me. Photo op, I thought, then slowly crept down the slope and under the three young birds, and got several good snapshots of them. As I did this, the parent birds growled at me, as only shrikes can growl, and I was a little fearful about what these so-called "butcher birds" might do. So I didn't dally long after taking the pictures, and hightailed it over to where the others were puzzling about where to ford the creek without having to take off their boots and socks.

Dennis and I solved the problem by building a little footbridge with some large boulders we grabbed from the edge of the creek and threw across in a snake-like line. "Voila!" I said, "There's always more than one way to skin a cat," and we quickly tip-toed on top of the rocks over to the other side. Then we climbed up to a small hillock overlooking the valley and peacefully ate our lunch. Peacefully, that is, until Kirk Sweetsir flew by with the last of three loads of rafters, which I supposed was part of Bob Dietrich's high-end bird-lister bunch that Kirk dropped eight miles downriver at the so-called bench strip. It was an expensive trip for those who wanted to add only one or two birds to their life lists, including the coveted Gray-headed chickadee whose whereabouts Dietrich knew was in the balsam poplar groves just downriver from the bench strip. He was extremely possessive of this knowledge, and when my friend John Breiby once asked him about their location for me a few years before, he wouldn't tell him. So I simply found the chickadees myself when I was through there in 2004. It made for a good story, and Dennis shook his head with obvious displeasure at Dietrich's behavior.

When we started our walk in the morning the day was overcast, but by the time we reached the limestone canyon the sky was perfectly blue, matching the color of the forget-me-nots we found at the mouth of the canyon. These flowers are not common in this part of the Brooks Range and seem to be found mostly where Dall sheep gather, either to rest or find shelter from the elements. A half-mile or so through the canyon, and about 150 feet up on the north side, there is a shallow cave that sheep often use to escape the torrential thunderstorms that sometimes occur here. Just outside the entrance to the cave and all along a small ridge overlooking the canyon is a veritable garden of the diminutive blue and yellow flowers. Once, when

I was up there a few years earlier checking on a Say's phoebe nest, I counted more than a dozen other wildflower species mixed among the forget-me-nots. Little wonder, since the cave floor was covered in a carpet of sheep turds several inches thick.

We didn't go as far as the sheep cave this year because of the high water that filled the canyon from side to side. And Dennis was curious about a marble formation that he'd found and wanted to spend some time exploring. The marble had broken off the steep edges of the canyon and lay in blocks on the valley floor, so it was easy to check them out. Since marble was metamorphosed limestone, Dennis said, it meant this little canyon was very ancient. While he was examining the rocks, I searched for signs of Say's phoebes and their possible nesting cavities in the cliffs. I spotted several of the birds, but couldn't determine which cavities they were using for their nests. I told the others that in 2003 I'd found a nest down-canyon, which was actually several cup-like nests layered year after year on the same ledge inside the cave, and that in the uppermost cup were five perfectly white eggs. "And why white?" I asked. "Well, white was the best color for the parents to spot them in the dark, and besides, they didn't need camouflage, since they weren't outside, visible to any would-be predators." I smiled, telling them it was a good Keim theory anyway. Dennis smiled, too, when I picked up a swatch of recently shed sheep hair, put it in a plastic bag and handed it to him with the comment, "Now you can tell your friends you bagged a sheep while you were in Alaska."

We arrived back at camp at dinnertime, but I was sweaty and felt it was time for a bath, so I snagged my towel and soap and went in search of a small pool of warm water I'd found the night before about 200 yards upriver. How luxuriant it was to douse myself in sun-warmed water up to my knees, to suds off all my oily sweat, and then to rinse almost completely submerged in the clear water. When I was finished I felt like a million bucks, as my dad used to say. Then I was ready for dinner, which we had decided would be one of our last Mountain House packages of dried rice and chicken. The water was already hot, so it took just a few more minutes for the meal to steep, and I called Jen to come out of the tent and eat. She was totally bushed, but put on her boots and joined us by the fire where we chatted about the day's adventures. Over a surprise dessert of chocolate pudding with cheesecake and graham crackers prepared by Keith and Susan, Stan reported that he had taken Anna and her daughter Rosie (on his back) up the tall mountain to the northeast of camp. He said she giggled the whole way up. To cap the evening off, Dennis played his harmonica while Sue sang some of their favorite ditties. The rest of us sang along the best we could. They are quite the musical couple. Dennis had been our son Steven's first guitar teacher when we taught together in the village of Marshall. He is an original thinker and I enjoyed chatting with him.

What a lovely evening it was as we sang, with a pale blue sky as a backdrop and the rosy tinge of alpenglow on the stratified limestone mountains behind us. White-crowned sparrows caroled along with us in the willows until finally just before midnight it was time to turn in.

This was to be our last full day on the Marsh Fork and we wanted to use it well, especially since the sky was so clear and the sun beamed bright and warm. But *warm* also meant more mosquitoes in our neighborhood, and I thought a good way to avoid them for most of the day would be to head up the South Fork to explore the the huge expanse of aufeis that is always present on that part of the river at this time of year. Mosquitoes don't like the cold air associated with aufeis, and who knew what surprises might be awaiting us there? I couldn't convince Jen and Stan to come with us, though. Stan wanted to spend the day with Anna and Rosie, and Jen wanted to take some R and R, so it would be just the five of us.

A mile or so up the river we decided to get off the cobbles and follow an animal trail on the left bank. Only a few minutes later six bull caribou passed directly below us on the riverbed, running stiff-legged with their ant-lered heads high in the air the way they do when they're in a hurry. They'd been spooked by something, and we didn't think it was us, since we were downwind from them. Just in case it had been a bear, though, we thought it worthwhile to be on our guard. But nothing showed up as we continued along the bank. I was glad we chose that route, not only because I didn't like the jarring effect of cobbles on my knees and back, but because there were so many wildflowers there. In places, the Lapland rosebay overwhelmed me with their redolence of allspice. And although no fragrance radiated from the Jacob's ladders, their bluish violet color always seduced me into leaning down to inspect them closely and sniff for at least the hint of a sweet smell.

Finally, when we had walked about a mile past the start of the aufeis and there was still no bear in sight, we clambered down the bank to the cobbles to search for a place to cross the river so we could climb onto the surface of the ice. It took a while to find just the right spot, but when we came to a braided patch of riffles next to a steep section of aufeis we knew that's where we would take off our boots and begin our ford. I volunteered to go first, in bare feet. The water was frigidly cold, since it had just been converted from solid ice to liquid water, one of those seeming miracles that we take for granted until we have to wade in it for several minutes. Dennis did the same and took the consequences, but Susan and Keith as usual forded the river in their boots, and Susan threw hers back across to Sue so she would have the comfort of only cold feet when she finished crossing.

The edge of the aufeis was too high and steep for us to step up on, so we had to search for a spot where it had broken off in a large chunk and leaned into the cobbles. It didn't take long, since the ice was now melting quickly and gigantic blocks broke off at regular intervals with a muffled thunderous roar into the river, then lay there until the running water did its trick of almost sudden conversion. When we found a route up, we wound our way down the middle of the ice back toward camp. Dennis and Sue had never had an experience like this in their life and marveled at the magical qualities of the ice we were on, and at how much easier it was to walk on its surface instead of over the irregular knee-breaking myriad of stones on the riverbed itself. As much as I searched, I couldn't find them any large ice "pingos," places where the pressure of the river at the terminal end of the aufeis pushed up big bubbles of thick ice. But I did discover a couple of small ones – "blowouts," I called them – that had already collapsed and were now only raised circles of candle ice with a pool of glacier-blue water in the middle of them. Keith and I agreed these pingos were probably formed during warm weather when a large volume of melt-water flowing under the ice caused pressure so great at the terminus, especially in places where the ice was thinner and more plastic, that it pushed it up into what looked like a series of Eskimo igloos. When Dennis and Sue stood on the edge of one of them, looking down into the clear water, I told them of the much larger ones Jen and I had run across in this area only two years earlier during our hike over from Spring Creek.

Shortly after we left the pingos Dennis stopped and began staring at the mountainside. He stated, "Ice isn't the only thing plastic enough to bend and fold into weird shapes." Pointing at the colossal twists and turns in the rock strata on both sides of us, he said this process had begun happening more than 200 million years ago when the area was more tectonically active. The same dramatic shifting and warping of the earth is still going on, especially in the Andes and Himalaya Mountains, he added.

On the last tongue of still intact aufeis projecting north on the cobbled riverbed, we found a big boulder in the middle that we thought was probably an erratic that had been carried down on top of a glacier during the height of the Pleistocene Epoch more than 15,000 years ago. Keith suggested we sit on top of it and eat our lunch. So for an hour we chewed our food slowly and debated one of Dennis's "recondite abstrusities," as I referred to some of his theories, about a mother civilization of long heads in Peru that far predated any of the other high cultures on Peru's south coast. Finally, agreeing to disagree, we clambered down from our rocky perch onto a ribbon of flat dryas terrace that offered us a much better walking platform for our back and knees than the ubiquitous river cobbles, and headed back to camp.

The mosquito activity picked up as soon as we stepped off the ice, but as long as we kept moving they didn't bother us much. We were a little worried about what it might be like in camp, though, and when the wind began picking up just as we reached a cluster of giant limestone blocks at the end of the airstrip, we breathed a sigh of relief. It remained that way all evening and kept the mosquitoes at bay as Jen and Sue prepared dinner for the seven of us. Stan's friend Anna and her baby were visiting for supper, but she prepared their own meal. We noticed that Rosie had a mosquito jacket on, and Jen told me she had given her one of ours in the morning when they had come over for a visit. The mosquitoes were eating her alive, she said, so she had made the offer, which was readily accepted. After dinner, on my way down to the river to wash the kitchen utensils, I surprised a yearling caribou near the willows. He was a lovely caramel color, and I hoped the others would see him, too, but he spooked and dashed for cover into the heavy willows, and we never saw him again.

That evening around the fire we chatted about our most memorable experiences over the past two weeks, and, bar none, it was our crossing of the engorged and muddy Ivishak River and the immense relief we felt as we stepped out on the other shore. Some of the crew thanked Jen and me for the trip and told us we were "grate" people because we had brought along our little metal fire grate to make cooking over wood fires so much easier.

June 17 –

It was our last day in the Arctic Refuge, and right away while eating our breakfast we were visited by a red fox carrying a dead parky squirrel in her mouth. She strode right through the middle of camp like she owned the place. She was on a mission, and we figured she was headed for her lair where she had hungry kits waiting for her. She had vibrant red fur and walked so fast that her white-tipped tail trailed behind her like a horizontal exclamation point. It was a thoughtful moment for us, and emblematic of the wilderness we were in.

Our ride back to civilization in Dirk's Beaver wasn't scheduled till sometime in the afternoon, and I wasn't about to spend the rest of the day in camp waiting for him, especially with all the mosquitoes buzzing around us. I had never climbed very high on any of the three stately limestone mountains behind camp, so today would be the day. I chose the one in the middle because its shoulder seemed to offer the easiest access to a high perch from where I could take photos of the surrounding country, including the two forks of the river that defined the area. I invited the others to join me. Dennis and Sue were game, as were Stan and Anna, but Jen chose to rest in her tent, and Keith and Susan had to get ready for their pick-up with Kirk Sweetsir, who was due to arrive at about noon.

On the way up, the succession of wildflowers was just short of incredible. Starting with bear root, Lapland rosebay and sweet pea at the base of the mountain, various saxifrages and cinquefoils joined the fray about midway up, then boykinia (aka bear flower) followed me the rest of the way to a ledge I had spotted from below. Most of the plants were in the shale-slate strata of the mountain, and it seemed that only the cinquefoil liked the limestone. I climbed as far as a thick chalky-yellow layer of limestone about halfway up the mountain, since from then on the rock was just too rugged and steep to think about going any farther. When I stopped I noticed that no one had followed me, and I was alone. I sat for a long time on an old sheep perch probably used for millennia by rams to search for predators far below. Glassing with my binoculars, I spotted a couple of caribou in the middle of the aufeis we had been on during our second day at the Marsh Fork airstrip. I guessed they were trying to escape the worst of the mosquitoes, which by now were likely getting pretty bad in the tundra. I had avoided them almost completely by climbing the mountain.

Another good reason for being up there was to contemplate the people and events of the past fortnight. The "crew," as I thought of them, had been a good one, probably the best I had ever been with on a hike like this. It was Dennis and Sue's first trip to the Arctic Refuge and they were both a joy to have along. Dennis carried a pack at least 15 pounds heavier than mine with the patience of a Spartan and, in spite of Sue's back problem, she had a sprightly outlook all the way. Jen had stepped lively through some tough situations and once again proved her mettle. Stan set the pace most of the time, and the way he strode across the tundra reminded me of a caribou. Keith and Susan were in the same league, in spite of the brain tumor that sometimes hindered Keith's abilities.

While thinking these thoughts, Kirk had set down his Cessna 185 so far below that the noise of the plane was barely audible. After silently loading up, he turned the aircraft into the wind, gunned the engine, and lifted into the air. I waved goodbye and wished Keith and Susan well. It had indeed been a good crew, and I hoped most of us could get together again the next year to do a similar trip in the Refuge.

Special Note: Jen and I and a couple of others (Stan Justice and Laurie Leonard) did get together with Keith and Susan again the following summer in the Arctic Refuge. After landing on a small gravel airstrip about half-way up a northwestern tributary of the East Fork of the Chandalar River named Cane Creek, our plan was to cross a couple of high passes into the upper Marsh Fork of the Canning River and walk down to the airstrip where we had ended up the previous summer. However, after remaining for four days at our camp on Cane Creek, Keith and Susan decided that Keith wasn't up to the long hike and called our pilot Kirk Sweetsir to come in and get them. With sadness we bid them goodbye and continued the trek without them. It was to be Keith's final visit to the Arctic Refuge.

PHOTOS

1. Jen and crew hiking up from Ivishak River
2. Dennis sniffing Lapland rosebay
3. Keith Echolmeyer

Chapter 10

On the Brink Delta Wild and Scenic River
June 2013

I hadn't planned on writing about this canoe trip. I'd floated the Delta Wild and Scenic River so many times before that I thought it would be routine and uneventful. It didn't turn out that way.

Four of us arrived at Round Tangle Lake (17 miles west of Paxson on the Denali Highway) on Wednesday afternoon and launched our two canoes at the BLM campsite on water as flat as a windowpane. My canoeing partner Fran Mauer was a retired USFWS biologist and had done this trip with me three summers before. Larry Fogleson captained the other canoe, with his paddling mate Mike Spindler in the bow. Larry was a semi-retired carpenter and Mike the manager of the Kanuti Wildlife Refuge in Alaska's Interior. All four of us had paddled together in the past on other Alaskan rivers.

Round Tangle Lake

We glided quietly along the western shore of the lake for a mile or so until we were away from the noise of the campground, then began to search for a campsite on the bald pates of the scores of small knolls left behind by a Pleistocene glacier as it melted more than 12,000 years ago. We finally spied one that looked promising on the other side of the lake. But before heading there, we watched a small raft of 10 male Long-tailed ducks floating listlessly next to the shoreline. I had never seen Long-tails there in such numbers, and I wondered if it had anything to do with the cold spring we'd just come through in the Interior. With their piebald mottling and two long thin tail feathers, they are unique birds to behold. Mike hoped they would vocalize because their call was so different from that of other ducks. To me it sounded like a melodious yodel, as did the Yup'ik Eskimos of the Lower Yukon River, where I'd taught for so many years. Their name for it was "Aarrangyaraq," I told Mike.

The campsite turned out to fit our needs perfectly, and we located our tents along the ridgeline of the moraine on top of sprays of yellow arnica flowers, just beginning to bloom. And, in spite of some smoke from a forest fire that had crept in during the day, we had a lovely view of the lake and the rugged mountains surrounding it on all sides.

After a late dinner at the water's edge and some good stories we retired to our tents. Fran shared my tent, and we gabbed for a while about our last trip through this remarkable series of lakes, wondering about what might be in store for us the next day, until I finally closed my eyes and listened to a couple of loons yodeling back and forth in the distance.

When I crawled out of the tent early the next morning the mirror surface of the lake echoed the crisp outline of the mountains and a few ragtag trailing clouds, and it seemed the calm water might last until we paddled to the end of the lakes and started down the river. Below our tents there was a large flush of snow where the early light reflected a tinge of red from the surface. I was curious, so on my way down to the shoreline I decided to venture onto it to inspect what I thought might be red algae. Even with the warm weather, the snow was still quite firm and when I scooped up a handful and looked at it through the objective lens of my binoculars, sure enough, there were tiny thin strands of algae tentacling in every direction through the cracks and crevasses of the snow crystals. I later checked this stuff out at home and found that it's called snow algae or red snow (*Chlamydomonas nivalis*), and is actually a green alga that carries a red carotenoid pigment in addition to chlorophyll. It is referred to as "cryophilic" because it thrives in freezing water.

The sun was already getting hot and threatening to get even hotter the later we dallied, so it wasn't long after breakfast till we loaded up and shoved off for the portage around a waterfall and a series of four major rapids between the upper and lower rivers.

We paddled leisurely on the glassy water of the chain of lakes that came before the river outlet. Scores of ducks rested in every little nook and cranny, many of them females that just seemed to be hanging out with the males. When we neared the end of the lakes, there were large rafts of scaups and widgeons mixed with a few Green-winged teals and Common goldeneyes, and at least 20 swans. I had never seen so many Tundra and Trumpeter swans on the lake during the summer, and Mike said it was possible they were failed nesters. Early-arriving birds such as swans may have been hit hard by the record cold spring we had in the Interior.

I hadn't noticed so many muskrats before either. Several were idly floating in the middle of the lake, as though trying to escape the heat of the land. Just across the water from one of the muskrats we were watching, Fran pointed out several rafts and canoes pulled up on shore. A large group of people were camped there, and as we passed them a young fellow hailed us, introducing himself as Dan, the pastor of a Fairbanks Baptist church. He asked where we were going to camp that night, and I replied, at the first campsite just below the canyon. He said he knew where it was and that they planned to camp at the larger site about three hours downriver from there. Since there were so many of them, I understood why. It was the only place I knew that was big enough to accommodate them all.

By now, we could feel the increased tug of current as we paddled toward the entrance to the river, then very soon afterward started down the first small rapid. The upper river isn't very long, but there are a few rapids where we practiced our paddle strokes to prepare for the much more challenging white water in the mile-long canyon below the portage. I had never had a problem in that section, and the last time Fran and I were on it we managed to get through it with little difficulty, in spite of the low water level of the river. But we knew that others had not had the same luck, so we weren't taking any chances.

Just upriver from the take-out for the portage we spotted the Bald eagle nest that had been there for so many years. And there was an adult on it, most probably incubating eggs. At least the eagles hadn't been affected by the late spring, but only time would tell whether their young would be mature enough to fledge three months later. Winter sets in early in this area.

After quickly beaching, then unloading our gear, we pulled our canoe out of the way so Larry and Mike could land their own boat. Fran and I started over the portage right away, hefting the canoe up the small hill and over the quarter-mile or so of trail to a little lake where we placed it in the water. Three loads later we were ready to start across the lake, then stage for the more difficult part of the portage down the steep rocky grade to the lower river. Meanwhile, Larry and Mike did their own much heftier portage. Larry hadn't remembered the nature of the trail from the last time he had floated the river many years before, and he had brought some really heavy items, including a camp box with two small stainless steel kitchen sinks in it. "Never again with that stuff," he panted.

As we carried our loads, a Merlin flew over, calling its typical *kyee kyee kyee kyee kyee*. When I heard a Hermit thrush sing, Mike told us it was a different race of the bird, with its own dialect, similar to the situation with the Fox sparrows we had heard earlier on the lake. Mike said they, too, were a distinct race, with darker plumage than ours north of the Alaska Range, which have rust-colored feathers.

On the downhill side of the portage we had to be extra careful not to slip and drop the canoe on the sharp rocks, or, more important, not to hurt ourselves. By now we were committed to go the rest of the way down the river and we wanted to be in our best form to negotiate the rapids through the canyon. At the bottom of the trail we had to skirt a section of *aufeis*, seasonal ice that had been deposited during the long winter by water trickling down the mountain slope through the talus accumulated there over the eons. Although it was the first time I'd ever seen this phenomenon in this spot, it did serve as a good base to slide our canoes across to the landing where we would push off into the rapids. By now we were bushed and ready for some lunch before going back up to the top to check out the falls and the four huge rapids we avoided by taking the portage. Larry and Mike hadn't seen them the last time they were through here several years earlier, so I told them I'd give them the tour.

I led the way up an old trail, used for many years as a portage before the new one was built to a viewpoint overlooking the river, and noticed immediately that the water was running so high it was going to be difficult to approach the edge of the falls. We halted about 150 feet from the top of the falls when we spotted a dozen handsome male Harlequin ducks clustered directly above the lip of the drop. I told the others that the ducks usually wait there to dive under the foaming water just ahead of the falls to snatch black fly larvae that hang along the edge of the underwater rocks. The ducks are experts at this and we watched them skitter across the surface and make the plunge twice before they became aware of us and peeled off downriver. Both Mike and I took photos of them, then I hopped over some big rocks and headed for the roar of the falls.

I still don't know how it happened, but one moment I was peering over the brink of the falls at the frothing water bouncing and leaping down the narrow cleft in the rock wall below me, and the next thing I knew I was on my back in the middle of a water trace pushing me feet first toward the falls. For a moment, I thought I could grab the edge of the rock on my right and crawl out, but the current was racing too quickly and if I released my left fingers from the rocky bottom I was certain I would be swept into what looked like an abyss below. So I held on, and for the first time in my life shouted for help to the guys behind me. At first no one came and I started to slip and yelled again. Then Mike was beside me, and I told him to grab my right hand, "now!" In another eternity of moment, he did that and I was back on my feet staring at my left hand. It was covered with black fly larvae and the middle finger was bent completely up at a right angle then out like a stair step. Instantly I knew the joint was dislocated and I had to pull it out and down again to get it back in place. I asked Fran to help me, and he grabbed it as I pinched and yanked hard outward. In another second the knuckle was straight, but I still felt no pain. Everything was so sudden that I could only wonder aloud how it had happened, finally deciding it was due to some mud I had picked up on my boots that had caused me to slip.

But for the moment I was soaking wet, along with everything in my pockets, including my camera. I fished it out and figured it was a total loss, except maybe the photo card, which I immediately ejected and gave to Fran for safekeeping. Maybe when I got home, if I dried the camera out in the oven I could salvage it. I didn't really have much hope for that, though, and resigned myself to having to replace it with another one. Too bad, because some of the Harlequin ducks were still hanging around and I could have gotten some good photos of them.

In no way did I want to interrupt the flow of our "tour" around the falls, so I regrouped and asked everyone to follow me along the brushy trail leading to a series of overlooks that gave us a good view of each of the four big rapids following on the heels of the falls. Only an ace kayaker could even think about getting through those, Larry told us. The last section of the trail was almost impenetrable with shrub birch and alders, and the word "bush-whacking" lived up to its literal meaning as we slowly picked our way back to the main trail. Finally, we were down to the canoes again, and right away we secured the loads in case we made a wrong calculation and went belly-up in the canyon of rapids lying ahead of us.

Fran and I shoved off first and paddled slightly upriver to where we could get a clear shot at the deepest water. The current was running fast and a maze of sharp boulders loomed ahead of us, but we briskly wove our way through a straight stretch of water laced with foaming rocks, quickly took a dogleg to the left, then pushed hard for another half-mile in and out of sections of frothy tossing whitewater interspersed with short spaces of dark calm. Finally, when the river began to braid out we knew we were through the worst of it, and relaxed a little. There were still a few tricky spots, but the first of a series of large beaver lodges told us we no longer had to worry about any more serious rapids. We also knew our camping spot was only a short distance away and that we should look for some dead standing spruce to use as firewood. Over the years the campsites on the river had been picked clean of dry wood for fires, so we had to collect whatever wood we needed before landing at camp.

After spotting a stand of beetle-killed spruce, we pulled ashore and started to hack away at a dead standing tree with our small hatchet. When Larry and Mike arrived a few minutes later, though, Larry got out his handy dandy pack saw and we used it to cut enough firewood for the night. Then we loaded it on board and headed for our campsite.

When we hefted the canoes up on shore, memories of previous camps at this spot surged through my mind. I remembered to the others that I had set my tent up here back in 1964 when I first floated this little river with my brothers in our uncle Chuck's aluminum Grumman canoe. He had called the valley we were now in his "hidden valley," and every time I floated through it I could see why he spoke of it with such reverence. I was happy it had been included in the 1980 Alaska Lands Act as a Wild and Scenic River, and I had floated it with friends and family probably 25 times since then.

After erecting our tents and building a small fire, Larry set up his camp table and began preparing dinner. He had not only brought a camp box with two small kitchen sinks, he had also come with a cooler full of fresh vegetables and some elk meat he planned to use with our evening meals. He cut up the meat and veggies into small pieces, then stir-fried them with some olive oil in a skillet. At the same time, he put some pasta on the fire to cook, and when both were ready we ate one of the tastiest camp meals I've had in many years. While eating, we listened to the purling sound of the river next to us and the singing of the many small birds around camp. One of them, a Western wood peewee, was new to me on the river, perhaps because I usually floated it later in the season. In fact, there seemed to be several of them calling from different places. Mike and I both recognized their breezy *brrrzeeee*, and remarked on how this flycatcher compared to the more common Alder and Hammond's flycatchers. Mike said it was a little larger than its *Empidonax* cousins, and of a different genus, *Contopus*. Its calls mingled with the melodious chorus of other birds, including Varied, Gray-cheeked and Hermit thrushes and Tree and Fox sparrows, all of which made our campsite a musical place indeed. With 24-hour light, it also meant we heard the chorus all night long.

The next morning, I opened my eyes to the *tweedling* of a Spotted sandpiper flitting along our shore and back and forth across the water. We'd been seeing more of these since starting down the river. I presumed it was the female, since the male was probably incubating the eggs. This species of sandpiper is one where there is a complete reversal of parental roles, similar to that of the phalaropes. It was our wakeup call, though, and Fran and I crawled out of the tent, built a small fire and put on some coffee water. Larry joined us next, followed by Mike, and coffee cups in hand we chatted about the night sounds we'd heard and whether there would be another camping spot as nice as this one farther downriver. Fran and I told them of a place where we had tried camping three summers earlier, but a family of motor boaters was already there, so we had set up our tents on a small island just upriver. It had been a nice camp but hadn't given us access to the ridge to the east, which I thought might be a good hike. Since the church group we had briefly spoken to on the lake still had not come by, we thought we might try that one for a night.

So on down the river we went, along with much of the firewood we had collected earlier. The next three hours or so were a real pleasure just rid-ing the swift current and only once in a while having to avoid a few sweepers or turtleback boulders in the middle of the river. While listening for bird song along the banks we heard Wilson's and Myrtle warblers, Savannah, Fox and Tree sparrows, plus a few Northern waterthrushes. There were also Red-breasted mergansers on the river, and Bald eagles perched on the tall spruce on both sides of us. It was an idyllic scene, bringing back many mem-ories of previous floats down the river with family and special friends. I still hadn't taken the trip with any of my grandkids, though, and hoped one day to be able to do that.

Fran and I recognized our old island campsite just upstream from the larger one where we planned to camp that night, and we remembered all the birds and bird song we had seen and heard there. The Arctic terns had been a special delight, the way they had dazzled us with their deft fishing skills. Hovering with rapid wing beats about twenty feet above the river, they suddenly dove into the clear water, disappeared for a split second under the surface, then in an explosion of spray flew upward with a small minnow in their mouth. It had been quite a show.

There were no terns to greet us this year, but we were pleased there were no people either. The church group still had not arrived and we expected they wouldn't until the next day because of the difficulty of the portage for such a large number of people with huge rafts and small children. So Fran and I tied the canoe to the nearest stout willow, unloaded our gear, and waited for Larry and Mike to pull in – which they did a few minutes later. They had enjoyed the river, too, and Mike reported he had heard a Golden-crowned sparrow with its telltale song, *oh dear me, oh dear me*, repeated mournfully over and over again. I had never heard one on this river, but the brushy habitat was perfect for them. They are such a furtive bird you'd never know they were there except for their woeful call.

After setting up our tents and having some lunch, I suggested a hike up to the ridge I'd mentioned earlier. Walking was fairly straightforward along a caribou trail, I told them, and once on top we would have a superb view of the river valley as well as of the mountains to the west. So off we went for the next two hours, following an animal trail up the broad shoulder of a ridge that paralleled a large stream named Garrett Creek, then along the summit of the ridge to an overlook where we perched for a while to get our bearings and see what we could see. We had already run across a lot of recent caribou dung and knew the animals were hiding somewhere, but so far, we had only seen one small cow caribou back at the lake. Moose were around, too, by all the sign in the brush on the ridge, but we'd seen nary a one so far. When we looked back toward camp, I noticed a Bald eagle standing on the edge of its nest at the top of a tall white spruce. It was the same nest I'd spotted almost

30 years earlier but had been vacant the last few times I'd stopped there. It seemed it was being used again, although even with my binoculars, I couldn't see any young birds. Maybe the eagle had not nested at all and was simply resting on it. We would probably find out later. Meanwhile we chatted about the chert flake I had found coming up the trail and the way the Natives in the old days had likely used the ridge as a vantage point to hunt for caribou and moose, much like they had in the Tangle Lakes area we had just canoed through. This whole region was full of Early Man sites, and for good reason had been designated a Special Archeological District by the BLM.

When we were back at camp again it was time to think about dinner, so Larry used the rest of his elk meat and more of the veggies he'd brought along and repeated the chef's delight of the night before. Fran and Mike and I shared some of our own stuff, so by the time we finished we had eaten a camp meal fit for kings. Right in the middle of eating we even had a ringside seat to some high entertainment. The eagle from the nest we'd been watching from the ridge top cruised over us, circled above the river, glided down across the marsh in front of our camp, then abruptly plummeted and began to jump around. With my binocs, I could see it had something in its talons, something furry with a long skinny tail. By the looks of it, the eagle had pounced on a muskrat and was making sure it was dead before eating it. But instead of eating the animal, it lifted the now lifeless form into the air and made a short beeline back to its nest. So our question was answered. The eagle did have young, and she was feeding them.

After dinner, I ambled over to the nest tree and confirmed what she was up to. And perhaps the nest had been more active than I'd thought over the past few years, for directly under the tree the grass and wildflowers were dense from the food detritus that had fallen over the edge of the nest. Raising a couple of young eagles takes a lot of food, and the leftovers and projectile guano from the chicks all end up on the ground to fertilize the plants there, hence such lush undergrowth below.

Later in the evening we were proven wrong about the church group. They arrived, thirteen strong, along with four kids, in their rafts and canoes and parked along the bank while their pastor Dan came ashore to chat with us. I apologized for misunderstanding him and invited him and his small congregation to camp with us. There was plenty of room farther back in the woods, I told him, but he said there was another spot just around the corner next to the mouth of Garrett Creek, and they would camp there. It would only be for one night because they were also planning to head out the next day. Then Dan stepped back into his canoe, and they were off downriver again. It wasn't long, though, till we heard them pull ashore and start putting up their own tents. So they would be neighbors, after all.

For the rest of the evening we watched a pair of beavers from a nearby lodge working eagerly in the placid backwater just out from our campfire. I remarked to the others that I was sure beavers belonged to a labor union, since they only begin to work at about five in the afternoon and finish their shift at around seven the next morning. Nonetheless, for laborers it was still a long workday.

While brushing my teeth I noticed the mosquitoes were worse than at our previous camps. But on the whole, they were better than I'd expected, especially since coming from one of the worst mosquito seasons Fairbanks has had in recent memory.

The explosive splash of a beaver diving woke me up in the morning, and I heard wind in the trees. Not that the two noises were related, but when I looked at my watch it was 6:30, and I knew we'd probably better sound reveille for the others because the wind was strong and contrary and would make for some slow paddling on the long calm stretches of the clear water part of the river coming up. It could also make it tricky on the much swifter silty section beginning at Eureka Creek.

The wind did turn out to be a problem, but by hugging the right bank of the river we managed to stay in the lee and avoid the worst of it. There was no need to hurry, though, and at one point we pulled ashore to check out the four-wheeler trail I had found a number of years ago. Fran and I had taken a look at it three summers before and weren't happy that the BLM didn't seem to be enforcing the Wild and Scenic Rivers Act, which stated that all motorized trails had to be located at least a half-mile back from the river's edge. I later learned that BLM claimed this "motorized" trail predated the 1980 ANILCA, when Alaska's Wild and Scenic Rivers were first established. Since this was the case, they maintained the trail was legal. But I have my suspicions about these preexisting claims because I don't remember the trail being there in the 1970s.

Since my own camera had gone for a swim when I fell in the water at the falls, Mike volunteered to snap some photos of the recent damage by four-wheeler motor-heads to the muddy trail. Fran referred to these people as "exhaust breathers," and all four of us agreed they were the scourge of wild lands everywhere. As we pulled out onto the windy river again, the ugly memory of the trail momentarily dimmed when I spotted two cow caribou peering at us from the other shore. Partly hidden by willows, they were almost invisible and at first Fran had difficulty seeing them. Camouflage is a wonderful thing. If the animals had remained completely still, and the wind was in their favor, a wolf or bear would probably not have seen them either. For me, what gave them away was their eyes; the way their dark pupils focused on us like lasers was uncanny.

It wasn't long till we spied where the muddy glacial waters of Eureka

Creek joined the clear water of the part of the Delta River designated as Wild and Scenic. I remembered to Fran when back in the 1970s this lovely wild river had been surveyed and marked with white 4x4 stakes almost all the way up to where we had camped the night before, and how I and many others had fought to protect it from the clutches of miners who said they wanted to dredge it for gold. Thankfully, the 1980 Alaska Lands Act saved it, and we can continue to enjoy it as we always have. We both agreed that we had to remain forever vigilant to assure that federal and state land managers of the area enforced the law.

We pulled in for a lunch break at a place I called Fossil Camp because of all the fossils I had found over the years in the rocks there. It was right at the verge point where silty water collided with the mainstream and there was a perceptible drop in the river, thus quickening its pace to about the speed we saw in the canyon. This was where geologists say the earthquake prone Denali Fault runs through the Alaska Range, therefore explaining the drop in the river and perhaps also the plethora of fossils. The little creek that flowed into the river there was cold and crystal-clear and carried the fossils down from the mother lode farther toward the ridge. I had mentioned earlier that we might climb up there for some exploration after we ate, but as lunch and chat about the river rambled on I wondered if the others really wanted to check the area out. As though he read my mind, Larry asked if we still planned to take our little jaunt up the creek.

We snaked our way through the willows till we got to where at this time of year it had always been lush and green and replete with wildflowers. Not so this summer. Instead, most of the area was still covered with a large flush of snow draping down the draw of the creek. Only the steep south-facing portion of the draw was green and filled with the color of bluebells, wild geraniums, anemones and shooting stars. We had to step gingerly on the hard snow to get up to the limestone and shale fossil formation on the cliff beside the creek, taking special care to avoid places where flowing water had thinned the snow and left open holes.

We didn't tarry long up there, and after Mike took some flower pictures, we headed back to the boats and chatted about the possible dangers downriver where Eureka Creek met the Delta River. With higher water and gusty winds, Larry and Mike were a little worried about this spot. Water moving quickly into other water at almost right angles can be dangerous, as I had learned many years ago on the Yukon River when, after floating upstream in a fast-moving back eddy, my brother and I had turned directly into the mainstream of the big river. The canoe tipped to the side and half-filled with water and we just about ended up in Davy Jones Locker. So, I advised them to be careful and enter the confluence at a diagonal, and when they were past the dangerous water to keep an eye out for Peregrine falcons, since for many years there had been an active aerie high in the crags above that part of the river.

We saw no Peregrines, but the river took us next to one of the most spectacular geological formations I had ever seen, an area that eons of years ago had undergone sudden tectonic faulting and subsequent exposure of a very thick alternating series of light and dark strata. These colored layers were probably part of the same fossil-laden limestone and slate we had just explored back at Fossil Camp. I had a few small chunks of the rock at my feet in the canoe, and when I got home I was sure I would find the remains of all sorts of crinoids and even shellfish, which would date the formation to the mid to late Paleozoic Era, making them approximately 250 million years old. That was something to think about as we sped down the last stretch of the river toward our take-out on the Richardson Highway. But it wasn't long until our attention was diverted by other things, such as a young Bald eagle perched at the edge of the river, the lisping song of a Savannah sparrow in the willows, blooming red dwarf fireweed being blown sideways by the wind, and shallow water in the braided sections of the river that would hang us up momentarily on the gravel bottom. And there was the ubiquitous silver phallus of the Alaska pipeline crawling along the ridge on our right, a sad reminder of how Alaska had changed since I arrived here in 1961.

Just before we reached the pullout we passed a couple of G.I.'s on the river who seemed to be having difficulty maneuvering their canoe in the wind. When they beached a short time after we did, they complained they had been buffeted by the strong winds all morning and that they had an especially rough time getting through the braids just upriver. They hadn't been on the river before and didn't really know where to take out, so when they saw us pass they figured we knew what we were doing and followed us to the landing. While chatting with them they told us they'd been bear hunting, but hadn't had any luck. Mike and I both wondered whether hunting was allowed at this time of year and whether these guys even had permits. They said they worked at the Black Rapids Training Center just down the road.

By the time the two G.I.'s had packed up and headed for home, Fran and Larry were on their way to Round Tangle Lake in Fran's truck to get Larry's pickup. As Mike and I chatted about the church group, wondering how they were doing in such windy weather with their huge rafts, we glanced upriver and, speak of the devil, two of their canoes were just then skirting the mouth of Phelan Creek, searching for a place to land. I motioned for them to pull in to where we were, then chatted with Dan the pastor about their trip. He said it had been gusty but they hadn't had any problems and that the rafts would be showing up shortly. And they did, much to our amazement. But little wonder, when we saw the guys who were rowing the boats. They were young and muscular and would have been able to use their raw sinew to power the rafts through anything. As Dan and his wife unloaded their canoe, their son Elias came over with a handful of fossils and showed them to us. One of his friends did the same. I told them what some of the ancient forms of life might be and asked them how old they thought they were. When Elias said a couple hundred years old, I suggested, "How about a couple hundred million years old?" Elias looked at me and said, "Well that's pretty old, isn't it?" I glanced over at his parents in the distance, and pondered what they would have thought about that. I somehow knew they wouldn't have agreed with me.

Fran rolled in first in his truck, and we waited and waited for Larry, but he didn't show up. Mike thought he'd seen him pass by on the highway heading for Fairbanks, which meant he had missed the turnoff. Then he saw him again going the other direction, and again passing the turn to the pullout. Finally, five minutes later he figured it out and drove down to where we were beside the river. After joking a bit about Larry's confusion, it didn't take us long to heft our canoes on top of the pickups, stow our gear inside, and head for our next camping spot high on the flank of Rainbow Mountain, about seven miles away.

Many years ago, I started calling this campsite, Fossil Trail Camp, because of its location at the head of a "trail" that leads up a creek containing rocks replete with fossils of all descriptions. For this reason, I'd been told it was used every year by UAF students studying the Denali Fault and its associated geology. A geologist once said to me there are examples of rocks from as far away as the South American Andes Mountains that likely became a part of the amalgam even before the existence of Gondwanaland, more than 200 million years ago. The age of the place and its geological diversity are part of what brings me back there year after year, although the sheer beauty of the surrounding country and its wildlife are even more important reasons.

After driving the trucks up the steep grade, we found the campsite the same as it was the year before. Since the level spot I had cleared in the gravel so long ago was only big enough for one large tent, Larry and Mike found two other smaller sites that had been cleared in the past and set up their tents on these. It was late, so we immediately started thinking about dinner, and I got out all the fixings for quesadillas: tortillas, cheese, onions and Frank's hot sauce. Larry had a package of dried refried beans, and he tossed that into the mix. As always, they hit the spot, along with the last of Fran's dessert cognac, although at one point in the preparation of my own plate I mistakenly poured too much hot sauce on my quesadilla. No worries, I said, and I simply added more refried beans to the mess on my plate and ate it anyway. Of course, the others mentioned their concern about the state of my innards while riding back to Fairbanks the next day, especially since beans are such a musical fruit.

During dinner, I pointed at a familiar plant hugging the ground near the campfire, and asked Mike if he'd ever seen it before. He said he hadn't, although he recognized that it was in the legume family because of its bean pods. It was a legume, I said, and its crescent-shaped pods identified it as a Nootka milk vetch, which is found in alpine areas from the Brooks Range south. The light purple flower was an early bloomer, hence all of the bean pods already lying on the ground. Conversation then turned to our walk up the mountain the next day and what we might find there. Fran was hoping to find more forget-me-nots, like we did three summers before when we took the same hike. After a few more minutes of chitchat, Larry excused himself and went to bed, as I did soon afterward while Fran and Mike chatted around the campfire till well into the white night.

My alarm the next morning was a Hermit thrush singing its lovely, *oh holy holy, ah purity purity, ee sweetly sweetly*! I listened for a difference in the song between this one and those we have farther north, but couldn't hear any, so maybe they spoke the same dialect. While building our breakfast fire I also heard Wilson's warblers across the creek and a Merlin in the distance, remembering I'd heard these same bird species the previous year when I was there camping with my grandsons.

Larry prepared some of his eggs for breakfast, and, thus fortified, we headed up the creek to see if we could find Fran's forget-me-nots. Right away I noticed there had been a lot of melt water come down the creek all at once sometime in spring, because part of the trailhead had been washed out. Then only a few hundred yards from there we came across a series of mounds of fine gravel that had washed down on top of the ice formed in the draw over the course of the winter. I hadn't seen this before, and we had to carefully pick our way over this stretch, which reminded me of the terminal moraine of a glacier, but on a much smaller scale. After jumping clear of the gravel, we skirted a belt of old ice snaking up the draw, then followed a recently used caribou trail onto the south-facing flank of the mountain that broadened out to form a wide swath of hard tundra. On the way up a steep incline we came across some forget-me-nots, but not in the large sprays we found when Fran and I climbed up there three summers earlier. While walking on the tundra we were astounded by the array of different wildflower species blooming there, including snow buttercups and a lily called false asphodel, which I hadn't seen there before. They dazzled us as we ambled across the open meadows above the creek.

Once on top we walked another hundred yards or so to the brink of the saddle overlooking McCallum Creek, one of the tributaries of Phelan Creek. At one time McCallum Creek was the main headwaters of Phelan Creek. But, according to glaciologist Larry Mayo, in the 1950's the federal Alaska Road Commission (now DOTPF) had rerouted the bed of the glacial river issuing from the Gulkana Glacier so that it would no longer flow directly into Summit Lake. He said this was so they wouldn't have to build a bridge over the Richardson Highway big enough to take the spring-summer runoff from the glacier. As a result, Phelan Creek now received most of its water from the glacier.

After finding a perch we shared snacks and chatted about the rugged country across the valley and the carpet of wildflowers surrounding us. As the others focused on the view, I watched a small pale brown bird skulking behind some rocks just below me. Raising my binoculars, I saw that it was an American pipit with an insect in its beak, and it looked like it was on a mission, probably to feed its young somewhere. I made a brief foray down to try to locate the nest but didn't search for long, since I didn't want to interfere with the mother bird's feeding routine.

When the wind picked up it started getting a little cool, so Larry suggested heading for home. No sooner had we begun retracing our steps down the mountain than I heard a familiar squeak. Mike heard it too. I pointed at the talus rocks to our left and half whispered, "pica"! He had asked me just an hour before if I'd ever run across what he and Fran called "rock rabbits" in these parts, and I told him I hadn't, till now. He informed me that this cute little critter with the big ears was in danger of disappearing, especially in the Lower 48, because of warmer weather in the alpine regions caused by climate change. They flourish only in cool temperatures, he said. In spite of the bad news, it was nice knowing they continue to survive on Rainbow Mountain.

About halfway down I detected a familiar fragrance and looked around for its source. I was right in the middle of a copse of willows, and on a hunch, I plucked a few of the leaves from a nearby tree and smelled them. Sure enough, they were the source, and when the others caught up I told them that I had once asked a willow expert if any willows in Alaska were fragrant at any time of the year. He said no, although I explained that I had smelled them countless times in early summer while canoeing on rivers in Alaska's Interior. Mike said he had smelled them at that time, too. I later looked the willow up and identified it as *Salix alexensis*, felt-leafed willow.

After decamping from Rainbow Mountain, I rode back to Fairbanks with Larry. When we arrived at his place and began transferring gear from the bed of his pickup to my car, he glanced at my swollen left middle finger. Then he turned, smiled, and remarked that I probably wouldn't forget this trip for a long time.

PHOTOS

1. Fran, Larry and Mike chewing the fat at first camp
2. Harlequin ducks above the falls
3. Portaging around the falls

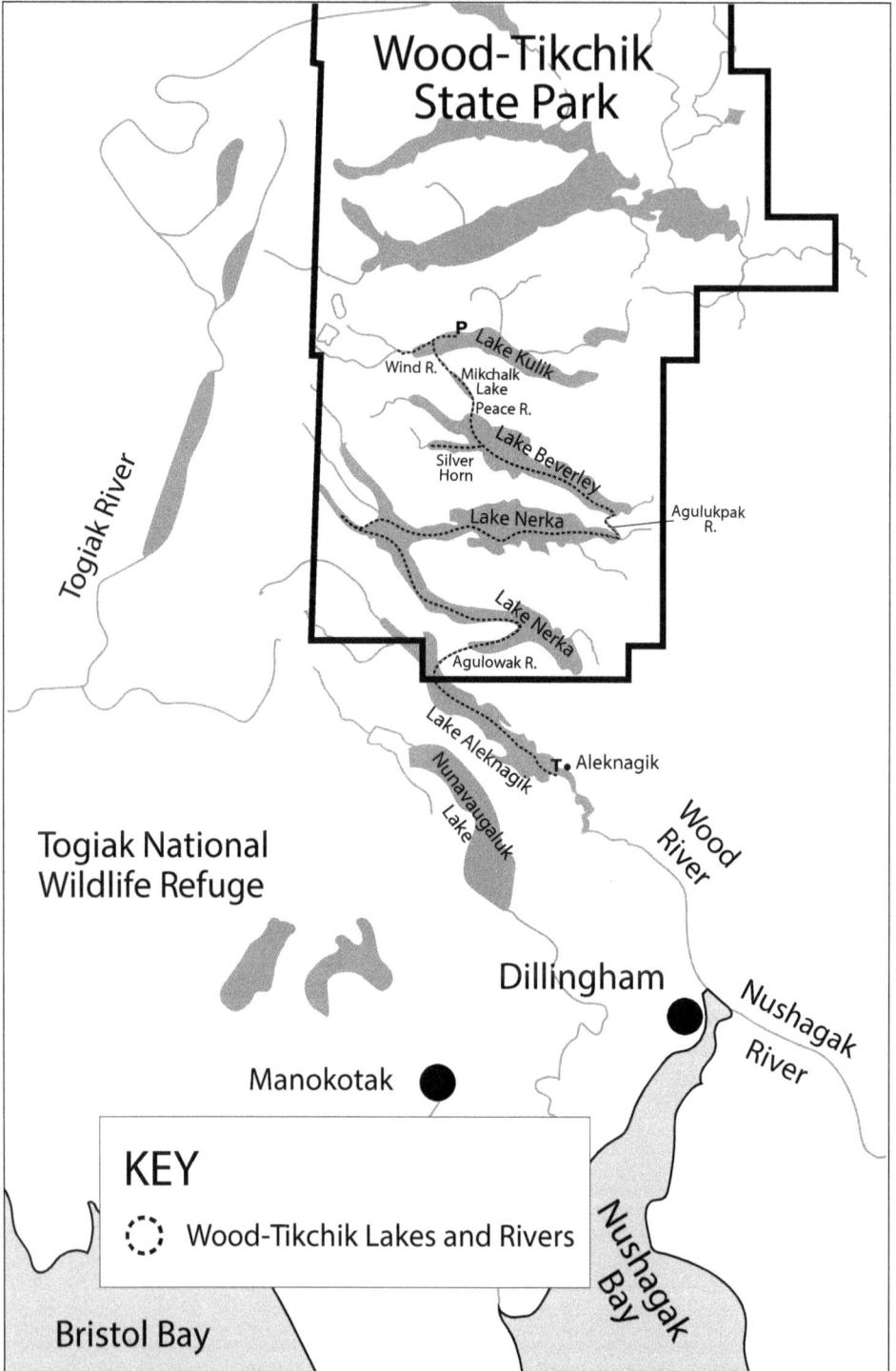

Wood-Tikchik
State Park

P Lake Kulik
Wind R.   Mikchalk
Lake
Peace R.

Lake Beverley
Silver
Horn

Lake Nerka   Agulukpak
R.

Lake Nerka

Togiak River

Agulowak R.

Lake Aleknagik
Nunavaugaluk   T• Aleknagik
Lake

Togiak National
Wildlife Refuge

Wood
River

Dillingham   Nushagak
River

Manokotak •

KEY

◌ Wood-Tikchik Lakes and Rivers

Nushagak
Bay

Bristol Bay

Chapter 11

Yodeling of Loons Wood-Tikchik Lakes and Rivers
June 9-June 24, 2019

It was short notice, but when Don and Tracie Pendergrast called and made me the offer, I couldn't refuse. They asked if I would be interested in going with them on a two- week canoe paddle north of Dillingham, Alaska, in the Wood-Tikchik Lakes State Park, starting at Kulik Lake in the north and ending at Aleknagik Lake in the south. The route would take us ninety miles down four connecting rivers through Beverley and Nerka Lakes, the latter, one of Alaska's longest lakes (thirty-six miles). These freshwater lakes, and others even farther north, are located in the eastern part of the Ahklun Mountains, the highest Alaskan mountain range west of the Alaska Range. Many of the tallest summits still have the only existing glaciers in western Alaska, although with climate change their ice fields had diminished by fifty percent over the past thirty years and are predicted to disappear completely within a few decades. The highest peaks of the mountains and their remnant glaciers are found in both the Wood-Tikchik State Park and the Togiak National Wildlife Refuge, which abuts the park to the west.

Kulik Lake

By the end of the ninety mile canoe trip, I found these mountains and their lakes and glaciers to be one of the most stunningly beautiful regions of Alaska. However, I had no idea of their majesty when I first signed on as a part of the crew, who were: Don and Tracie Pendergrast, Torre and Janet Jorgenson, and Brad Fleener. I had known Don while he was a board member of the Northern Alaska Environmental Center in Fairbanks, but I'd never met his wife, Tracie. Torre and Janet Jorgenson were neighbors and walking friends, but Brad Fleener, a teacher who lived in Anchorage, was a stranger. I would soon meet Brad, who was to be my canoeing partner, at the Anchorage airport on our way to Dillingham.

June 9 –

Torre and Janet picked me up early Sunday morning and took me to the airport, where we met Don and Tracie and quickly began to reorganize our gear so it would all fit into three large bags each, which is what Alaska Airlines allotted Alaskans to take with them free of charge. Then after meeting Brad in Anchorage, I sent my last messages to family and sat back and enjoyed the hour ride to Dillingham. When we arrived there the terminal was a madhouse of fisherman traveling in to work on the fishing boats during the sockeye salmon season, scheduled to open in just a few days. Our friend Paul Liedberg met us there and helped load our gear into two vehicles awaiting us that belonged to Rick and Denise Grant, the owners of the charter service, Tikchik Adventures, who were to fly us up to our starting point on Kulik Lake. Bad weather intervened, however, and we couldn't leave until early the next morning. Meanwhile, Denise took us out to their property on Aleknagik Lake, where I set up my tent on a flat spot not far from the lake edge. The others slept in the bunkhouse, but I wanted to hear the birds sing during the twilight nights they had at this latitude during the summer. And for much of the night they did just that. Some of the especially vocal songbirds I recognized were the Ruby-crowned kinglet, Myrtle warbler, and all five of the thrushes found there: Swainson's, Varied, Gray-cheeked, Robin, and my favorite, the Hermit thrush. Common loons added their loud bawling and jubilant yodeling to the medley of gentler avian voices. As I wrote in my journal, those singing birds reminded me of the joy a person could still find in this troubled world of ours.

Yodeling of loons greeted me in the morning as I walked down to the lakeshore. Right away I noticed a few red (sockeye) salmon jumping as they migrated into Aleknagik Lake from the Wood River, which began its twenty-five mile run to Nushagak Bay at precisely the spot where I was standing. Some of those salmon we would see again far up the lake and river system that comprised the Wood-Tikchik State Park.

After breakfast, we heard a deep drone of an airplane over the water, then a soft kerplush as Rick Grant from Tikchik Adventures touched down in his DeHaviland Beaver. Turning slowly in the river, he headed back upstream toward the dock where we had been instructed to place our gear in preparation for our charter north. I was part of the first load along with Torre, Brad and Don. Tracie and Janet would be on the next flight along with the second canoe. Our first canoe had been flown in the day before on a piggyback flight with another client. It took a couple of tries for Rick to get us up on step because of a momentary fouling of one of the nine cylinders of the Beaver, but we were finally in the air and heading for the northwest shore of Kulik Lake, one of the four enormous lakes that we planned to paddle during our ninety mile canoe journey.

Our flight trajectory took us over an eastern segment of the Ahklun Mountains, and after landing and unloading our gear I mentioned to Torre that the words, "akleng," or "nakleng," were Yup'ik Eskimo expressions of sympathy. A huge massif of craggy peaks to the west made me wonder if there was good reason for this name. I'd never imagined there was such a high mountain range on the southwest coast of Alaska, and with so many alpine glaciers visible at the west end of the lake. I later read that those were only remnant glaciers, and would soon be gone – a chilling thought.

While Brad and I inflated his SOAR inflatable canoe, I noticed the plants were not as advanced as they were in Dillingham, indicating that Kulik Lake, and the mountains they were part of, probably created a slighter cooler microclimate. There were also no mosquitoes or black flies, at least, not yet. And the amount of alder, lady fern and false hellebore undergrowth that blanketed the lower topography of the mountains stole some of our incentive to do as much mountain climbing as we'd originally planned. Tuning into the bird song, I recognized many of the same birds I'd heard the night before, especially the five thrushes, Golden-crowned kinglet and Northern waterthrush. There were also Tree swallows wheeling and bobbing over the now placid surface of the water, and a Greater yellowlegs loudly complaining of our presence in his nesting area.

Just as Brad and I finished attaching the outboard kicker unit to the SOAR, Rick splashed down with Tracie and Janet inside and our second canoe lashed on the left pontoon. Although I realized this method of carrying hard shell canoes on Beavers and Otters was a long practice in Canada, I hadn't seen it done yet in Alaska.

We quickly offloaded the canoe and gear and set to organizing it into the boats. At first, I feared we might not be able to fit everything in the canoes, but I'd forgotten how much capacity the SOAR could manage. When we finally set sail for a camping spot on the far northwest end of the lake, Brad's inflatable looked a little like a river barge. It even sounded like one with its tiny Chinese, Nankai, 3.5 horsepower kicker steadily chugging along behind the other canoes. It was a different experience for me, since I had never been a part of a semi-motorized expedition before. But that's what I'd signed on for, although Torre had told me there would probably be an opportunity for paddling in his canoe because of a shoulder injury Janet had sustained earlier.

As we approached the high mountains at the end of Kulik Lake, we could make out the craggy pinnacled peaks with their attendant alpine gla-

ciers that we'd seen from the air. I mentioned how surprised I was about
their existence to Brad, and also wondered about their geological origins.
I thought they might be the result of tectonic uplift caused by subduction
of the Bering Sea plate under the Alaska (North American) plate. I later
learned that a major fault line called the Denali-Farewell Fault exists where
these high mountains are located, which I guessed was partly caused by this
ancient undersea movement in the Bering region to the west.

We found a good campsite on the north shore directly opposite the
entrance to the Wind River on the south shore of the lake. We would be
heading over there in a couple of days. Located on the outwash plain of a
small creek, our campground had plenty of firewood, good tent sites and a
glorious view of the mountains, made even more spectacular when the wind
died and reflected the snow flushes, fluffy clouds and intense emerald greens
of ferns and hellebore from the lake surface. Seldom had I experienced such
a combination of beauty anywhere in the world. And we were completely
alone on the lake, as we found out after dinner when Torre, Janet and I paddled even farther west into a fiord-like arm where the tall pinnacled peaks
and their alpine glaciers loomed even closer. To see them from a bird's eye
view, we pulled ashore and climbed a small knoll mantled with a variety of
different ferns, including one I'd never seen before, which I thought might
be a fragile bladder fern (*Crystoperis fragilis*). As I watched a Common loon
and Arctic tern hunt for fish below us, I marveled at their completely different diving strategies – one deep down below the lake surface, and the other
steeply from the air to pluck food from just under the mirror of water. Across
the bay, waterfalls pulsed in the lustrous evening sunlight as a huge storm
cell with its attendant rainbow slowly rolled our way from the east. As we
paddled back to camp loons yodeled from both sides of the lake.

Torre had set bear alarms on the food barrels before going to bed,
but had not given me the complete instructions on how to disarm
them, so everyone was suddenly awakened by a combination of bells and si-
rens and other noxious blaring sounds that startled even a Raven perched in
a nearby tree. By fiddling with the contraptions, I finally stopped the clamor,
then poured me a cup of strong coffee to settle my nerves. After brewing
more coffee over the fire, I flipped a large batch of hearty pancakes for the
crew using a recipe I'd found in an old cookbook titled, *Recipes For a Small
Planet*, by Ellen Ewald. The alarms, of course, were a part of the breakfast
chatter, and by going back to the drawing boards with the manual, Torre
figured out what had gone wrong.

By mid-morning everyone was ready for a paddle to the head of the
lake to do some exploration. Once there we consulted our map, and it showed
a smaller lake on the other side of a small berm. So, after scoping it out, Torre

and the younger men pushed and pulled the canoes up and through an al‐der–tangled creek and across a beaver dam so that we were able to continue paddling almost to the bitter end of the extensive basin that the lake was a part of. At some point Janet thought she spotted a way through the under‐brush of alders to a knoll where we could eat our snack while taking in the stunning scenery. It was a welcome change to sedentary camp life and we all hoofed to the top and perched on an overlook that encompassed a view of the rugged mountain massif to the west, the Wind River to the south, and beyond the river to what was probably the upper drainage of Nerka Lake. Directly below us was a pothole lake with many pairs of ducks on it that I recognized through my binoculars to be Greater scaup and probably Bar‐row's goldeneyes. On the way down from the knoll, I found a lichen-studded rock pedestal with fur and bone pellets on it where a hawk or owl had burped up the remains of a small animal it had snatched from somewhere nearby. Closer to shore, I remarked to Janet, our official botanist, on the choco‐late lilies everywhere, and on the large numbers of plant species in general. Ferns especially were ubiquitous, including clumps of lady ferns and shield and oak ferns, as well as others. Twisted stalk, false hellebore, rosemary, and Labrador tea with their still immature rusty umbrella-like flower heads were also present. My head was truly spinning at the many bouquets of different wildflowers. The word, *abundance*, was not big enough to describe them.

We still had plenty of time in the day to throw out a line and troll for trout while crossing the lake to a waterfall where a spring avalanche had dumped an enormous load of snow along the shoreline. Its margin was about 500 feet long and had eroded from wind and waves to where it looked like a tidewater glacier. There were even recently calved icebergs that completed the comparison. Brad and Torre and I climbed the steep but still firm snow pack to where the water pulsed and splashed down on the snow causing a deep crevasse that gave me the shivers when I imagined slipping into its maw. I had the same feeling while carefully stepping down the 300 feet or so of dangerously sharp slope to the bottom, and breathed a sigh of relief when we finally reached the canoes. One slip and I knew we could have ended up in the icy waters below.

That evening, Tracie and Don prepared an Italian Gnocchi dinner with a cheesecake dessert. Then after washing the dishes, I joined in some camp gossip around the fire until a swarm of pesky red biting flies convinced me to retire for the night. It had been a full day.

With Torre's new instructions, I was able to disarm the bear alarms quietly in the morning, then start a fire and brew some coffee for the rest of the crew. While waiting for the coffee I watched an aggressive interaction between a pair of Northern shrikes and a Raven. The shrikes had been perched in a couple of white spruce just above camp when a Raven approached nonchalantly from uplake. Immediately the two shrikes went into combat mode and intercepted the much larger bird, bouncing down and striking his head and back and finally routing the Raven to the top of a faraway stand of spruce. I had noticed the same pair do this the morning before, but thought it was just a momentary territorial tiff between these two predatory bird species. But as I continued to watch, I noticed one of the shrikes repetitively going in and out of a spot on one of the spruce trees, and it looked to me like it might be her nest location. Which would explain their behavior every time the Raven flew over on its scouting mission.

While everyone was drinking their coffee and chatting around the morning fire, I spotted a lone fledgling duck aimlessly approaching us along the lakeshore. I wondered where the mother duck was and how long the little guy might last without the protection of the adults. He floated like that in front of camp as we ate breakfast and packed up to leave for the far shore, where Torre and Brad wanted to do some fishing at the entrance to the Wind River. I wished the duckling good luck as Brad and I pulled out in his blue barge about a half-mile behind everyone else so they could paddle in solitude across the placid lake to the Wind River, one of the two rivers connecting Kulik Lake to the next big one called Beverley Lake. I could never find the real origin of the name for this one, but I did find the meaning of "kulik," or "kulich," which in Russian means "Easter bread," perhaps because the billowy shape of the surrounding mountains reminded the original Russian explorers of their special bread.

Brad and I tied up at the head of the river in some alders, where he joined Torre to try his luck at fishing. While waiting for them a brightly colored mixed flock of Harlequin ducks raced back and forth above the river. I imagined the reason why there were still females in the flock was because they still hadn't finished nesting, since after Harlequin females lay all of their eggs, the males split for good, forming their own small bands. After Torre caught one large grayling, we departed downriver to see if we would have better luck in a small lake at the end of the river called Mikchalk, or "mikcuaq," meaning tiny in Yup'ik. We didn't have much luck there either, so continued into the next short river known as the Peace River to where it emerged into Beverley Lake. There we stopped at Fishing Bear Lodge, a small lodge, where after Jordon the young guardian told us about the run of Arctic char right off the beach, Torre and Brad whipped out their rods and reels and quickly caught more fish to add to our two graylings, which we planned to eat over the next two days.

I then joined Janet in her canoe as the sternsman and set out with Don and Tracie for the other side of Beverley Lake to try to outrun a fast approaching thunderstorm that was already whipping up small whitecaps.

Luckily, the wind allowed us to cut diagonally across the flow of bouncing water to the protection of a covey of small islands studded with hundreds of nesting Glaucous-winged gulls. More hundreds were floating or flying in circles, shrilly reminding us not to approach any closer. I never realized these gulls nested in colonies, and that the colonies were on islands on these lakes. We would see more of them later on other lakes. Meanwhile Tracie and Janet decided they wanted to camp before the rain from the storm hit, so we took in on a beach that seemed like it might be adequate for our needs. As we quickly erected our tents, however, we were viciously attacked by an onslaught of biting blackflies. Thankfully, we had brought head nets to protect us. Gloves protected our hands, and Don and Tracie erected the bug tent they had included in the gear kit for just such an occasion. There were so many of these pesky demons we dubbed this camp, Blackfly Camp. When Brad and Torre putted in later with our fish dinners, they agreed this was an all too appropriate name for the campsite.

As it turned out, the worst of the storm missed us, and dumped most of its heavy rain on the north shore of the lake. Through the raindrops, I watched the lightning and thunder dance off the distant mountains, providing us with a dramatic spectacle of light and sound that would be memorable for quite a long time. Torre and Brad cleaned fish through it all, then Torre prepared the tasty pink flesh of the char for a feast that we consumed comfortably inside the bug tent. The fish was so delicious that most of us ate even the skin. It was probably one of the best meals of the trip.

While eating, I heard what sounded like the creaky calls of a Bald eagle somewhere above us. I immediately unzipped the tent and searched skyward. Sure enough, an adult eagle was flying around over the nearby shoreline and stirring up the Mew gulls nesting there. He finally grew tired of their mobbing and settled down on top of a tall white spruce next to our bug tent. He looked a little ruffled from his run-in with the gulls, but I knew he would eventually find an opportunity and run the gauntlet through the wall of gulls to quickly light on one of their nests and gulp down a few eggs. The imperative of hunger will do that to any animal, including us.

As I brushed my teeth down by the lake, I reflected on how privileged we were to have eaten such a delicious trout meal while so many other humans were starving all over the globe. Not long after I retired to my tent and zipped the fly shut, raindrops began falling, and over the next hour we were hammered by the most ferocious thunderstorm we'd had yet – so hard that it set off the bear alarms a few times. It seemed as if the sky gods had unleashed their anger on us. Maybe a reminder? I wrote in my journal during the rain, and as the raindrops slowed I peeked through my tent vestibule to watch the ragged remnants of the storm disappear to the south, revealing more pinnacled peaks to the west that were part of the same Ahklun Mountains that we saw on Kulik Lake. There appeared to be extensive snowfields toward the summits of those peaks also.

I again managed to successfully disarm the bear alarms without awakening everyone, although Brad was already up and ready for a cup of tea. We built a fire on the shoreline from some dry wood that had been stashed under the bug tent, then brewed a pot of hot water. While drinking my first cup of coffee, I wandered over to the lone spruce tree near our canoes to examine more closely the evidence of bear scratching on the tree trunk that we'd found the evening before. The bark on the lakeside had been completely worn off with rubbing and bites and scratches made by big grizzly bears with light brown and blondish hairs. I tried to imagine the ecstasy they felt as they massaged their backs on that tree. Just as I turned to go back to the fire, I almost stepped on a fresh pile of bear dung I hadn't noticed when we first pulled in, and wondered if it had been deposited during the night while we were sleeping.

Since we were taking the day off to explore the upper part of the Silver Horn Arm of the lake and do some walking there, we took our time eating breakfast and securing the camp. I was Torre's bowman again, while Janet sat up front in Brad's SOAR and Don and Tracie paddled in their canoe, for about four miles to the end of the Arm, where we found a small fishing cabin owned by someone from Dillingham. From there, Silver Horn Mountain was in plain view and tempting us to hike up the glaciated valley it was part of. The six of us started along a rudimentary trail through the alders for a few hundred yards, when Don and Tracy decided to leave us and go back to their canoe to do more exploration on the water. The rest of us continued through the tangle of alders until we reached a snow flush, then another larger one where we had a full view of Silver Horn. Its massive naked face looked as if it had been stripped of its glacier fairly recently, maybe 11,000 years ago at the end of the Pleistocene glaciation when the same lakes we were canoeing on were left behind as giant tarns. At that point, Brad and I decided to turn around and go back to the cabin while Torre and Janet fought the alders to try to reach some larger snow patches farther up the valley. The cabin was a welcome respite from the blackflies and a good place for some visiting. Later, as Brad napped I went outside to take another look at our surroundings. As we'd suspected earlier, the water level of the lake seemed about two feet higher than normal, since it had almost reached the staircase to the cabin.

About an hour after leaving us, Torre and Janet returned, saying they had reached the snow flushes toward the middle of the valley where they could see the remnant glacier at the base of the mountains. Then we all left the cabin to return to our camp. Torre paddled with his wife, and I sat in the bow of the blue barge while Brad steered his Nankai kicker. We made it back first, in time to help the Pendergrasts prepare their couscous and char dinner by gathering firewood and hauling water. Brad and I did the dishes, and afterward I watched a Myrtle warbler catch flies around our water station, then turned in to write in my journal.

I closed my eyes to the yodeling of loons.

And I opened my eyes to the yodeling loons. What a wonderful alarm in the mornings. Then it was a small fire and coffee and tea again with Brad officiating, and a Varied thrush doing flybys as it did the day before on its way to and from its nest, probably located in a nearby spruce tree. I told Brad this robin-like bird was one of my favorite thrushes, not only because of its lovely fluting song in the early morning and at dusk but also because of its vivid orange color accented by a black chest crescent and a wide black eye streak resembling a mask.

We broke camp at about 10 in a light breeze. I started as usual in the bow of the barge, then later spelled Janet in Torre's canoe so she could rest her shoulder. We paddled hard in steadily increasing winds and waves along the lake edge until we spotted Brad and Janet, who had beached the SOAR on a narrow strip of pea gravel, where they wanted to eat lunch. Unfortunately, the onshore wind fetched stronger and stronger, forming white caps on the lake, and the conditions remained that way for the next few hours while we hiked over to a bog mire just behind the wooded strip we'd parked ourselves on. Once on the mire, though, we decided it was worth sticking around there until morning. The mire was just too interesting to give only a cursory examination. For plant biologists, Torre and Janet, it was especially intriguing because it was a large island of bog and fen vegetation located in the middle of a subarctic forest. I wasn't a botanist, but felt the same way, since it was an opportunity to rediscover plants I saw much less of in the Interior. I think our fascination was contagious because the others began checking out the plants too – species such as sphagnum mosses, buck bean, yellow pond lily, cotton grass, a tiny sedge I'd never seen before, and both round-leafed and long-leafed sun dew with crane flies hopelessly caught in the sticky goo on the tiny hairs of their leaves. In two cases, a pair of gooey leaves shared their victims.

As we walked on, the first mire led to a series of others with many similar plants, plus others I hadn't noticed before. A shrub, which I recognized from the Interior but couldn't put a name to (but Torre could), called sweet gale, whose aromatic leaves were once used to flavor English ale and still used to make a sweet tea and food spice as well as to give a pleasant scent to linens and clothing. The buds and bark were also used as a dye by some Native American tribes. In addition, we found various willows, including Barclay's and diamond-leaf, blue flag irises, and more species of sedges that I wasn't familiar with.

We were resting in the tundra near a large pond when an Osprey flew over us in the direction of Beverley Lake. At first, we thought it was a Bald eagle, but I noticed its telltale flight pattern, which was slightly above the horizontal with a bend at the wrist. It was also smaller than an eagle and moved its wings more often. My binocs made the definitive ID. It was to be our only Osprey during the trip. A real surprise for me was a much smaller bird I never expected to find in the area, an Arctic warbler. I was tailing behind the others on our way back to camp when I heard the song of a bird that sounded a little like a Cactus wren in the Southwest but higher pitched and with less of a deep murmur. Listening closely, I could distinguish two males singing in a stand of willows and birch along a small creek, and finally got a good look at them with my binocs. The last time I'd seen them was in June, 2015, during a long hike up the Anaktuvuk River in the Gates of the Arctic National Park with my wife Jennifer and three friends. When I checked my Audubon bird app, it indicated they were only seldom seen in the Wood-Tikchik area, but here they were in front of my eyes. I wondered if we would encounter more of them.

I didn't have to wait long. While eating a shepherd's pie dinner prepared by Tracie, I heard the bird's telltale song again and again right over our tents, which we'd had to erect in a tangle of mixed alder, willow, birch, spruce and fern taiga. I continued to hear it as I sat on the beach watching the wind die on the lake, then later in my tent while writing in my journal.

How lucky could I be? The same warbler began singing as I prepared coffee in the early morning. Then while Brad and I chatted, I pointed out another familiar bird sound overhead, a Wilson's snipe winnowing with its tail feathers as it raced down from the heights above, bounded back up, then dipped toward the ground again in a sort of graceful dance. Along with Golden-crowned sparrows, water thrushes, a Varied thrush, Wilson's warbler, and loons yodeling on the lake, it was a glorious wild bird orchestra of Nature's original music.

After a hearty breakfast of grits with bacon and cheese, we left what I dubbed as Arctic warbler camp. The primitive camp had been more of a bivouac, but it possessed the redeeming features of the bog mire with its unusual plants and Arctic warblers. There was no wind and the surface of the water was calm as Torre and I set out, reaching the end of the lake and Agulukpak River in about two hours. At the mouth of the river we found a comfortable ranger station and a campground with an opportunity for a long walk. The station had evidently been built several years earlier when Alaska still had money to burn, and it was closed until the beginning of the sockeye (red) salmon migration in another few days. Torre said he'd read there were rainbow trout to be caught there, so he, Brad and Don fished while Janet,

Tracie and I walked the river trail. About midway, we came across another large mire and ventured onto it for a ways to check out some of the plant species. But it was not as interesting as the one we'd visited the day before, and shortly afterward Janet and Tracie turned around. I continued on what in places was a muddy trail paralleling another long bog mire, and followed it to its end, then doubled back. I walked more slowly then, and twice stopped to listen closely to two birds I hadn't heard much since we'd started the trip, a Fox sparrow and Lincoln's sparrow. Both of these have among the sweetest songs that exist in the bird world. The clear rapid whistle of a Whimbrel, which I'd heard call overhead the night before, also caught my attention. I'd seen this large sandpiper with its down-curved bill many times in the Arctic and on the Lower Yukon Delta, but it was new for me here.

When I got back to the canoes Janet and Tracie told me the others had caught a mess of rainbows, and would be ready to leave as soon as they landed one more fish. Within ten minutes they had their eighth fish, a big grayling, and were eager to find a campsite farther along so they could clean and fry four of them for dinner. First, though, we had to float the short but challenging Agulukpak River down to Nerka Lake, the longest of the four big lakes we would encounter on our two-week canoe trip. The Agulukpak River is wide and fast-flowing and takes its meaning from the Yup'ik Eskimo, "big channel connecting two lakes." Nerka Lake has two arms that join at the west end. On the map it looks a little like a snaggle-toothed male salmon with its mouth opening to the west. In fact, Nerka derives from the Yup'ik name, *neqa*, for "food," and specifically refers to the red salmon that spawn in the lake and have been one of the main staples in their diet for thousands of years.

At the mouth of the river, Brad and I stopped to watch a feeding frenzy of Bonaparte's and Arctic terns as they consumed what were probably part of a downriver migration of red and king salmon fry, which were in turn feeding on the effluent of the river. I confirmed that with my binocs while watching them pick the tiny minnows from the surface of the water. I was amazed at the different hunting strategies of the two birds while observing them. Where the little Bonaparte's gulls swooped in like jet planes and sortied down to snatch their prey from the surface, the Arctic terns hovered about ten feet above the level of the water, then dived straight down into it to capture their victims, instantly flying back up again with minnows in their mouths. The terns were by far more successful than the gulls, proving them to be the virtuosos of the two species, and explained in part why they were the world's long distance bird migratory champions, traveling an average of almost 80,000 kilometers (49,700 miles) in one year. We are always lucky to see them in summers in Alaska, because for about nine months of the year they are pelagic, only found over the world's oceans.

Janet and I switched again after landing for a short snack break, then Torre and I continued paddling west till we reached a small rarely used campsite on an island. With its steady breeze, ample wood supply, and many wild flowers, including chocolate lilies and cranesbills, it would have been a nice campsite, but it was too early to camp, so we only stayed briefly and headed west again. During our break Torre jury-rigged a primitive sail, which he asked me to hold while he steered the canoe. But the breeze wasn't strong enough to make much difference, so we returned to our paddling. It was a good idea whose time hadn't come.

At about 6:00 pm, a sudden strong wind surged in from the north, whipping up breaking waves and dangerous canoeing conditions. We knew we should pull in to camp, but we were in the middle of a cluster of islands where the rough terrain made it almost impossible to find a suitable campsite. We finally had to settle for a small pea gravel beach on one of the islands in the lee of the wind that proved fine as an anchorage and for cooking over a wood fire but only marginal when it came to setting up our tents. As Brad and I were searching for good tent sites, I came across a huge mound of fresh dark purple bear dung similar to the pile I'd found at one of our other campsites. I showed it to Brad, lifting my forefinger to my mouth, then covered it with fresh vegetation.

After Torre cleaned the rainbow trout, Brad fried them over a wood fire. Tracie added a side dish of lasagna, then we ate like Italian kings. Later I built what I called a "masking fire" over the spot where the trout had been cleaned so there would be less of a chance for any bear on the island to sniff the scent of fresh fish. There was never a guarantee it would do that, but I thought it might help. After dinner, it was my turn to dig a small outhouse hole and mark the trail so everyone could find it. I connected my phone to Torre's small solar array so I could take pictures the next day, then retired to my tent where I set to repairing my head net. As I sewed, I thanked myself over and over for bringing it, since it was probably the piece of gear I used more than any other on the trip so far. Without protection from the onslaught of black and red flies, I would not have enjoyed the beauty of the place as much as I did.

I closed my eyes to the yammering of a nestful of hungry young Ravens.

At 6:00 a.m. light rain tapped on my tent, but I got up anyway to brew coffee for the others, and to lay out the cooking utensils that I thought Janet might need to prepare her breakfast of powdered eggs and hash browns for the crew. Shortly afterwards we struck camp and continued through the maze of islands on water as flat as glass and mirroring the vegetation like butterfly wings on both sides of us. I started out in the barge, as usual, and immediately spotted seven Surf scoters, which took off with heavy flapping when we were still quite distant from them. I'm sure part of what frightened them was the loud chugging noise of the one cylinder Nankai kicker on the back of the boat. After a couple hours, we pulled over on a north-facing shore of upper Nerka Lake and waited for the rest of the crew on one of the nicest pebble beaches we'd found so far. And there were no black flies! It was so idyllic and flat that I instantly went into my yoga mode. I was board-stiff from sitting so long in the barge, and felt I really needed the stretches, in spite of my fear of inflicting it on the others.

Then it was back to the peace and quiet and conversation of Torre's canoe for a few hours. Over the days, Torre and I had chatted about a range of topics, but this time we focused on our environmental culture heroes, including Olaus and Margaret Murie and other scientists. Two hours later we spotted yet another fine beach, actually a pebble spit located on the south-facing shore of the west end of the upper lake. This one turned out to be the loveliest beach of our trip, and we milked it for all it was worth, lunching and lounging, taking cold baths and photographing a plethora of wild flowers including chocolate lilies, wild geranium, Bering chickweed, bluebells, blue flag and others under a vast sunny dome of sky. All good things must end, though, and when we noticed an ominous wall of dark clouds approaching from the west, we thought it might be a good idea to start paddling across the lake to the other shore where my binocs told me there was a low bench with an open area that seemed ample enough for all of our tents and the kitchen area. After some hesitation by the group, we finally all agreed the bench should be our goal and pushed off. As it turned out, we made it just in time to avoid a minor williwaw with fierce cross winds and rainsqualls. We immediately set up camp on the bench above the shoreline, which, in addition to having plenty of firewood and clear water for drinking, had a lot of gull and loon activity out front. As Brad and I cleared our tent sites, I listened to the wailing of nearby loons through careening blasts of wind and rain squalls, and commented to Brad how lucky we were to hear those wild haunting calls of the loons.

Torre fried the remaining four rainbows, and we ate those for dinner plus a tasty fruit dumpling dessert that Janet prepared. They made a good team. To celebrate Father's Day, we drank a small glass of Jen's cloudberry wine I'd brought along. We saluted fathers everywhere, our good luck to have outrun the storm, and that we'd found yet another great campsite. This one was scattered with so many chocolate lilies I proposed another toast to remember it as Chocolate Lily Camp.

The storm and choppy waves of the lake subsided almost suddenly after I returned to my tent to write in my journal, and the setting solstice sun cast soft shimmers of light and shadow on the lake surface until it faded below the distant Ahklun Mountains behind us. Again, I closed my eyes to the singing of loons.

The night before we had decided if the weather was auspicious in the morning we would declare another layover day so we could explore more of the upper end of Nerka Lake. It turned out to be what we'd hoped for in the wake of a brief bout of early morning rain, and after listening to the yodeling of loons for a few more minutes, I was out of the tent by 7:00 and eager to start preparations for my flapjack breakfast.

On our way to the end of the lake we stopped by the Alaska State fish research station and chatted with Dan Schindler, a seasoned researcher from the U. of Washington who had been spending the last twenty-five summers there studying the various species of fish in the Wood-Tikchik Lake system. He answered some of our questions about Arctic char and rainbow trout, and also told us a little of the geology of the area. Pointing to the skirt of the mountain to the south, he explained that the three glacial benches visible there, and everywhere above the lakes, were sixteen, fifteen, and fourteen thousand years old, with extremely rapid melting of the glacier taking place after 14,000 BP. I'd wondered about their chronology, and that took care of that question.

We left the researcher and his student assistant for the other side of the lake to paddle up the outflow creek leading to Little Togiak Lake, where we were greeted by a young Bald eagle cruising low and searching for unwary quarry to satisfy his youthful appetite. While Don and Tracie continued paddling to the head of the lake, the rest of us stopped and tied up on the alders about a quarter-mile along the north shore to try to find a way to the top of a high knoll with a good view of the lakes. Then we climbed straight up through one of the most god-awful tangles of alders and lady ferns I'd ever seen before. But wildflowers like Beauvard's spirea, Arctic arnica, starflower, cranesbill and the lovely sky-blue Jacob's ladder gave me some cheer through the blood, sweat and tears of the climb. And even better, hearing and seeing the birds, from the gaudy Harlequin ducks on the lake, the Spotted sandpipers along the shoreline, Savannah, Fox and Golden-crowned sparrows singing among the alders, two soaring Bald eagles, and a Merlin chasing one of the eagles, made my steps seem nimbler all the way to the top.

Although it was difficult getting there, the knoll offered us such a panoramic view of Little Togiak Lake and both arms of Nerka Lake that it made the tremendous effort worthwhile. We could also see the extent of the alder canker that had killed so many alders on the mountainsides, and had apparently allowed the subsequent release of nitrogen by the dying roots of the alders, leading to the prolific growth of the thickets of ferns in the region. On the way back to the canoes, we followed a much easier route down through grasses and ferns and only a few copses of alders, but en route I lost my dark glasses to the alders. I retraced my steps to try to find them, but soon had to give up the search and return to my friends who were patiently waiting for me at the bottom. Fortunately, I had a backup pair.

Torre and Brad fished in the outflow river and caught four large Char, which we ate for dinner. When I retired to my tent at about 10:00 p.m. the lake was perfectly calm, but not more than fifteen minutes later we were pummeled by another sudden williwaw with huge breakers hitting us square in the face. I was in my tent writing when it struck, and the noise of the angry waves on the shore was deafening. There were no loons wailing that night.

I awoke to a lake that had returned to calm, with tattered striations of white mist and cloud streaking the lower elevations of the mountains and the surface of the lake. As I prepared the wood fire and heated up the coffee water, I noticed a line of gulls perched atop every spruce tree on the island opposite our camp, all of them probably spotting for their breakfast.

Tracie prepared our breakfast of corn grits, and soon afterward we broke camp and headed for the opposite shore and the wide neck of water that led to the southern arm of Nerka Lake. Later, I learned the length of both of Nerka's arms was 36 miles. The canoes pulled out first, then when they faded into the distant mist Brad and I set out in the barge. As we left shore, I pointed to a small flotilla of Common mergansers that included three adult females, five adult males and three first year males. I racked my brain but couldn't remember ever seeing a mixed flock of this sort so late in the spring before. It was probably because of the longer warm season in this part of Alaska. Farther north all birds had to get down to business earlier.

Nearer the south end of the lake, we could make out three small islands that had been concealed by the mist but were now visible and crowded with mobs of gulls either perched on dry scrapes between patches of green grass or flying and swimming near their rocky shores. After glassing the birds, I saw they were Glaucous-winged gulls, and they were nesting on the islands. I had never seen so many of them gathered together in one place at the same time, or realized that they were colonial in nature. It was another new experience for me, and I was so excited I took about 20 photos of the gulls and their islands. They reminded me of the nesting cliffs of the Black-legged kittiwakes in Prince William Sound and the colonial nesting sanctuaries of the gannets, razorbills and Atlantic puffins in Newfoundland.

Brad and I caught up with the rest of the crew just as they were going ashore on the lee side of a large island to have a hot drink to warm up from the cold north wind that had sprung up only an hour before. While there Tracie pointed out a dead Pelagic cormorant that had recently washed ashore. I couldn't find any wound on it, so there had been no foul play by either humans or predators, and I wondered if it had anything to do with food shortage due to climate change.

The way conversations usually go, we wandered from the topic of food shortages and climate change to camping preferences. When Tracie told us she "eschewed" certain types of campsites, I said I'd never heard "eschew" used in that context before, and being a person who appreciated the power of words, I asked where she'd learned that substitute for avoiding something or somebody. She said she really didn't remember where she'd picked it up. I gave her a thumbs-up on it, though, then began chatting about the origins of words and phrases.

I canoed with Torre from there, and as we crossed the windy channel to the mainland we noticed some large patches of dead alder probably killed by the same canker fungus that had recently wiped out so many of them on the north arm of the lake, and in Alaska's Interior about twenty years ago. We stopped to wait for the others in a tangle of what looked like alder mangroves because of the high water level on the lakes. The likeness of the water-hugging shrubs to mangroves convinced us that we should dub this particular species of alder, *Alnus mangrovensis alaskana*.

When the others caught up we continued along the south shore. Just as the wind began to abate we spotted an open beach where we saw the possibility of a snack around a warming fire. Torre built a nice bonfire and was relaxing around it when Janet noticed a large bird's egg on the spot where she was going to sit down. It was a dark olive color covered with brown splotches, and she wondered if it could belong to the tern she'd just seen fly off the beach when we first landed. I looked at it closely and told her she was right, explaining why it was so huge for such a small bird. Like sandpipers and plovers, terns are ground-nesting birds whose first strategy for survival is to beget precocial young that can leave the nest almost as soon as they hatch. Hence the big eggs. I looked around and saw both parents circling near shore, and Janet and Tracie were concerned they might not come back to their nest. I told them not to worry because there was still only one egg and it did not have to be incubated yet. Only when the full clutch of two or three eggs was laid would the three-week incubation count begin. And when that time came the pair would defend their nest almost to the death. They also had an excellent tactic for dissuading would be predators from coming too close to the nest. They dive bombed them, sometimes pecking their heads on the upswing or even crapping on them. I added that their Yup'ik names, *Teqiyaaraq* and *Teqirayuli*, both loosely meant "the dear little bird that is good at using its bottom to disadvantage others."

This information, plus the example from Yup'ik lore, I think, allowed everyone to rest a little easier by allaying some of their fears, so we stuck around a little longer, chatting about early environmentalists and their organizations such as the Audubon Society and the New York City, D.C., and San Francisco women's garden clubs that had helped in the political battles to stop the late 19th century millinery trade, and supported the Sierra Club and President Teddy Roosevelt in their efforts to establish and protect National Parks and other public lands throughout the United States. I mentioned that Peter Matthiessen's trilogy, The Killing of Mr. Watson, was a good source for learning about the history of those battles.

After snuffing out the fire, Torre and I paddled together again for another three-and-a-half miles until we found what I thought was probably our best campsite yet. I dubbed it Beach Rye Camp because of all the beach rye grass we found there, much of it, along with most of the willows, now underwater because of the high level of the lake. After setting up camp, I worked for a while on the cedar owl I'd been carving, then did some yoga, and helped Brad realign the struts on the floor of the SOAR that were attached to the little kicker. They'd come loose from all the bouncing around in the waves generated by the last wind event.

Tracie served us a tasty tamale pie for dinner, then Torre and Brad and I paddled quietly over to where they had earlier spotted a Common loon sitting on her nest in a hidden corner of the lagoon next to our camp. When she'd slid off the nest and headed for deeper water, she had revealed two olive brown eggs. She was back on her nest again when we silently floated by, but now hunched low, beak toward the water, waiting for us to leave, which we did right away, photographing as we paddled. Back at camp I mentioned that it was only the second time in my life I'd seen that behavior. The topic quickly changed to other things, though, like Torre's experience doing climate research on the Yukon Delta; what we would do with our personal collections after we kicked off; and how much we'd enjoyed our afternoon on the bog mire just a few days before. Then I retired to my tent to catch up on my journal and listen to a yellowlegs yelping at our presence on his nesting ground. At first, I didn't know which one it was, a Greater or Lesser yellowlegs, but finally decided it was a Greater because of its hoarser yelp – a trivial mental pursuit for most people, I thought, but not for me.

While brewing the coffee I noticed the bark of a nearby tree had been chewed up pretty badly by a porcupine. Pointing it out to Brad, who'd joined me around the fire, we both wondered why we still hadn't seen any porkies on our trip. But later in the day during a lunch stop Don and Tracie reported they finally saw a big porcupine along the water's edge, proving there was at least one of them hanging around the lakes. With that, Torre announced that we had spotted something a bit bigger on that same stretch of lake, a bull moose with huge antlers. As it turned out, this was the only moose we were to encounter during the whole trip, and we thought perhaps the reason for their scarcity was the lack of good habitat. There were just too few willows and too many alders.

When we reached a turn of the lake to the south and into a bay that would take us towards the Agulowak River, Torre and I noticed an aggregation of Bonaparte's gulls and Arctic terns out in the middle, maybe waiting for salmon fry that were headed down to Aleknagik Lake and Nushagak Bay. Suspecting there might be bigger fish out there feeding on the fry, he took out his fishing pole and began trolling. But there were no big ones to be caught, so he left his line out, and we joined the rest of our crew and paddled to another camping spot on the western shore. Just before landing, Torre reeled in his line, and to his surprise he had a twenty-inch Arctic char on his hook.

Our camp turned out to be infested with a plague of black flies, so we named it Black Fly Camp II. Only on the windy spit were there fewer of the little buggers, so we cooked, ate our dinner and socialized out there. Torre fried up the big fish he'd caught and prepared some tasty sides to add to it, so again we dined like royalty. The meal left such an afterglow in our stomachs that we visited on the spit until 9:30. While chatting, we were entertained by a chorus of bird song, including tunes from Wilson's and Orange-crowned warblers, a medley of thrushes, and a Wilson's snipe and Northern water-thrush. For me, it was all a part of the social mix.

Before calling it quits for the night, I noted in my journal a change in the makeup of the flotillas of mergansers I'd observed on the lake during the day. They were almost exclusively composed of males, which meant the females had laid the last of their eggs and were now into serious brooding mode. At this point, the males turned all of the family business over to the females, virtually abandoning them and forming "men's clubs" once again.

It was overcast when I awoke, but I heard Brad rummaging around, so together we built a wood fire, boiled some water for coffee and tea, then chatted about his five years of teaching in two Yup'ik Eskimo villages along the Kuskokwim River, not far from where Jennifer and I had taught. He told me the students in his Small Engines class had fixed so many of the village snow machines and outboard kickers that he felt sorry for the teacher that replaced him after he left.

When everyone was out of their tents I brewed some more coffee and made a pot of oats for them. Soon afterward we packed up and headed for Lake Aleknagik, which would be the last of the four great lakes we paddled on.

As Brad and I began floating into the Agulowak River, we spotted a school of about three dozen sockeye salmon heading upriver to spawn in one of the northern lakes. It was probably the vanguard of the sockeye migration, since the salmon had still not turned red as they do when they approach their spawning grounds. Brad immediately threw his fish line out to try to catch one, but had no takers because by that stage the fish had something more important in mind.

When we caught up to the others they were pulled over below another bog mire, so we joined them for a lunch break and a cursory check of the plant life. The mire wasn't as large as the one we'd explored on Beverley Lake, but it was interesting nonetheless, especially for Torre who wanted to examine the various species of sedges and grasses there. As we were leaving, he said he discovered a sedge, *Carex pauciflora*, that wasn't previously recognized to grow in the area.

Torre and Brad were able to try their luck at fishing again a little farther down in front of the GCI fishing lodge, where we stopped for a couple of hours. While they fished and Don and Tracie explored the premises, Janet and I hiked up the mountain behind the lodge to see what we could see. We weren't able to take photos of the river because we'd both forgotten our cameras, but we enjoyed the exercise and the beautiful views of the area. I was also able to identify the call of a bird that I'd originally mistaken to be that of a flycatcher. It turned out instead to be the primary call (not the song) of a Gray-cheeked thrush.

After all of their effort fishing, Brad and Torre were only able to land one grayling and one char, but they would have another opportunity to fish at the mouth of the river. So we soon hopped back in our boats and began paddling downriver for Lake Aleknagik. Brad and I hadn't expected the river to be so rough, but that it was, and offered us the most exciting white water yet.

As we pulled in at the mouth of the Agulowak River, who should we meet standing next to his airplane but our friend from Dillingham, Paul Liedberg. He said he had seen us from the air as we were floating downriver and decided to land and wait for us, just in case we needed any information about camping spots on our final leg home. It was nice to see him again, and we chatted for about an hour until he took off for Dillingham. He informed us that the GCI lodge where we'd stopped to hike and fish was the same one where Senator Ted Stevens had stayed just prior to the airplane accident that had killed him a few years earlier. Before leaving, Paul told us that, because of the high water on the lake, the only decent place we would find to set up our tents for the night was at the Seventh Day Adventist summer camp down the lake about four miles.

Torre and I partnered up again for the remaining paddle to the Adventist camp. After getting underway I asked him if we could slow down a bit to watch the large rafts and flocks of gulls and terns hunting and pecking for sockeye salmon fry where the river collided with the lake, churning and swirling and bringing the fry to the surface as it did so. I'd never seen such a feeding frenzy before. At that moment there must have been a massive movement of the small minnows into the lake, hence the gull activity.

It was fascinating to observe the different hunting techniques of each of the three species of gulls. Although the Bonaparte's gulls plunged head first into the water, they didn't submerge their bodies entirely; the Arctic terns, on the other hand, first hovered above the surface to locate their quarry, then dove straight down into the water, submerging their bodies completely, then quickly flying up again as if the weight of the water made no difference in either direction. But the giant Glaucous-winged gulls just floated lazily along, every once in a while ducking their heads under the surface to catch a minnow.

Once at the Adventist summer camp, we asked the foreman of a volunteer crew from Seattle doing building repairs where we could camp for the night. He told us anywhere we wanted would be fine, so most of us set up our tents in the tall grass about a hundred feet from the beach. In spite of the out buildings, it was a comfortable campsite, made even better because of the few black flies. One disadvantage, though, was that we couldn't have a campfire. No matter, because Torre cooked another gourmet fish dinner over our backup gas stove, added to by Janet with some savory spaghetti and a fine dessert cobbler.

As I closed my eyes, I heard the yodeling of loons in the distance again – for me, a joyful final night on the lakes.

June 21 –

I awoke to variable winds, wondering what sort of luck we would have with them as we made our way east to the end of the lake where we'd started our trip. Mother Nature was kind, though, and granted us calm water for the rest of our journey. I was in Torre's canoe first, then later in Brad's barge, as we paddled and putted on a trajectory that took us near the north shore, then through a small cluster of islands.

We stopped for lunch at a broken-down dock that had been left high and dry away from a muddy shore on one of the islands where a village family at one time had a fish camp. After an hour or so, I joined Torre again on calm water, and set off in his canoe, first past the village of Aleknagik, and finally ending up in the early afternoon back where we started at the dock owned by Tikchik Adventures. Since the current of the Wood River was still running strong because of high water, we had to be extra careful we didn't miss our mark, or it would have been a long twenty-mile float to Dillingham.

Soon after our arrival, we were met at the dock by Paul Liedberg and Alan Jubanville with their vehicles to help us haul our gear to Paul's house in Dillingham. There Paul and Alan introduced us to their wives, Mary Ann and Sharon. Alan and Sharon told me they now lived in Fairbanks.

Later in the evening, during a small party with some of Paul's friends, I was able to visit with all of them for a while. I especially enjoyed discussing the local geology with Todd Radenbaugh, and some of the birds I'd seen over the past two weeks with Bob Henry, the husband of Susanna Henry, who was Paul's replacement as Manager of the Togiak National Wildlife

Refuge. As Bob and I were chatting about birds, an Arctic warbler began singing in Paul's backyard, which I said was a further revelation to me of how far they had extended their range south since their fairly recent spill-over from Asia into Alaska. This qualified them as "Old World Warblers," I told him, and put them in the *Silviidae* family, making them more closely related to kinglets. But this warbler was only in Alaska during the summer months, then headed back to its wintering grounds in Southeast Asia. I also mentioned that in Yup'ik the bird's name was *cungakcuarnaq*, meaning little greenish-yellow bird, deriving from the Yup'ik words, *cungak*, "bile," and *cungaq*, "gall bladder," hence the color. Trivia for most people, I imagined, but for me it seemed important.

Susanna was listening to the conversation, and segued into a discussion of her difficulties approaching the Yup'ik people in the Refuge area about their tradition of collecting the eggs of Aleutian terns in spring, which she said had resulted in the decimation of their nesting habitat and a ninety percent reduction of their numbers over just the last fifteen years. I suggested a different way of dealing with the people and their leaders about the problem. Rather than a head-on Western approach of mandating prohibitions, she might try a more oblique one, especially using some key Yup'ik words like "piuguvet," meaning, "if you want to." This always gave those who collected the eggs the idea that it was their decision to stop doing it, not the Government's. I had used it during my twenty-one years teaching in the Lower Yukon Delta, and it seemed to work well. It was at least worth a try, I said.

After Paul's guests went home, we got together with him and planned for our next two days of set net fishing. He told us we could use his permit and net gear at his beach site only a few miles down the road and catch our limit of both red and king salmon. We all looked forward to the possibility of catching fresh salmon to take home.

That night, Brad and I slept on the concrete floor of Paul's garage, but I confess I missed the fresh air and the yodeling of loons as I went to sleep. On both of the following days we were successful in catching our limits of salmon. It was an exciting time pulling in the nets together and reaping our harvest as the high tide flowed in then ebbed back out. I was always mindful that we were killing animals so we could eat them, and I thanked each fish as we dispatched them. The preparation of the fish for transport back to Fairbanks was less enjoyable, but with Paul's guidance we all pitched in and got the job done.

During the three days and nights we were with the Liedbergs, Paul must have noticed my ability to distinguish birds by their songs and calls, because on Sunday evening he asked me if I would get up early in the morning and sit with him on his back porch and help him identify the songs of his backyard birds as they began their dawn medleys. Over cups of coffee, we sat for a couple of hours and listened to the sweet warbling of Ruby-crowned kinglets, the bold staccato chipping of Wilson's warblers, and the reedy wolf-whistles of Gray-cheeked thrushes – and a little later, the buzzy trills of the Arctic warbler, which I'd heard during his small party on Friday evening. There were many others, too, including the familiar whispering whinnies of adult robins as they fed their cheeping fledglings in the deep marsh grass in his front yard facing Nushagak Bay.

Later in the day we packed up and said our final goodbyes at Dillingham's small airport, then boarded the jet for Anchorage and Fairbanks. From then on it would all be memories and dreams of the people we'd met and the places where our trails had taken us. But we had followed them to their end, and we were richer for what we'd done.

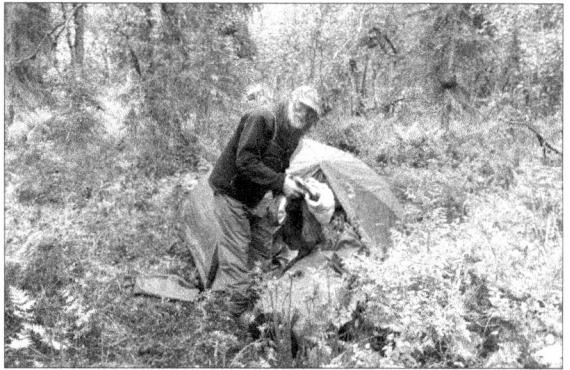

PHOTOS

1. Ahklun Mountains
2. Tracey, Janet and Don on Kulik Lake
3. Frank setting up tent in a cosmos of ferns

www.ingramcontent.com/pod-product-compliance
Lightning Source LLC
Chambersburg PA
CBHW052108030426
42335CB00025B/2882